1994

INTRODUCTION TO THE HOSPITALITY INDUSTRY

WILEY SERVICE MANAGEMENT SERIES

TOM POWERS, *Series Editor*

Introduction to the Hospitality Industry
Tom Powers

Introduction to Management in the Hospitality Industry
Tom Powers

Marketing Hospitality
Tom Powers

Supervision in the Hospitality Industry
Jack E. Miller
Mary Porter

The Management of Maintenance and Engineering Systems in the Hospitality Industry
Frank D. Borsenik
Alan R. Stutts

The Bar and Beverage Book: Basics of Profitable Management
Costas Katsigris
Mary Porter

Purchasing: Selection and Procurement for the Hospitality Industry
John M. Stefanelli

INTRODUCTION TO THE HOSPITALITY INDUSTRY

SECOND EDITION

TOM POWERS
School of Hotel and Food Administration
University of Guelph

JOHN WILEY & SONS, INC.

NEW YORK • CHICHESTER • BRISBANE • TORONTO • SINGAPORE

Photo researcher: Grace How

Library of Congress Cataloging-in-Publication Data

Powers, Thomas F.
    Introduction to the hospitality industry / Tom Powers : study
  guide prepared by Jo Marie Powers. — 2nd ed.
    p. cm. — (Wiley service management series)
  Includes index.
  ISBN 0-471-53054-9 (paper)
    1. Hospitality industry. I. Powers, Jo Marie, 1935-
  II. Title. III. Title: Hospitality industry. IV. Series.
TX911.P62 1992
647.94'068 — dc20   92-2523

Printed in the United States of America

10 9 8 7 6 5 4 3

This book is dedicated with affection to my father, the late F. Urban Powers, a pioneer in the application of modern management techniques to the hospitality industry, who taught me to understand the relationship between the particular and the general and to guide practice with theory.
1898–1980

PREFACE

The rapid rate of change in the hospitality industry makes life difficult for authors revising textbooks. A simple updating of facts and statistics is not enough—although that has been done aggressively here. The real question is, "Which facts are relevant in analyzing today's industry?" Large parts of this edition are new: there are new chapters on service, the international hospitality industry, and restaurant operations. Within chapters retained from the previous edition, there are numerous new sections, including new material on developments in lodging, tourism, and food services.

The separate chapters on marketing and franchising have been eliminated in this edition, and much of their content relocated to their proper context in other chapters. (The marketing mix is discussed in Chapter 4, but a concern with hospitality marketing pervades Chapters 2 through 12. Franchising is discussed in Chapter 3 and again in Chapter 7.)

The basic commitments of this book remain the same: (1) to present hospitality as a single, interrelated industry and (2) to emphasize problem-solving *tools* rather than answers, and industry-wide *trends* rather than facts and figures. This is not a "how-to" book. The first edition's emphasis on the importance of field experience and personal observation should still come through loud and clear in Chapter 1 and in the rest of the text. Finally, and most fundamentally, students are challenged throughout to realize that in building a career in hospitality they are building their own business and a way of life as well.

There is a new theme in the lives of the hospitality and travel industries: maturity. They are increasingly being recognized as economically important and significant industries whose leaders should be heard. At this point in our evolution, however, also come more and tougher competition and a slower growth rate that parallels the growth of the economy as a whole. This more intense competition and the resulting changes in the market are reflected throughout this edition.

The addition of Chapter 13, on service, is a recognition that this element of our product, especially personal service, is increasingly important. For among today's more standardized hospitality offerings, it is service that differentiates one from another, especially in the upper end of the price range.

Another force driving the changes in today's hospitality businesses is the globalization of the industry. A European firm now owns the largest budget lodging chain in North America; Asian investors are also prominent in North American lodging. Food service shares in this trend as well. Overseas players compete in our home market, and overseas markets represent a major avenue of growth for North American hospitality firms. This international context is discussed in Chapter 14.

In Part 2, the new forms of food service competition represented by drive-through, takeout, and delivery operations illustrate the continuing evolution toward a multitiered industry with many levels of quality and service. In the upscale segments, the introduction of casual theme restaurants based on market research marks a trend toward more professional management and more deliberate development of hospitality concepts.

Chapter 3 has been added in Part 2 to deal with restaurant operations. There we review the tasks, responsibilities, and roles found in managing food service and consider how they are supervised in the front of the house, the back of the house, and the administration areas. We also consider the chain and independent restaurants and their advantages and drawbacks and look at franchised restaurant systems in depth. For students who are serious about getting into business for themselves, these are key sections.

Chapters 4 and 5, on forces and issues affecting the restaurant business, contain a number of new sections. The new shape of *demand for food service* evolving from the changing age distribution of our population, especially the aging of the baby boomers, is really the foundation for discussion in several later chapters related not only to food service but to lodging and tourism as well. Graphs emphasizing the main trends help make them more apparent. These chapters also emphasize the intensifying competition both within food service and from other, related retailers.

The impact of environmental concerns is an everyday fact of life in the 1990s. For food service, the problem boils down to changing the way we think about garbage. Today's operator must learn to help manage the waste stream through reduction, reuse, and recycling. Technology has a bearing here, too, as it does on every other sector of food operations.

In Chapter 6, on institutional food service, a new section addresses the opportunities and challenges of caring for the elderly in retirement communities and brings out the growing role of contract companies in institutions.

The chapters in Part 3, Lodging, emphasize meeting guest needs. This is a useful context in which to introduce new concepts such as the limited-service and hard-budget operations, at one end of the price spectrum, and all-suite and extended-stay operations, at the other. These chapters also reflect the increasing force of market segmentation—differences in demand for services not only between business and pleasure travelers but also between "upstairs" guests, who choose a hotel on the basis of the guest room and rate, and "downstairs" guests, who are willing to pay more for the other amenities of the full-service hotel. These chapters also recognize the increasing significance of computerization in lodging operations. In today's lodging business, the concept of yield management is necessary to an understanding of how rooms are actually sold. Finally, we will consider the industry-wide problems of overbuilding and the more positive outlook for renewed growth that is likely as we move out of an overbuilt period.

The travel and tourism chapters in Part 4 give greater emphasis to the importance of overseas guests to the North American industry. We also look at the trend toward shorter vacations and at what one industry leader referred to as a society in which leisure is increasingly the most important fact of social and economic life. Sections on urban revitalization, smaller recreation centers, winter festivals, and cruise lines highlight important destination-oriented developments. Coverage of travel agents and their role has been expanded. The interconnection between all central reservation systems, one of the most important developments in businesses serving travelers, is considered here as well.

In Chapter 13 we take an in-depth look at service, while Chapter 14 considers the international dimension of hospitality.

Chapter 15 offers a view of what the industry will face in the near future and beyond. Expanded sections on the use of natural resources, transportation, and the world environment explore some possible implications for the industry.

The dynamic and ever-changing hospitality industry is a hard taskmaster for all of us who work in it. But it is exciting. I can only hope that students will take some of the pleasure in reading this text that I found in writing it.

ACKNOWLEDGMENTS

In the current volume, I must acknowledge many who have helped in shaping this book, even at the risk of inadvertently overlooking friends and colleagues who have also helped me. My wife, Jo Marie Powers, who is also a colleague in HRI, is the source of many ideas found in this text—not all, I'm afraid, properly acknowledged. Her advice and critical reactions have been vital to developing the text over the course of earlier editions, and that continues to be true with this one. She also made major contributions to the test bank developed for the instructor's manual. Michael Nightingale, Director of the School of Hotel and Food Administration at the University of Guelph, has borne generously with a research and writing project that took a year longer than originally planned. He was also kind enough to read and comment on several new sections of the book. My colleagues in the school, particularly James Pickworth and Michael Haywood, were also generous with their time, reading several sections and making numerous helpful comments. Jim Pickworth was also a valuable collaborator in preparing the instructor's manual and is its co-author. Several colleagues at other institutions read and commented on new material and helped shape it in important ways. Leo Renaghan at Cornell, Carl Riegel at Washington State, and Donald Dinkelman, Peter D'Souza, and Leland Nicholls at the University of Wisconsin–Stout were most helpful in this way.

It is a special pleasure for me to acknowledge the contribution to this edition of my son, Mike Powers, principal of Circle Consulting, a waste management consulting firm. His understanding of this fast-changing field shaped both my research and my treatment of this vital topic. His review of an earlier version of the section on waste management resulted in numerous improvements in that material.

Security analysts John Rohs at Wertheim Schroder, Michael Culp at Prudential Bache, Michael Mueller at Montgomery Securities, and Daniel Lee at First Boston were kind enough to share the results of their research with me. They have each made important contributions to this text.

The Institutional Foodservice Manufacturers of America (IFMA) sponsors an annual meeting, COEX, featuring the latest research on food service market trends. I am indebted to them for generously allowing me to attend that conference and make extensive use of its *Proceedings* not only in this book but in developing my own understanding of the industry. Their help has been important in earlier editions of this text as well. I acknowledge, in particular, the leadership of George D. Rice in bringing the discipline of modern marketing to bear on food service management.

Technomic Consultants provided invaluable guidance in the literature of hospitality in their publication *TRA Foodservice Abstracts*. I have acknowledged that publication in numerous footnotes, but should point out that it has also helped me in keeping track of a topsy-turvy industry. In particular, Ron Paul, both in his editorials there as well as in personal communications, has helped me understand the unfolding food service panorama.

The Hospitality Industry Investment Conference, held annually in New York, has provided yet another key to understanding the patterns emerging in lodging as well as an invaluable source of information. Steven Brenner, president of Steven Brenner Associates, and Arlene Lesser and her colleagues at New York University have generously permitted me to attend that conference. The conceptual underpinnings of the chapters on lodging have, as a result, been greatly enriched.

The Burtenshaw Lectures at Washington State University have been important to my understanding of contemporary hospitality. Dr. Terry Umbreit has made copies of these lectures at Washington State available to me and I have appreciated his help. The 1990 Burtenshaw Lecture by Richard Komen, president of Restaurants Unlimited, makes an important new contribution to the present edition.

At the Marriott Corporation, Trudy Marotta has run interference for me and, as a result, secured the cooperation of many Marriott executives. Robert Fox at McDonald's gave me several interviews both by phone and in person. Kenneth Hornback, Chief Statistical Officer of the National Park Service, assisted me in obtaining research materials published by the Park Service and provided me with copies of his own papers. His insights on public-sector recreation also added to this book.

Smith Travel Research publishes an invaluable monthly newsletter, *Lodging Outlook,* and I have drawn from it repeatedly. Randall Smith was generous with his time and was most helpful to me in understanding the changing relationships between owner, franchisor, and operator in the lodging industry. The CKC Report is an industry newsletter devoted to technology; Lawrence Chervenak, its publisher and president of Chervenak Keene and Company, gave generously of his time in an interview related to the emerging central reservation technology, a subject on which he has also written eloquently. His work is cited in several chapters of this book.

The writing of a book involves not only developing material and the actual writing, but also a mountain of work related to preparing a usable manuscript. You would not be reading this but for the patient and meticulous efforts of Kay Fairfull in typing the manuscript — much of it two or three times. She bore with numerous revisions, marches, and countermarches with unusual patience, for which I am grateful.

When I set out to revise this text, several colleagues provided me with reviews of the first edition that resulted in valuable insights that shaped this latest edition: Bob Bennett, Delaware County Community College; Mary Martin, Anderson College; Irving Anderson, Warwick Hotel, Philadelphia, Pennsylvania; Marcille Dalgleish, Grand Rapids Community College; Jack Plummer, Joliet Junior College; Suzanne Beckley, Lake Michigan College; Jayne Pearson, Manchester Community College. In addition, the following colleagues reviewed the manuscript and made valuable suggestions: Carol Kizer, Columbus State Community College; Ed Sherwin, Essex County Community College; Carl Riegel, Washington State University; Andy Schwarz, Sullivan County Community College; Fred Faria, Johnson and Wales University; Cliff Wener, College of Lake County.

In spite of all the help I have had, there doubtless still remain errors and deficiencies in this text for which, of course, the author must accept responsibility.

TOM POWERS

Moon River, Ontario
June 1992

CONTENTS

PART 3 LODGING

CHAPTER 9 FORCES SHAPING THE HOTEL BUSINESS   284

PART 4 TRAVEL, TOURISM, AND THE
HOSPITALITY INDUSTRY

CHAPTER 10 TOURISM: FRONT AND CENTER   316

PART 5 SPECIAL TOPICS IN
        HOSPITALITY MANAGEMENT

INTRODUCTION TO THE HOSPITALITY INDUSTRY

P A R T 1

PERSPECTIVES ON CAREERS IN HOSPITALITY

C H A P T E R 1

THE HOSPITALITY INDUSTRY AND YOU

THE PURPOSE OF THIS CHAPTER

Your own career choice is probably the most important *management decision* you'll ever make—at least from your point of view. This chapter has been designed, therefore, to help you analyze a career in the hospitality industry and correlate that analysis with your field experiences while in school. It will also help prepare you for the first career decision you make just before or after you graduate. This chapter, in short, discusses the career decisions ahead of you over the next three to five years.

THIS CHAPTER SHOULD HELP YOU

1. Know what kind of businesses (and other establishments) make up the hospitality industry.

2. Know why people study in hospitality management programs—and what advantages these academic programs may have for you.

3. Think of your career decision in terms of a life's work, not just a job.

4. Start planning your field experiences—again, not just as jobs, but as crucial parts of your education.

5. Relate your education—both class and field experiences—to your employment goals at graduation.

6. Evaluate the employment outlook in the various sectors of the hospitality industry, and learn where the "hot spots" and "soft spots" are.

3

WHAT IS HOSPITALITY MANAGEMENT?

When we think of the *hospitality industry,* we usually think of hotels and restaurants. But the term has a much broader meaning. According to the *Oxford English Dictionary,* hospitality means "the reception and entertainment of guests, visitors or strangers with liberality and good will." The word *hospitality* is derived from *hospice,* a medieval "house of rest" for travelers and pilgrims. A hospice was also an early form of what we now call a nursing home, and the word is clearly related to *hospital.*

Hospitality, then, includes hotels and restaurants. But it also refers to other kinds of institutions that offer shelter or food or both to people away from their homes. Moreover, these institutions have more than a common historical heritage. They also share the management problems of providing food and shelter—problems that include erecting a building; providing heat, light, and power; cleaning and maintaining the premises; and preparing and serving food in a way that pleases the guests. Of course, we expect all of this to be done "with liberality and good will" when we stay in a hotel or dine in a restaurant, but we can also rightfully expect the same treatment from the dietary department in a health-care facility or from a school lunch program.

The hospitality professions are among the oldest of the humane professions, and they involve making a guest, client, or resident welcome and comfortable. But there is a more important reason that people interested in a career in these industries should think of them collectively. Today, managers and supervisors, as well as skilled employees, find that opportunities for advancement often mean moving from one part of the hospitality industry to another. For example, a hospitality graduate may begin as a management trainee with a restaurant company, complete the necessary training, and in a short time take a job as an assistant innkeeper in a motor hotel. The next job offer could come from a hospitality conglomerate, such as ARA Services. ARA provides food service operations not only in plant and office food services, but also in such varied areas as recreation centers, college campuses, health-care facilities, airline food services, community nutrition centers, and gourmet restaurants. Another such conglomerate is Marriott, which some people think of as a hotel company (which it is) or an institutional food service company (which it is). But Marriott is also expanding rapidly in the retirement center market and is a major factor among the companies offering restaurant food service along turnpikes and interstates and in airline terminals. Likewise, Holiday Inns, as everybody knows, is in the motor hotel business, but it is also one of the largest food service companies in the United States.

The point, of course, is that the hospitality industry is tied together as a clearly recognizable unit by more than just a common heritage and a commitment to "liberality and good will." Careers in the industry are such that your big break may come in a part of the industry entirely different from the one you expected. Hospitality management is one of the few remaining places in our specialized world of work that calls for a broadly gauged generalist—and

Saga Food Service, a Marriott subsidiary, provides food service on the ferries that serve travelers commuting to Seattle through one of North America's most beautiful waterways, Puget Sound.

the student who understands this principle increases the opportunity for a rewarding career in one of the hospitality industries.

THE MANAGER'S ROLE IN THE HOSPITALITY INDUSTRY

As a successful manager in the hospitality industry, you must exhibit many skills and command much specialized knowledge, but for now, let's discuss three general kinds of hospitality objectives:

1. *A manager wants to make the guest welcome personally.* This requires both a friendly manner on your part toward the guest and an atmosphere of "liberality and good will" among the people who work with you in serving the guests. That almost always means an organization in which workers get along well with one another.

2. *A manager wants to make things work for the guest.* Food has to be savory and hot or cold according to design—and on time. Beds must be made and rooms cleaned. A hospitality system requires a lot of work, and the manager must see that it is done.

3. *A manager wants to make sure the operation will continue providing service and making a profit.* When we speak of "liberality and good will," we don't mean giving the whole place away! In a restaurant or hotel operated for profit, portion sizes are related to cost, and so menu

and room prices must be related to building and operating costs. This enables the establishment to recover the cost of its operation and to make enough additional income to pay back any money borrowed, as well as to provide a return to the owner who risked a good deal of money—and time—to build the establishment. (This situation is surprisingly similar to subsidized operations such as school lunch or health-care food services. Here the problem is not to make a profit but to achieve either a break-even or zero-profit operation, or a controlled but negative profit—that is, a loss covered by a subsidy from another source.) The key lies in achieving a controlled profit, loss, or break-even operation. A good term to describe this management concern is *conformance to budget*.

Managers, then, must be able to relate successfully to employees and guests, direct the work of their operation, and achieve operating goals within a budget.

WHY STUDY IN A HOSPITALITY MANAGEMENT PROGRAM?

One way to learn the hospitality business is actually to go to work in it and acquire the necessary skills to operate the business. The trouble with this approach, however, is that the skills that accompany the various work stations (cook, waitress, and so forth) are not the same as those needed by hospitality managers. In earlier times of small operations in a slowly changing society, hospitality education was basically skill centered. Most hospitality managers learned their work through apprenticeship. The old crafts built on apprentice-ships assumed that knowledge—and work—were unchanging. But for reasons that later chapters will make clear, this assumption no longer holds true. As Peter Drucker, a noted management consultant, pointed out, "Today the center [of our society's productivity] is the knowledge worker, the man or woman who applies to productive work ideas, concepts, and information."[1] In other words, *studying* is a necessary part of your preparation for a career as a supervisor or manager.

Of course, many people argue that the liberal arts provide excellent preparation not only for work but also for life. They're quite right. What we've found, however, is that many students just aren't interested in the liberal arts subject matter. Because they are not interested, they are not eager to learn. On the other hand, these same people become hardworking students in a career-oriented program that interests them. Besides, there's no reason for educational preparation for work to be separate from preparation for life. We spend

[1] Peter F. Drucker, *The Age of Discontinuity* (New York: Harper & Row, 1968), p. 264.

Luxury food service relies on a highly skilled team made up of people in the front and back of the house. (Courtesy of the Hilton Corporation)

at least half our waking hours at work. As we will learn shortly, work lies at the heart of a person's life and can lead directly to "self-discovery."

Business administration offers a logical route to management preparation. Indeed, many hospitality managers have prepared for their careers in this field. But business administration is principally concerned with the manufacturing and marketing of a physical product in a national market. By contrast, the hospitality industry is a service industry, and the management of a service institution *is* different. Food is, of course, a restaurant's product, but most of the "manufacturing" (often all of it) is done right in the place that offers the service. The market is local, and the emphasis is on face-to-face contact with the guest. Hospitality operations are also smaller; so the problems of a large bureaucracy are not as significant as are the problems of face-to-face relationships with employees and guests.

Our point is not that there is something wrong with the liberal arts or with business administration. The point is that hospitality management programs are usually made up of students who are interested in what they're studying and that there is a difference between the hospitality service system and the typical manufacturing company.

Now, why might anyone want to study in a hospitality management program? Perhaps the best answer is the reasons that students before you have chosen to study there. Their reasons fall into three categories: their experience, their interests, and their ambitions. Figure 1.1 lists the various reasons that students cite, in order of frequency. As you can see, many students become interested in hospitality because a job they once had proved particularly attractive. Others learn of the industry through family or friends working in the field.

One important consideration for many students is that they like and are interested in people. As we just saw, working well with people is a crucial part of a manager's job in our industry. Many students, too, have a natural interest in food, and some are attracted by the natural glamour of the hospitality industry.

In addition, the employment outlook (as we'll see later in this chapter) is excellent in most segments of the hospitality industry, particularly for managers. Many people are attracted to a field in which they are reasonably sure they can secure employment. Others feel that in a job market with more opportunities than applicants, they will enjoy a good measure of independence, whether in their own businesses or as company employees. Many students are drawn to the hospitality industry because they want to get into their own business. One way to do that is through franchised operations, in either food service or lodging. Others, with good reason, suspect there are opportunities for innovation off the beaten track of the franchise organizations. And there are many examples of success.

Many young entrepreneurs have chosen catering as a low-investment field that offers opportunities to people with a flair for foods and careful

EXPERIENCE
    Personal work experience
    Family background in the industry
    Contact with other students and faculty in hospitality management programs
INTERESTS
    Enjoy working with people
    Enjoy working with food
    Enjoy dining out, travel, variety
AMBITION
    Opportunity for employment and advancement
    Desire to operate own business
    Desire to be independent

FIGURE 1.1 The reasons that students select hospitality management programs.

service. Catering is a fast-growing segment of food service, and is also a business that students sometimes try while in school, through either a student organization or groups of students setting up a small catering operation.

In the lodging area, one enterprising young couple expanded in an ingenious way the services of a small country inn. Once they and their tiny inn had been established in the community, they arranged to represent a large number of rental-unit owners in the area, offering marketing services to the owners and providing "front office" and housekeeping services for their guests in some 50 units, ranging from one-bedroom condominiums to larger condos and even houses.[2] The magazine *Restaurant Business* described this "new breed of independents" as follows:

> They practice modern management techniques rather than seat of the pants management, and they understand the importance of personnel policies, marketing and promotion, well-defined business strategies, and staying abreast of the industry.[3]

The biggest appeal to being in business for yourself, cited by two thirds of entrepreneurs, was not money but being your own boss.[4]

There are many other opportunities as well — for instance, people with chef's training may open their own business, especially if they feel that they have a sufficient management background. In the health-care area, home-care organizations are expanding in response to the needs of our growing senior citizen population and offer a wide range of opportunities to entrepreneurs. This interest in independent operations reinforces the need for studying hospitality management.

Whether you're studying hospitality management because you want to start a business of your own or because you found your past work experience in the business especially interesting — or perhaps just because the continuing growth in the area makes the job prospects especially attractive — management studies are an important preparation for budding entrepreneurs. Hospitality management students tend to be highly motivated, lively people who take pride in their future in a career of service.

PLANNING A CAREER

WHY DO WE WORK?

We all have several motives for going to work. Of course, we work to live — to provide food, clothing, and shelter. Psychologists and sociologists tell us,

---

[2] *Lodging,* September, 1984, pp. 68–71.

[3] *Restaurant Business,* January 20, 1986, p. 96.

[4] *Nations Restaurant News,* October 15, 1990, p. 14.

Marriott uses major franchise brands in many of its institutional and travel service operations. (Courtesy of Marriott Corporation/Host International)

however, that our work also provides a sense of who we are and binds us to the community in which we live. The ancient Greeks, who had slaves to do menial tasks, saw work as a curse. Their Hebrew contemporaries saw it as punishment. Early Christians, too, saw work for profit as offensive. But by the time of the Middle Ages, work began to be accepted as a vocation, that is, as a calling from God. Gradually, as working conditions improved and work became something that all social classes did, it became a necessary part of maturation and self-fulfillment in our society.

Today, workers at all levels demand more than just a job. Indeed, work has been defined as "an activity that produces something of value for other people."[5] This definition puts work into a social context. That is, it implies there is a social purpose to work as well as the crude purpose of survival. It is an important achievement in human history that the majority of Americans can define their own approach to a life of work as something more than mere survival.

Work contributes to our self-esteem in two ways. First, by doing our work well, we prove our own competence to ourselves. Psychologists tell us

[5] *Work in America* (Cambridge, Mass.: MIT Press, n.d.), p. 3.

that this is essential to a healthy life, as this information gives us a sense of control over both ourselves and our environment. Second, by working we contribute to others—others come to depend on us. Human beings, as social animals, need this sense of participation. For these reasons, what happens at work becomes a large part of our sense of self-worth.

Education for such a significant part of life is clearly important. Indeed, education has become essential in most walks of life. There is, moreover, a clear connection between education and income. In one study extending over several years, high school graduates and high school dropouts had similar *reductions* in annual inflation-adjusted income, while those with some college had a modest gain, and graduates of baccalaureate programs experienced substantial gains.[6] The evidence, then, is that your commitment to education will pay off.

The next section explores career planning in regard to employment decisions that you must make while you are still in school. We also will discuss selecting your first employer when you leave school. If you've chosen the hospitality industry as your career, this section will help you map out your job plans. If you are still undecided, the section should help you think about this field in a more concrete way and give you some ideas about exploring your career through part-time employment. Of course, a large number of readers of this text already have significant working experience, many in hospitality fields. Because not everyone has such experience in their background, however, this is a subject that does need to be covered. Perhaps those with more experience will find this a useful opportunity to review plans they've already made. A fresh look at your commitments will probably be worthwhile.

It's hard to overstate the importance of career planning. Young people, particularly in high school, find that their career plans change constantly. But by the time they've graduated from high school, their career plans have begun to take definite shape. There still may be more changes, however. For example, people who start out studying for a career in the hotel business may find the opportunities they want in food service. Others may begin preparations for the restaurant industry only to find they prefer the hours offered in industrial food service. This kind of change in plans will be easier to cope with if you have a plan that can guide you until your experience enables you to judge the "fit" between yourself and the available opportunities. As a prospective manager, give at least as much time and attention to planning for decisions that affect your career as you expect to give to decisions you will be making for your employer. Remember that no matter whom you work for, you're always in business for yourself, because it's *your* life.

---

[6]*American Demographics,* May 1, 1988, p. 12.

EMPLOYMENT AS AN IMPORTANT PART OF YOUR EDUCATION

Profit in a business is treated in two different ways. Some is paid out to the owner or shareholders as dividends (returns on their investment). Some of the profit, however, is retained by the business to provide funds for future growth. This portion of profit that is not paid out is called *retained earnings.* WE NEED A CONCEPT OF RETAINED EARNINGS TO CONSIDER THE REAL PLACE OF WORK EXPERIENCE IN CAREER DEVELOPMENT.

PROFITING FROM WORK EXPERIENCE

The most obvious profit we earn from work is the income paid to us by an employer. But in the early years of your career, there are other kinds of benefits that are at least as important as income. The key to understanding this statement is the idea of a lifetime income. You'll obviously need income over your entire life-span, but giving up some income now may gain you income (and, we ought to note, enjoyment, a sense of satisfaction, and independence) just a few years later. There is, then, a *job-benefit mix* made up of both money and knowledge to be gained from any job. Knowledge gained today can be traded with an employer for income tomorrow: a better salary for a better qualified person. The decision to take a job that will add to your knowledge is thus a decision for retained earnings and for acquiring knowledge that you can use later.

Every job, therefore, has to be weighed according to its benefit mix, not just in terms of the dollar income it provides. A part-time job as a supermarket stock boy (well, it is a "food-related" job in a way) might seem attractive because it pays more than a busboy's job does. But if you think about the learning portion of the benefit mix and your *total* income, including what you learn, your decision may – and probably should – be for the job that will add to your professional education.

There is another important point to consider about retained earnings and the benefit mix. Very often the only part-time job in the industry available to students is an unskilled one. Many people find these jobs dull, and they often pay poorly. But if you think about these jobs in terms of their total income, you may change your perspective. The work of a busboy or a dishwasher won't take you very long to learn. But you can improve your total profits from such a job by resolving to learn all you can *about the operation.* In this way you can build your retained earnings – the bank of skills and knowledge that nobody can ever take away from you.

Learning Strategies for Work Experience

When you go to work, regardless of the position you take, you can learn a good deal through careful observation. Look first at how the operation is organized. More specifically, look at both its managerial organization and its physical organization.

Managerial Organization.   The topic of organizational structure requires separate consideration. You will probably take the topic up later in your course of studies—and perhaps even in this course. Even now, however, you can begin to think about this problem. Who is the boss? Who reports to (or works directly with) him or her? Is the work divided into definite departments or sections? Is one person responsible for each department? To whom do the department staff members report? If you can answer these questions, you will have figured out the *formal organization* of the operation. Indeed, most large companies will have an organization chart that you can look at. If your employer doesn't have such a chart, ask him or her to explain the organization to you. You'll be surprised at how helpful to hospitality management students most employers and supervisors are.

While you're thinking about organization, it is also important to notice the "informal organization" or the "social organization" of the group you are working with. Which of the workers are influential? Who seem to be the informal leaders, and why? Most work groups are made up of cliques with informal leaders. After you identify this informal structure, ask yourself how management deals with it. Remember that someday the management of these "informal organizations" will be *your* problem; in time, you will be helping to plan the organization, and you will need their cooperation. In the meantime, this firsthand experience will help you both in your studies and in sizing up the real world of work.

The Physical Plant.   You can learn a great deal about a physical plant by making a simple drawing of your workplace, like the one shown in Figure 1.2. On this drawing, identify the main work areas and major pieces of equipment. Then begin to note on it where you see problems resulting from cross traffic or bottlenecks. For example, if you're working in the *back of the house,* you can chart the flow of products from the back door (receiver) to storage and from there to preparation. You should also trace the flow of dishes. Dirty dishes come to the dishroom window and go to the clean-supply area after washing. How are they transported to the cooler or to the pantry people for use in service? If you are working in the back of the house, you will be looking mostly at the flow of kitchen workers and dishes from the viewpoint of the kitchen, dishroom, or pantry. A similar flow analysis of guests and servers (and plates) can also be made from the *front of the house* (that is, the dining room).

A study of guest flow in a hotel lobby can be equally enlightening. Trace the flow of room guests, restaurant guests, banquet department guests, and service employees arriving through the lobby. Then note where you observe congestion.

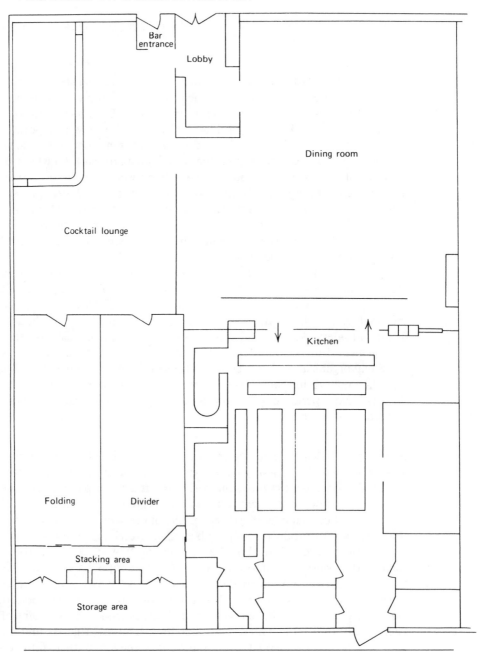

FIGURE 1.2 A sample layout.

These simple charting activities will give you some practical experience that will be useful for later courses in layout and design and in food service operations and analysis.

Learning from the Back of the House

Things to look for in the back of the house include how quality is assured in preparation, menu planning, recipes, cooking methods, supervision, and food holding. (How is lunch prepared in advance? How is it kept hot or cold? How long can food be held?) How are food costs controlled? For instance, are food portions standardized? Are they measured? How? How is access to storerooms controlled? These all are points you'll consider a great deal in later courses. But from the very beginning you can collect information that is invaluable to your studies and your career.

Learning from the Front of the House

If you are working as a busboy, waitress, or a server on a cafeteria line, you can learn a great deal about the operation from observing the guests or clients. Who are the customers, and what do they value? Peter Drucker called these the two central questions in determining what a business is and what it should be doing.[7] Are the guests or clients satisfied? What in particular seems to please them?

Employees in the hospitality industry derive personal satisfaction from pleasing the guests. So be sure to find out whether or not your job will allow you this satisfaction. Would you change things? How?

In any job you take, your future work lies in managing others and serving people. Wherever you work and whatever you do, you can observe critically the management and guest or client relations of others. Ask yourself, "How would I have handled that problem? Is this an effective management style? In what other ways have I seen this problem handled?" Your development as a manager also means the development of a management style that suits you, and that is a job that will depend in large part on your personal experience.

GETTING A JOB

Hospitality jobs can be obtained from several sources. For example, your college may maintain a placement office. Many hospitality management programs receive direct requests for part-time help. Some programs maintain a job bulletin board or file, and some even work with industry to provide internships. The "help wanted" pages of your newspaper also may offer leads, as may your local employment service office. Sometimes personal contacts established through your fellow students, your instructor, or your family or

---

[7] Peter F. Drucker, *Management: Tasks, Responsibilities, Practices* (New York: Harper & Row, 1974), pp. 80–86.

Atlanta's Peachtree Center offers a most dramatic and beautiful "front of the house." (Photo by Alexandre Georges)

neighborhood will pay off. Or you may find it necessary to "pound the pavement," making personal applications in places where you would like to work.

Some employers may even arrange for hospitality management students to rotate through more than one position and even to assume some supervisory responsibility.

Getting in the Door

But it is not enough just to ask for a job. Careful attention to your appearance is important too. For an interview, this probably means a coat and tie for men, a conservative dress for women. Neatness and cleanliness are the absolute minimum. (Neatness and cleanliness are, after all, major aspects of the hospitality product.) When you apply for or have an interview for a job, if you can, find out who the manager is; then, if the operation is not a large one, ask for him or her by name. In a larger organization, however, you'll deal with a personnel manager. The same basic rules of appearance apply, regardless of the organization's size.

Don't be afraid to check up on the status of your application. Here's an old but worthwhile adage from personal selling: It takes three calls to make a sale. The number *three* isn't magic, but a certain persistence—letting an employer know that you are interested—often will land you a job. Be sure to identify yourself as a hospitality management student, because this tells an employer that you will be interested in your work.

Learning from a Job

Let's look at some ideas about learning on the job. One key is your attitude. If you are really interested and eager to learn, you will, in fact, learn a great deal more, because you will naturally extend yourself, ask questions, and observe what's going on around you.

Many hospitality managers report that they gained the most useful knowledge on the job *on their own time.* Let's suppose you're working as a dishwasher in the summer and your operation has a person assigned to meat cutting. You may be allowed to observe and then perhaps help out—as long as you do it on your own time. Your "profit" in such a situation is in the "retained earnings" of increased knowledge. Many job skills can be learned through observation and some unpaid practice: bartending (by a waitress or waiter), clerking on a front desk (by a bellman), and even some cooking (by a dishwasher or cook's helper). With this kind of experience behind you, it may be possible to win the skilled job part time during the year or even for the following summer.

One of the best student jobs, from a learning standpoint, is a relief job, either day-off relief or vacation relief. The training for this fill-in work can teach you a good deal about every skill in your operation. Although these skills differ from the skills a manager uses, they are important for a manager to know. This is because the structure of the hospitality industry keeps most managers close to the operating level. Knowledge of necessary skills gives them credibility among their subordinates, facilitates communication, and equips them to deal confidently with skilled employees. In fact, a good manager ought to be able to pitch in when employees get stuck.[8] For these reasons, one phrase that should never pass your lips is "that's not my job."

Other Ways of Profiting from a Job

In addition to income and knowledge, after-school part-time employment has other advantages. For example, your employer might have a career for you upon graduation. This is particularly likely if your employer happens to be a fairly large firm or if you want to remain close to the area of your schooling.

In addition, you may choose to take off a term or two from school to pursue a particular interest or just to clarify your longer term job goals. This does have the advantage of giving you more than "just a summer job" on your résumé—but be sure you don't let the work experience get in the way of acquiring the basic educational requirements for progress into management.

Wherever—and for however long—you work, remember that through your employment you may make contacts that will help you after graduation. People with whom you have worked may be able to tell you of interesting opportunities or recommend you for a job.

Don't underestimate a recommendation. Even if your summer employer doesn't have a career opportunity for you, a favorable recommendation can give your career a big boost when you graduate. In addition, many employers may have contacts they will make available to you—perhaps friends of theirs who can offer interesting opportunities. The lesson here is that the record you make on the job now can help shape your career later.

EMPLOYMENT AT GRADUATION

Graduation probably seems a long way off right now, but you should already be considering strategies for finding a job when you finish your formal education. Clear goals formed now will direct your work experience plans and, to a lesser degree, the courses you take and the topics you emphasize within those courses. If you have not yet decided on a specific goal, then this question deserves prompt but careful consideration as you move through your education. You still have plenty of time.

The rest of this section offers a kind of "dry run" postgraduation placement procedure. From this distance, you can view the process objectively. When you come closer to graduation, you may find the subject a tense one:

---

[8] If they get stuck too often, of course, management must find out why and correct the problem. If a manager has to pitch in frequently, it can be a sign of inadequate organization.

People worry about placement as graduation nears, even if they're quite sure of finding a job.

GOALS AND OBJECTIVES: THE STRATEGY OF JOB PLACEMENT

Most hospitality management students have three concerns. First, many students are interested in such income issues as starting salary and the possibility of raises and bonuses.

Second, students are concerned with personal satisfaction. They wonder about opportunities for self-expression, creativity, initiative, and independence. Although few starting jobs offer a great deal of independence, some types of work (for example, employment with a franchising company) can lead quite rapidly to independent ownership. Students also want to know about the number of hours they'll be investing in their work. Many companies expect long hours, especially from junior management people. But other sectors, especially the institutional operations, make more modest demands (and generally offer more modest prospects for advancement).

Third, many students, particularly in health-care food service, want to achieve such professional goals as competence as a dietitian or a dietetic technician. Although professional goals in the commercial sector don't lead to formal certification, they are clearly associated with developing a topflight reputation as an operator. These three sets of interests are obviously related; for example, most personal goals include the elements of income, satisfaction, and professional status. Our point is that although it may be too early to set definite goals, it is not too early to begin evaluating these elements. From the three concerns we've just discussed, the following are five elements for your consideration:

1. *Income.* The place to begin your analysis is with the issue of survival. How much will you require to meet your financial needs? For example, your needs will be greater if you plan to support a family than if you need to support only yourself. If your income needs are modest, you may decide to forgo luxuries to take a lower paying job that offers superior training. Thus, you would make an investment in retained earnings—the knowledge you hope someday to trade for more income, security, and job satisfaction.

2. *Professional status.* Whether your goal is professional certification (as a dietitian, for example) or a reputation as a topflight hotelier or restaurateur, you should consider the job's benefit mix. In this case, you may choose to accept a lower income (but, of course, one on which you can live and in line with what such jobs pay in your region). Although you shouldn't be indifferent to income, you'll want to focus principally on what the job can teach you.

3. *Evaluating an employer.* Students who make snap judgments about a company and act aggressively in an interview often offend potential employers, who, after all, see the interview as an occasion to evaluate the student crop. Nevertheless, in a quiet way, you should learn about the company's commitment to training. Does it have a training program? If not, how does it translate its entry jobs into learning experiences? (Inquiries directed to your acquaintances and the younger management people can help you determine how the company really scores in these areas.) Because training beyond the entry-level basics requires responsibility and access to promotion, you will want to know about the opportunities for advancement. Finally, you need to evaluate the company's operations. Are they quality operations? Can you be proud to work there? If the quality of food or service is consistently poor, can you help improve things? Or will you be misled into learning the wrong way to do things?

4. *Determining potential job satisfaction.* Some students study hospitality management only to discover that their real love is food preparation. Such students may decide, late in their student careers, to seek a job that provides skill training in food preparation. Other students may decide they need a high income immediately (to pay off debts or to do some traveling, for example). These students may decide to trade the skills they have acquired in their work experiences to gain a high income for a year or two as a waitress or waiter in a topflight operation. Such a goal is highly personal but perfectly reasonable. The key is to form a goal and keep moving toward it. The student who wants eventually to own an operation will probably have to postpone his or her goal while developing the management skills and reputation necessary to attract the needed financial backing.

5. *Accepting skilled jobs.* Students sometimes accept skilled jobs rather than management jobs because that is all they can find. This happens, sometimes, during a period of recession. Younger students, too, are prone to suffer from this problem for a year or two, as are students who choose to locate in small communities. The concept of retained earnings provides the key to riding out these periods. Learn as much as you can and don't abandon your goals, because (as the next section will make clear) the prospects for people with management aspirations remain bright.

THE OUTLOOK FOR HOSPITALITY MANAGEMENT

The factors that underlie the changes that the hospitality industry faces are so important that we will refer to them repeatedly throughout the text, especially

Classic Residences by Hyatt offer luxury accommodations to senior citizens.
Retirement housing represents a major new area of activity for hotel companies.
(Courtesy of Hyatt Hotels Corporation; Photo by Stan Ries)

in the chapter on forces shaping food service and the final chapter that views the future. Still, at the outset we can give a quick overview of some key trends. In general, we can expect a dramatic increase in the peak age groups that use hospitality services, and this growth will extend until the turn of the century. Accompanying this growth will be a general labor shortage brought on by a reduction in a key labor market for the hospitality industry: young people.

DEMAND FOR HOSPITALITY SERVICES

People in their middle years—35 to 54—are in their peak earning years. People 35 to 44 years of age are those most inclined to travel, and people 45 to 54 spend the most on food away from home. The middle years, then, are peak years for spending on hospitality services. Both of these populations will be growing throughout the decade of the 1990s.

People over 65 are generally retired. They are another group of likely hospitality customers. Retirees today, especially those between the ages of 65 and 75, are predominantly active people—and obviously people with a lot of leisure time. While their income is not as great, neither are the demands on that income: as a rule, their children are grown and the mortgage is paid. The bumper sticker "I'm Spending My Children's Inheritance" that we see on retirees' cars suggests that older people *are* in a more openhanded mood than might once have been the case.

So, on the one hand, several strong demand segments are likely to provide healthy growth for the hospitality industry. On the other hand, food service, lodging, and tourism are all three mature industries that, as a whole, are likely to grow at about the same rate as the economy. Some sectors (take-out food service, economy lodging, and urban entertainment centers, for instance) will grow at much more rapid rates than others. Thus, there will be areas of exceptional opportunity in every field, and most of hospitality will offer solid prospects. However, *your* opportunity in hospitality management is only partly dependent on the industry's growth prospects.

Hospitality Labor Supply

There is a continuing shortage of qualified managers in the hospitality industry. Moreover, the age group that supplies most entry level managers, the college-age group, will be in decline until the mid-1990s, and the next older age group, also prominent in the operational levels of management, will be in decline throughout the decade of the 1990s. The shortage of operating managers, then, is likely to continue because the age groups from which they are drawn are getting smaller. Though some will need to make their initial start out of school in the hourly ranks, getting an entry level manager's job should not be difficult for the well qualified.

Not all the labor supply news is good news, however. Young workers play a major role in the hospitality industry in hourly jobs. While the number of teenagers has begun to rise, that rise is from a low level, and it will be the end of the decade before that population group reaches its 1980 level. As we just noted, the number of college-age people will be in decline until 1995 and only then will begin a slow climb. Overall, then, young workers will be in short supply. As a manager in just a short time, you will be faced with the need to manage this problem. Anything you can do in your education to improve your people-management skills will be time and effort well spent.

Industry Conditions

The industry faces more competition from within and from other retailers—convenience stores, for instance, and grocery store deli counters. Moreover, there is significant competition for the leisure dollar from other industries such as home entertainment.

Firms that successfully meet this competition will be service oriented. They will know what their customers want and see to it that it is delivered. Service is so important that we devote an entire chapter to that subject (see "The Role of Service in the Hospitality Industry").

Hospitality is going global. That means there will be competition from foreign firms and from U.S. firms purchased by foreign owners with "deep pockets," that is, a lot of money to invest in their U.S. affiliate, heightening competition in North America. That also means there are *some* opportunities in the international environment for people who are willing to undertake the necessary preparation. The chapter on managing international hospitality discusses these prospects.

With heightened competition and an even greater emphasis on service, the successful hospitality firm of tomorrow will need topflight managers. Your decision to *study* to prepare for the challenging industry that lies ahead is an excellent business decision. The industry needs and wants qualified people and offers more rewarding careers than ever before. Welcome, then, to your hospitality studies, and good luck in a promising career.

SUMMARY

The hospitality industry includes hotels, restaurants, and other institutions that offer shelter and/or food to people away from home. A manager in the hospitality industry, therefore, must have the following three objectives: (1) making the guest welcome personally, (2) making things work for the guest, and (3) making sure that the operation will continue providing service and meeting its budget.

There are many reasons for studying in a hospitality program, among them being a good past experience working in the field, interests in the field, and ambitions in the field.

We also discussed why people work and how to get the most from a job, including weighing both retained earnings and the job-benefit mix. We pointed out that in the hospitality industry you can learn a lot from the physical plant and from the front and the back of the house.

We then turned to ways to get a job—including preparing for an interview—and how to gain the most from whatever job you do find. We also talked about what you should consider in regard to a more permanent job: income, professional status, your employer, potential job satisfaction, and accepting an interim, less-skilled job.

Finally, we began our book-long discussion of the outlook for the hospitality industry, which we found to be bright.

KEY WORDS AND CONCEPTS

To help you review this chapter, keep in mind the following:

Hospitality	Job-benefit mix
Hospitality industry	Back of the house
Retained earnings	Front of the house

REVIEW QUESTIONS

1. What kinds of institutions or establishments does the hospitality industry include?
2. What is the role of a manager in the hospitality industry?
3. Why study in a hospitality management program?
4. What are some of the reasons that people work?
5. What is retained earnings?
6. What is a job-benefit mix?
7. What are some things to learn from the front of the house? the back of the house?
8. What kinds of things can you learn from a part-time or summer job that are not strictly part of the job?
9. What are three principal concerns in regard to a job after graduation?

P A R T 2

FOOD
SERVICE

C H A P T E R **2**

Courtesy of Hyatt Hotels Corporation (Photo by Mary McAleer)

THE RESTAURANT BUSINESS

THE PURPOSE OF THIS CHAPTER

This is the first of several chapters devoted to restaurants and food service. They should give you a useful perspective on the largest component of the hospitality industry. This chapter looks at the major types of restaurants. Combined with your own field experience and the experiences of other students as related in class discussions, this chapter should help you consider—and eventually shape—your career decisions.

In this chapter we describe some restaurant categories designed to help you visualize the variety of commercial food service operations. First, we consider *full-service restaurants* (operations that feature extensive menus, prepare most of their food on the premises, and offer table service). Full-service restaurants can be contrasted to *specialty restaurants* (which offer limited menus and often feature self-service). The specialty restaurant category includes operations such as fast-food and take-out shops, family restaurants, budget steak houses, and pizza restaurants.

Restaurants can also be categorized according to the markets they serve. We will contrast the "dining market" (served by the fine-dining and casual restaurants) to the "eating market" (served by specialty restaurants). Because of the growing importance of the "casual" upscale operation, we will devote a separate section to that part of the full-service category. Another section of this chapter discusses restaurants that are parts of other larger retail enterprises, such as food courts located in malls.

THIS CHAPTER SHOULD HELP YOU

1. Estimate the relative and absolute size of the major components of the food service field and of food service as a whole.
2. Describe and contrast the major kinds of restaurant operations.
3. Learn why some restaurant types are growing while others are declining.
4. Become familiar with the process of developing a new concept.

THE VARIED FIELD OF FOOD SERVICE

Americans spend approximately 43.5 percent of their food budget on food away from home. The lion's share of that is spent in commercial restaurants. The term "restaurant" covers an extremely broad range of food service operations. The term is derived from the French word *restaurant,* meaning restorers of energy. The term was used as early as the mid-1700s to describe public places that offered soup and bread. Today, any public place that specializes in the sale of prepared food for consumption on or off premise can be described as a restaurant. Nearly 69 percent of the food purchased away from home is sold in restaurants, cafeterias, and taverns. Hotel, motel, and motor-inn restaurants account for another 6.3 percent. Sales in restaurants located in other retail establishments, such as department stores and drugstores, account for over 3 percent. Thus, nearly $8 out of every $10 spent for food service is spent in commercial operations.

Contractors and caterers (who serve food in places such as industrial plants and office buildings, health-care facilities, and schools and colleges) generate 7.5 percent of food sales, while just over 11 percent is sold by institutions that operate their own food service. Slightly more than 2 percent of sales are made through vending machines. As you can see, 20 percent of food-away-from-home expenditures are accounted for by the institutional market. These estimates are summarized in Table 2.1.

Food service is a mature industry; that is, it is growing at about the same rate as the economy as a whole.[1] Moreover, the proportionate shares of the market captured by the major segments identified in Table 2.1 tend to be quite stable from year to year. Such seeming stability, however, hides important evolutionary processes that are going on within these categories. In fact, the industry is in the throes of change. For instance, the number of units offering food for off-premise consumption (i.e., take-out, drive-through, and delivery service) is increasing roughly three times as fast as is the growth of units that do not offer that service. Fast food altered dramatically the *meaning* of what a

---

[1] John J. Rohs, *The Restaurant Industry: The Outlook for 1990 and Beyond* (New York: Wertheirm Schroeder and Company, February 1990), p. 7.

TABLE 2.1 The Major Areas of Food Service, 1991

	Sales	
Category	(millions of $)	%
Restaurants, cafeterias, fast food, bars, and taverns	$168.9	68.3%
Food service in hotels, motels, and motor hotels	15.7	6.3
Food service sales in retail stores	7.8	3.2
Vending and nonstore retailers	5.7	2.3
Contractors and caterers	18.5	7.5
Recreation and sports	2.9	1.2
Institutions operating own food service	27.6	11.2
	$247.1	100.0%

Source: National Restaurant Association.

Note: Dollar amounts and percentages shown are based on estimates for 1991 made by the National Restaurant Association in *Restaurants USA,* December 1990, p. 18.

restaurant was during the 1960s and 1970s. The trend toward off-premise consumption, which is now well established, suggests that another fundamental change in the business definition for restaurants may be in the offing.

Another set of changes involves fine dining, for years the mainstay of the upscale restaurant segment. In recent years it has been declining in relative importance while casual dining operations have been the fastest growing segment. Food *tastes* are changing as well, with growing emphasis on fresh and healthy foods. We will be examining these and numerous other changes in this and the next three chapters. Most of these developments result from changes in the age composition of North America's population. The huge generation that was born in the 20 years following World War II, called the "baby boomers," are entering middle age. As they do, their life-styles are changing.

Food service is a basic part of the North American way of life. Virtually everyone in North America has eaten in a restaurant, and roughly half the population eats in a restaurant at least once in any given month. Restaurants account for over a quarter of the lunches and dinners served (27 percent and 28 percent, respectively, according to the Gallup poll) and close to 1 in 10 breakfasts (7 percent) and snacks (7 percent).[2] Roughly 10 percent of the meals eaten in the United States are eaten in a restaurant.[3] While not all of the nonrestaurant balance of 90 percent represents market opportunity, a good bit of it does. In fact, as Figure 2.1 illustrates, food service's share of the food dollar has increased steadily over the last 35 years.

[2] *Restaurants USA,* August 1990, p. 44.

[3] George D. Rice, "Leveraging Resources in a Mature Market," *Proceedings of the 18th Annual Chain Operators Exchange,* Orlando, Florida, February 24–27, 1991 (Chicago: International Foodservice Manufacturers Association, 1991).

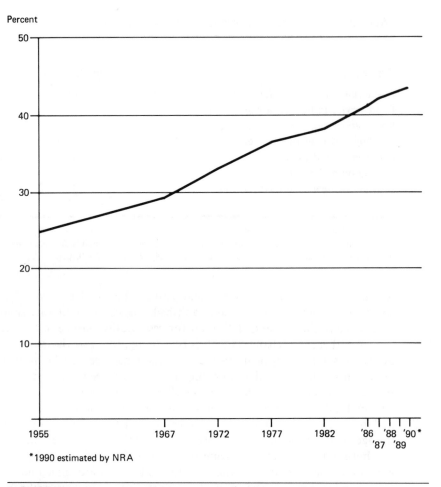

Percent

*1990 estimated by NRA

FIGURE 2.1 Percentage of food budget spent on food away from home 1955–1990. (*Source:* National Restaurant Association.)

THE RESTAURANT BUSINESS

One problem in describing the restaurant business is that it changes so fast that today's description may well be outdated tomorrow. Moreover, there are so many and varied types of restaurants that it is almost impossible to devise a model to fit all operations. Nevertheless, we need some basic terminology to describe the field even generally. Two obvious (and descriptive) terms are *full-service restaurant* and *specialty restaurant*.

FULL-SERVICE RESTAURANTS

The term *full-service* refers to the *style of service* in the dining room, to the *menu,* and to the *style of preparation.* A traditional full-service restaurant offers a wide variety of menu choices, and most full-service restaurants prepare most of their food "from scratch" (that is, from fresh or raw ingredients). Waitresses and waiters serve the food.

There are, however, really three kinds of full-service restaurants. First is the independent fine-dining restaurant specializing in haute cuisine.[4] Second, at the opposite end of the spectrum, are such lower priced operations as neighborhood restaurants with simple and inexpensive fare, usually prepared "from scratch," but offering table service. The second group of operations are sometimes called mom-and-pop restaurants because they are often family concerns in which one spouse supervises the cooking while the other looks after the front of the house. Mom-and-pop restaurants are increasingly threatened by newer competition such as fast-food, family restaurants, and budget steak house operations that offer competitive prices in more modern surroundings. It is more and more unusual, moreover, to find people who are willing to work the hours of the owner-managers in the mom-and-pop segment.

The third kind of full-service restaurant is the casual dinner house. Although most are also open for lunch, this restaurant category takes its name from its function as a "nice place to have dinner." Like other full-service restaurants, these operations offer a varied menu and table service, with prices ranging from mid- to upscale. The ambience, that is, the decor and "feel" of the place in these restaurants, is intended to support a dining experience that is fun and relaxing. To achieve this effect operations often use ethnic themes in both decor and food service, creating an evening's adventure in a far away place—or at least a place that gives the appearance of not being just around the corner.

In the midscale price range, chains predominate with operations such as TGI Friday's, Chi Chi's, Red Lobster, and Olive Garden. Upscale operations tend to be independents. It is increasingly common, however, to find fine-dining restaurants that are deliberately lowering their prices so that the average sale per guest will decrease from the $35-to-$50 range to one of from $15 to $25. At the same time, they are adopting a more casual style of ambiance and interaction with the guest. That is, the ranks of fine dining are thinning and those of casual dining are growing. We will have occasion to discuss fine dining and casual restaurants in more detail later in this chapter.

SPECIALTY RESTAURANTS

A wide variety of restaurants can be called *specialty restaurants.* Here, too, it is difficult to establish neat categories. All of the specialty operations tend to

---

[4] Loosely translated, the term means *elegant dining,* or food prepared in the manner of the classic French (or European) chefs.

Specialty restaurants often have lower operating costs that can be passed on to the guest in lower prices. (Courtesy of Buffets Inc.)

simplify their production processes, although to varying degrees, and most of them use at least some self-service. The result is a drastic reduction in labor in both the front and back of the house, as Table 2.2 shows. Because specialty restaurants require less labor, they can pass on their savings to the guests in the form of lower prices. Furthermore, these operations, even with their lower prices, have historically earned profits substantially higher than those of other operations. Although not all specialty restaurants are affiliated with chains or franchise groups, many are, especially in fast food. A few exceptions will be discussed later in this chapter. Specialty restaurants may look different from

TABLE 2.2   Productivity in Food Service Establishments

Food Service Type	Direct Labor Hours per 100 Guests
Luxury restaurants	72.3
Family restaurants	20.7
Cafeterias	18.3
Fast food	10.5

Source: Agricultural Research Service.

Theme restaurants offer an atmosphere that will entertain. Shown is Crawdaddy's Restaurant on the Tampa Bay Waterfront in Florida. (Courtesy of Specialty Restaurant Corp.)

one another but, to a surprising degree, they are all modeled on one pattern, dictated by the fast-food concept.

Fast Food: The QSR

Fast food is the largest single form of specialty restaurant and, in fact, the largest single form of restaurant of any kind, accounting for approximately 45 percent of restaurant sales.[5] While fast food has been the fastest growing segment, its growth has slowed in recent years. The everyday phrase, "fast food," is the most common name for the segment we are discussing, but operators of this kind of restaurant generally prefer their units to be called "quick-service restaurants" or QSRs. These operations have always had a rightful claim to the name *restaurant* but, given the increasing sophistication of physical plant and decor as well as the growing length of their menus, any

[5] *Restaurants USA,* December 1990, p. 18.

doubt about their claim must be dismissed out of hand today. We will use the terms *QSR* and *fast food* interchangeably in this text.

Automation is the key to the modern QSR. When we think of automation, we usually imagine a factory, masses of machinery, and repetitive tasks. But as Peter Drucker pointed out, "Automation is not 'technical' in character. Like every technology, it is primarily a system of concepts, and its technical aspects are results rather than causes."[6] Automation in this sense, then, refers to a way of *thinking about* production, and the nuts and bolts of operations follow from the ideas that spark that thinking process. Although mechanization and computerization are an important part of QSR operations, their fast-food restaurants are not automated in the sense of *depending* on new, automatic machinery. Some new variations of the traditional food service equipment are found in these operations, but it is really the customer who has been automated!

The *automating concept* in the fast-food operation is a reduction in menu choices, a sharp limitation on customer service, and different customer behavior. Through self-service, the customer replaces the entire front-of-the-house staff, even to the point of cleaning up. There may be some choice in regard to cleaning up, but absolutely no choice in regard to self-service. Moreover, because fast-food operations offer a simple menu, very specialized, highly efficient kitchens can be built around this limited food choice.

The fast-food operation is, in many ways, more like a manufacturing enterprise than a traditional restaurant. One management scholar put it this way:

> McDonald's has created a highly sophisticated piece of service technology by applying the manufacturing mode of managerial thought to a labor-intensive service situation. If a machine is a piece of equipment with the capability of producing a predictably standardized, customer-satisfying output while minimizing the operating discretion of its attendant, that is what a McDonald's outlet is. It produces, with the help of totally unskilled machine tenders, a fairly sophisticated, reliable product at great speed and low cost.
>
> McDonald's represents the industrialization of service—applying, through management, the same systematic modes of analysis, design, organization, and control that are commonplace in manufacturing. These more than anything account for its success.[7]

Fast Food's Unique Characteristics. Tim Zagat, editor of a prestigious newsletter on New York City's fine restaurants, surveyed his regular subscriber list not long ago to find out what they knew about fast food. He discovered that even his upper crust clientele was very knowledgeable about QSRs and

[6] Peter Drucker, *The Practice of Management* (New York: Harper & Row, 1954), p. 19.

[7] Theodore Levitt, "Management and the Post-Industrial State," *The Public Interest,* Summer 1976, p. 89.

that they had formed marked preferences among fast-food restaurants in addition to their fine-dining preferences. Indeed, as Mr. Zagat remarked, "Eating in fast-food chains is an undeniable part of the American life-style today."[8] As a matter of fact, the presence of fast-food operations in every market of any size is a key characteristic of fast food and one of the main factors supporting the growth of QSRs over the past 25 years. Because they are, almost literally, everywhere, they make eating out convenient. That convenience reinforces patronage.

We have already noted that simplified menus and operations that use unskilled labor result in a price that has been very attractive to the consumer. This simple operating format results in fast service and has earned fast food its name. Self-service is built into the operating format, reinforcing both speed of service and lower cost, especially in the absence of any tipping.

Fast food is dominated by chains, and this introduces an interesting note of complexity into a segment that at first appears to be straightforward. While the operation of any single QSR unit is relatively straightforward compared with other, more service-intensive restaurants, the operation of the *restaurant chain as a whole*—that is, as a system of interactive parts—is highly complex. With over 8,500 restaurants in the United States alone, McDonalds requires a huge management structure to make all the parts of the system function together in a consistent fashion that the consumer can depend on.

The introduction of a new product offers a useful example of this complexity. In a more traditional restaurant, with its flexible kitchen, introducing a new product is just a matter of developing a recipe, putting it in the menu, and trying it out. Managers introducing a product in fast food, however, must take account of the equipment changes required in thousands of restaurants; the preferences and perceptions of consumers in widely different geographic markets; the packaging requirements for the new product; and the marketing cost of persuading customers across the country or the world to try the product.

When a large company with thousands of units adds an item, supplier markets must be considered too. A few examples will illustrate the point. When Church's Fried Chicken decided to change the portion size of a catfish product it was in the process of introducing, a $5 million promotional campaign had to be stopped in midstride and then restarted because Church's discovered that the producers were unable to deliver sufficient numbers of the new portion sizes for a time.[9] When Wendy's began offering baked potatoes, a product ordered *hundreds of thousands of times daily,* the U.S. potato market was disrupted.[10] When McDonald's rolled out Chicken McNuggets, it had to

[8] *Wall Street Journal,* October 5, 1988, p. B1.

[9] *Nations Restaurant News,* August 19, 1985, p. 100.

[10] Michael Culp, "Wendy's International Company Report," *Prudential Bache Securities,* March 8, 1985, pp. 8–9.

TABLE 2.3 What Makes Fast Food Different?

Location strategy (they are everywhere!)
Highly limited menu
Sales volume: very high and highly variable
Fast service; high degree of self-service
Numerous part-time employees with various schedules
Use of unskilled labor—and highly skilled management
Key role for unit managers
Highly competitive prices
Chain domination
Simple unit; complex system

arrange to have a total of 5 million pounds of chicken delivered *each week* to the 6,200 restaurants it then operated across the United States. When Burger King introduced the bacon cheeseburger, those three strips of bacon (times millions of customers) so increased the demand for bacon that it disrupted the national commodity markets in pork bellies.[11]

While we have asserted that a fast-food unit is a relatively simple operation, it is *not* true that managing one is in any way a simple or easy task. Managing the very tight quality and cost controls on which QSR operations depend is also extremely demanding. The very large and highly variable sales volume that QSRs experience requires managers to hire numerous part-time employees whose schedules vary from day to day and week to week. Keeping this crew properly trained and motivated is a major task. Given the costs associated with turnover, such as lost training time as well as management time required to hire and train new employees, maintaining staff morale is also a major factor in controlling payroll costs. Table 2.3 summarizes some of the most significant distinguishing characteristics of QSRs.

The Evolving QSR. Some of the factors cited in Table 2.3 that make QSRs different have begun to blur, while others are in a state of flux. The limited menu of most QSRs has been broadened to the extent that QSRs are, to some degree, competing with family restaurants and coffee shops. The menus have been expanded with salads and "lite" entrees to meet consumer needs and concerns such as nutrition and health. To attract customers who don't like just burgers, chicken and fish have been added at McDonald's and other hamburger chains. To please health-conscious customers, decaffeinated coffee is available. The effect of this cumulatively, however, is to add requirements for space, equipment, and labor. All of this also adds to operating costs and, incidentally, can slow service times.

---

[11] *Wall Street Journal,* January 5, 1984, p. 21.

As people's tastes in restaurants have become more sophisticated, fast-food companies have upgraded the restaurant unit, first adding seating, then simple decor and, in more recent years, costly enhancements to ambiance and often special features appropriate to the locale. Fax and "ticker tape" machines, for instance, have been added in areas near stock brokerages as have antiques in upscale neighborhoods. A Wall Street outlet has a reception room and a menu offering cappuccino and espresso — and, of course, the equipment to go with it.[12] This enhancement of physical plant, however, is hard to offset with additional sales.

One key factor in the success of QSRs is productivity. This is a factor that we usually think of in terms of labor. Investment productivity is increasingly important as well, however, as physical facilities become more elaborate. In fact, moderately priced table-service operations such as Shoney's or Sizzler have sales that are 1.25 to 1.75 times the investment cost of a restaurant. A QSR, on the other hand, has a dramatically lower sales-to-investment ratio, from 1:1 to 1:1.05.[13] Put another way, fast-food operators have to spread their capital cost over fewer sales. As a result, they reduce profit at a proportionately greater rate.

In the last half of the 1980s, *rising* operating *costs* and investment in plant and equipment resulted in *rising prices* in fast food. McDonald's prices, for instance, consistently rose more rapidly than the consumer price index from 1985 to 1989.[14]

As traditional fast-food companies have increased prices to the consumer to offset rising operating and investment costs, they have created opportunities for smaller, simpler operations that are more like the original fast-food concept. For this reason, conventional QSRs find themselves facing increasing competition from simplified fast-food operations such as the double drive-throughs and take-out operations that serve the consumer who wants a convenient, inexpensive meal in a hurry. As *The Wall Street Journal* put it, the drive-through customer "looks at it more as a fuel stop than a dining experience."[15]

Double drive throughs typically provide neither seating nor parking. Hence they can use smaller, less-expensive real estate. The small building they use is also much less expensive and requires less equipment.[16] With a simple menu, fewer employees are required and transaction times of less than a minute ensure high productivity of both labor and capital. Other low-invest-

---

[12] *TRA Foodservice Digest/Chicago Tribune,* October 30, 1990, sec. 3, p. 1.

[13] Michael G. Mueller, "Why the Mid-Priced Restaurant Is More Attractive than Fast Food," *1989 Restaurant Industry Trends and Analysis* (San Francisco; Montgomery Securities, October 16, 1989), Table 9.

[14] Michael G. Mueller, *Company Update: McDonald's Corporation* (San Francisco: Montgomery Securities, January 26, 1990), p. 3.

[15] *The Wall Street Journal,* June 22, 1990, p. B1.

[16] *Restaurants USA,* March 1991, pp. 26–28.

ment units, such as carryout pizza and sub and sandwich shops offering "value and convenience above everything,"[17] are also responding to the opening created by rising prices in established QSR chains. We will return to the topics of drive-through, take-out, and delivery operations later in this chapter.

Some of the new operations following the simplication trend, we should note, show that a good thing can be carried too far. Yogurt restaurants have found that their "special" featured product was one that all its fast-food competitors could add to their menus quite easily. As a result, yogurt specialty restaurants have seen their market share threatened. Perhaps for this reason, some simplified operations have begun to add menu items and facilities as competition in their market niche has increased. Cookie Factory, for instance, added soups, sandwiches, muffins, croissants, cinnamon rolls, and puff pastries to their menu and added seating in some of their units.[18]

There are clear indications that rapid price increases in QSRs are at an end and, indeed, that rising competition between giants such as Pepsi's Taco Bell and McDonald's has set off what *Nations Restaurant News* called a "value stampede." Price competition has been a problem for QSRs in slow-volume periods, particularly in the winter months, for years. In the late 1980s, however, Taco Bell introduced the value menu featuring 59-cent items. When it became clear that these lower prices were a permanent feature at Taco Bell, the initiative resulted in a basic change in competitive patterns. Other fast-food chains sooner or later followed Taco Bell's lead and price competition became, instead of a seasonal aberration, a regular fixture in QSR competition.

It is interesting to reflect on why this strategy worked for Taco Bell. First of all their (food) product cost was lower than many other main line fast-food chains. Moreover, before the introduction of "value pricing," they were seen by customers as a specialty chain with limited appeal. When they offered a bargain, however, the number of people trying Taco Bell increased dramatically—and they liked what they found and came back. The move paid off, with unit volumes soaring. Customer counts rose 35 percent and dollar sales increased by about 20 percent in a period when traffic increased less than 8 percent and dollar volume rose only 1 percent at other chains.

The picture we see, then, is of fast food having broadened menus and upgraded decor with the result that cost of operation has increased. They now face competition from lower priced QSRs and other specialized concepts as well as heavy discounting and price competition from within the established QSRs. McDonald's, we should note, however, is still feeding well over 20 million people a day.[19] QSRs have adjusted to changed competitive conditions with lowered prices, tighter operations, increased promotional expenditures,

[17] *Nations Restaurant News,* March 11, 1991, p. 7.

[18] *Nations Restaurant News,* December 3, 1990, p. 44.

[19] *Wall Street Journal,* June 22, 1990, p. B1.

and still more new products. Nevertheless, the days of unimpeded growth are over for fast food.

The Future of Fast Food. Perhaps the most difficult challenge the QSRs face is the shift in the composition of the population, that is, the aging of the baby boomers. Baby boomers (people born between 1946 and 1964) played a major role in creating demand for fast food when they were children and for its gradual upscaling as they entered their teens and twenties in the years just before and after 1970. In 1990, the youngest baby boomer was 26 and in 1995 will be over 30. As they leave their youth behind and enter middle age, baby boomers' tastes are naturally changing. They are able to afford a more expensive restaurant and prefer a more upscale environment and more extensive service. All of these operators have made major efforts to adapt to the preferences for healthier foods and a more pleasant dining environment. The QSR simply no longer fits their needs as well as it did when they were younger. At the same time, the segments of the population who are natural customers for fast food are becoming a smaller segment of the population. While QSRs will be sought out by people of all ages when speed or cost are especially important, the market for fast-food services is no longer expanding and may even be shrinking.

While fast food may have passed its prime in terms of growth, this does not mean that QSR employment opportunities will shrink. Indeed, with so many units in operation, even without growth the large number of units all require staffing, and this in the face of a persistent shortage of qualified managers and considerable turnover. Note, too, that some kinds of QSRs, such as those featuring Mexican and Asian food, are likely to grow faster than the rest of fast food. True, the number of fast-track opportunities that have characterized this segment of the industry will probably fall. Nevertheless, QSRs are still likely to offer attractive opportunities. They give significant responsibility to new managers and generous compensation to those who can deliver results, and their many units mean opportunities for advancement.

Other Specialty Restaurants

Although other specialty restaurants may not *look like* fast-food operations, the heart of all specialty operating systems closely resembles the QSR format. Their back-of-the-house production system has been simplified by a specialized menu that reduces skill levels, thus holding down wage costs and speeding service. Specialty restaurants might therefore be called "moderately fast food," for although the guests in these operations are prepared to wait a bit longer for food, they will not have to wait much longer. We will discuss three of the most numerous specialty restaurant types: family restaurants, budget steak houses, and pizza operations.

Family Restaurants. Family restaurants, sometimes referred to as coffee shops, depart quite a bit from the fast-food format in that they offer waiter or

Adventure in an exotic atmosphere is part of the experience offered by Benihana of Tokyo, where foods are cooked in front of the guest on a "hibachi table" by a Japanese chef. (Courtesy of Benihana)

waitress service as well as self-service in the form of salad bars, breakfast bars, and dessert bars. Family restaurants usually offer breakfast, lunch, and dinner. Another similarity to full-service restaurants is the extensive variety of menu items they appear to offer.

This resemblance to full service is, however, deceiving. First, the preparation staff is limited to one or more short-order cooks. Almost everything is prepared to order, sometimes from scratch (as with the sandwiches and breakfast items that give the menu much of its variety), and sometimes from frozen or chilled prepared foods that are reconstituted to order. The production process is really almost as simple as the fast-food process.

Furthermore, the service the customers receive is anything but elaborate. Place settings usually consist of paper place mats and a minimum of china and silver. Most meals consist of a choice of soup or salad, an entrée with rolls and butter, and perhaps a dessert. This reduction in courses simplifies service. Platters, sandwiches, and salads are the mainstay of the menu, all attractively but simply served. Breakfast is the largest meal for some operators and a significant one for all the others. Snacks and coffee breaks are also an im-

TABLE 2.4 Leading Family
Restaurant Chains

Denny's
Big Boy
Shoney's
Friendly's Restaurants
Perkins Family Restaurants
International House of Pancakes
Bob Evans Farms
Waffle House
Cracker Barrel
Baker's Square

Source: Nations Restaurant News, August
1990, p. 79.

portant source of business, particularly for family restaurants that combine a
bakery with their unit. Table 2.4 shows the 10 leading family chains. In this
segment, chains dominate with something over three quarters of the market.

Given the relatively straightforward operating format of family restaurants, the cost of training new service employees remains manageable. And the
flexible menu permits operations to drop menu choices when their food costs
advance too rapidly and to substitute less costly items.

The guests who visit a family restaurant want to be waited on and, in
choosing a family restaurant, they are opting for an informal, simple, relatively inexpensive style of service. These operations generally offer a pleasant,
modern restaurant located near dense pedestrian or vehicular traffic and
convenient to shoppers and suburban family diners.

While QSRs face problems in adapting to changing demographics, family restaurants, with their more varied menus, table service, and modest price
level, offer considerable appeal to the aging baby boomer. For families,
children's menus are available that often cost less than feeding the same child
at a QSR. Another market that family restaurants have considerable appeal to
is the 55- to 64-year-olds, a segment of the population that will be in a growth
phase beginning in 1995. Many family restaurants offer budget menus or
special selections for seniors.[20] To appeal to all these market segments, family
restaurants are offering expanded menus featuring selections that are lighter
and healthier.

Family restaurants do face significant competition. On the one hand,
their customers can choose a QSR that offers less menu choice but lower price
and an ambiance that is frequently equal to that offered by a family restaurant. At the other extreme, they face competition from casual full-service

[20]*Nations Restaurant News,* August 6, 1990, p. 76.

Some specialty restaurants feature self-service and offer comfortable but spartan surroundings. Others, like Chi Chi's shown here, offer table service and lots of atmosphere. (Courtesy of Foodmaker Inc.)

restaurants, some of which offer prices that are not a lot higher. Like any operation in the middle, family restaurants have to watch out for price competition from those below and value competition from those on the next rung up. Thus their strategy must be to hold down prices while trying to improve their image, food, and service.[21] During the 1980s, midscale restaurants lost nearly 9 percent of their share of the market to QSRs.[22] On the other hand, as the 1990s opened, a sign that the tide may be turning is found in the breakfast market segment. Fast food lost nearly 3 percent of its market share—to midscale operators.[23]

Budget Steak Houses. In the early 1970s, budget steak houses grew rapidly. They relied, however, on steak as a main product. When the price of beef began to soar, they felt serious cost pressures. Moreover, they relied principally on the evening meal for most of their sales. Finally, their main target

[21] *Nations Restaurant News,* August 6, 1990, p. 76.
[22] Rice, "Leveraging Resources in a Mature Market."
[23] Rohs, *The Restaurant Industry,* p. 22.

market in the 1970s was the blue-collar family. During the recession of the early 1980s, many of these operations found they had to turn to other formats. The blue-collar work force was not growing as fast as white-collar employment, and the vulnerability of steak houses to blue-collar unemployment in a recession became painfully apparent. Their experience is often described by the term *repositioning*. Repositioning involves changing not only the operating format but the target market that a firm is pursuing while shifting into an area where competition is not as intense.

Family steak houses have diversified their menus by adding chicken and fish entrées, sandwiches, and elaborate salad bars. In an effort to widen their market, some steak houses have also added breakfast bars, thus expanding into another part of the day. The consumer's continuing interest in health and nutrition has led to even greater emphasis on chicken and seafood. Today these operations' sales of steak are less than 50 percent, while food bars account for as much as 45 percent of sales. Because of their broadened menu, "budget steakers" are in more or less direct competition with family restaurants.

Franchising brands are becoming increasingly common in travel plazas along interstates and other expressways. (Courtesy of Pizza Hut, Inc.)

Pizza Restaurants. Pizza restaurants, like budget steak houses, once depended almost exclusively on a single item. But in recent years, pizza restaurants have extended their product line to appeal to more customers. New items include the deep-dish, Chicago-style pizza; pizza with thick or thin crust; specialty two-crusted pizza; and, at lunch, individual-sized pizzas. All have added variety and choice to the menu. In addition, many operations have added other Italian dishes to their menu and, at lunch, submarine sandwiches. But despite all their menu and service expansion, these operations are still principally pizza restaurants. The cost of their food product itself is relatively low, and these operations also have low labor costs. Pizza's continuing popularity with consumers ensures its remaining in the front ranks of growth concepts.

Pizza is an interesting product in itself and would merit our attention on that basis. The pizza segment of the industry, however, is especially interesting for having pioneered home delivery. Domino's was the first to show on a broad national scale that delivery was an economically viable concept. This subject of delivery deserves more attention and we will return to it later in this chapter.

There are, of course, numerous other specialty restaurants, featuring, for instance, chicken, seafood, ice cream, Mexican food, and Asian food. They generally fit the pattern already described: limited menus, highly efficient productivity based on an "automated customer," and a product characterized by a relatively low food cost.

THE DINING MARKET AND THE EATING MARKET

One of the twentieth century's most innovative restaurateurs, Joe Baum, summed up the challenge of food service in this way:

> A restaurant takes a basic drive—the simplest act of eating—and transforms it into a civilized ritual; a ritual involving hospitality and imagination and satisfaction and graciousness and warmth.[24]

Restaurants serve both our social and our biological needs. To show the restaurant business from both of these perspectives, we will divide restaurants into those serving predominantly our social needs—the *dining market*—and those serving our biological needs—the *eating market*. Of course, nearly all meals eaten in public have a social dimension, just as the most formal state dinner has its biological aspect. The main purpose, however, is usually clear.

The specialty restaurants we have been discussing are more or less part of the eating market. Although many of them seem to emphasize decor and service, they really concentrate on economy and speed. The dining market,

---

[24] *Restaurants & Institutions,* February 5, 1986, p. 16.

serving our social and recreational needs, emphasizes personal service, food excellence, and often entertainment.

DINING WELL

From research by the National Restaurant Association, we have some clues to the motives of diners: to escape from boredom, to socialize, to avoid drudgery, to be waited on, to have foods different from those served at home. Finally, consumers find that dining out is convenient.[25]

Because dining (as opposed to eating) is predominantly a social event, service is important. Research on what consumers value in *service*[26] revealed that the server in a good restaurant is expected to anticipate the guests' needs and to be attentive, but not disruptive. At lunch, and to a lesser degree at dinner, guests value promptness and efficiency. At dinner, the service needs to be both timely (no long waits) and well timed ("when I'm ready"). The servers are expected to be friendly, as signified by a warm smile, and to be accurate. The role of the server is, therefore, ideally much more than a mechanical one. (Note that service is discussed in more detail in the chapter on the role of service in the hospitality industry.)

In the expensive restaurants serving the dining market, the operation that falls short on significant measures of service is likely to lose customers quickly. The demographics of such customers, as always, are important. The older consumer who dines in a fine restaurant is well-educated, has a higher than average income, and is accustomed to dining out and to traveling. As Don Smith, Taco Bell Distinguished Professor at Washington State University, put it recently, "We're dealing with an aging, more experienced society."[27]

The importance of service was illustrated in a Gallup survey which indicated that service strongly influences whether guests will return and whether they will recommend the operation to others. "It's incredible how much diners will put up with if they are treated properly. Mediocre food, too much noise, cramped tables all appear to be accepted as long as people are greeted with a welcoming smile and are made to feel that the management cares about them."[28] In the dining market, food is a primary consideration, but good service is essential too.

Fine-Dining Restaurants

Most full-service, fine-dining establishments are small, independent operations, some seating fewer than 100 guests. Despite their modest capacities,

[25] *NRA News* January 1986, p. 39.

[26] Ron Dimbert, "An Evaluation of Service Requirements," *Proceedings of the 12th Annual Chain Operators Exchange,* Miami, February 17–20, 1985. (Chicago: International Foodservice Manufacturers Association, 1985).

[27] *NRA News,* March 1986, p. 14.

[28] *NRA News,* March 1986, p. 14.

these restaurants succeed because of their excellent quality. Many are staffed by trained professional chefs who have brought with them a craft tradition that dates back to the Middle Ages and, incidentally, to a time when wage costs were relatively lower and labor intensity was more practical. Many operations, however, provide excellent food prepared by American staffs who are often less formally trained.

Excellence is the absolute prerequisite in these operations because the prices they must charge are high. An operator may do everything possible to make the restaurant efficient, but the guests still expect careful, personal service: food prepared to order by highly skilled chefs and served by expert waiters or waitresses. Because this service is, quite literally, manual labor, only marginal improvements in productivity are possible. For example, a cook, waitress, or waiter can move only so much faster before she or he reaches the limits of human performance. Thus, only moderate savings are possible through improved efficiency, which makes an escalation of prices inevitable. (It is an axiom of economics that as prices rise, consumers become more discriminating.) Thus the clientele of the fine restaurant expects, demands, and is willing to pay for excellence. In fact, only about 1 percent of table-service restaurants fit in this category.[29]

These distinguished operations generally require a "critical mass" of three different kinds: market, skilled workers, and devoted management. First, because of the high prices they must charge, most are located in or near large population centers or in major tourism areas. As a result, there is a sufficiently large number of people with high incomes to ensure a satisfactory sales volume. Table 2.5 shows the cities and areas with the heaviest concentration of fine-dining establishments. You will notice that they are all located in major population centers or an important tourist destination area. Table 2.6 shows the states that have the largest number of fine-dining establishments. The picture that emerges is one of areas with either a very large population base or with very large tourist volumes. In either case, the critical mass of a substantial number of customers is necessary because visit frequency is, according to CREST, only slightly more than once a month.[30]

A second requirement of these restaurants is chefs and service personnel with highly polished skills. It is, of course, difficult to find such workers anywhere, but they are most likely to be found in big cities. A third and most important requirement for successful fine-dining restaurants is a special devotion from the key operating personnel, especially their owners. The hours tend to be long, and the owners, although amply compensated, generally devote their lives to their work.

---

[29]Estimate based on the number of restaurants with a per person check average of $30 or more in the most recent 1987 Census of Business. *Restaurants USA,* February 1991, p. 31.

[30]Rice, "Leveraging Resources in a Mature Market." CREST is the acronym for Consumer Reports in Eating Out Share Trends, a series of market research studies based on diaries that consumers keep for researchers.

TABLE 2.5 Top-Ranked Metropolitan Areas for Fine Dining Based on Establishments per Capita

Rank	Metropolitan Area	Resident Population per Fine-Dining Establishment	Number of Fine-Dining Establishments
1	Portsmount–Dover–Rochester, NH–ME	11,300	19
2	Ft. Myers–Cape Coral, FL	22,700	13
3	Salinas–Seaside–Monterey, CA	26,400	13
4	NY, Northern NJ, Long Island, CT	31,900	566
5	Las Vegas, NV	46,200	13
6	Portland–Vancouver, OR–WA	55,300	25
7	Miami–Ft. Lauderdale, FL	55,700	53
8	West Palm Beach–Boca Raton–Delray, FL	56,400	14
9	San Francisco–Oakland–San Jose, CA	63,300	94
10	Philadelphia–Wilmington–Trenton, PA, DE, NJ	70,100	84
11	New Orleans, LA	77,700	17
12	Honolulu, HI	83,100	10
13	Hartford–New Britain–Middletown, CT	88,100	12
14	Atlanta, GA	88,600	30
15	Washington, DC, MD, VA	91,200	40
16	Los Angeles–Anaheim–Riverside, CA	93,500	144
17	Chicago–Gary–Lake County, IL, IN	99,400	82
18	Sacramento, CA	95,400	14
19	Boston–Lawrence–Salem, MA, NH	110,600	37
20	Denver–Boulder, CO	116,300	16

Source: National Restaurant Association analysis of *1987 Census of Retail Trade.* From *Restaurants USA,* February 1991, p. 31.
Note: Fine dining = per person check of $30 or more

The field requires a person to invest in long training periods to achieve competency. However, for those attracted to this kind of operation, the satisfactions go far beyond monetary compensation. To be sure, key people in fine-dining restaurants earn comfortable livings, but their most important reward comes from the professional satisfaction and respect found only in the achievement of excellence.

TABLE 2.6 Top 10 States Based on Number of Fine-Dining Establishments

State	Number of Fine-Dining Establishments	Sales (millions)
New York	465	$654.2
California	307	334.1
New Jersey	116	87.2
Florida	102	106.6
Pennsylvania	92	73.6
Illinois	82	92.3
Massachusetts	79	58.9
Texas	65	64.9
Michigan	42	39.8
Colorado	42	35.5

Source: National Restaurant Association analysis of *1987 Census of Retail Trade.* From *Restaurants USA,* February 1991, p. 32.
Note: Fine dining = per person check of $30 or more.

Fine-dining operations showed no growth in 1989 and an actual decline of nearly 7 percent in 1990.[31] The National Restaurant Association indicates that this category of restaurant probably "peaked in 1987."[32] George Rice, a leading authority on food service trends in the United States, points out that what is required is "perfection,"[33] a difficult standard for all but the very finest operations. A sophisticated customer with educated tastes expects that the very high prices of haute cuisine will be matched by excellence — and anything less leads to loss in patronage.

Some part of the loss in sales may come, as well, from changing demographics. Older patrons, who inevitably leave the market, were accustomed to the kind of service rituals that characterize these operations. Younger customers who have grown up with less formal ways, as they progress in income and age to the point where they are logical customers for fine dining, are apparently put off by overly formal fine dining and prefer an upscale experience that is less stuffy.

Casual Dinner Houses

The variety of forms the casual dinner house takes is suggested by Table 2.7. In contrast to family restaurants, which offer a wide variety of product at

[31] Rice, "Leveraging Resources in a Mature Market."

[32] *Restaurants USA,* February 1991, p. 32.

[33] Rice, "Leveraging Resources in a Mature Market."

TABLE 2.7   Leading Dinner House Chains

Chain	Specialty
Red Lobster	Seafood
Olive Garden	Italian
TGI Fridays	Full menu
Chili's Grill & Bar	American food
Bennigan's	Full menu
Chi Chi's	Mexican
Tony Roma's	Full menu
Ground Round	American food
El Torito	Mexican
Steak and Ale	Steak and seafood

Source: Adapted from *Nations Restaurant News,* August 6, 1990, p. 74.

modest prices, dinner houses usually have a more distinctive, specialized menu and prices that range as high as double those of a family restaurant. These operations are restaurants that have taken to heart the advice of William Rice, the food editor of *The Washington Post* and a restaurant consultant:

> The single-minded vision of the restaurant as a temple of gastronomy is too narrow today. The restaurant is becoming an urban recreation center. Customers want crowds, noise and distraction. Cooking should be free form. Dining should be fun, informality is the rule. Uniform is out. Menu language is casual. Creature comforts are few but the energy level is high. No longer in this country is "restaurant" a French word. Today's restaurants are being designed to *accommodate* customers.[34]

Asked by the Gallup Poll whether they preferred a casual or fine-dining atmosphere, half of those responding preferred casual while only 18 percent chose fine dining. Twenty-three percent enjoyed both equally. As Table 2.8 indicates, the occasion for the meal out had some influence on relative popularity, with birthday celebrations giving fine dining a marginal (but not a statistically significant) advantage. Gallup found that customers rate fine and casual dining about equal on food but give fine dining a higher approval level on decor and service. Casual operations, however, have a higher approval rating on value.[35]

The most popular casual restaurants, based on CREST traffic counts, are Italian restaurants, steak houses, and units with a Mexican theme (see Figure 2.2). One of the most interesting facts emerging in Figure 2.2 is not just

---

[34] *Nations Restaurant News,* November 4, 1985, p. 14.

[35] *Restaurants USA,* March 1990, pp. 41–42.

TABLE 2.8 Percentage of Adults Saying They Would Be Likely to Eat at a Restaurant on Each Occasion

	Type of Restaurant	
Occasion	Fine Dining	Casual
Dinner out with children	16%	40%
Saturday night treat with friends	26	43*
Dinner out with spouse/friend instead of cooking at home	44	57*
Business lunch	26	26
Birthday celebration dinner	52	48

Source: National Restaurant Association Gallup Survey, *Restaurants USA,* March 1991, p. 42.
* Significant difference.

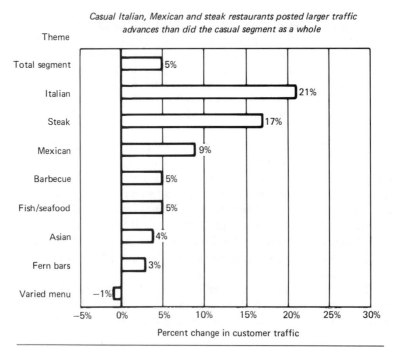

FIGURE 2.2 Change in traffic at casual restaurants, for year ended August 1990. (*Source:* NPD CREST/*Restaurants USA,* February 1991, p. 29)

the popularity of themed operations but that the only category with an actual decline is varied menu operations. This suggests the possibility that 25 years of experience with limited menu restaurants has established in consumers' minds the notion that specialists are better—as, in fact, may be true.

Making "Casual" Happen.   The rising success of casual operations over the past decade and their current increasing rate of success justifies our giving extended consideration to what it takes to develop a successful casual restaurant. "Casual" success, we are not surprised to find, is no accident.

The key to successful restaurant design in the casual segment is very careful study of the consumer. Richard Komen, president of Restaurants Unlimited, a firm that operates casual full-service restaurants in 15 cities from Honolulu to Philadelphia, described the design process that his firm has developed in a Burtenshaw Lecture at the School of Hotel and Restaurant Management at Washington State University.[36]

During the 1970s, Restaurants Unlimited operated theme restaurants. By 1980, operating results began to signal a need to reassess the company's approach to the marketplace. Using restaurant consultant George Lang and the market research firm of Yankelovich, Shelly and White, Restaurants Unlimited looked at what was happening to their guests and how that was affecting restaurant preferences.

The picture that emerged was one of massive social change. By 1980, the oldest of the baby boom generation was 34 and the median age was 25. One of the major forces was the maturing of younger women who had gone to work in unprecedented numbers during the 1970s. Two-income families had the money to dine out more. The well-educated boomers—and other upscale customers—were sophisticated by their education and exposure to media as well as travel, and they had had lots of experience in dining out. As to what customers wanted, Komen and his colleagues discovered:

> They wanted reality more than just about anything. They wanted real food . . . light and natural and healthy. They demanded that they be treated with respect and given recognition and excellent service.[37]

The units Restaurants Unlimited were operating in 1980, as Komen put it, "were stage sets . . . they were fake and our cooking was semi-fake." At Lang's urging, managers concentrated more effort on the cooking process, with resulting improvement in food quality. In 1981 they converted one of

---

[36] The Burtenshaw Lecture brings an industry leader to Washington State University's campus to discuss a key contemporary topic with students, faculty, and industry executives. Restaurants Unlimited, in addition to 21 themed restaurants, operates Cinnabon, a specialty bakery operation that features cinnamon rolls. There are 130 Cinnabon locations, of which 60 are franchised.

[37] This, and the balance of the quotes in this section, unless otherwise identified, are taken from Richard Komen, "Upscale Restauranting in the 1990s," Burtenshaw Lecture, April 1990.

their theme restaurants into Morgan's Lakeplace, which they styled an "urban bistro,"[38] embodying insights that grew out of the Yankelovich life-style studies. The remodeled restaurant nearly doubled sales during the first year of operation.

The firm's continuing study of customers leads Komen to the conclusion that there is

> a melding of what we call *traditional values* with *new values*. It doesn't mean there is a compromise between the two. But what it means is that people now are appreciating many of the good things that have happened in the past. Some of the values that were good for people in the past are now being embraced by modern people.

In addition to a decor that complements the guest's new respect for traditions of the past, Komen describes their service expectations as embodying not only professionalism but a person-to-person exchange. Guests want not just real food and decor but real people to wait on them. Guest recognition is also important for regular guests, and Komen's judgment is that today's guest, if treated well, will be more loyal than has been true in the past.

Dining in an upscale environment, he points out, has a "significant component of emotional satisfaction" because "dining is a highly charged emotional experience." Understanding the emotional needs of guests, "separates upscale dining from just eating. . . . Upscale restauranting is the business of making guests feel good."

The design of a casual restaurant begins with the careful definition of a target market and study of that market's needs and preferences. From this study, a "vision statement" is developed. For one of Restaurants Unlimited operations, the Palomino in Seattle, that statement is:

> An urban bistro with a strong European feel, an Italian cooking style but using fresh Northwest ingredients and other products that would challenge our target guests but also be understandable to them.

The vision statement details tabletops, floors, servers, and their apparel.

The next step is to create a brand personality. The brand personality developed for Palomino is as follows:

> You have seen me before, but you can't quite remember when . . . Milan, Rome, Nice, perhaps Manhattan. Sort of a blend of the old and the new

---

[38] In Europe, a bistro is a family-operated table-service restaurant offering a limited selection of hearty foods of the region and a selection of wines by the glass or carafe. The decor is generally quite simple. In the United States, the term *bistro* is used to denote a casual table-service operation, generally upscale, with a distinctive European style in decor and menu. For a fuller discussion of the meaning of the term *bistro,* see the introduction to Patricia Wells, *Food Lovers' Guide to Paris* (New York: Workman Publishing, 1988), p. 3.

world. I am high heel click with downtown buzz. I walk tall and hold my head high. I am alluring and sensuous, but not outlandish or simplistic. Grand is right. Shimmering and sleek, not fussy or self conscious.

There is just a good spark about me. A combination of feelings. Urban, European, Mediterranean, Seattle. Fifth Avenue, grilled salmon, pizza! What can I say?

I am no kid's place—a world away from trendy. I am fashion with rich color, fine woods, polished marble, and a glow you can cut with a knife. Energy abounds—a gathering place with the big woodburning ovens, huge rotisserie, vaulted ceilings. I am Mediterranean adventure making an important Northwest statement.

With a clear agreement on what is intended, a Project Development Team that includes a team leader, marketing people, designers, and one or more chefs begins the process of development. Generally only the team leader and one chef work on the project full time. The rest are frequent consultants as ideas begin to take shape. Periodically there are meetings of the team with senior executives in restaurant operations, human resource, and finance.

What we have seen is that the restaurant may be casual but its development is not. A carefully studied process is used to develop a place to dine that has a feel of authenticity, that is real, not fake. Food that embodies top-quality ingredients and preparation is served in a distinctive ambiance with excellent, person-to-person service. The entire effort is targeted on a clientele that is upscale not only in income but preferences and tastes.

Note, though, that Restaurants Unlimited does not assume that its customers are indifferent to price. As the marketing vice-president put it, "We don't want to price ourselves out of the market. The higher the guest-check average goes, the more likely we'll be perceived as a special occasion restaurant, which is exactly what we don't want to happen."[39]

''Casualizing'' Fine Dining. A growing number of fine-dining establishments, finding traffic dropping, have changed menus to introduce lower prices either as an addition to their traditional menu or as a completely new, lower priced replacement.[40]

It is clear, however, that for many, more is involved than just lowering prices. A fine-dining operation, the Blue Horse in St. Paul, Minnesota, indicates that it hopes to alter an image of being "a stuffy traditional, special occasion restaurant to more of a casual, elegant type of restaurant," according to the owner. The number of menu items has been reduced from 45 to 16, and they have stopped the ritual of displaying a tray of raw items at each table. In Detroit, the Van Dyke Place has adopted a lighter decor, more contemporary

[39] *Restaurant Business,* February 10, 1985, p. 166.
[40] *Nations Restaurant News,* August 13, 1990, p. 8.

menu items, and a fixed-price menu that has lowered the check average. According to the owner, it is "still a formal place but it's just not intimidating as much as it used to be."[41]

We should be careful not to conclude that fine dining is on its last legs. Rather, what remains, according to *Nations Restaurant News,* is a number of small, very upscale operations with an average check of $80 and up and an international clientele.[42] Marketing efforts in the full-service segment are on the increase, too. Advertising expenditures are rising, and frequent-diner programs, a rarity even a year or two earlier, were being offered in increasing numbers in the early 1990s.[43]

The future of the dining market seems secure—even if its definition for many customers is changing to a more casual one. In a *Wall Street Journal* survey of executives and professionals, a favorite "indulgence" was a meal at an expensive restaurant, which ranked second after buying a book or magazine.[44] If you consider the much higher price for a fine meal than for a book or magazine, you will probably agree that dining out achieves a favorable price/value perception with its target audience.

EATING MARKET DYNAMICS

Fast food, which we looked at in some detail earlier, is patronized by nearly every household; and, on average, some member of each household visits a fast-food operation twice a week (29 visits per quarter). Roughly 8 out of 10 customers (82 percent) visit specialty operations, such as family restaurants, with a visit frequency of once a week.[45] These customers are clearly the heart of the eating market. These components of the eating market are highly competitive, and we have already characterized them as mature, that is, growing at about the same rate as the economy as a whole.

There is, in addition, substantial growth in the eating market. That growth, however, is in the emerging off-premise sector. Table 2.9 highlights the trends in off-premise and on-premise consumption. On-premise consumption has grown very little and, in several years, declined. Off-premise consumption, on the other hand, has accounted for virtually all the growth in restaurant sales in the last half of the 1980s. This growth came from food picked up by the customer at a carryout counter (40 percent) or a drive-through window (23 percent). The rest (23 percent) came from increases in delivery sales. We need to consider these three important growth sectors in more detail.

---

[41] *Nations Restaurant News,* January 21, 1991, p. 3.

[42] *Nations Restaurant News,* January 7, 1991, p. 40.

[43] *Nations Restaurant News,* January 21, 1991, p. 3.

[44] *Wall Street Journal,* January 9, 1990, p. B1.

[45] Rice, "Leveraging Resources in a Mature Market."

Fuddruckers, an early leader in the gourmet hamburger segment, merchandises a sense of plenty with its self-service condiments and trimmings bar. Because the meat is ground on the premises in the butcher shop (shown in the background), customers are convinced that they are receiving fresh, all-beef hamburgers. (Courtesy of Fuddruckers, Inc.)

Take Out

Take out is an old and established part of food service but its recent rapid growth increases its prominence. Almost half of the consumers queried by a Gallup poll in 1990 indicated that they would be likely to purchase ready-to-

TABLE 2.9 Customer Traffic Growth Industry, On Premise and Off Premise 1986–1990

Year	All Restaurants	On Premise	Off Premise
1986	+ 2.1%	− 1.1%	+ 6.8%
1987	+ 3.5	+ 0.9	+ 7.1
1988	+ 0.5	− 2.1	+ 3.8
1989	+ 1.4	− 0.6	+ 3.9
1990	+ 1.7	+ 0.3	+ 3.4

Source: George D. Rice, "Leveraging Resources in a Mature Market." *Proceedings of the 18th Annual Chain Operators Exchange,* Orlando, February 24–27, 1991 (Chicago: International Foodservice Manufacturers Association, 1991).

TABLE 2.10 Proportion of Table-Service Restaurants Providing Take-Out Services by Check Size

	Under $8	$8 to $14.99	$15 to $24.99	$25 and up
Take-out meals	93%	87%	77%	52%
Retail sale of items by the pound	31	31	23	19
Off-premise catering	30	46	42	44

Source: Restaurants USA, December 1990, p. 28.

eat, take-out meals if they were offered by table-service establishments. Not surprisingly, operators have responded to consumer interest in take out. Nearly all fast-food operations offer take-out meals and fast-food operations account for roughly three quarters of take-out sales. As Table 2.10 illustrates, the vast majority of midscale table-service restaurants also offer take out, and so do many in the upscale segments of the industry. Thus, increased sales of

Many QSRs offer drive-through service to people in a hurry and on the go. (Courtesy of Foodmaker Inc.)

take-out food are fueled not only by consumer preference but by the wide availability of take-out food service.

The evening meal has historically received the lion's share of take-out sales but, in recent years, take-out luncheon sales have been rising at twice the rate of dinner sales, and weekend sales are booming as well. The majority of take-out food for the evening meal is purchased for the whole family and eaten at home. The reverse is true of lunch, with the majority being purchased by individuals and eaten away from home. Pizza restaurants and sandwich operations such as McDonald's account for nearly two thirds of all take-out purchases.[46]

Drive-Through

Initially, drive-through service was introduced as a part of an existing fast-food restaurant—and that is still an important use of drive throughs. Drive throughs have come of age, however, and now are the sole means of service to the guest in a new, rapidly growing segment emphasizing convenience, speed, and low price.

The double drive through requires only a very small building. Compared with $1 million or more for a major chain operation, a drive through can be built for as little as $250,000. Featuring highly simplified menus and service times of under a minute—often only 30 seconds—operations such as Rally's (headquartered in Kentucky), In N Out Burgers (California), and Fast Track (Louisiana) offer menus that are significantly lower priced than conventional fast food.[47]

The advantage of low price and the convenience of speed of service give these operators significant advantages for the target market for whom a meal is essentially a refueling stop.

The double drive throughs don't have an untroubled outlook, however. They have plenty of competition from established QSRs and numerous operating problems to contend with as well. Staffing, for instance, is a challenge. "Squeezing 5 to 7 people in close quarters several hours at a time" puts those people under considerable pressure, particularly managers. Zoning restrictions are also proving to be a problem in some areas because of traffic problems these operations might create.[48] Still, for the segment of the population that wants speed of service and low price, the double drive through has major advantages and seems certain to carve out a wider niche in food service. The entry of industry leader Pepsico, through the purchase of a drive-through chain, indicates that expansion of this segment will be backed by the "deep pockets" of large corporations.

---

[46]*Restaurants USA,* August 1988, p. 39.

[47]*Nations Restaurant News,* November 20, 1989, p. 1.

[48]*Nations Restaurant News,* November 20, 1989, p. 7.

TABLE 2.11   Delivery Service from
Table-Service Restaurants

Check Average	Proportion Providing
Under $8	14%
$8 to $14.99	15
$15 to $24.99	15
$25 and up	17

Source: Restaurants USA, December 1990, p. 28.

Delivery

Delivery operations do not fit well with table-service operations. Not only does demand peak just when the dining room is busiest (as is also true with take out), but the parking lot and its aisles are jammed with customers' cars just when delivery vehicle traffic in and out is at its peak. In fact, only about 15 percent of such operations offer delivery service (Table 2.11). Pizza Hut decided to limit delivery operations principally to separate delivery units for these reasons — and because delivery units can be located on less-expensive real estate.

The largest single player in the delivery market is almost exclusively a delivery and take-out operation. Domino's Pizza offers delivery in the United States from over 5,000 units, reaching sales of $2.65 billion or some 350 million pizzas. Domino's set the industry's delivery standard of 30 minutes, adhered to by most food-service delivery companies.

Each Domino's Pizza unit has its own phone, but some delivery chains use a single number for all units. Often a catchy phone number is used as a handy focus for promotion. Take, for example, Toronto's Pizza Pizza. Its 967-11-11 (try saying it rhythmically) has become so widely known that Canadian immigration officials sometimes use it as a quick check on the authenticity of people claiming residence in Toronto.

The single number is much more than a promotional trick, however. At the central answering facility, employees taking calls work at computer terminals. When a customer places an order, the operator asks for his or her phone number and address. Using this information, the order is passed to the nearest unit for dispatch. At the same time, the customer's name and order goes into the computerized guest history system. Then, on subsequent calls, the operator is able to call up the customer's record, using their phone number. Thus, when John Doe calls, the operator can say, "Good to hear from you again Mr. Doe. Would you like to have your usual pepperoni and mushrooms? Shall we deliver it to the side door again?"

The single-number system is spreading. It is being used not only for pizza but for a wide variety of products. For instance, companies as varied as T.G.

Quickly's Barbecued Chicken and "Confucius Says" Chinese food[49] are using it, and Kentucky Fried Chicken (KFC) is reportedly considering use of a single number nationwide when it rolls out delivery to all units.[50]

Specialized delivery firms, such as Take Out Taxi, deliver food for several operations. The company buys the food at wholesale prices from the restaurants and charges the customer a delivery fee. The company reports wide acceptance in its market area in Northern Virginia, with 85 percent of its business coming from repeat customers.[51]

One of the problems encountered by delivery companies is driver safety. Domino's Pizza was denied a license in a downtown area in a California city because the city council was concerned that the 30-minute delivery requirement would make delivery drivers speed, to the hazard of the local citizenry.[52]

A different kind of problem is suggested by the concerns of KFC franchisees. KFC's commitment to system-wide delivery will require each franchisee to make a substantial investment in plant and equipment to offer delivery in their units. Franchisees have estimated that it will take at least three years to pay for new equipment. They are naturally concerned that the franchisor not set up delivery-only units in their territory because it would cannibalize their sales. Costs and concerns of franchisees and the weight of existing investment make it difficult, as this example illustrates, for existing companies with many operating units in place to enter the delivery market.

RESTAURANTS AS A PART OF A LARGER BUSINESS

Thus far, this chapter has examined freestanding restaurants — separate and distinct operations. A substantial part of the food service industry is, however, made up of operations that are the food service arms of larger organizations. A major area that we should consider briefly is restaurants in retailing. Some of these are in department stores and truck stops. Others are found in shopping centers. It is interesting to see how trends in these catering establishments match those in the restaurant business elsewhere.

RESTAURANTS IN RETAIL STORES

Restaurants in department stores and drugstores were originally built as store services; a shopper who had to leave the store for lunch might resume shopping in some other store. The restaurants, therefore, helped keep the shoppers in the store and often helped attract them there in the first place. Increasingly,

[49] *Nations Restaurant News,* November 6, 1989, p. 7.

[50] *Nations Restaurant News,* October 8, 1990, p. 1.

[51] *Washington Business Journal,* January 30, 1990, n.p.

[52] *Nations Restaurant News,* August 27, 1990, p. 1.

Morrison's Cafeterias aim to expand their share of the eating market with "Home Cooking to Go" take-out centers which feature both a pickup counter and a drive-through. (Courtesy of Morrison Incorporated)

in-store restaurants are becoming in themselves worthwhile businesses that often generate higher profit margins than do the store's other retail sales. In fact, if properly merchandised, restaurants can *bring* shoppers into the store, not just *keep* them there.

The economics of restaurant operations that gave rise to the specialty restaurant are now at work in retailing. Retailer-housed restaurants are being pressed to adopt specialty restaurant (especially fast-food) service patterns to hold costs in line and to meet the guests' demand for speed.

RESTAURANTS IN SHOPPING MALLS

Thirty years ago, Americans did 5 percent of their shopping in malls. Today malls account for well over half of nonautomotive retail sales. Malls have become a place to relax, as well as shop. Insulated from the weather, with excellent security, they are a clean and comfortable place to stroll. Malls have been thought of as "places to buy," but they are becoming "places to be." One of the major purposes that consumers give for visiting malls is browsing. And one of the major attractions of the larger malls are their food service establishments.[53] The food court idea, first developed in malls, offers the consumer

[53] John Marinovich, "The Malling of America," *Proceedings of the 17th Annual Chain Operators Exchange,* Orlando, Florida, February 25–28, 1990 (Chicago, International Foodservice Manufacturers Association, 1990).

significant choice yet gives each operator a chance to specialize and achieve high productivity because of the large volume of customers provided.

The composition of mall food service is quite similar to the restaurant industry as a whole. QSRs capture about two thirds of visits; midscale restaurants, about a quarter; with the balance going to upscale concepts. Mall locations have been growing at twice the rate of food service in general for several years. Less traditional units and ethnic units have fared the best in malls. The dominant food service operators are independents and small chains.[54] This is probably true because the mall provides a basic volume of visitors, and the smaller operator does not have to support major advertising expenditures. About three quarters of mall food service customers are shoppers, while one quarter are mall employees.[55]

RESTAURANTS AT TRUCK STOPS

Another significant set of operations that are part of a larger system are located in truck stops and other roadside complexes that serve the interstate highway system and road travelers in general. Restaurant operations in truck stops generally feature a family restaurant or a coffee shop style of operation that offers travelers a break in their journey—a chance to eat and to sit for a few minutes in a comfortable atmosphere. In addition, these operations usually provide special sections for truckers who need superquick service. As this segment of the business develops, theme truck stop restaurants are on the increase, with a steamboat theme operation in Fulton, Minnesota; American colonial in Connecticut; and a wharfside restaurant in Warren, Indiana.

The truck stop restaurant is almost always part of a larger service package that includes gas and diesel fuel, truck repair facilities, gift and sundry shops, and often a motel. Originally intended as an ancillary service, truck stop restaurants now do about a tenth of the dollar volume of all truck stop business. Marriott operates in a related area, controlling 80 percent of the travel plazas on interstate highways.[56]

SUMMARY

Food service is big business, accounting for 43.5 percent of the American food budget, with most of that spent in restaurants (Table 2.1). Nearly everyone in the United States has eaten in a restaurant, and roughly half the population eats in a restaurant in any given month.

---

[54] "Leveraging Non-traditional Opportunities," *Proceedings of the 17th Annual Chain Operators Exchange,* Orlando, Florida, February 25–28, 1990 (Chicago, International Foodservice Manufacturers Association, 1990).

[55] "Leveraging Non-traditional Opportunities."

[56] *Nations Restaurant News,* January 7, 1991, p. 22.

The truck stop restaurant is generally a part of a larger roadside service center. (Courtesy of Truck Stops of America)

Specialty restaurants limit menus and simplify work. As a result, they have much higher productivity. Fast food (the QSR) is the most common kind of specialty restaurant. Its success is based on automating the customer through limiting choices, and reducing needed employee skills. Fast food has become "part of the American life-style," and one of the keys to the QSRs' success is universal location (Table 2.4). QSRs are evolving to meet changing needs but, as they do so, their costs are being raised because of broader menus and enhanced amenities. This has resulted in rising fast-food prices, which creates an opportunity for lower cost options such as take out and double drive throughs. Price competition, moreover, is eroding profit margins at a time when the age of the baby boomers is taking many of them out of the QSR market. Conventional QSRs face competition from each other, from lower cost operations, and also from other low-priced specialty operations offering table service. The automation concept used by fast food also applies to family restaurants, budget steak house operations, and pizza restaurants.

The dining market serves *principally* a social need while the eating market serves principally a biological need. Fine-dining restaurants represent only about 1 percent of the market and have been in decline in recent years. Casual dinner houses, on the other hand, have been one of the major growth areas in food service. Operators work very hard to achieve a casual relaxed atmosphere for the sophisticated guest. Many fine-dining restaurants have been repositioned to compete for the customer who prefers a casual atmosphere.

In the eating market, the main growth vehicles are drive-through, take-out, and delivery operations. These three account for almost all the growth in *total* restaurant sales that occurred in the last half of the 1980s. Restaurants in retailing resemble the industry as a whole in operation type but support the goals of some larger enterprises. Most restaurants have a higher proportion of independent operators.

KEY WORDS AND CONCEPTS

To help you review this chapter, keep in mind the following:

Full-service restaurant	Budget steak houses
Specialty restaurant	Pizza restaurants
Haute cuisine	Dining market
Mom and Pop	Eating market

Food-service productivity
   of labor
   of capital
Fast food
QSR
Automation
Automating concept
Limited menu
Service intensive
Simple unit/complex system
Family restaurants

Fine dining
Casual dinner house
Vision statement
Brand personality
Off-premise sector
Take out
Drive through
Double drive through
Delivery
Restaurants in retailing

REVIEW QUESTIONS

1. What are the three elements of a full-service restaurant?
2. What kinds of restaurants are defined as full-service restaurants?
3. What are the characteristics of a specialty restaurant?
4. What kinds of restaurants are defined as specialty restaurants?
5. Describe the process of introducing a new menu item in a fast-food restaurant.
6. How do the dining market and the eating market differ?
7. What kinds of restaurants are included in each market?
8. What are the growth concepts in the dining market and the eating market?
9. What larger businesses do restaurants serve?

C H A P T E R 3

Courtesy of Hilton Hotel Corp.

RESTAURANT OPERATIONS

THE PURPOSE OF THIS CHAPTER

The best opportunities for advancement in food service are in operations. Staff specialists such as marketers, accountants, and human resource people all play an important role in food service chains, but most restaurant chains (and institutional operations) have operations people in the top jobs. Of course, an independent restaurant operator is and must be principally an operations executive who often does most of the staff specialist work as well. Indeed, most senior executives boast of having started at the bottom in food service operations. While their time in the dish room or other unskilled job may have been only a few months—perhaps a summer—while in school or college, many executives feel that that kind of operational experience helped them understand the work of the employees they lead.

In this chapter we want to develop an overview of the all-important topic of restaurant operations. The opening section reviews the key responsibilities in major operational areas and describes a typical day in the life of food service. This should help you to start thinking about the paths to advancement that best suit you.

The second section of the chapter looks at how restaurants are organized, that is, their status as a chain, an independent, or a franchise. Each of these organizations offers somewhat different opportunities and advantages that you should take into account as you consider your plans. The chapter concludes with a final section on profitability in food service operations and a summary of the financial statements that are used to track operating results, that is, income, expense, and profit.

THIS CHAPTER SHOULD HELP YOU

1. Form an overall impression of what people do in food service operations.

2. Provide a basis for your own observation of food service. Whether your work is for a summer, part time while in school, or full time, learning from your work should become part of your professional life.

3. Identify the main divisions of activity in food service, what work is done in each, and what the main responsibilities and jobs are.

4. Understand the strengths of both independent operators and chains and to see the relative advantages of each.

5. Size up what a franchise offers to a franchised operation.

6. Determine whether seeking to become a franchisee would be a good decision for you.

7. Identify the major approaches to making a profit and the major means of keeping score in food service operations.

RESTAURANT OPERATIONS

The best way to become familiar with operations in a restaurant or other food service operation is to work in one. The next few sections, however, should give you useful background and a framework for thinking about your experiences. We will focus on three areas of the restaurant: the front of the house, the back of the house, and "the office." Within each section, we will look at the principal responsibilities of each area, the tasks they perform, and the kinds of roles played in the food service drama by employees working in that area. Finally, we will look at the general supervisory and managerial positions typical of that area.

Because our concern is with the whole range of restaurants, from QSR (that is, quick service restaurants or fast-food operations) to haute cuisine, the amount of detail we can deal with will be limited. In general, we'll take as our model a medium-priced, casual table-service restaurant. Where there are substantial variations in fast food or fine dining, we'll note those, however.

THE FRONT OF THE HOUSE

This is the part of the operation everyone is familiar with because they can see it. It is more complex, however, than it at first appears. The front of the house is at once an operating system, a business place, and a social stage setting. As an operating system, it is laid out to provide maximum efficiency to workers and ease of movement to guests. As a business, it is a marketplace that provides an exchange of service for money, which requires appropriate controls. Finally, it is a social place where people not only enjoy their meals but enjoy one another's company, good service, and a pleasing atmosphere.

Responsibilities

Probably *the* key responsibility of the front of the house is *guest satisfaction,* with particular emphasis on *personal service.* A later chapter on the role of service in the hospitality industry discusses service in more detail, but here we can just note that service goes beyond the mechanical delivery of the food to include the way the guest is served by the people in the restaurant.

The kind of service that should be delivered has a great deal to do with what the guest wants and expects; that is, in a fast-food restaurant guests expect economy and speedy service at the counter and self-service—even to the point of discarding their own used disposables after they are finished eating. While there is emphasis on speed and economy, the guest is entitled to expect a friendly greeting, accuracy in order filling, and a cheerful willingness to handle any problems that occur. In midscale restaurants, the table service provided raises the level of interaction with the guest. While speed of service is still usually expected, the success of the guest's experience is more dependent on the server's personal style. A grouchy waiter or waitress can ruin a good meal; a pleasant manner can help out even when things go wrong.

In fine dining, guest satisfaction and service requirements have a considerably different frame of reference. As a rule, fine dining implies a leisurely meal, so speed as such is not as important as the timely arrival of courses, that is, when the guest is ready. The higher price the guest pays raises the level of service they expect. A server in a coffee shop may serve from the wrong side or ask who gets which sandwich without arousing a strong reaction. Errors should *not* happen there, either, but when the price is modest, guests' expectations are usually reasonable. On the other hand, when people are paying $50 or so for a meal, they quite reasonably expect professional service and a high degree of expertise on the part of staff.

While service is the most obvious job of the front of the house, those who work there share in the responsibility for a *quality food product.* This means food isn't left to get cold (or baked dry under heat lamps) at a kitchen pickup station. If there *is* an error in the way food is prepared, the front of the house is where it is likely to show up in a guest complaint. People in the front of the house, therefore, need to be ready to deal with complaints. That requires at least two things. First, there must be a willingness to listen sympathetically to a guest's complaint. Second, a system of operation must be in place that permits the server or a supervisor to correct any error promptly and cheerfully. In other words, employees must be *empowered* to satisfy guests' needs. (Empowerment, which is discussed in the chapter on service, refers to an approach to managing people that gives employees discretion over as many decisions as possible affecting the quality of service.) An unhappy guest is much more expensive than a lost meal. Customers represent potential future sales *and* powerful word-of-mouth advertising.

The front of the house is a place where food product and service are sold and a lot of money changes hands. *Control* aspects of the operation that are important involve check control and cash control. Guest check control—being sure that every order taken is on a guest check—prevents servers from "going into business for themselves." An unscrupulous server *might* take orders, serve the food, and pocket some or all of the money. Today, point-of-sales systems make this kind of scam much more difficult, but there are still ways around even the most scientific system. Because money is *the* most valuable commodity, ounce for ounce, that a person can steal, extreme vigilance is called for in controlling cash.

Tasks

From the above description of responsibilities, you can see the kinds of tasks performed in the front of the house:

- Greeting the guest
- Taking the order
- Serving the food
- Removing used tableware
- Accepting payment and accounting for sales, charge as well as cash
- The closing: thanking the guest and inviting comments and return business

Roles

The tasks are performed, of course, quite differently in different levels of restaurants. The *hostess* or *host* (in very upscale operations, the headwaiter or waitress or maître d'hôtel) *greets* the guests, shows them to their table and, often, supervises the service. Some large, very busy restaurants separate greeting and *seating,* with hostesses or hosts from several dining rooms ("seaters") taking guests to their table after the guests have been directed to them by the person at the main entrance called "the greeter." At the opposite end of the scale, in QSRs, the counterperson is the greeter, thus making the smile and personal greeting there more important than casual observation might suggest.

The *cashier's* main duty is taking money or charge slips from guests and giving change when the check is paid. In some smaller operations, however,

The *greeting* the guests receive can set the tone for their entire visit. (Courtesy of the National Restaurant Association)

the cashier doubles as a host or hostess. The cashier is also sometimes responsible for taking reservations and making a record of them.

In table-service operations, the waitress or waiter takes the order then looks after the guest's needs for the balance of the meal. The server spends more time with the guest than any other employee. What the guest expects regarding service is based on the type of operation. More elaborate service rituals, potentially longer interactions as a result of consultations on choices of food and wine, and highly expert behavior on the part of the server are all expected in more expensive operations. In family restaurants and fast-food operations, while the length and intensity of interaction is much lower, the guest may assume a genuine interest in the customers on the part of the server, a friendly and cheerful manner, and competence in serving the right food promptly to be minimum—and reasonable—expectations. At all levels of restaurant service, excellent service is crucial to success in an ever more competitive market.

Servers are generally assigned to a specific group of tables called a station. In some restaurants, servers work in teams to cover a larger station, often with the understanding that only one of them will be in the kitchen at a time so that at least one of them will be in the dining room and available to the guests at all times. In European dining rooms and those in North America patterned after them, a *chef de rang* and *commis de rang*—effectively, the chief of station and his or her assistant—work together in a team. In less formal operations, waitresses and waiters are supported by a *bus person* who clears and sets tables but provides no service directly to the guest except, perhaps, to pour water or coffee. The bus person's job is basically to heighten the productivity of the service staff and to speed table turnover and service to the guest. Their personal appearance and manner, however, are a part of the guest's experience.

Supervision

The front of the house supervision is ideally exercised by the senior manager on duty. Most managers should be expected to devote the majority of their time to the front of the house during meal hours to see to it that guests are served well. This also enables the manager to greet and speak with guests. In this sense, the manager is expected to be a public figure whose recognition is important to the guest—"I know *the manager* here." At the same time, she or he can deal with complaints, follow up on employee training, and generally assess the quality of the operation. In some cases, of course, the manager finds it necessary to spend more time in the back of the house if there are quality or cost problems there.

In larger operations, a dining room manager is delegated responsibility from the general manager to manage service in a specific area or in the whole front of the house. In many operations, the job of host or hostess includes supervisory responsibility for the service in the room or rooms for which he or she is responsible.

In addition to supervising service, managers in the front of the house have responsibility for supervising cleaning staff, cashiers, and for opening and closing procedures in the restaurant. These last are sometimes discharged by a lead employee.

THE BACK OF THE HOUSE

In many ways, the back of the house is like a factory. Some factories are assembly plants, while others manufacture goods from raw materials. A similar distinction can be made regarding restaurants. Some are really an "assembly operation," where food is simply finished and plated by kitchen staff. This is true of operations that use a lot of prepared foods such as portioned steaks or a sandwich operation such as a QSR. In others, the product is actually "manufactured" on premise or, as we more commonly say, cooked from scratch.

Responsibilities

The principal responsibility of the back of the house, clearly, is the *quality of the food* the guest is served. That is a matter not only of food taste but also of food safety and sanitation. *Sanitation,* then, is also an extremely important responsibility. Finally, *cost control* with respect to food, labor, and supplies

There are varying skill levels for cooks but the guests'
demand for a high standard of quality applies to all
of them. (Courtesy of Domino's Pizza Inc.)

are make-or-break responsibilities for the back of the house. Because prompt,
timely service is dependent on being able to get the food out of the kitchen on
time, the kitchen has a major responsibility in service.

Tasks

Food production stands out as the predominant work done in the back of the
house. *Controlling quality and cost* are usually parallel activities. In other
words, standardized recipes and carefully thought-out procedures, used consistently, will produce food that has the correct ingredients; that ensures both
quality and cost if properly planned.

An important dimension of cost control is *portion control*. Say a sandwich that calls for 2 ounces of ham has 2½ ounces. While "only" a half ounce
overweight, that is 25 percent additional meat and probably represents an
increase of 20 percent in cost. Portion control has a quality dimension as well.
Assume two guests order fish and the planned portion is 8 ounces. If one
receives a 7-ounce portion and the other 9 ounces, although the overall size is
the same and, therefore, costs won't be affected, the guests are likely to notice

the discrepancy. Portions should be the same for a guest at every visit — and should be the same for every guest.

Dishwashing and *pot washing* are not skilled jobs, but they are certainly important work. Anyone who has been in a restaurant that ran out of clean dishes in the middle of the meal or pots during a heavy preparation period can testify to this. These are activities that use a significant amount of labor in any operation that serves food on permanent ware and has a varied menu (i.e., most operations outside of fast food). *Labor cost control* is, therefore, an important element in planning ware washing. Because detergent is a commodity that restaurants use in large quantity, costs of supplies are a significant concern. Quality work, which relates not only to the workers' performance but to adequate water temperatures and soap solutions, is absolutely essential.

Cleanup work is important in both the front and back of the house but, because it relates to *sanitation,* back-of-the-house cleanup is especially significant. While in most operations workers clean up as they work during the day, the heavy cleanup is usually done at night when the restaurant is closed.

Roles

Cooks come not only in all sizes and shapes but in varying skill levels. In fine dining, cooking is generally done by people with professional chef's credentials, received only after serving a lengthy apprenticeship. The much talked about "hamburger flippers" of fast-food operations are at the other end of the scale. It is not surprising that the "flipper's" work can be learned quickly, because the operation has been deliberately designed to reduce skill requirements. In between these extremes lie the short order cook, the grill person, the salad preparation people, and many others who have a significant amount of skill but in a narrow range of specialized activities. Whatever the skill level, it is really crucial to the success of the operation that this work be done well.

Dishwashers are often people who have taken the job on a short-term — and often part-time — basis. Because the job is repetitive, monotonous, and messy, it is not surprising that it has a high turnover. We ought to note, however, that an inquisitive, observant person working in the dishroom — or on the pot sink — is in a position to learn a lot about what makes a restaurant run.

Some operations employ handicapped people in dish and pot work as well as in salad and vegetable preparation. Mentally handicapped employees find the routine, repetitive nature of the work suited to their abilities. Not surprisingly, they find that their dignity as individuals is enhanced by their success in doing an important job well. As a result, employers, such as the Marriott Corporation, who have developed successful programs for handicapped workers report significantly lower turnover among this group of workers.

An important role we haven't touched on yet is that of the *receiver*. One person may be responsible for this function or the job may be shared by several employees. The receiver's function is to be responsible for accepting shipments to the restaurant and checking them for accuracy in weight or count as well as quality. In most operations the receiver will also check to be sure that the goods received were ordered in the number and quality delivered.

In large operations such as hotels and clubs, the receiver reports to the accounting department since the work relates to control. The receiver needs a good working relationship with kitchen staff, whatever the formal reporting relationships. In most operations, the receiver has duties closely involved with kitchen operations such as storing food and keeping storage and receiving areas clean and sanitary. Some restaurants distribute the tasks of the receiver among two or more people. In a hotel the author ran, for instance, *counting and weighing* of goods received was done by the pot washer while verifying *quality* was the responsibility of the restaurant manager on duty.

Supervision

Because a variety of titles are used in different organizations, we will focus on three functional areas: food production, washing and cleanup, and closing. Food production is headed by a person carrying the title of chef, executive chef, or food production manager. In smaller, simpler operations the title may be head cook, or just cook. In these latter operations, the general manager and her or his assistants usually exercise some supervision over cooks, so it is important that they have cooking experience in their own background.

Dishwashing, pot washing, and cleanup in very large organizations, particularly hotels and clubs, is supervised by a *steward*. In smaller organizations the manager on duty takes on this responsibility.

Closing responsibility is very much related to these activities but deserves separate discussion because of its importance in relation to sanitation and security. The closing manager is responsible for the major cleanup of the food production areas each day (and probably has the same responsibility in the front of the house). That person also oversees the putting away of valuable food and beverage products into secure storage at the end of the day and for locking up the restaurant itself when all employees have left. The job is not a very glamorous one but it is clearly important.

THE "OFFICE"

We have put "office" in quotes because it has many organizational designations, from "manager's office" to "accounting office." The functions relate to the *administrative coordination* and *accounting* in the operation.

Responsibilities and Tasks

The office has as its first task *administrative assistance* to the general manager and his or her staff. The office staff handles correspondence, phone calls, and other office routines. These activities, while routine, are essential to maintaining the image of the restaurant in the eyes of its public. Ideally, managers should not be bogged down in this time-consuming work. It is essential to have office staff to free managers to manage.

A second major area of responsibility is *keeping the books.* Very often, the actual books of account are kept in some other place (a chain's home office, or an accountant's office for an independent), but the preliminary processing of cashier's deposits, preparation of payrolls, and approval of bills to be paid are all included in this function. Prompt payment of bills is very important to a restaurant's good name in the community; so whether this is done in house, at a home office, or by a local bookkeeping service, it deserves careful and prompt attention. Either on premise or off, regular cost-control reports must be prepared, usually including the statement of income and expense (which is discussed in the closing section of this chapter).

Roles

The *manager's secretary* or administrative assistant often functions as *office manager.* Independent operators often employ a *bookkeeper* or *accountant* full or part time or use an outside service while chains handle most accounting centrally. Very often the secretary/office manager is responsible for filling out forms that serve as the basis for the more formal reports.

Supervision

As noted, the person who supervises on-premise clerical work usually reports to the general manager, as does any in-house accountant. We should note, however, that there are many smaller operations whose low sales volume will not support clerical staff. In these cases, the clerical and accounting routines are usually handled by the managers themselves. In chains, particularly fast-food chains, there has been very extensive effort to automate reporting systems. Here, most reports are prepared from routine entries made in the point-of-sales register and transmitted directly to the central accounting office automatically over the phone lines.

GENERAL MANAGEMENT

We should now add one additional category to our framework for observing a restaurant, that of the general managers and their assistants. It is essential that there be someone in charge whenever an operation is open. One possible schedule is as follows: An assistant manager comes in before the restaurant opens and oversees all the opening routines. These include turning on equipment, unlocking storage areas, and seeing to it that all of the crew has shown up and that all the necessary working stations are covered. The general manager arrives in midmorning and stays at least through the evening meal rush. The closing manager arrives sometime in the afternoon and is usually the last person to leave, locking up for the night. The schedule just described, of course, fits a restaurant in which major meals are lunch and dinner. Checklists are often used as reminders and are a good way to document the tasks. An operation with different hours of operation would have a different schedule in some of the details, but the essential functions identified here would all have to be covered in some way. A key point is that someone in the unit is in charge at all times.

We should note that, in talking about management, we have really been describing *management presence*. We may not always see the title "manager" used, however. Many of the duties of management are carried out by supervisors. In fast-food and smaller restaurants, managers and their assistants are often supplemented by crew chiefs and lead employees.

We have used the title "general manager" in this section but should note that that is a title used principally in larger operations. The function of overall direction, however, is the same even if the title used is unit manager or simply manager. Since the general manager can't be present every hour of the day, her or his assistants, whatever *their* titles, stand in for the manager when he or she cannot be physically present. A key point is that managers act as a team to give direction to the unit, to maintain standards (quality *and* cost), and to secure the best possible experience for their guests.

Daily Routine

As we have said, opening and closing a restaurant require specialized work. The highest levels of activity, of course, occur during the meal periods. Between the rush hours a lot of routine work is accomplished. The following is a look at the major divisions of a restaurant's day.

Opening. Somebody has to unlock the door. In a small operation it may be a lead employee; in a large operation it will probably be an assistant manager. As other employees arrive for work, storage areas and walk-ins must be unlocked. If a junior level supervisor was in charge of closing the night before, it is especially important that the first manager on duty inspect the restaurant and especially the back of the house for cleanliness and sanitation.

In larger restaurants, a considerable amount of equipment has to be turned on. Sometimes this process is automated, but in other operations equipment is turned on by hand following a carefully planned schedule. One element of a utility's charge relates to the amount of power used, but another relates to the peak demand level. If someone throws all the electrical panel switches, turning on air-conditioners, lights, exhaust fans, ovens, and so forth all at once, that will create a costly, artificially high demand peak. Schedules to phase in electrical equipment over a longer period may be followed by the person who opens up to avoid this problem.

As we noted earlier, it is important to be sure that all stations are covered; that is, that everybody is coming to work. If an employee calls in at 6:30 A.M. to say he or she can't make it, or if somebody just doesn't show up, appropriate steps must be taken to cover that position. This could mean calling the appropriate supervisor at home to let that person know of a problem. Or the opening manager might also handle it more directly by calling in someone who can cover the position.

Before and After the Rush.   Much of the work done outside the meal period is routine. Probably the most important is "making your *setup*"; that is, preparing the food that will be needed during the next meal period. In a full-menu operation, this will likely involve roasting and baking meats, chopping lettuce and other salad ingredients, and other tasks. In more specialized operations, it may involve slicing prepared meats or simply transferring an appropriate amount of ready-to-use food from the walk-in to a working refrigerator. It is essential that safe food-handling procedures always be followed to prevent food contamination. In some QSRs, a key portion of the setup actually occurs just as the meal period is about to begin, when product is prepared and stored in the bin, ready for the rush that is about to commence. The key element in making the setup is to do as much as possible before the meal to be ready to serve customers promptly.

Sidework is another important activity done by waitresses and waiters on a regular schedule. Sidework includes such tasks as cleaning and filling salt and pepper shakers, cleaning the side stands and, in many restaurants, some cleaning of the dining room itself. This is work that can't be done during the rush of the meal hour. The front of the house has a sidework setup for every meal period, too. Side stands must be stocked with flatware, napkins, butter, sugar packets, or whatever guest and food supplies might be needed during the coming rush.

Other routine work such as calling in orders, preparing cash deposits and reports on the previous day's business, preparing and posting work schedules—all are tended to by management staff or under their supervision. It is important that this routine work be done during off-peak hours so that managers on duty can be available during rush hours to greet guests, supervise service, and help out if a worker gets stuck. When you see a manager moving through the dining room pouring coffee, that manager is (or should be) using that work as a way of greeting guests and helping busy servers rather than covering a shortage in the service staff.

The Meal Periods.   Not every meal is a rush in terms of the restaurant's seating capacity. Employees are scheduled, however, to meet the levels of business, so there should be no extra help around. Accordingly, those who are there will probably experience most meal periods as a rush. Each meal has its own characteristics—probably slightly different in different operations—and the service offered needs to be adapted to that style. In hotels the author ran, breakfast guests came from the hotel. They were slightly abstracted, thinking about the day ahead, and more interested in their newspaper or breakfast companion than in visiting with dining room staff. Lunch was mostly local business people on a business lunch with clients or in a party of co-workers. The emphasis at both breakfast and lunch was on speed and efficiency. Most guests had to go somewhere else on a fairly tight schedule.

In contrast, dinner was a more relaxed meal. The day was over and people were not in as much of a hurry. There were more single diners, and many were quite happy to visit for a few minutes with staff.

Closing.   We have noted in earlier sections the importance of the housekeeping, sanitation, and security duties involved in closing activities. We might just note that, in addition, there is the guest contact work of easing the last few people out of the restaurant without offending them—or of waiting until they're ready to leave, depending on house policy. Special care must be employed in operations serving alcohol with guests who may be intoxicated to avoid liability for the operation for any harm they might do to themselves or others. There should be written house policies covering this contingency.

Life in the Restaurant Business

Whether to work in the restaurant business is really a decision about the kind of life you want to lead. Weekend and holiday work is common, and workweeks of 50 and 60 hours are too, especially while you are working your way up in management. The work is often physically demanding because you are on your feet, under pressure, and in a hurry for most of the working day.

On the other hand, it is an *exciting* business. It involves working with people—both employees and guests—in a way that is very rewarding. Every day—every meal—is a new challenge, and there are literally hundreds of opportunities to make people feel good. Few things are as pleasant as the end of a meal when a restaurant crew can take satisfaction in the success of its joint effort.

In 1990, the *Restaurants and Institutions* job survey found that, on average, an assistant unit manager made $24,000 per year while a unit manager made $29,500. General managers earned $38,900, and area and regional managers, $49,800. Executive chefs, on average, received $34,000. While dietitians earned $30,300, we should note that their raises were among the largest in that year and their salaries appear to be moving up. Including senior executives and all other ranks, food service executives in 1990 made an average of $34,900.[1] Clearly, most people fresh out of school may not start at a high salary, but it is good to know what the longer term rewards are.

ORGANIZING OPERATIONS: CHAIN, INDEPENDENT, OR FRANCHISE?

Even though we sometimes hear that the day of the independent is past and the chains will soon gobble up the entire food service market, nothing could be further from the truth. Chains do have enormous advantages in some markets,

[1] *Restaurants and Institutions,* September 5, 1990, p. 38.

One of the big advantages of a major franchise is a well-known brand name.
(Photo courtesy of McDonald's Corp.)

but in others they have disadvantages. It is useful, therefore, to examine the
competitive advantages of both the independents and the chains and franchisees. In our discussion, we will treat franchised restaurants much like
chains. If there are important differences, we will point them out.

CHAIN SPECIALTY RESTAURANTS

Chains have six strengths: (1) brand recognition or preference, (2) site selection
expertise, (3) access to capital, (4) purchasing economies, (5) centrally administered control and information systems, and (6) personnel program development. All of these strengths represent *economies of scale:* the savings come, in
one way or another, from spreading a centralized activity over a large number
of units so that each absorbs only a small portion of the cost but all have the
benefit of specialized expertise or buying power when they need it.

Brand Recognition

More young children in America recognize Santa Claus than any other public figure. Ronald McDonald comes second! Because McDonald's and its franchisees spend well over a billion dollars on marketing and advertising, it's no wonder more children recognize Ronald than, say, Mickey Mouse, Donald Duck, or the Easter Bunny. Indeed, McDonald's has created a generic item— the Big Mac. The company has done for the hamburger what Coke did for cola, Avon for cosmetics, and Kodak for film. The reasons for this success are threefold: simplicity of message, enormous spending, and the additive effect.

The *message* of modern advertising is affected by the form in which it is offered: 10-, 30-, or 60-second television commercials, for instance. Even in the printed media, the message must be kept simple, because an advertisement in a newspaper or magazine has to compete with other ads and news or feature stories for the consumer's casual attention. The message of the specialty restaurant resembles its menu. It boils down to a simple statement or a catch phrase. In fact, marketing people generally try to design a "tag line" that summarizes the benefits they want an advertising campaign to tell the consumer. Some years ago, Wendy's Restaurants used the slogan, "Ain't no reason to go anyplace else." Although this slogan set off a letter-writing campaign complaining about the grammar (apparently organized by high school English teachers), Wendy's officials judged it effective in "breaking through the clutter." Classic tag lines of the past are still memorable:

"We do it all for you."

"You deserve a break today."

"Finger lickin' good."

Television advertising, even at the local level, is very expensive. National or even regional television advertising is so expensive that it is limited to the very largest companies. Chains can pool the advertising dollars of their many units to make TV affordable. Few except the largest independents, however, can afford to use television.

Independents and units owned by chains offering table service spend roughly the same percent of sales—between 1.5 and 2 percent—on advertising. Franchise table-service chains collect an advertising royalty on all sales and so have a large war chest for promotional campaigns. In fact, franchise table-service units spend roughly twice as much on advertising as do independents or chain-owned units, between 3 and 4 percent. Fast-food units also spend twice as much on advertising, about 4 percent for company-owned units and 8 percent for franchised operations.[2]

---

[2] *Restaurant Industry Operations Report* (Washington, D.C.: The National Restaurant Association, 1990).

Of course, all this advertising will be effective only if consumers get exactly what they expect. Therefore, chains concentrate on ensuring consistency of quality and service in operations. Customers know exactly what to expect in each McDonald's and, in an increasingly mobile society, that is important. For people on the go as tourists, shoppers, or businesspersons, what is more natural than to stop at a familiar sign? If that experience is pleasant, it will reinforce the desire to return to that sign in the local market or wherever else it appears.

Site Selection Expertise

The success of most specialty restaurants is also enhanced by a location near the heart of major traffic patterns. The technique for analyzing location potential requires a special kind of knowledge, and the chains alone can afford real estate departments that possess that expertise.

Access to Capital

Most bankers and other money lenders have traditionally treated restaurants as risky businesses. So an independent operator who wants to open a restaurant (or even remodel or expand an existing operation) may find it difficult to borrow the needed capital. But the banker's willingness to lend increases with the size of the company: if one unit should falter, the banker knows that the franchise will want to protect its credit record. To do so, it can divert funds from successful operations to "carry" one in trouble until the problems can be worked out. Thus, banks not only make capital available to units of larger companies, but they also lower the interest rates on these loans, sometimes substantially.

Purchasing Economies

Chains can centralize their purchasing either by buying centrally in their own commissary or by negotiating centrally with suppliers who then deliver the products, made according to rigid specifications, from their own warehouses and processing plants. Chains obviously purchase in great quantity, and they can use this bargaining leverage to negotiate the best possible prices and terms. Indeed, the leverage of a large purchaser goes beyond price. McDonald's, for instance, has persuaded competing suppliers to work together on the development of new technology or to share their proprietary technology to benefit McDonald's.[3] In addition, chains can afford their own research and development laboratories for testing products and developing new equipment.

Control and Information Systems

Economies of scale is the important concept here. Chains can spend large sums on developing accounting procedures and procedures for collecting market

[3] *TRA Foodservice Digest/Prepared Foods,* November 1988, p. 40.

A site convenient to local auto traffic and with adequate parking is essential to success in fast foods. (Courtesy of McDonald's Corp.)

information. They can devise costly computer programs and purchase or lease expensive computer equipment, again spreading the cost over a large number of operations. Moreover, in most chains, an expert staff dispatched from central headquarters reviews the units' efficiency. Unit managers may not always enjoy these inspections, but they make them stay on their toes.

Personnel Program Development

Some restaurant chains have established sophisticated training programs for hourly employees, using audiovisual techniques such as films, tapes, and slide shows to demonstrate the proper ways of performing food service operations. These standardized procedures in turn lower the cost of training and improve its effectiveness. This economy is especially advantageous in semiskilled and unskilled jobs, which traditionally experience high turnover rates and, therefore, waste considerable training time.

Management training also is important, and the chains can usually afford the cost of thorough entry-level management training programs. ARA Services, for instance, estimates the first-year direct costs for training a management trainee fresh out of college to be $12,500. This includes the trainee's salary, fringe benefits, and travel and classroom costs, with an additional

Fast-food restaurants do offer fast service, but they also provide a relaxing, pleasant place to eat. (Courtesy of McDonald's Corp.)

$3,500 estimated as the cost of managers' time to provide on-the-job training. In effect, this company spends as much as or more than a year of college costs on their trainees, a truly valuable education for the person who receives it.[4]

Because of their multiple operations, moreover, chains can instill in beginning managers an incentive to work hard by offering gradual increases in responsibility and compensation. In addition, a district and regional management organization monitors the managers' progress. Early in a manager's career, he or she begins to receive performance bonuses tied to the unit's operating results. These bonuses and the success they represent obviously are powerful motivators.

Chains' Market Share

The 100 largest restaurant chains control nearly half (46.6 percent) of restaurant sales. As Table 3.1 indicates, the largest chains controlled less than a third of sales in 1972.[5] The proportion of sales controlled by chains, then, has increased by over 50 percent in less than 20 years. Chain sales grew nearly 9 percent (8.8 percent) in 1989 compared with the total industry's growth of just over 6 percent (6.2 percent).[6]

---

[4] Joel Katz, director of Human Resource Development, ARA, personal communication to author.

[5] *US Chain Restaurant Companies, 1990* (Chicago: Technomic Consultants, 1990).

[6] *Nations Restaurant News,* August 6, 1990, p. 4.

TABLE 3.1 Market Share of 100
Largest U.S. Restaurant Chains

Year	Percentage of Sales
1972	30.2%
1978	40.2
1983	44.7
1989	46.6

Source: Data from Technomic Consultants, Chicago.

Because successful chains have "deep pockets" (i.e., adequate financial reserves), they are able to ride out recessions. Indeed, some larger chains look on a recession as a time when they can purchase smaller or less successful chains having trouble weathering the economic storm. While most experts expect the concentration of chains to continue, fierce competition from regional chains, shifting consumer preferences, and competitive patterns ensure that few if any players will establish anything resembling market dominance except on a local or temporary basis.

OPERATING ADVANTAGES OF THE INDEPENDENT

Although chains undeniably have advantages in the competitive battle for the consumer's dollar, the independents also enjoy advantages that ensure them a continuing place in the market, a different place from that of the chains, perhaps, but a significant place nevertheless.

We can use the same method to analyze the strengths of the independents that we used to examine the chain specialty restaurants. The advantages of the chains derive basically from the large size of their organization. The advantages of the independents derive from a somewhat different common core. The independent's flexibility, the motivation of its owner, and the owner's closeness to the operation affect its success. Flexibility and a highly focussed operation, then, are the independent's edge.

Although the following analysis does not deal directly with the issue, we should note that economies of scale also are important in the independent restaurant. The small operation—the mom-and-pop restaurant—finds itself increasingly pressed by rising costs. We cannot specify a minimum volume requirement for success, but National Restaurant Association (NRA) figures show that, in each size grouping, the restaurants with higher total sales achieve not only a higher dollar profit but a higher percentage of sales as profit.[7]

[7] *Restaurant Industry Operations Report,* pp. 34, 63, 90–91.

Brand Recognition

Ronald McDonald may be a popular figure, but he is not a real person. The successful restaurant proprietor, however, is real. In fact, successful restaurateurs often become well known, are involved in community affairs, and establish strong ties of friendship with many of their customers. This local celebrity can be especially effective "standing at the door," greeting guests by name as they arrive, moving through the dining room, recognizing friends or acquaintances, dealing graciously with complaints, and expressing gratitude for praise. "Thanks and come back again" has an especially pleasant ring when it comes from the boss—the owner whose status in the town isn't subject to corporate whim or sudden transfer.

Although the chain may have advantages among transients, the operator of a high-quality operation enjoys an almost unique advantage in the local market. Moreover, word-of-mouth advertising may spread his or her reputation to an even larger area. The key to recognition for the independent is more than just personality; it is, first and foremost, quality. To build a reputation, the operation must be different from others and noticeably better than the ordinary restaurant. This is hard to achieve with a "hamburger or chicken" menu. Hamburgers or chicken can be good, but not so distinctively better as to make a difference.

Site Selection

The chain operation continually faces the problem of selecting the right site as it seeks new locations for expansion. The established operator, however, gives location less attention. Of course, over the long term, an independent operator must adjust to changing urban patterns and real estate values. Because independent units tend to stay put, the problem of choosing a location is encountered infrequently. Independents nevertheless do sometimes face the need to change the location of a restaurant. When contemplating such a move, a local operator can supplement his or her own knowledge of the area by hiring a consulting firm to conduct a location study. It's an expensive service but valuable if it is needed.

Access to Capital

In most cases, the chain will have the most ready access to capital. Nevertheless, the successful operator can often establish contacts with local financial institutions and investors.

Purchasing Economies

Once again, the chain enjoys substantial advantages in its purchasing economies. But the independent's problem may differ somewhat from the chain's. Because of the importance of quality in the independent operation, the price advantages in centralized purchasing may not be as important as an ability to find top-quality products consistently. Thus, long-standing personal friendships with local purveyors can be an advantage for the independent.

Control and Information Systems

Because of its simple menu, the chain specialty restaurant can take advantage of the sort of information on marketing and sales patterns produced by computerized routines. This practice is, in fact, essential to companies operating many units in a national market. But the complex menu of the single, independent, full-service restaurant lends itself to the operator's subjective interpretation, impressions, and "hunches" about the changing preferences of the guests. Moreover, the independent operator can easily analyze some simple data (such as menu popularity counts) without paying for programming or computer time.

Computers and standardized software put sophisticated cost control and sales analyses within easy reach of most independent operators. A survey of full-service restaurants, for instance, showed that most operators (over 85 percent) used computers for accounting and bookkeeping, over half used them for inventory control, and nearly half also used them for recipe costing. Over one third used computers in purchasing, and half of larger full-service operators (those with over $500,000 sales per year) used the computer to report time and attendance and to do food production forecasting. Only slightly more than one in five, however, used computerized routines for scheduling, but that proportion is likely to increase.[8]

Cost-control procedures may be more stringent in the chain operation, but if an owner keeps an eye on everything from preparation to portion sizes to the garbage can (the amount of food left on a plate is often a good clue to the overportioning), effective cost control can be achieved even when an ECR/POS system to fit the operator's needs is not available or when the cost of such a system seems prohibitive. By using the uniform system of accounts and professional advice available from restaurant accounting specialists, independents can readily develop control systems adequate to their needs.

This description of the independent operator suggests what has become a food service axiom: Anyone who cannot operate successfully without the corporate brass looking over his or her shoulder will probably be out of business as an independent in less than a year.

Personnel

The independent proprietor can and usually does develop close personal ties with the employees, a practice that can help reduce turnover. But even though "old hand" employees can act as trainers, the cost of training new workers tends to be higher for the independent because of the complex operation and because he or she lacks the economies of a centralized training program.

Although advancement incentives are not as abundant in independent operations as in the chains, some successful independents hire young people, train them over a period of several years to become effective supervisors, and

[8] *Nations Restaurant News,* March 25, 1991, p. 14.

then help them move on to a larger operation. Often, too, the independent finds key employees whose life goals are satisfied by their positions as chef, host or hostess, or head bartender. These employees often receive bonus plans similar to those offered by the chains.

Independents have a special attraction for employees who are tied by family obligations or a strong personal preference to their home community. Clearly, the problem of being transferred is unlikely to arise with independents. With chains, however, the probability is that advancement is dependent on a willingness to relocate.

The Independent's Extra: Flexibility

One strength that the independent boasts is the flexibility inherent in having only one boss or a small partnership. Fast decision making permits the independent to adapt to changing market conditions. And because there is no need to maintain a standard chain image, an independent is free to develop menus that take advantage of local tastes. Finally, there are many "one of a kind" niches in the marketplace, special situations that don't repeat themselves often enough to make them interesting to chains. Yet these situations may be ideally suited to the strengths of independents. Can you see a chain mass-marketing delicate meals featuring freshly gathered wild mushrooms in the way that a fancy little independent operation in Reading, Pennsylvania, does?

Between Independent and Chain

Between the independent and the chain lie at least two other possibilities. First, some independent operations are so successful that they open additional units, without, however, becoming so large as to lose the "hands-on" management of the owner-operator. *Nation's Restaurant News* refers to these as *independent group operators* which are not exactly chains but which because of their success are no longer single unit operators. The other possibility, and one that is pursued by thousands of business people, is a franchised operation.

FRANCHISED OPERATIONS

A conversation with a franchisee is likely to yield this contradiction: The franchisee clearly thinks of himself as an independent businessman but is likely to refer to the franchisor in the course of the conversation as "the parent company." "Many franchisees," one report suggested, "do not really wish to be independent at all but are tempted by the opportunity to be part of a large group, sharing in its success image, and yet also maintaining an "individual identity."[9]

Nearly half the restaurant sales in the United States are made by franchised units. Half of these sales come from operations specializing in hamburgers, which comprise 40 percent of franchised units. Steak and full-menu

---

[9]E. Patrick McGuire, *Franchised Distribution* (New York: The Conference Board, 1971).

Food service franchises offer a successful business format that includes detailed marketing and operating plans. (Courtesy of DAKA International)

operations account for 17 percent of sales, and pizza operations are next with 15 percent. Restaurants specializing in chicken come fourth, with 7.4 percent of sales.[10]

There are two basic kinds of franchising. Product and trade name franchising, such as a soft drink or automobile dealership, confers the right to use a brand name and to sell a particular product. The type of franchising found in the hospitality industry, however, is called *business format franchising*. Business format franchising "includes not only the product, service and trademark, but the entire business format itself—a marketing strategy and plan, operating manuals and standards, quality control, and continuing two way communication."[11]

The franchisee has a substantial investment, ownership (of the franchise and very possibly of land, building, furniture, and fixtures or a lease on them). Beyond that, he or she has full day-to-day operating control and responsibility. For instance, franchisees are responsible for determining the need for hiring employees, supervising the daily operation (or managing those who do that supervision), and generally representing themselves in the community as independent businesspeople. The degree of franchisee control over key issues varies from one franchise group to another, but many franchisees share considerable freedom of advertising, choice of some suppliers, and additions to and renovations of physical plant. Although some aspects of the unit's

[10] *Restaurants USA,* March 1990, pp. 39–40. Figures given are from an International Franchise Association publication, *Franchising in the Economy, 1988–1990.*

[11] Andrew Kostecka, *Franchising in the Economy, 1984*–86 (Washington, D.C.: U.S. Government Printing Office, 1986), p. 3.

budget are governed by the franchise agreement, the franchisee retains signifi-cant budgetary discretion under most agreements and, in practice, exercises even more.

On the other hand, the essence of almost all franchises in the hospitality industry is an agreement by the franchisee to follow the form of the fran-chisor's business system in order to gain the advantages of that business format. The franchisee has indeed relinquished a great deal of discretion in the management of the enterprise and is a part of a system that largely defines its operation. The franchisee's relationship is neither that of an employee nor that of an independent customer of the franchisor.

The most common characteristics of a franchise agreement are as follows:

1. A contractual relationship sets forth the rights and responsibilities of each party.

2. The purpose of the arrangement is the efficient distribution of an entire business concept.

3. Both parties contribute resources to establish and maintain the franchise.

4. The contract describes the contribution of each party and the specific marketing and operating procedures.

5. The franchise is a business entity that requires the full-time business activity of the franchisee or his or her representative.

6. The franchisee and franchisor participate in a common public identity.

7. There is customarily a payment of an initial franchise fee, continuing royalties, and usually a required contribution to a common advertising fund.[12]

Fees for selected franchisors are shown in Table 3.2. Services provided the franchisee can be divided into those that are especially important to the new franchisee and those that are offered on a continuing basis.

The New Franchisee

The franchisor offers to an investor, who often has no previous experience, a proven way of doing business, including established products, an operating system, and a complete marketing program. The franchise minimizes risk. Small Business Administration studies indicate, for instance, that somewhere between one fourth and one third of all businesses fail during their first year, and 65 percent fail within their first five years. On the other hand, the failure rate for franchised businesses is well under 5 percent, and the failed businesses amount to less than a one-half percent of total franchise sales.

[12] Adapted from McGuire, *Franchised Distribution;* and Kostecka, *Franchising in the Economy, 1984–86.*

TABLE 3.2 Fee Structure for Selected Restaurant Franchises

Franchisor	Development Fee	Royalty Fee	Advertising Assessment
		(% of gross revenue)	
Kentucky Fried Chicken	$20,000	4%	2%
Denny's	35,000	4	2
Popeye's	25,000	5	3
Hardee's	15,800	3.5–4	5

Source: Data from Shelly Piedmont and Donald E. Winterhead, "The Franchise Business," *Cornell Hotel and Restaurant Administration Quarterly,* February 1990, p. 77.

In addition to an overall concept, the franchisor provides a number of specific services to the newcomer.

Screening.   Being screened to see whether you are the right person to be sold a franchise may not seem like a service. A moment's reflection, however, will show that careful franchisee selection is in the best interests not only of the company and other, existing franchisees, but of the prospective franchisee as well.

Site Selection and Planning.   Franchisors maintain a real estate department staffed with site-selection experts. The franchise company also has its pooled experience to guide it. Given the importance of location to most hospitality operations, the availability of expert advice is important. The physical layout of the operation, from the site plan to the building, equipment, and furnishings, and even a list of small wares and opening inventory, will be spelled out in detail.

Preopening Training.   Virtually all franchise organizations have some means of training the franchisee and his or her key personnel. This service ranges from McDonald's Hamburger University to simpler programs based on experience in an existing store.

Operations Manuals.   The backbone of the operating system is typically a set of comprehensive operations manuals that cover operating procedures from opening to closing and nearly everything in between. All major equipment operations and routine maintenance are described in the operations manual or in a separate equipment manual.

Continuing Franchise Services

Once a unit is open and running, the first year or two of advice and assistance is the most crucial. Even once a franchisee is sufficiently experienced to manage his or her unit without close assistance, the advantages of a franchise

---

INTERESTED IN BECOMING A FRANCHISEE?

Here Are Seven Basic Questions for a Prospective Franchisee

1. Is the company itself reasonably secure financially, or is it selling franchises to get cash to cover ongoing expenses?
   - Is the company selective in choosing franchisees?
   - Is it in too big a hurry to get your money? Is this deal too good to be true?

   Today, sweetheart deals are few and far between.

2. Does the company have a solid base of company-owned units? If it does,
   - It is in the same business as its franchisees.
   - It is in the company's interest to concentrate on improving marketing and operating systems.

   If *your* primary business is operations and *theirs* is selling franchises, the system is headed for trouble.

3. Is the system successful on a per-unit basis? To find out, look at several numbers:
   - Comparable average sales of stores that have been open longer than one year (sometimes first-year sales are very high and then drop off).
   - Unit-level trends: What is really needed are sales data adjusted for inflation or, better yet, customer counts at the unit level.

   A business is really only growing when it's serving more people.

4. Is the franchisor innovative across all parts of its business?
   - The company should be working on operating and equipment refinements.
   - Ask what it is doing in purchasing, recruiting, training, and labor scheduling. Is anyone working to make uniforms more attractive, durable, and comfortable, for instance?

   The best companies are consistently trying to upgrade every component of their business.

5. Does the company share sufficient support services with its franchisees?
   - In general, the company should provide guidance and strategic direction on marketing and excellent operations training. In addition, every franchisee should have contact with a company employee whose primary responsibility is a small group of franchised restaurants.
   - There are some services that a company can't provide, such as setting prices. And others are risky, such as getting involved in franchisee manager selection or outside financing.

   Support services must be shared in such a way that they respect the franchisee's independence.

6. Does the company respect its franchisees?

- In addition to formal publications, there should be regular informal forums or councils in which selected franchisees meet face to face with top management to discuss both problems and opportunities.
- Corporate staff should collect ideas, test them, and, if they look good, involve franchisees in expanded testing.

Franchisees should actually participate in the development of any change that will affect their units.

7. Does the franchisor provide long-term leadership for the entire system?

- Franchisee participation is no excuse for franchisor abdication of its leadership responsibilities. Somebody has to make the formal decisions, and that must be the franchisor.
- A primary function of the franchisor is to protect the value of each franchise by actively and aggressively monitoring operations, demanding that each unit live up to system standards.

Perhaps a necessary long-term decision is not popular. Making tough decisions and following through may be the best real test of leadership.

Source: Adapted from Don N. Smith, Burton Shaw Lecture, Washington State University, Fall 1985.

---

are still impressive. These services relate to operations and control and to marketing.

Operating and Control Procedures. The franchisor strives to present operating methods that have control procedures designed into them. For instance, McDonald's not only specifies the portion sizes of its french fries but also has designed packages and serving devices that ensure that the portion size will be accurately maintained. Similarly, Long John Silver's specifies a procedure for portioning fish that, if followed, will minimize waste.

The essential ingredient in a successful franchisor's "proven way of doing business" is not just a great idea but an *operational concept.* The concept works and is accepted by customers, and its results can be tracked so that its continuing success is measured and assessed. We should note here, too, that the product and service that underlie the franchise must be continually redeveloped to remain current in the marketplace. Several specialized areas of operations and control franchisor services are discussed below.

Information Management. Accounting systems furnished by franchisors normally integrate the individual sales transactions from the point-of-sales terminal with both daily management reports and the franchisee's books of account. This makes current management and marketing information available in a timely way and helps hold down the cost of accounting services.

One of the most valuable assets that comes with a franchise is the right to use an established brand name. (Courtesy of Pizza Hut Inc.)

Quality Control. Inspection systems help keep units on their toes and provide the franchisee with an expert — if sometimes annoying — outsider's view of the operation. Quality control staff use detailed inspection forms that ensure systemwide standards. Inspectors are trained by the franchisor and their work is generally backed up by detailed written guidelines.

Training. In addition to the opening training effort, franchisors prepare training materials, such as videotapes for common tasks in a unit, as well as training manuals and other training aids.

Field Support. There is general agreement on the importance of field support: "It is the quality of field support that ultimately determines how good a franchise system is."[13] The backbone of field support is an experienced franchise district manager. One of the most serious problems with unsuccessful franchise systems is a lack of field staff or field staff lacking in expertise. One experienced franchisee commented of a failing franchise system, "We started to get pretty annoyed when we found we had to train the franchisee's field staff if we wanted to keep them from messing things up."

[13] McGuire, *Franchised Distribution*, p. 93.

Purchasing. Most franchised restaurant companies have purchasing cooperatives. The co-op offers one-stop shopping for virtually all products required in the operation: food, packaging, and equipment, and often insurance programs. In addition, the co-op periodically publishes a price list that the units can use in negotiating prices with local distributors. The co-op may also publish a newsletter containing information on pricing and trends in equipment, food products, and supply.

Although attractive price and the convenience of one-stop shopping are important purchasing franchisee benefits, particularly with the co-ops, perhaps the most important advantage in the purchasing area is quality maintenance. The lengthy product development process includes careful attention to each product ingredient and the development of detailed product specifications. Often the franchisor will work with the research department of a supplier company to develop a product to meet these specifications and to anticipate market fluctuations. Moreover, it is common for franchisors to maintain a quality control staff in supplier's plants and maintain rigorous

Franchise units follow a common advertising theme developed by the franchisor and bring a national campaign into local media. (Courtesy of Country Kitchen International, Inc.)

inspection systems that monitor the product from the fabrication plant to regional storage centers and then to the individual operating unit.[14]

Marketing. Second only in importance to providing franchisees with a unique way of doing business is the ongoing development and execution of the system's marketing plan. Although franchisees usually are consulted about the marketing program, the executive responsibility for developing and implementing the system's marketing program lies with the franchisor's top management and marketing staff.

Advertising. Many franchisors assist in operating advertising co-ops that are funded with franchisee advertising contributions. National advertising co-ops typically provide copies of the company's television and radio commercials to franchisee members for a nominal price, as well as mats for both black-and-white and color newspaper ads. Co-ops also develop point-of-purchase promotional materials such as window banners and counter cards. Regional and local co-ops devote their efforts to media buying and to execution of the advertising program in their area. The pooling of media buys at the local level yields substantial savings, makes advertising dollars go further, and secures a frequency of advertising that heightens effectiveness. Local and regional co-ops also often coordinate local promotional programs such as those using coupons, games, or premium merchandise.

New Products. The marketplace changes constantly, and it is the franchisor's responsibility to monitor and respond to those changes. The company's marketing department carries out a program of continuing market research. When a need for a new product emerges, either from research or from suggestions from franchisees, the company develops a new product in its test kitchens and tests it for consumer acceptance with taste panels and for fit with the operating system in a pilot store or stores. If test marketing in selected units is successful, the product will be "rolled out" systemwide, with standard procedures for operation and extensive promotional support.

Drawbacks for the Franchisee

Some of the more obvious drawbacks of obtaining a franchise have been implicit in our discussion: loss of independence and payment of substantial advertising assessments and franchise fees. If the franchisee has picked a weak franchising organization, field support and other management services may be inadequate.

Franchising is *not* risk free. The franchisee is generally completely dependent on the franchisor not only for marketing but often for purchasing and

---

[14]For a fuller discussion of the significance of the logistical function in multiunit operations, see Thomas F. Powers, "Complex Food Service Systems," *Cornell Hotel and Restaurant Administration Quarterly,* November 1979, p. 55.

other operations-oriented assistance. If a franchisee concept is not kept up to date—as many argue was the case for Howard Johnson's Restaurants, for instance—or loses its focus, it is difficult for the franchisee to do much about it.

What happens when things really go bad is illustrated by the case of Arthur Treacher's Fish and Chips.[15] A successful and growing franchise in the mid-1970s, Treacher's then had serious difficulties that ended in bankruptcy. Its national marketing efforts virtually ceased. Its product quality control system broke down, yet the franchisees were contractually obligated to purchase only from approved suppliers. The franchisees also were required to pay both advertising fees and royalties but claimed they received little or no services in return. Many franchisees withheld payment of fees and royalties and then became involved in lengthy lawsuits that were expensive in both executive time and attorney's fees. While some Treacher franchisees weathered the series of setbacks, virtually all suffered serious losses, and many left the field.

The Franchisor's View

The franchisee makes most—often, all—of the investment in a new unit. As a result, franchising gives the franchisor the means to expand rapidly without extensive use of its own capital. By expanding rapidly, the franchising organization achieves a presence in the marketplace that is, in itself, an advantage. Moreover, the more units a company has in a market, the more advertising media it can buy. In addition, the better geographic coverage there is, the easier it will be for people to visit often; the restaurants are simply closer and more convenient. Finally, continuous exposure of all kinds—seeing television commercials, driving past the sign and building, as well as actually visiting the restaurant—contribute to "top-of-mind awareness," that is, being the first place that comes into people's minds when they think of a restaurant. Clearly, then, being *in place* in a market is a crucial advantage and one more readily secured quickly through franchising.

The franchising organization gains highly motivated owner managers who require less field supervision than owned units do. A district manager supervising owned units is usually responsible for from 4 to 8 units. A supervisor (or consultant, as they are sometimes called) overseeing franchised units is likely to cover somewhere between 15 and 30 units.[16] This permits a large company like McDonald's to operate with a much smaller organization than would be possible if it had to provide close supervision to all of its thousands of units.

[15] The difficulties of a franchise system in trouble are told from the point of view of a successful multiunit franchisee in case history form in Thomas F. Powers, "MIE Hospitality" (Guelph, Ont.: Advanced Management Program for the Hospitality Industry, 1983).

[16] Don N. Smith, Burton Shaw Lecture, Washington State University, Fall 1985.

Franchising companies also draw on franchisees as a source of know-how. According to Don N. Smith, president of Perkins Pancake Houses, input from the grass-roots level "creates a check and balance that enables the corporate functional support groups to keep a proper perspective on the business." Smith also stressed the value of practical ideas that franchisees running daily operations can bring to the solution of operating problems:

> A simple example is the sour cream gun at Taco Bell. Everyone in the Taco Bell system knew it was needed for better portion control and faster speed of service. After spending several years and several hundred thousand dollars with no practical solution in sight, the company gave up. Finally, a franchisee showed them how it should be done. On a much larger scale, breakfast at McDonald's had been tried without success until a franchisee came up with Egg McMuffin.[17]

Franchising Disadvantages to Franchisors

The bargain struck with franchisees has its costs to franchisors. Although their experience varies, many franchise companies find that their owned stores yield higher sales and profit margins. And if the company owned all its units — if it could overcome the organizational difficulties of a much larger, more complex organization — the profits earned from the same stores would be higher than the royalties received from a franchised store.

We should note, too, that not all franchise royalty income is profit. Usually 2 percent of sales is needed to service a franchise system. And because of start-up costs for a new franchised unit *for the franchisor,* it may be three years before the royalties begin to contribute to the franchisor's profit. In addition, the franchisor will already have made a considerable investment in legal and accounting costs, executives' time, and consultants' and managerial time.

Franchising: A Middle Way

The franchisee is not fully independent but neither is he or she as much at risk as the independent. Taking part in a larger organization that provides vital services while still allowing a considerable measure of financial and managerial independence has much to say for it. A person who is unable to work within a tightly prescribed system would be uncomfortable as a franchisee. Those who can live within such a framework, however, can reap significant rewards with much less risk than they would have in their own business.

---

[17] Smith, Burton Shaw Lecture.

MAKING A PROFIT
IN FOOD SERVICE OPERATIONS

Restaurants have several business purposes. One is to serve the customer. Another is to provide a good place to work and a decent living for employees. At bottom, though, the purpose that underlies the logic of any business is to make a profit. Without profit, funds to renew the business — to remodel, to launch new products or services, to expand to serve a changing market and keep employees on the payroll — are just not available. Moreover, owners, like all of us, need some reward for their effort and risk. Profit fulfills these vital roles in a business.

There are two basic approaches to increasing profit. One is to increase sales, while the other is to reduce costs. Most commonly, operators try to do both to the limits of what is possible.

INCREASING SALES

The two basic approaches to raising sales are to sell to more people or to sell more to your present customers — or to do both. Increasing the customer base is usually thought of as the job of advertising and promotion. We should also note, however, that a *superior* operation that achieves a good reputation may build its customer base through word-of-mouth referrals.

Another approach to raising sales is to increase sales to the customers you now have; that is, to increase the check average. One obvious way to do this is simply to raise prices. But, unless the price level of the competition is also going up, this will most probably result in losing customers. Effective approaches to increasing the average check are menu redesign and suggestive selling.

One of the most common menu redesign strategies is the combination meal. Several items that are sold separately — for instance, a hamburger, french fries, a soft drink, and dessert in fast food — are sold together for a price that is less than the price of each separately. If this is a good value to the customer, it is likely to persuade a certain percentage to buy more than they might otherwise have done. In a table-service restaurant, this kind of combination is referred to as a complete dinner (or lunch) or table d'hôte. The higher check average results in an increase in sales.[18]

---

[18] Another result is likely to be a slightly higher food cost percentage because selling price is reduced but food costs remain the same. On the other hand, since total dollar sales have increased and, almost certainly, no additional labor has been scheduled, labor cost percentage will be lower. The intent would be to have the higher food cost more than offset by the reduced labor cost percentage.

Suggestive selling is another effective technique for raising sales. Common targets for increased sales are appetizers, side dishes, wine, desserts, or after-dinner drinks. The service staff is crucial to this effort: "May I suggest something from our wine cellar? A bottle of Pommard would complement the roast beef perfectly." Operators often offer prizes or bonuses for the server most effective in selling.

REDUCING COSTS

Just as raising prices faster than the competition will drive off customers, so will cheapening quality through use of inferior ingredients or smaller portions. Thus, reducing costs must result from improved efficiency, which is a fit subject for not one but several books.[19] We will content ourselves here by noting that some of the most common techniques for reducing costs in food service involve more careful scheduling of employees, improved portion control, and more careful monitoring of the issue and use of supplies such as soap, paper goods, and other disposables. Generally, the key to reducing costs is a careful review of the operation to find places where waste can be reduced without loss of quality. Following such a review, realistic standards are set and performance is monitored against those standards. Figure 3.1 shows some common techniques for monitoring cost performance with examples of the kind of measurement used.

Provided that reduced costs come from improved efficiency rather than cheapening the operation, it will have a greater impact on profit. A dollar saved in cost, after all, is a dollar more profit. An increase in sales, however, will be accompanied by some increased cost—the variable cost, such as food cost, for instance—and so will not produce as much profit.

KEEPING THE SCORE IN OPERATIONS: ACCOUNTING STATEMENTS AND OPERATING RATIOS

A discussion of operations is not complete without a brief review of the common score-keeping methods used in the field. Elsewhere in your hospitality curriculum you will undoubtedly study the subject of control at more length. As part of your introduction to the hospitality field, however, this section will discuss briefly some key food service control terms and accounting statements and operating statistics.

[19]For an extended discussion of topics related to cost reduction and control, see Thomas F. Powers and Jo Marie Powers, *Food Service Operations: Planning and Control* (New York: John Wiley & Sons, 1984).

Cost Group	Technique	Example of Measurement
Food	Yielding	Dollar cost or weight per portion served
Labor	Productivity standards	Number of guests served per waitress hour or per dollar of service payroll
China, glass, and silver	Breakage/loss counts	Guests served per broken/missing piece
Supplies	Usage monitoring	Gallons/pounds of soap used per 100 guests

FIGURE 3.1 Some common cost-control techniques.

COST OF SALES

The *cost of sales* refers to the cost of a product consumed by the guest in the process of operations. The principal product costs include:

- *Food costs.* The cost of food prepared for and consumed by guests.
- *Beverage or bar costs.* The cost of alcoholic beverages and other ingredients, such as juices, carbonated water, or fruit, used to make drinks for guests.

Note that these (and all other) costs are customarily stated both in dollar amounts and as a percentage of sales. For example, if your food cost is $25,000 and your food sales are $75,000, then the food cost percentage will be $25,000 ÷ 75,000 or 33.3 percent. Although dollar costs are essential to the accounting system, the percentage of the cost (that is, its size relative to sales level) is more useful to managers because the percentages for one month (or for some other period) can readily be compared with those of other months, with a budget, and with industry averages.

CONTROLLABLE EXPENSES

Controllable expenses are costs that may be expected to vary to some degree and over which operating management can exercise direct control. Controllable expenses include:

- *Payroll costs.* Payroll costs are the wages and salaries paid to employees.
- *Employee benefits.* Employee benefits include social security taxes and such social insurance as workers' compensation, pension payments.
- *Other variable costs.* Other costs that generally vary with sales are laundry, linen, uniforms, china, glass and silver, guest supplies, cleaning

supplies, and menus. Some costs in the category of controllable expenses have both a fixed and variable component (utilities cost), while others are fixed by management decision, which is subject to change (advertising and promotion, utilities, administrative and general, and repairs and maintenance).

- *Capital costs.* This group of costs varies with the value of the fixed assets — usually land, building, furniture and fixtures, and equipment. The higher the value, for instance, the higher the property taxes or insurance. The same is true of depreciation, which is a bookkeeping entry to write off the cost of a capital asset. Interest varies, of course, with the size of the debt and the interest rate.

By categorizing cost information as we have above, we focus attention on the operation's key variables. The cost percentages also reflect the efficiency of various segments of an operation. Food costs reflect management pricing and the kitchen crew's efficiency. Labor costs reflect efficiency in employee scheduling and the adequacy of sales volume in proportion to the operation's crew size. Results can be improved by either reducing employee hours or increasing sales.

Two key operating statistics are *covers* and *check averages*. The number of covers refers to the number of guests. (*Guest count* is an alternative term.) The *check average* can be what it sounds like, the average dollar amount of a check. But because parties (a group of guests seated together) vary in size, the check average is usually quoted as the average sale per guest. This figure is found by dividing total dollar sales by the number of guests served during the period and is sometimes referred to as the *average cover*.

Figure 3.2 shows an example of a restaurant statement of income and expenses (also called an operating statement or a profit-and-loss statement). This statement shows the relationship of the costs we have just discussed and also how the check averages are computed.

As a final way to compare and contrast differing restaurants, Table 3.3 presents selected *average operating ratios* for the kinds of restaurants we were describing in the previous chapter.

SUMMARY

A good way to structure your observation of food service is around the major divisions of the front of the house, back of the house, and the "office" or the administrative function. Guest satisfaction, personal service, and accounting for sales are the major responsibilities of the front of the house. Food quality as well as good safety, sanitation, and food cost control are crucial in the back of the house. The office staff provides administrative assistance to managers and han-

---

STATEMENT OF INCOME AND EXPENSE
Suburban Restaurant
Year Ending December 31, 19XX

SALES		
Food	$962,400	80.2%
Beverage	237,600	19.8
Total sales	1,200,000	100.0
COST OF SALES		
Food	$348,400	36.2%
Beverage	66,100	27.8
Total cost of sales	414,500	34.5
CONTROLLABLE EXPENSES		
Payroll	$338,400	28.2%
Employee benefits	62,400	5.2
Direct operating expenses	64,800	5.4
Music and entertainment	3,600	0.3
Advertising and promotion	22,800	1.9
Utilities	38,400	3.2
Administrative and general	46,800	3.9
Repairs and maintenance	21,600	1.8
Total controllable expenses	598,800	49.9
INCOME BEFORE CAPITAL COSTS	$187,200	15.6%
CAPITAL COSTS		
Rent, property taxes, and insurance	$ 84,000	7.0%
Interest and depreciation	46,800	3.9
Total capital costs	130,800	10.9
NET PROFIT BEFORE INCOME TAXES	$ 56,400	4.7%

Number of covers served	74,918
Food check average	$12.85
Beverage check average	$ 3.17
Total check average	$16.02

FIGURE 3.2 Restaurant statement of income and expense.

dles routine accounting and cost-control functions. It is vital to see that there is some kind of management presence whenever an operation's employees are at work. The food service day revolves around opening and closing routines and rush periods at meals.

Restaurants are organized into groups in chains or franchise organizations or stand alone as independents. Chains and independents can be compared on the basis of brand recognition, site selection, access to capital, purchasing economies, information and control

TABLE 3.3 Comparison of U.S. Restaurant Operating Statistics

	Quick-Service Restaurant	Limited Menu Table-Service Restaurants	Table-Service Restaurants
Food cost[a]	34.3%	35.6%	36.2
Beverage cost[b]	32.3[f]	28.2	27.8
Product cost[c]	34.6	34.2	34.5
Payroll and related cost[d]	29.2	31.1	33.4
Prime cost[e]	63.8	65.3	67.9
Other operating costs	13.7	15.9	16.5
Occupancy and capital costs[g]	14.4	12.1	12.4
Profit before income taxes	8.2	4.3	3.2

Source: Restaurant Operations Report (Washington, D.C.: National Restaurant Association, 1990); median figures are used.

[a]Food cost as percentage of food sales.

[b]Beverage cost as percentage of beverage sales.

[c]Total food and beverage cost as percentage of total food and beverage sales.

[d]Includes employee benefits.

[e]Total of product cost and labor cost.

[f]Applies to some operations.

[g]Includes "other deductions."

systems, and personnel programs. Chains' strengths come largely from economies of scale, while the independent's advantages lie in flexibility and the closeness of the owner-manager to the operation.

Franchising offers operators a degree of independence but requires a willingness to work within a defined operation. Franchisees must give up some control over the operation but, in return, their risks are lowered dramatically. Franchisees generally pay a development fee, a royalty fee, and an advertising assessment. The franchisor provides a proven system of operation and expert field staff as well as a marketing program.

Food service operations can be made profitable by increasing revenues or decreasing costs. Sales can be increased by selling more to existing customers or by broadening the customer base. Costs must be reduced through greater efficiency rather than by cheapening the product and service. In operations, the effectiveness of results is measured with financial statements, particularly the statement of income and expense, and in operating statistics and ratios.

KEY WORDS AND CONCEPTS

To help you review this chapter, keep in mind the following:

Front of the house
Guest satisfaction
Back of the house
Food quality
The "office" function at the unit
    level
Opening and closing routines
Management presence
Specialty restaurant
Economies of scale
Independent restaurants

Flexibility
Business format franchising
Services to the new franchisee
Services to the established
    franchisee
Increasing sales
Reducing costs
Cost of sales
Controllable expenses
Cover
Check average

REVIEW QUESTIONS

1. What are the most important elements of quality in food service? How are they attained?

2. What is meant by "management presence"? Why is it important? How have you seen it provided in operations you have worked in?

3. What characteristics do you think are important in a person who chooses to work in food service operations?

4. In which areas of operation are chains and independents likely to be most effective? What strengths do they bring to the marketplace?

5. What are the differences between a franchisee and an independent? What are the advantages and disadvantages of each?

6. What are the benefits *to the franchisor* of franchising? What are their disadvantages?

7. What pitfalls can you see in the attempts to raise sales? To reduce costs?

8. What are the major approaches to increasing profit? Which is the best way? Why? What are its dangers?

9. What are the main controllable costs? Why are they called controllable?

C H A P T E R 4

Courtesy of Bob Evans Farms

FORCES SHAPING FOOD SERVICE

THE PURPOSE OF THIS CHAPTER

The food service business, as it is today and will be tomorrow, is the result of the interaction of basic market forces. In this chapter we will look at three of the most basic of the forces. The first is the *demand* for food service from consumers. Second, we must consider the *supply* of those things required to provide service, such as new food products and food service labor. Finally, food service changes so often because its highly competitive nature leads to constant adaptation. Accordingly, we will consider *competition* both within the industry and with other sectors that compete for consumers' food dollars.

THIS CHAPTER SHOULD HELP YOU

1. Understand the impact of the changing demographics of the North American population on demand for food services.

2. See how changes in the proportion of women working and alterations in family structure affect consumers.

3. Identify the key factors of supply required by food service organizations and become familiar with trends that are changing their relative cost.

4. Assess the change in competitive conditions in food service as that market matures.

5. Recognize the major elements of competition within food service.

6. Appreciate the growing significance of competition from other industries serving our customers' food service needs.

DEMAND

Demand, ultimately, means customers. We will look at customers from three different perspectives. First, we need to understand what the population's changing age patterns are and how they affect demand for food service. Next, we will look at other patterns of change such as the increase in working women, the transformation of the family structure, and the change in income and spending patterns. Finally, when we have reviewed these factors, we should be able to draw some numerical and qualitative conclusions about demand.

THE CHANGING AGE COMPOSITION OF OUR POPULATION

We have mentioned the impact of the baby boom on food service in earlier chapters. It is now time to examine that central fact of the population of North America more carefully and set it in the context of other population groups. We can begin by describing just what the baby boom is. Beginning with the Great Depression, the birth rate fell dramatically and remained low throughout the 1930s. Then came World War II, which also produced a low birth rate. After the war, however, family formation rose dramatically and, beginning in 1946 and lasting until 1964, the number of births rose as well. The boom in births was out of all proportion to anything the country had experienced before. The resulting "baby boomers," that is, people who were born between 1946 and 1964, have, as a generation, had an unprecedented impact on all facets of American life from economics to social change, and certainly on food service.

Fast food grew up to feed the boomers when they were children and when their parents, still young, had limited incomes and needed to economize. Then, starting in the late 1950s, the boomers, as young people, began to have money to spend on their own. McDonald's, Burger King, and other fast-food operations suited their taste and their pocketbooks. In the late 1960s and early 1970s, however, the boomers were becoming young adults—and Wendy's, among others, developed an upscale fast-food operation to meet their moderately higher incomes and more sophisticated tastes. Similarly, in the early 1980s, as a significant number of boomers passed the age of 30, the "gourmet hamburger" restaurant appeared.

Following the baby boom years, the boomers' parents passed out of the prime childbearing years. By this time the children born during the low-birth-rate Depression and war years were of an age to begin their own families. This meant fewer people in the childbearing ages. The period from roughly 1965

Decor designed to meet special customer interests helps make eating out a pleasant experience. The merry-go-round motif at this McDonald's dining room is aimed at young customers. (Courtesy of McDonald's Corp.)

until 1975 was the time of the "birth dearth." Then, in 1975, we saw the children born during the baby boom years—that is, the boomers themselves—come into the family formation age. The boomers began to have children. The increase in the number of children born during the late 1970s has been referred to as the "echo" of the baby boom. As the huge generation of boomers came into the childbearing years, births rose simply because there were more potential parents. The echo boom, however, was smaller because the boomers chose to have much smaller families than *their* parents had had.

Figure 4.1 graphs the number of children under the age of five from 1950 to 1990. The period of the baby boom, the birth dearth, and the echo boom are identified in this figure. The figure also shows the U.S. Census Bureau's projection of the population of children five and under to the year 2020. (Note: The higher the curve is over a certain year, the more people it is projected will be in the age segment that year.)

Children

Turning again to Figure 4.1, it is apparent that from 1977 until 1989, the number of young children increased in number. During this time, emphasis on children's menus, playgrounds, and the like was appropriate. At one restaurant in Denver, for instance, a playroom adjoined the dining room where

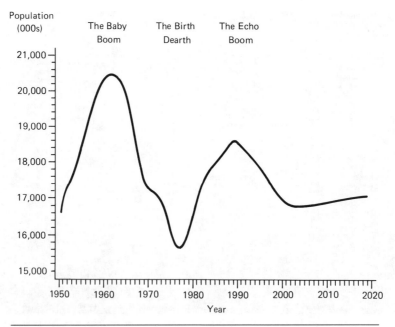

FIGURE 4.1 Number of preschool children, 1950 to 2020. (*Data:* U.S. Department of Commerce, Bureau of the Census.)

children could both eat and play while their parents kept an eye on them through a one-way window.[1] The early 1990s saw the number of families with young children decline. From 1990 to the year 2000, the number of children under five will drop by nearly 10 percent and increase only very gradually thereafter. This *doesn't* mean children's menus will disappear, but it does mean there will be less emphasis on a market segment that, although still significant, will be getting smaller.

Figure 4.2 shows children of grade school age. Once again we can see the shape of the baby boom. The grade school population peaked in 1969 and then declined by 20 percent until the "echo" children began to go to school. It is interesting to note that a national study has indicated that children aged 4 to 12 have about $9 billion to spend, over 20 percent of it on snacks and fast food. Now that families often have two working parents, there are more "latchkey children" who have a significant degree of independence as consumers.[2]

[1] *Restaurants and Institutions Alert,* January 9, 1991.

[2] George D. Rice, "Leveraging Resources in a Mature Market," *Proceedings of the 18th Chain Operators Exchange* (Chicago: International Foodservice Manufacturers Association, 1991).

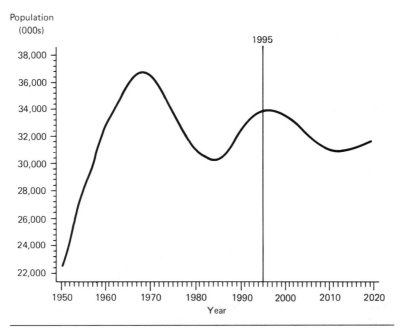

FIGURE 4.2 Number of elementary school-age children, 1950 to 2020. (*Data:* U.S. Department of Commerce, Bureau of the Census.)

Young People

Teenagers are a significant market in their own right. They spent a total of $71 billion[3] in 1989 and have a substantial effect on family decision making. A Roper poll, for instance, reveals that over half of parents said their children had influence in deciding which full-service restaurant to visit, and that was true for three quarters of them on a QSR choice. Over half of the families polled involve their children in deciding where to spend a vacation, and three quarters consulted them on family recreation activities. This strong-minded, vociferous group of consumers, as Figure 4.3 shows, has been growing very slowly through the 1990s and will have slow growth until it begins to decline in 2000.

As Figure 4.4 shows, the age group from 18 to 24 has been declining in size since 1981 and will continue to do so until 1995, with adverse impact on college food service and on fast food. When the "echo" generation moves into their college years, however, we will see this group begin to grow once again.

[3] *American Demographics,* April 1990, p. 15.

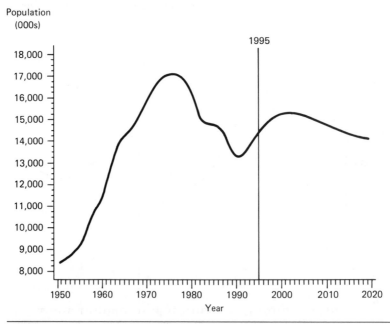

FIGURE 4.3 Number of teenagers, 1950 to 2020. (*Data:* U.S. Department of Commerce, Bureau of the Census.)

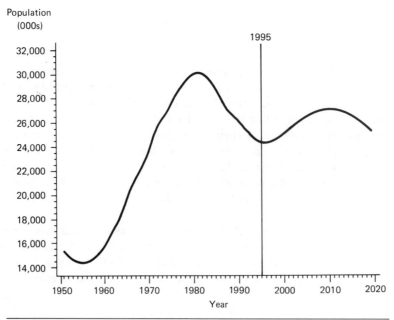

FIGURE 4.4 Number of college-age people, 1950 to 2020. (*Data:* U.S. Department of Commerce, Bureau of the Census.)

Young Adults

The ages 25 to 34 are family formation years. This is a time when young families are still near the starting point in the job market, and their incomes are correspondingly limited. At the same time, however, they are taking on the responsibilities of furnishing and equipping a home and bringing children into the world. During the first half of the 1990s, this group forms the trailing edge of the baby boom. In 1990, the youngest baby boomer was 26, and the median age of the baby boom generation was 34. During the 1980s, when this age segment of the population was growing rapidly to a peak in 1990, their desire to move upscale from fast food led to the development of restaurants specializing in "gourmet hamburgers." In the entertainment-food-and-alcohol segment, they supported the growth of the roadhouse. Figure 4.5 leads us to wonder what the growth for such operations will be as this age group declines throughout the decade of the 1990s.

The Baby Boomers Turn Middle Age

In 1995, the youngest baby boomer will be 31 and the median age will be 39; the oldest boomers, born in 1946, will be 49. Because of their huge numbers, the baby boom generation has had an enormous impact on everything and everyone living in the last half of the twentieth century. Their arrival in middle

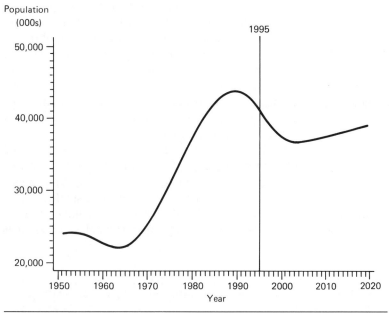

FIGURE 4.5 Number of people 25 to 34 years old, 1950 to 2020. (*Data:* U.S. Department of Commerce, Bureau of the Census.)

TABLE 4.1 Meals Purchased Annually at Restaurants, Carryouts, and Other Food Service

Age Group	Dollar Expenditure	Percent of Average Expenditure
Average household expenditure	$1,358.05	100%
Under 25	$ 977.91	72%
25–34	1,446.62	106
35–44	1,741.90	128
45–54	1,763.78	130
55–64	1,339.39	99
65–74	850.24	63
75 and over	586.26	43

age is no different. The growing popularity of the casual upscale restaurant, for instance, almost certainly reflects the casual tastes of the rebels of the sixties and seventies, now all grown up.

Table 4.1 highlights the significance of the growth of the middle-aged population segment for food service. Middle age is a time when people become more settled in their jobs. Their incomes expand, and they can afford to eat out. While people aged 25 to 34 eat out more frequently, people aged 35 to 54 spend more on eating out. In fact, middle-aged people spend roughly 30 percent more than the average household at restaurants and carryouts.

The 35- to 44-year-old population segment will grow until the year 2000. People in this age group are most likely to have young children living at home. For that reason, the number of people in their party is, on average, somewhat larger but their average spending *per person* is somewhat lower. They are more likely to be price conscious. If the person in this age group is single or married but without children, however, they are likely to have a higher disposable income and to be much less price conscious.[4]

The prosperous 45- to 54-year-old segment is growing and will continue to grow until 2010. These people are likely to have grown children living at home or away at college—or to be empty nesters.[5] They tend to eat out less often than younger boomers and to have, on average, a smaller party size and a higher check average.[6] Figures 4.6 and 4.7 show the changing relative sizes of the 35-to-44 and 45-to-54 population groups. Table 4.1 shows spending on

[4]NPD CREST, "Baby Boomers—New Life-Styles, New Needs," *Proceedings of the 17th Annual Chain Operators Exchange* (Chicago: International Foodservice Manufacturers Association, 1990).

[5]Empty nesters are people whose children have grown up and left home.

[6]NPD CREST, "Baby Boomers—New Life-Styles, New Needs."

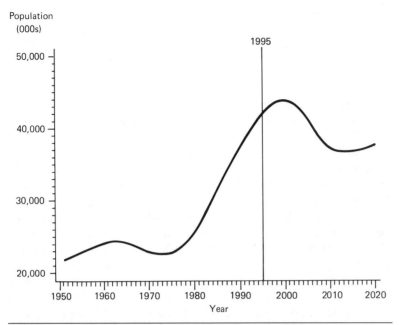

FIGURE 4.6 Number of people 35 to 44 years old, 1950 to 2020. (*Data:* U.S. Department of Commerce, Bureau of the Census.)

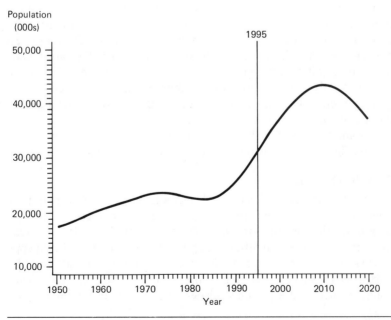

FIGURE 4.7 Number of people 45 to 54 years old, 1950 to 2020. (*Data:* U.S. Department of Commerce, Bureau of the Census.)

food service by age group. Notice that people aged 35 to 54 spend well above the average expenditure. Their free spending makes them prime customers.

The Aging

People aged 55 to 64 are a declining segment of the population and have been since the early 1980s. Not until the oldest baby boomers begin to turn 55, at the turn of the century, will this group begin to grow. We might, however, note that this group presents a long-range challenge that will become more and more important for food service after the year 2000. People in the 55 to 65 age bracket tend to have more leisure. If not already retired, they usually are in their peak earning years. Those who are retired have somewhat lower incomes but, on average, they have substantial *wealth*. For instance, their house and car are commonly paid for and they often have substantial savings in the form of pension entitlements, investments, or both. Moreover, because they usually have no dependent children, their *disposable* income is high relative to their total income. Finally, they have more leisure than most of the population and so have lots of time to spend their income. They *should* be good customers.

The lower spending in restaurants shown for this age group in Table 4.1 raises a question, however. Does the reduction in spending shown there really reflect a natural tendency to eat out less as people age? We can't be sure of the answer. The people who are 55 or over in 1995 were born in 1940 or earlier, children of parents who had lived through the Depression years. Their families had to be careful with money to survive. Eating out for them was a treat, a luxury. The evidence is that from the age of 35 on, eating-out *frequency* begins to decline. Some of the limitations in the 55- to 64-year-old market is undoubtedly due to this age effect. But the tendency of those over 55 *today* to eat out less may also reflect their upbringing. It could be that when the baby boomers arrive at 55, things will be different. They were, after all, weaned on McDonald's, grew up on Wendy's, and moved on to gourmet hamburgers before fueling the current boom in upscale casual restaurants. Baby boomers are a generation that has eaten out all its life. It will certainly be crucial for the success of the restaurant business after the turn of the century to keep a high percentage of this group. Figure 4.8 shows the impact of the baby boomers turning 55.

People Over 65

For much of this section, we have been looking at one of the major population phenomena of the twentieth century—the baby boomers and their impact as they move through the life cycle. We need, now, to shift our attention to a different but no less significant population development. Few people realize how radical the changes in aging have been in the last 100 years. In the late 1800s, only a small proportion of the population survived past the age of 50; "old age" began in a person's thirties.[7] But by the beginning of this century,

---

[7]For an extended discussion of this issue and its more general social consequences, see Peter Drucker, *The Unseen Revolution* (New York: Harper and Row, 1976).

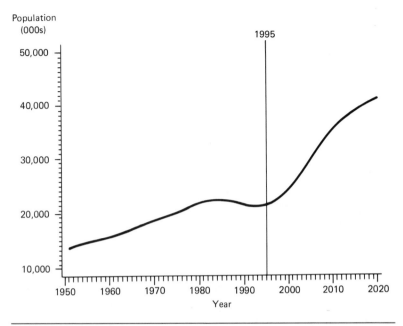

FIGURE 4.8 Number of people 55 to 64 years old, 1950 to 2020. (*Data:* U.S. Department of Commerce, Bureau of the Census.)

improved health care, better nutrition, better control of communicable diseases, and many other factors led to a radical increase in life expectancy. The strong influence of retirees in our society began, as Peter Drucker has pointed out, when the babies born in the 1890s did not die in the 1940s, as they would have a generation earlier. We are, in fact, the first society in history in which a large proportion of our population has survived not just past 50 but well into their sixties, seventies, and eighties.

America's elderly population is already large, as Figure 4.9 shows, but it will continue to grow at a steady rate through the first decade of the next century. In 2010, when the first baby boomer turns 65, however, this population group will soar.

People aged 65 to 74 tend to be active, lively people whose *career* has become leisure. From age 75 to 84, however, ill health takes a much greater toll, and most people who survive beyond 85 experience some impairment of their activities. As seen in Table 4.1, the people in this age group have demonstrated a tendency to spend less on eating out but, as their numbers grow, they will be a more and more attractive target market and food service marketers will want to reach them. Certainly, they have the time and, to a very large degree, the financial ability to eat out.

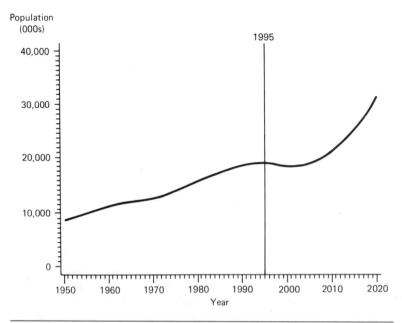

FIGURE 4.9 Number of people 65 to 74 years old, 1950 to 2020. (*Data:* U.S. Department of Commerce, Bureau of the Census.)

OTHER DEMOGRAPHIC FACTORS

We need to consider four other basic structural changes that have occurred or accelerated during the last half of the twentieth century. The increase in the proportion of women working, a falling birth rate, changes in family structure, and an altering income distribution are all interrelated. We will consider each briefly below.

Working Women

Over the past 35 years, the changes in our views of women and the family have had an enormous impact on food service in general. The best objective measure of the change in the role of women appears in the proportion of women employed outside the home or seeking such employment. This proportion is referred to as the *female labor force participation rate.*

In 1900, about 20 out of every 100 women in the United States entered the labor force. In 1920, after World War I, this number was only about 23 in 100, an overall change of less than 14 percent in the participation rate. From 1920 to 1940, the rate rose to just under 26 in 100; again, a change of just under 14 percent.

Following World War II, the rate rose from just over one quarter of the women working in 1940 to nearly one third in 1947, a rate of increase in that

TABLE 4.2 Growth in Female Labor Force Participation Rates, Projected and Actual, 1947–1995

| Age Group | Participation Percentages | | | | | Rate of Change | |
	1947	1970	1980	1990	1999*	1947–1990	1990–1999*
16–17	29.4%	34.9%	43.6%	41.9%	49.4%	42.5%	17.9%
18–19	52.2	53.5	61.9	60.5	68.7	15.9	13.6
20–24	44.8	57.7	68.9	71.6	77.6	59.8	8.4
25–34	31.9	45.0	65.5	73.6	81.7	130.7	11.0
35–44	36.3	51.1	65.5	76.5	84.3	110.7	10.2
45–54	32.7	54.4	59.9	71.2	76.1	117.7	6.9
55–64	24.3	43.0	41.3	45.3	48.7	86.4	7.5
65 and over	8.1	9.7	8.1	8.7	7.6	7.4	− 12.7
Total	31.8%	43.3%	51.5%	57.5%	62.2%	80.8%	8.2%

Source: Bureau of Labor Statistics, *Employment and Earnings,* January 1991.
*Projected.

7-year period of approximately 23 percent. In the 20 years between 1954 and 1974, the participation rate of women in the labor force jumped even higher, increasing from 34.6 percent to 45.6 percent. This was a *change* of 32 percent, or more than twice the rate of change experienced during the first two 20-year periods in this century.

Table 4.2 shows the change in female labor force participation from the period just after World War II to 1990 and provides a projection by the Bureau of Labor Statistics for 1999. The rate-of-change columns tell the story in summary fashion. From 1947 to 1990, the *rate* of women working rose by 80 percent. Labor force participation increased dramatically for women in the age groups normally associated with raising children (ages 20 to 54), with the growth in the number of working women between the ages of 25 and 34 being particularly pronounced.

In 1947, it was unusual for mothers to work; two thirds did not. By 1990, the unusual woman was the one who did *not* work — only a little over a quarter of women in the childbearing years. The second rate-of-change column tells a slightly different story. While the trend continues, most of the change has already taken place. The change in the next 10 years will be modest because so much has happened already.

The result of these changes, of course, is that many more women are midday food service customers. In families in which both spouses work, moreover, cooking dinner at the end of a day's work is likely to be easy to give up for a restaurant meal, and two incomes make that quite affordable. In Chapter 6 we will see that these trends have had a major impact on demand for government and employer services to help working women, too.

It seems likely that the statistics we have cited actually *understate* women's work roles. Women enter and exit the work force more frequently than men to accommodate other life changes such as marriage and childbirth. Counted as nonparticipants are many women who are not working *at the moment* but who expect to return to work shortly. In fact, *American Demographics* estimates that 90 percent of women aged 18 to 49 are in the work force sometime during a two-year period.[8]

Family Size

People are postponing marriage and, once married, are postponing the birth of their first child. They are also having fewer children.[9] The average number of persons in a family fell from 3.67 in 1960 to 3.17 in 1988,[10] reflecting this tendency toward smaller families. A longer period before marriage means more singles, and singles are among the restaurant industry's best individual customers. Delays in having children after marriage mean more dual-income families without children, another affluent group of excellent restaurant customers. Smaller families also mean more disposable spending power for the parents. On the other hand, the fact that many are postponing the birth of their first child means that many families will have dependent children later in life, delaying their entry into "empty nester" status. Empty nesters are also among the best food service customers.[11] The industry gains from the rising number of singles and two-earner couples without children but will have to pay for it later with delayed entry of some of these people into the empty nest stage.

Family Structure

Family breakup through divorce is changing consumer patterns, creating a large group of female-headed families. Female-headed families tend to have among the lowest incomes. Probably because of their lower incomes, single parents eat out 25 percent less often than the average American. As we have noted, most single parents are women. When and if they remarry, of course, they leave the ranks of single parents. There is a concern, however, that a large number of these women and their children will be permanently economically disadvantaged. In fact, mothers with no husband present was one of the fastest growing demographic groups in 1990.[12]

---

[8] Horst H. Stipp, "What Is a Working Woman?" *American Demographics,* July 1988, pp. 24–25.

[9] *American Demographics,* March 1990, p. 12.

[10] *American Demographics,* November 1988, p. 22.

[11] George D. Rice, "The World We Live In," *Proceedings of the 14th Annual Chain Operators Exchange* (Chicago: International Foodservice Manufacturers Association, 1987).

[12] Thomas Exeter, "Lifestyle Change Into the 90's," *Proceedings of the 17th Annual Chain Operators Exchange* (Chicago: International Foodservice Manufacturers Association, 1990).

As Americans become differentiated in their life-styles, their food service needs, too, become more differentiated. In large part, the emergence of the highly varied forms of food service that we have today is a function of the other changes in the way we live.

SUPPLY

The key factors of supply that concern us are food and labor.[13] We will consider food supply—that is, raw ingredients—further in the last chapter. For now we will simply note that while the cost of food may vary from season to season, for the most part these variations affect all food service competitors roughly the same. Food service price changes would have to reflect any change in raw food cost. But, foreseeable food supply conditions do not suggest any major price changes in North America, although a premature frost or dry summer can always drive up some prices temporarily.

LABOR

The National Restaurant Association expects employment in food service to grow 1.8 percent annually, half again as fast as the 1.2 percent annual growth rate projected for the total labor force. This growth in employment will be necessary to support projected industry growth. Many, however, are concerned about whether the industry can attract new recruits in those numbers. As one industry authority put it,

> Without a doubt, the single greatest problem facing the food service industry in the 90's is the lack of available staff and store management personnel. . . . and the resultant negative impact on profits through lower sales (poor customer service) and higher costs (lack of productivity, waste and theft).[14]

A review of Figures 4.3 and 4.4 shows one source of this concern. The hospitality industry in general and food service in particular has put great reliance on younger people as workers. The number of teenagers and people of college age has been declining for some years. While the worst of the decline is over, taken together, these two groups will be declining in numbers by about 2.5 percent from 1990 to 1995 and will only regain their 1990's total by the year 2000.

Another source of labor supply for the hospitality industry's growth has been the growing number of women entering the work force. We have just noted, however, that the *rate of increase* in working women is slowing dramat-

---

[13] Capital is a third factor of production of concern to the industry but is beyond the scope of this text.

[14] Rice, "Leveraging Resources in a Mature Market."

ically. Both women and young workers have played an especially important role in the part-time and seasonal food service labor force. The shortfall in these groups reduces staffing flexibility and leads to more pressure on costs.

Because of the shortage of workers, some operators have found expansion plans hindered and others have even had to close units for lack of staff.[15] Many operators have launched successful efforts to recruit older workers. With labor shortfalls putting increasing pressure on operators, some companies have moved to doubtful employment practices. For instance, the U.S. Department of Labor filed a suit in 1990 against Burger King, indicating that many of their units were employing workers under 16, working young workers more hours than permitted, working them during prohibited hours, and placing them in prohibited duties such as cooking.[16] At about the same time, over 7,000 restaurants were charged with violating child labor laws.[17]

One factor that may reduce the shortfall of young workers, however, is immigration, both legal and illegal. For some years immigrants, particularly from Mexico and other Latin and Caribbean countries, have swelled the food service work force. The effect of this source of labor, however, is limited to a few geographic areas.

Many immigrants have limited education, and some don't speak English when they arrive. This means that an immigrant family is able to obtain only unskilled jobs during its first generation in America. In fact, problems arise because some unscrupulous employers take advantage of these people, particularly if they are illegal immigrants.

Illegal immigration is like floodwater around a dike, always there and always seeking entry through any hole in the structure. Repeated crackdowns, like temporary repairs to a dike, staunch the flow for a time. But as long as the employment outlook in the United States is so much better and wages several times higher than in the lands to the south, it is likely that immigrants will continue to be an important source of labor supply in the regions to which immigrants move.

WORK FORCE DIVERSITY

Historically, the main component of the work force has been the white male. Even with the increasing female work force participation rate, in 1991 almost 50 percent of those entering the work force were white males. The black labor force, however, is growing nearly twice as fast and the Hispanic work force four times as fast as the white male work force. Because female employment is also growing faster than male employment, we can forecast a dramatic change in work force entrants. Compared with 50 percent today, white males will account for only 12 to 15 percent of new entrants to the work force by the year 2000. These trends suggest that diversity in the work force will increase and

[15] *TRA Foodservice Digest/Amusement Business,* October 1, 1988, p. 14.

[16] *The Wall Street Journal,* March 9, 1990, p. C18.

[17] *Nations Restaurant News,* October 15, 1990, p. 3.

Traditional table service restaurants are labor intensive, and as long as services are maintained, it is difficult to make great improvements in productivity. There is an absolute limit, for instance, to how fast this waitress can move.

that an even larger component of workers will come from disadvantaged backgrounds with poorer educational preparation.[18]

Given the relative shortage of workers, we can expect wage rates to continue to rise. This suggests that rising wage rates may push food service prices up at a rapid rate during the 1990s. The food service industry has recognized the labor crisis for some time, however. In addition to raising wages, many operators have enhanced benefit programs and instituted support services such as day care and more generous family leave policies. It is no accident, either, that hospitality educators at their annual conferences increasingly see industry leaders anxious to speak to them and, through them, to recommend their companies to students. Indeed, except when recession strikes, recruiting activities at Hotel, Restaurant and Institutional Management (HRI) schools and programs are at an all-time high. On the job, every effort is made to recognize superior performance and to offer career ladders to employees to retain them once their schooling is finished.

It is certainly gratifying to be sought after — but before taking too much satisfaction in your popularity with recruiters, you will do well to realize that in a short time you will be on the other side of the game, dealing with the difficulties of labor shortage and leading people who will often have many

[18]Rice, "Leveraging Resources in a Mature Market."

other employment options. Accordingly, building a solid understanding of how to deal with people successfully needs to be at the top of your list if your goal is a management career in the restaurant business.

Having considered supply and demand as they affect food service, we can now turn our attention to the third basic force that shapes the industry, competition.

COMPETITION WITHIN HOSPITALITY

Competition in the hospitality industry has always been intense. There are many buyers and many sellers, a condition that makes it hard for any company to achieve control over the market. The nature of the competition, however, has changed from the heady days of the growth of new concepts in a rapidly expanding market — roughly from 1950 to 1975 — to a time today when established food service giants struggle with each other over a much more slowly growing market.

Since the 1950s, the industry has been growing rapidly. As more women went to work, more families could afford to eat out — and were pressed by time to do so. In spite of intense competition, firms had lots of opportunities in an expanding market.

Moreover, the competition between *new concepts* was largely to fill unmet demand. The challenge was to grow rapidly enough to snap up the available locations in existing and new territories — before a competitor got to them.

While there was competition between new concepts for locations, to a large extent newer operations were competing for the customer's attention and patronage principally against outmoded, independent operations. It was relatively easy for new, well-advertised, low-priced operations to take business from old, tired units that had a high, fixed cost structure and usually indifferent, expensive service.

In the 1980s, however, conditions began to change. Already in the 1970s it had become harder to find good locations as most had been taken. Moreover, the marketplace changed from one that was anxious to try a new concept to one already saturated with restaurants constructed in the past 10 or 15 years. Competition now was more and more between established operations with sophisticated marketing and a proven, accepted operating format. In hamburgers, for instance, competition had gone from being Joe's Diner versus McDonald's to McDonald's versus Burger King versus Wendy's versus Hardee's — all struggling aggressively for market share. Nevertheless, the industry continued to expand in numbers of units. Between 1985 and 1987, 40,000 restaurants opened. By the end of the 1980s, the leading chains were growing more rapidly in numbers of units than in real sales.[19] By the early

[19]Ron Paul, "The Squeeze Is On," *TRA Abstracts,* December 1989, p. 2.

1990s, moreover, popular, new, low-cost concepts such as double drive-through, take-out, and delivery operations complicated the competitive scene further.

At the same time that competition intensified, market growth slowed. The basic factors that fueled earlier growth were growing numbers of women working and rising household incomes. While the number of women working continues to increase, it does so, as we have already noted, at a slower rate. Household income growth has slowed dramatically as well.

Some kinds of food service have been more seriously affected by these changes than others. While casual restaurants benefit from the changing age of the population, QSRs appeal less to aging baby boomers, and many younger people seem to be drawn to those lower cost, "faster food" units just mentioned. Competition from parallel service providers, like convenience stores, and other industries, such as supermarkets, is multiplying, too.

Indeed, some companies left the field—or a substantial part of it. Marriott, for instance, sold off most of its restaurant and fast-food divisions, choosing instead to concentrate on lodging, institutional food service, and retirement communities. Basically, the reason for that decision appears to have been limited food service profits in a crowded industry and competitive pressures that were likely only to get worse. The established players had a dominance that even a company as large and accomplished as Marriott could not challenge.[20]

As noted in Chapter 2, competition between established concepts that characterized the 1980s led to continuing service and facility enhancements and to broader menus. These new units cost more to operate, adding rising cost pressures to the already difficult competitive picture.

The change in the competitive scene is summarized in Figure 4.10, using the evolving situation of the QSR as a case history. With this overview of the evolution of competition, we can turn to an examination of current competitive practices. We will look first at competition within the food service field and then consider interindustry competition.

COMPETITION WITHIN FOOD SERVICE

The task of marketing is accomplished by a program of interrelated actions and policies usually called the *marketing mix*. This mix is made up of four basic elements: product, price, place, and promotion.[21] Because marketing efforts are aimed at offsetting those of competitors, the marketing mix provides a good way to organize our examination of contemporary competitive practices.

---

[20] For an extended discussion of Marriott's decision to leave these markets, see Christopher Muller, "The Marriott Divestment: Leaving the Past Behind," *Cornell Hotel and Restaurant Administration Quarterly,* February 1990, pp. 7–13.

[21] Thomas F. Powers, *Marketing Hospitality* (New York: John Wiley & Sons, 1989).

Early Growth	The 1990s

Expanding market:
   More two-income households
   Rising incomes
	Static market:
	   Growth in number of working women slowing

Growing population segments prefer fast food	Aging baby boomers prefer casual table-service operation
Demand growing faster than supply	Number of units increasing faster than increase in sales

Expand to fill good locations fast
   Get there first and beat the competition
	Good freestanding locations saturated
	   Meet the competition head to head

Slim, cost-effective concepts	Enhanced concepts, costly to operate
The newest concept priced below the existing competition (i.e., mom and pop)	Prices close to nearest higher priced competitors and much higher than lower tier operations such as double drive-through and take-out operations

FIGURE 4.10 The changing competitive climate: The case of the QSR.

Product—and New Product

The most popular products today, as indicated by customer traffic in restaurants, are indicated in Figure 4.11. The greatest growth has been in Italian, Mexican, and oriental restaurants.

In the 1980s, *new products* were a key strategy in securing sales growth in established chains. At the start of the 1980s, for instance, Wendy's used the salad bar and later the baked potato to target women. Both products—salads and baked potatoes—had the effect of increasing Wendy's market share among women. Interestingly, Taco Bell later introduced its large-portion tacos and burritos to increase its market share among men.

The pace of new-product introductions accelerated as the industry moved into the 1990s. There were, for instance, 273 new product introductions mentioned in the trade press in 1990, more than double the 124 of the previous year. A study by one of the leading food service market research firms found that good menu variety was rated by 58 percent of customers as critical to their selection of a quick-service restaurant (QSR), and an overwhelming 84 percent rated it critical in their selection of a full-service restaurant. While not *all* products need to be new, it is clear that to achieve and maintain "good menu variety," new products are required from time to time—and on a regular basis. Between one fifth and one quarter of consumers rate new products in themselves as critical.[22]

---

[22] George D. Rice, "Leveraging Resources in a Mature Market."

Category	1982	1989	$ Chg.
Pizza	8.6%	13.2%	78
Mexican	2.8	4.2	74
Oriental	1.9	2.8	68
Italian	0.9	1.2	52
Other sandwich	4.5	5.8	45
Hamburger	24.1	24.8	19
Chicken	4.8	4.8	15
Family style	3.7	3.5	9
BBQ/other spec.	2.2	2.1	9
Varied/unclass.	21.3	18.7	2
Fish/seafood	3.0	2.6	2
Ice cream	4.6	4.0	1
Total steak	2.8	2.4	NC
Retail	5.2	4.4	−3
Donut	2.2	1.6	−18
Cafeteria chains	0.9	0.6	−18
Hotel	2.8	1.9	−19

FIGURE 4.11 Restaurant category customer traffic. [*Source:* George D. Rice, "Leveraging Resources in a Mature Market," *Proceedings of the 18th Annual Chain Operators Exchange* (Chicago: International Foodservice Manufacturers Association, 1991).]

The term *new product* can mean products that are a genuine innovation—that is, a product that hasn't been served before commercially. These are sometimes referred to as "new-to-world." Examples are the Egg McMuffin and Chicken McNuggets, products that set off major sales growth for McDonald's when they were introduced. Other new products, often introduced defensively, are referred to as "new-to-chain" and are essentially an imitation of a successful new product offered by another operator. KFC's chicken nugget product is an example of this category. KFC introduced it as a defensive measure when the McNugget had made McDonald's the biggest "chicken chain" in North America.

A third kind of change is the "line extension," a new product that is an extension of an existing product, such as a different-sized portion or some other minor alteration. This is a less risky new product because it requires little if any change in the operation and its acceptability to the consumer is already established. Typical line extensions are extralarge orders of french fries at a QSR or an extralarge coffee in a donut shop. Both are products that require only packaging changes. On the other hand, some line extensions result in the cannibalization of sales of the product they are adapted from (i.e., replace those sales without any real increase in total sales volume). This has been the case in some hamburger operations that introduced a new sandwich. They found they were competing with themselves and ended up dropping one of the

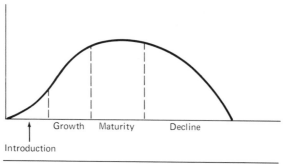

Growth   Maturity   Decline

Introduction

FIGURE 4.12 The product service life cycle.

sandwiches. Moreover, a line extension lacks the interest of the innovation and so creates less excitement. They are seen as the "same old thing." Looking at the three options, one authority put the overall picture this way:

> The "big hits" are riskier and more expensive to develop but we believe that for many operators they yield the greatest return. . . . It is our belief that menu enhancement is one of the most potent strategic weapons available to restaurant marketers.[23]

Many successful new products appear to follow a style cycle similar to one for products in fashion-dominated industries. Figure 4.12, which depicts industrywide sales, shows new product sales growing rapidly during the introduction and growth stages. At the peak of the cycle, total sales of the product are at their highest largely because everybody is selling it. Many new products can't maintain the consumer's interest when everybody else is offering the same or similar products. Consumers tire of them as the novelty wears off, as seems to have happened with salad bars in some QSRs. As one authority points out, however, that is hardly a reason to dismiss new products.

> The repeat purchase patterns show a rapid growth and then sharp decline in frequency from trial periods. Does this suggest that the new product introductions were not valid builders of business? To the contrary, it indicates that significant traffic growth was achieved by first (and later) companies which clearly helped to keep them competitive but that the growth is neither forever nor, in many cases, can it sustain itself against a combination of competitive market factors including similar introductions by others.[24]

---

[23]Nancy Kruse, "Winning the Battle for New Products and New Profits: Strategies and Tactics for New Product Development," *Proceedings of the 18th Annual Chain Operators Exchange* (Chicago: International Foodservice Manufacturers Association, 1991).

[24]Rice, "Leveraging Resources in a Mature Market."

We should note that a broader view of "product" in a service industry such as ours embraces the whole of the *consumer's experience.* This line of reasoning leads us to see the whole restaurant concept—product and service, location, ambiance, and price level—as a product. Concepts pass through style cycles much as do individual food products. The reaction to maturity in a *concept,* however, is to change the concept in an evolutionary way to renew the consumer's interest, as illustrated in Figure 4.13. Indeed, Figure 4.13 captures the gradual evolution and upgrading of concepts that major chains—and independents—have engaged in over the past generation.

McDonald's was initially a drive-in restaurant. Gradually, however, the building was increased to allow a small amount of seating, and then a larger number of seats was provided. Initially, bare, off-white walls greeted the guest who chose to eat inside the restaurant. These were gradually softened by limited decoration and then, gradually, by upgrading to a level of decor competitive with many more upscale operations. We have noted elsewhere that this added to the cost of the operation, but we need to see here that it also added to its appeal. It was a way of redeveloping a concept to renew its appeal.

As we look to the future, food service competition will continue to rely on the introduction of individual new products to liven consumers' interest in

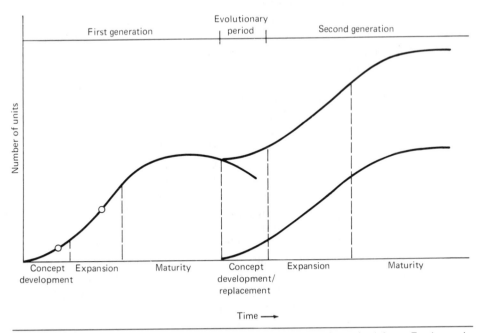

FIGURE 4.13 Restaurant concept life cycle. (*Source:* Adapted from Technomic Consultants.)

the operation. It seems likely that most of these will generate initial interest and sales, then will gradually fall from favor and be dropped. They will, however, have served a useful competitive purpose. New food products serve, too, as a means to upgrade and revitalize *concepts* that have begun to lose consumer interest. Other tactics as various as decor, promotion, and price will also be used to revitalize the total product offering we refer to as concept.

Price

The price competition of fast food was virtually unheard of in upscale operations until quite recently. As noted in Chapter 2, however, many fine-dining operations have adopted new menu and service formats featuring a more casual style of operation—and lower prices. Moreover, while couponing is not something you'd expect at *Chez Haute Cuisine,* frequent-diner cards *have* become increasingly common in upscale operations of late—and they are really a form of discount.

In fast food, couponing and price reduction were once a seasonal practice followed mainly in the off season from January through March or early April. As competition heated up, however, the proportion of discounting and other "deals" increased from under 15 percent in 1986 to nearly 21 percent five years later in 1990, the highest level ever achieved. "Dealing" refers not only to coupons that reduce the cost of menu items but also to the use of premium merchandise and games. Dealing was a factor in one out of five sales in 1990.

One indirect measure of price change is the change in food cost over a protracted period of time. In effect, a significant reduction in food cost *percentage* can only be achieved by raising prices. In that connection, it is interesting to note that McDonald's food cost fell from 40 percent in the company's early years to 33 percent in 1991.[25] In fact, McDonald's prices rose faster than the Consumer Price Index throughout the last half of the 1980s—and most of fast food followed right along.

In 1989, however, a "value-pricing strategy" was introduced by Taco Bell that resulted in rapid increases in the customer traffic and dollar sales. When the strategy's success became clear, McDonald's and many others followed suit.[26] Moreover, as we have noted earlier, new, low-priced, off-premise food service operations (drive throughs, for example) have been introduced which put price pressure on all popular-priced operations.

Value pricing is the new trend in fast food, and frequent-diner discounts are becoming the rule in upscale operations. Midlevel table-service operations are driven in the same direction by competition from above and below. It seems clear, then, that the days of easy price escalation are gone, perhaps for good, and price competition is here to stay.

---

[25] Michael G. Mueller, *Restaurant Industry Trends and Analysis* (San Francisco: Montgomery Securities, January 1991), p. 34. The figure for the earlier year is taken from a security analysis by Mueller dated June 28, 1990, p. 36.

[26] *The Wall Street Journal,* October 23, 1989, p. B1.

Pressure on prices, we should note, has implications for other elements of the marketing mix. A climate that made price rises easy was a favorable climate for competition through innovation. The cost of upgraded decors, more extensive preparation equipment, and more preparation labor—all could be passed on to the consumer in higher prices. In the future, however, the test for innovation may be stiffer. Changes will have to create savings or major increases in sales volume. If innovations don't pass these stricter tests, they may have to be dropped, since their cost cannot be passed on in ever-higher prices.

Place

Location[27] is a key competitive variable. As we noted earlier, during the expansive phase for fast food and its table-service competitors in the late 1960s and 1970s, a key element in competition was to expand fast enough to get good locations before another organization did. It is hardly surprising, then, that it has been increasingly difficult to find new, freestanding locations. In fact, units of a number of regional chains have been purchased by larger organizations to secure their restaurant sites for conversion to the buyer's concept. This strategy has been followed, for instance, by Hardee's, Denny's, and Perkins Family Restaurants in some regions.

The scarcity of freestanding locations has driven up the price of a separate location. Costly and scarce freestanding locations made companies rethink the way they were approaching location. Chains have come to seek locations that used to be regarded as unconventional, such as in hospitals and motels, as well as on military bases and along expressways. The pressure to secure locations, of course, has enhanced consumer convenience. It makes up-to-date food service available in many more places.

Companies also began to develop units jointly with a noncompetitive food service operator—a donut or ice cream shop with a hamburger operation, for instance—or with a nonfood service company such as a gasoline company. The results of this "co-location" strategy were not only lower construction and operating costs but increased sales volume for both units as customers for one of the two eventually became customers for the other.[28] Pepsico, which owns Taco Bell, Pizza Hut, and KFC, among other companies, has gone one step further. Apparently assuming that each company's concept targets somewhat different markets, Pepsico has opened several "All 'n One" outlets featuring

---

[27] The word *place* is being used here solely to mean location. In a more complex view, place includes not only location but the presentation of the place in terms of appearance, ambiance, and layout. For a discussion of a broader definition of the concept of place, see Leo M. Renaghan, "A New Marketing Mix for the Hospitality Industry," *Cornell Hotel and Restaurant Administration Quarterly,* August 1981; or Thomas F. Powers, *Marketing Hospitality* (New York: John Wiley & Sons, 1990), especially Chap. 6.

[28] *The Wall Street Journal,* December 27, 1989, p. B1.

Taco Bell, Pizza Hut, and KFC units under the same roof with a single kitchen and cross-trained staff.[29]

Secondary markets, that is, smaller towns, have also been discovered as attractive targets. Hardee's has moved into smaller midwestern towns, some with a population of less than a thousand people. This was their way of moving into that part of the country without taking on McDonald's in head-to-head competition. These smaller towns can draw on a local trading area of 8,000 to 10,000 people or more. Hardee's pursues a very active, sustained public relations campaign to win loyalty in these communities.[30] McDonald's, on the other hand, is testing an alternative concept, a diner called the Golden Arch Cafe, for smaller towns that don't generate enough traffic for a conventional McDonald's. The cafe features a wider menu and limited table service.[31]

Only a very few restaurants warrant driving a distance to visit—especially because that drive is bound to be past plenty of competitors. Competitively, the more places a chain is in, the more customers they can serve. The competitive drive for market share, then, is a drive to be "in place" wherever there are a significant number of consumers to serve. The result of this expansion of locations, as we have noted, is greater convenience for the guest and more sales for the food service industry.

Promotion

We will limit ourselves here to a brief discussion of advertising.[32] Figure 4.14 shows that the cost of restaurant advertising exceeded $1.5 billion in 1989. The restaurant business is one of the three largest industries in terms of advertising expenditure.[33] McDonald's reports total marketing expenditures of over $1 billion.[34] During the decade of the 1980s, advertising expenditures increased to almost four times the level at its start.

COMPETITION WITH OTHER INDUSTRIES

It is an axiom of economics that people's wants will expand indefinitely but that their resources are limited. Most people would like a new car, a vacation in Europe or the Caribbean, as well as the latest in VCR, stereo, and computer equipment. They would also like to dine in the finest restaurants. The problem is, since few can afford all of that, most must choose. Give up dining out in the

---

[29] *TRA Foodservice Digest/Miami Herald,* June 5, 1990.

[30] *American Demographics,* February 2, 1990, pp. 44–45.

[31] *The Wall Street Journal,* August 30, 1990, p. B6.

[32] As the term is used here, *promotion* is defined as advertising. A broader meaning for promotion can include sales promotion, which we have treated under price, as well as other forms of marketing communication such as public relations. See Powers, *Marketing Hospitality,* especially Chap. 8.

[33] *TRA Foodservice Digest/RBI Executive Report,* April 30, 1990, p. 1.

[34] *Annual Report 1990* (Oak Park, Ill.: McDonalds Corporation, 1990), p. 17.

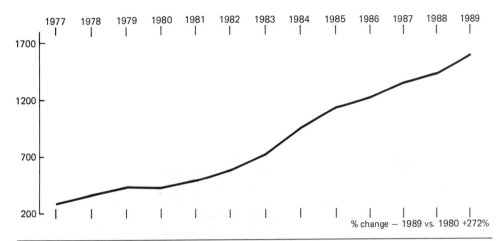

1977 1978 1979 1980 1981 1982 1983 1984 1985 1986 1987 1988 1989

1700

1200

700

200

% change — 1989 vs. 1980 +272%

FIGURE 4.14 Dollar spending to advertise restaurants (million). [*Source:* George D. Rice, "Leveraging Resources in a Mature Market," *Proceedings of the 18th Annual Chain Operators Exchange* (Chicago: International Foodservice Manufacturers Association, 1991).]

best the local restaurant scene has to offer for the next year or so and you may have the price of that vacation. Forgo lunch at your favorite restaurant and brown-bag it for six weeks and you can probably save the price of a new VCR. Thus, food service is, in a very real way, in competition with all other industries, and especially those providing leisure services and conveniences.

Some industries, however, challenge food service on its own turf, offering directly competitive products. These are the retailers on which we will concentrate our attention here. Convenience stores offer their own variety of fast food and from locations that are so numerous that they seem to be "just around the corner" from wherever you may be. Supermarkets are not as numerous as convenience stores, but they *are* conveniently located and virtually everyone visits them in the course of a week. Both are formidable competitors for food service.

Convenience Stores

While their most frequent customers are males under age 35, C stores, as they are often called, are visited at least twice a month by about three quarters of the adult population.[35] During the 1980s, their growth rates were high but, as the C store industry matured, that growth slowed to 2.7 percent in 1989. The number of units increased by 2.5 percent, less than half the rate of the previous year.[36] A significant part of C store sales are directly competitive with food-service sales, especially beverages and sandwiches. Because nearly all C stores have microwave equipment and offer prepared foods, these retail units can

[35] *TRA Foodservice Digest/Convenience Store News,* August 28, 1988, p. 29.

[36] *Restaurants USA,* January 1990, pp. 33–34.

Fast food has a tough competitor in convenience stores which offer meals as well as snacks. (Courtesy of Southland Corp.)

compete for more than the snack market. About one third offer a service deli. Another 14 percent offer pizza. French fries, salads, fried chicken, burritos, donuts, and a variety of desserts all account for significant portions of sales.[37] C stores are finding competition with food service tougher than they first expected, however. High equipment and labor costs have held back their food service profits. As a result, many C store operators are reducing their menus[38] or dropping in-store cooking.[39]

[37] *Nations Restaurant News,* October 8, 1990, pp. 25–26.

[38] *Restaurants and Institutions,* March 20, 1989, p. 86.

[39] *Restaurants and Institutions Alert,* July 24, 1989, p. 1.

The C store business experienced a dramatic change as the 1990s opened. The two largest C store chains, Southland's 7-Eleven (about 7,000 units) and Circle K (roughly 4,500 units), were driven into bankruptcy as a result of taking on heavy indebtedness.[40] At about the same time it became clear that the major petroleum companies would be the leaders of the C store industry of the 1990s. The third, fourth, and fifth largest chains are all operated by oil companies—Chevron, Mobil, and Marathon, respectively.[41] In addition, other oil companies—Texaco, Atlantic Richfield, Coastal Corp, and Shamrock—own more than 600 stores each.[42]

Oil companies have four distinct advantages over other C store operators. First, because of their large gasoline sales, they can afford prime corner locations. Second, they offer the backing of cash rich corporations. Third, they are able to sell gas at lower prices.[43] And fourth, consumers can use their gasoline credit card to make their purchase, which is a major convenience.

Oil companies have solid motives to expand operations. They want to make their petroleum products as widely available as possible. We can expect, therefore, continuing expansion and growing competition from these new industry leaders.

In fact, newer formats for C stores that feature wider aisles, upscale ambiance, more healthy foods, tighter target marketing to customers, and more careful tracking of product popularity promise to make C stores more effective competitors in the future.[44] Significantly, Amoco Oil is one of those announcing a new prototype, which it says will ultimately affect some aspects of all of its 1,300 stores.[45]

Supermarkets

Restaurateurs and retailers selling food for consumption at home have always been in competition. For some years, restaurants' share of that market has been increasing. During the 1990s, however, that struggle will intensify as a result of sharpened competitive practices in the grocery business and changing patterns in leisure-time usage. We will discuss the grocery business in this section and look briefly at the changing patterns in leisure in the next section, titled "The Home as Competition." Clearly the two developments are interrelated.

Supermarkets are heavily committed to offering take-out food, which makes them direct competitors for one of the fastest growing food service segments. To back this commitment, they are remodeling in-store delis, build-

[40] *The Wall Street Journal,* April 16, 1990, p. A3, and October 25, 1990, p. A14.

[41] *TRA Foodservice Digest/Convenience Store News,* August 5, 1990, p. 58.

[42] *TRA Foodservice Digest/Advertising Age,* April 23, 1990, p. 80.

[43] *TRA Foodservice Digest/Chicago Tribune,* June 11, 1989, p. 21.

[44] *The Wall Street Journal,* February 16, 1991, p. 1.

[45] *TRA Foodservice Digest/Convenience Store News,* January 6, 1991, p. 41.

Grocery store deli departments are working hard to get a share of the food service market. (Courtesy of Piggly Wiggly)

ing bakeries, and setting up salad bars and displays of prepared foods such as barbecued chicken and ribs. More than half of all supermarkets sell pizza made on premise, and 58 percent of those are made from scratch.[46] The overwhelming majority offer somewhere between 50 to 100 items of food prepared on premise or in their own central commissary.[47] Eight out of 10 American households buy take-out food from a supermarket at least once a month.[48]

Over two thirds of American households have a microwave oven.[49] This makes the grocery freezer case an ever more potent competitor, especially with the rise in microwave-ready packages. Frozen food manufacturers, moreover, are increasingly tightening the target market in designing products. Single-serving products, for instance, and products for children address the needs of the busy two-parent family. Recent developments in chilling rather than freezing are bringing chilled foods into stores in increasing numbers. While this chilled product is not yet as well established as the frozen,[50] refrigerated foods

[46] *TRA Foodservice Digest/Progressive Grocer,* January 1991, p. 125.

[47] *Restaurants and Institutions,* October 16, 1989, p. 80.

[48] *American Demographics,* January 1988, p. 22.

[49] *TRA Foodservice Digest/Frozen Food Executive,* November 1988, p. 11.

[50] *TRA Foodservice Digest/Supermarket Business,* January 1990, p. 30.

with a three- to five-day shelf life have advantages in better flavor, wider variety, and greater ability to fit local target markets than do frozen foods mass-produced for a national market.

Chilled foods also fit into the growing extension of catering services offered by supermarkets, ranging from dinner for 2 to dinner for 100.[51] Moreover, a number of grocery store chains are testing delivery, catalog shopping, and ordering by phone and fax.[52]

These new services are especially significant from two points of view. People really do not like grocery shopping. It ranked next to last in a list of family duties put to a panel of consumers—behind house cleaning![53] Simplifying shopping for the consumer will reduce a major obstacle to using a supermarket at the end of the day instead of a restaurant. Moreover, as restaurants rely more and more on off-premise consumption, they are vulnerable to convenience advantages of the supermarket and to the lower prices that many supermarkets charge.

As a famous New York restaurateur, Joe Baum, points out, supermarkets don't have the philosophy of service that restaurants have.[54] On the other hand, supermarkets offer something on the order of 2,000 items that can be considered single-service, quick-to-fix, or ready-to-serve items.[55]

Other Retail Operations

Specialized retail operations that compete with both restaurants and supermarkets are emerging. In the pizza market, for instance, a company called Take-and-Bake can sell for less than restaurants because they have neither seating nor ovens. The pizza, while fresh rather than frozen, is prepared for home baking.[56] Retail outlets devoted solely to refrigerated prepared foods are in test,[57] and an East Coast dairy offers delivery to customers who order from a menu that includes muffins, Danish, bagels, croissants, brioche, sliced bread, juice, and coffee in addition to dairy items.[58] Clearly, the number of businesses seeking to serve the customers' preference for staying home are expanding.

One other "competitor" ought to be considered here for the sake of completeness and that is not eating! Consumers skip an average of two meals per week. No breakfast accounts for 65 percent of skipped meals, followed by

[51] *TRA Foodservice Digest/Supermarket Business,* August 1989, p. 1A.

[52] *TRA Foodservice Digest/Miami Herald,* November 8, 1990, p. 17.

[53] *American Demographics,* April 1988, p. 2.

[54] Joe Baum, Remarks made during the Chain Operators Exchange, February 26, 1990.

[55] Rice, "Leveraging Resources in a Mature Market."

[56] *Nations Restaurant News,* November 28, 1988, p. 1.

[57] *Restaurants and Institutions Alert,* May 16, 1990.

[58] *TRA Foodservice Digest/Milling and Baking News,* May 5, 1990, p. 1.

no lunch, for 30 percent.[59] Nutritionists tell us that skipping breakfast is actually not good for us. It can result in weight gain because of insulin fluctuation and because of a tendency for the breakfast skipper to have a high-calorie snack later—or to overeat at lunch. Skipping breakfast also impairs performance, both physical and mental. Having just coffee and no breakfast has an even worse effect. The practice of skipped meals, then, might be thought of as a *marketing opportunity.* For example, individual restaurants or an industry group could use a public service format to urge people to have a nutritious meal to improve their chances of losing weight and to feel better and work more effectively.

The Home as Competition

As the baby boomers move into their middle years and greater family responsibilities, the attractions of staying at home increase. Indeed, the home is emerging as an entertainment center. The majority of people under 60, as Table 4.3 indicates, own a videocassette recorder (VCR) and make significant use of it. Moreover, people between 18 and 54 years of age watch between 14 and 15 hours of television programming a week while those aged 55 to 64 watch 18½ hours per week.

"The pleasure of leisure," as Ron Paul, president of Technomic Consultants, put it, "is control, and consumers have lost a lot of control in recent years."[60] The home is an environment that maximizes the consumer's control. It is *their* territory. The pattern of activity that emerges suits itself well to staying home with somebody's take-out meal. It is not surprising that plenty of competitors exist for that business.

The meal prepared at home and eaten elsewhere, the "brown-bag" competition, accounts for 56 percent of households. Sixty-eight percent of main meals (exclusive of snacks) are prepared in the home.[61] We might think there are cost advantages to home preparation that food service cannot meet. However, a study conducted by Purdue University's Department of Restaurant, Hotel and Institutional Management concluded that it is actually less expensive to eat fast food than it is to eat at home if meal preparation and cleanup time are given a realistic value.[62] The average consumer, of course, probably won't make the kind of cost study necessary to support this conclusion. The study does suggest marketing opportunities, however.

The future probably offers only more encouragement for "cocooning," as some call the practice of staying at home. *American Demographics,* for instance, predicts that "telephone technology will replace television as the

---

[59] John J. Rohs, *The Restaurant Industry* (New York: Wertheim & Co., 1985), p. 9.

[60] *Wall Street Journal,* November 22, 1989, p. B1.

[61] Rice, "Leveraging Resources in a Mature Market."

[62] *Nations Restaurant News,* August 19, 1985, p. 21.

TABLE 4.3 VCR Ownership and Usage

Age	Percent Own	Median Films Rented Per Month	Median TV Programs Taped Per Month
18–29	73%	3.8	1.7
30–44	77	3.0	1.6
45–59	70	1.4	1.4
60+	30	.9	1.0

Source: American Demographics, June 1990, p. 14.

dominant medium worldwide," though that development will occur gradually over the next few decades. As telephone technology expands further into consumers' lives, cocooning gets easier and easier.

> For consumers, the telephone will entertain (AT&T and Nintendo of America, Inc., are already talking), deliver mail (fax), connect households to local libraries and national data bases (on-line information services), and serve as a user-friendly interactive computer (with a link to city hall, to grocery stores, to supercomputers). If the phone companies string fiber optic cable to households, as is predicted when costs drop, the telephone will become a television set as well.[63]

SUMMARY

We have examined three basic forces shaping food service: demand, supply, and competition. To understand the underpinnings of demand, we first considered how the changing age of our population shapes patterns of demand. The baby boom, the birth dearth, and the echo boom each reflect age groups born in different periods. The huge baby boomer group has had a profound impact on every facet of our society, including food service. In the 1990s, the baby boomers move into middle age while the population of younger people declines in size. This shift changes the pattern of demand for food service. There is, for instance, less demand for fast food and increased demand for more casual, upscale dining. Another population and age phenomenon of importance is the growing senior citizen population. People in this age group are not as good customers for food service but represent a major marketing challenge for the industry.

[63] Cheryl Russell, "The Fifth Medium," *American Demographics,* October 1989, p. 2.

The growing participation of women in the work force has been a major force for growth in food service, but most of that change is now behind us. Smaller families and changing family structure are also giving rise to higher and lower income groups whose status as customers for food service is quite different.

The supply factors needed to make food service operations run include food and labor. Food prices are not expected to see any fundamental change in their level relative to other commodities in the foreseeable future. Scarcity of labor in the 1990s, however, is rated "the greatest single problem facing food service." The population groups that have staffed much of the expansion of food service for the last generation have been young people and women. Young people, as a population group, are in decline, and most of the change in the rate of women's participation in the work force is behind us. At low-skill levels, however, immigration may offset some of this problem. In any case, the way ahead will clearly see greater work force diversity and increased need for managers with people skills.

Competition within food service will use all elements of the marketing mix to attract customers. New *products* are important attractions to consumers and, as one product becomes stale, it is replaced by another. New products are also used to revitalize aging restaurant concepts. *Price* competition, it appears, is here to stay, and pressure on price makes innovation more difficult. *Locations (place)* are being expanded, making food service even more convenient to consumers. Finally, *promotion* has been increased fourfold in a 10-year period.

Competition with other industries is also heating up. Convenience stores and grocery stores both compete with restaurants by offering on-premise food service as well as ready-to-serve, take-out meals. Ultimately, the home may be food service's greatest and toughest competitor. Restaurants will have to offer consumers advantages, such as a philosophy of service that makes guests feel special when they dine out.

KEY WORDS AND CONCEPTS

To help you review this chapter, keep in mind the following.

Demand for food service
Changing age composition of
    the population

Female work force
    participation rate
Changing family structure

Worker shortage
Work force diversity
Changing nature of
competition
   Expanding market
   Static market
Elements of competition
   Product
   Product life cycle
   Concept life cycle
   Price

Value pricing
Place
Freestanding location
Promotion
Convenience stores
   Petroleum companies
Grocery stores
   In-store delicatessen
The home as competitor

REVIEW QUESTIONS

1. Which population groups seem to you to be the most attractive targets for food service? What are their attractive features?

2. Why is food service facing a labor shortage? What solutions would you recommend?

3. What is giving rise to work force diversity? What consequences is it likely to have for the industry? For you as a manager?

4. How has the competitive climate changed?

5. Discuss the significance of each element of the marketing mix in food service competition in your city. What recent developments strike you as significant in the local competitive scene?

6. What competitive practices have grocery chains in your area engaged in that will affect food service? How do you rate local C store competition against fast food?

7. What factors support the home as an effective competitor?

C H A P T E R 5

Courtesy of Caesars Palace

ISSUES FACING FOOD SERVICE

THE PURPOSE OF THIS CHAPTER

This chapter continues our discussion of the factors shaping the food service business. In the last chapter, we looked at the basic forces of demand, supply, and competition. In this chapter, we will consider food service's reaction to a number of pressing issues. Once again, we will begin with the consumer and consumer concerns, such as nutrition, and with the closely related consumerist movement. We will then turn to the impact on hospitality of rising consumer concern—as well as growing government action—related to the environment. Akin to the environment in many ways is the topic of energy scarcity and energy management. Finally, we will look at the challenges posed by technology and the technological responses to cost and quality problems with which food service now has to contend.

THIS CHAPTER SHOULD HELP YOU

1. Recognize consumer concerns for health and nutrition as part of the challenge of planning food service operations.

2. Understand the basis of the consumer movement and identify the major issues it raises with regard to food service.

3. Become familiar with a rising operational and environmental concern in the food service, that of solid waste management, which you are bound to encounter for the rest of your career in the hospitality industry.

4. Identify the major impacts of technology on food service from guest ordering and payment to food production and information management.

5. Develop a balanced view of the impact of the energy crisis on food service operations.

CONSUMER CONCERNS

The baby boom generation is generally affluent, well educated, and discriminating, and wants an active, pleasurable, and very long life. Not surprisingly, therefore, they are concerned about their health, nutrition, and fitness. They want to both stay alive and feel more alive and vigorous. These concerns very much involve food service.

HEALTH

Although nutrition and diet are much on the consumer's mind, they are a part of a larger concern regarding overall health and fitness. Drive down a residential street in the early morning or late afternoon and count the joggers, if you doubt it. This interest in health, in turn, has affected restaurants beyond their menus. For example, consumers' concerns about "secondhand" cigarette smoke have led to no-smoking sections in restaurants, very commonly by mandate of the local municipal government. Most North American airline flights have become no-smoking flights, and there is wide speculation that the banning of smoking in all public places, including restaurants, is not far off. The biggest impact of health concern for restaurants, however, is on menus.

NUTRITION

Statistics cited by *The Wall Street Journal* suggest that most people are at least conscious of the need to watch their diet, and so the proportion of *nondieters* who use diet products is surprisingly high: over three quarters of those who drink light beer are nondieters, as are nearly two thirds of those who buy light margarine, diet soft drinks, and sugar substitutes.[1] Clearly, "weight consciousness" is more prevalent than dieting. Restrictive dieters, in fact, account for only about one fifth of consumers. Research shows a fairly stable set of consumer preferences with regard to food. The market segments resulting from these consumer attitudes are shown in Table 5.1.

Foods that are low in calories, cholesterol, or fat have increased their sales each year since 1981. In 1981, for instance, 39 percent of consumers ate at

---

[1] *The Wall Street Journal,* December 11, 1985, p. 3.

TABLE 5.1 Major Food Service Segments by Nutritional Attitude

Segment	Description	Percentage of Consumers	Income Level	Typical Occupation of Husband	Education	Occupation of Spouse	Number of Households
Nutritionally fit	Most concerned with nutrition and health; less concerned with taste, convenience, or calories	30%	$25,000 and over	White collar	Well educated	Working wife	21 million
Conventional	Rates taste more important in selecting food than nutrition, convenience, or calories.	26%	$15,000 and under	Blue collar	Less educated	Homemaker wife	17 million
Busy urbanite; Convenience cook	Hates to cook; rates convenience as the most important item in selecting food items	24%	$25,000 and over	White collar	Well educated	Working wife	14 million
Restrictive dieter	Conventional tastes, older	20%	$25,000 and under	Blue collar; retired	Less educated	Homemaker wife	13 million

Source: George D. Rice, *Proceedings of the 11th Annual Chain Operator's Exchange* (Chicago: International Foodservice Manufacturers Association 1984); Harry Balzer, *Proceedings of the 12th Annual Chain Operator's Exchange* (Chicago: International Foodservice Manufacturers Association 1985).

least one "light product" every two weeks, but by 1989 that proportion more than doubled, to 64 percent. Red meat consumption has been declining steadily while poultry and fish sales have increased steadily. In 1990, 60 percent of consumers indicated that they try to avoid fried foods. As recently as 1985 only about one fifth of consumers agreed that they discouraged the eating of fried chicken but, in 1990, that proportion had doubled (to 39 percent), and 43 percent said the same thing of french fries. In spite of all this concern, roughly 6 in every 10 adults over age 25 are somewhat overweight, and half of those are more than 10 percent above their recommended weight. Not surprisingly, therefore, an average of 28 percent of Americans are on a diet (32 percent of women and 24 percent of men), a statistic that has remained constant since the mid-1980s.[2]

In addition to a concern with fat, consumers have become interested in the fiber content of various foods, as fiber has been shown to reduce cholesterol levels and the incidence of heart disease. It is also widely thought to lower the risk of cancer of the bowel and colon. Fiber includes all those components of foods that are not broken down in the digestive tract and absorbed into the bloodstream. The desirable levels of fiber intake — 25 to 50 grams per day — is as much as 2.5 times higher than most people's current level of consumption. Common servings of fruits, vegetables, and whole grain breads and cereals contain about 2 to 4 grams of dietary fiber per serving.

Dietary Schizophrenia

Despite their avowed concerns, however, consumers are not necessarily consistent in their responses to health, fitness, and nutrition consciousness. For instance, Steve's Ice Cream, specializing in ultrarich, high-butterfat ice cream, was asked to put an outlet in a major fitness center! When they expressed surprise, they were told that "people want to reward themselves for all that work."[3] And when companies developed low-salt soups to respond to people's widely expressed concerns about sodium in their diet, they were surprised when the products didn't sell well. Apparently people aren't as prepared to give up the taste of salt as they are to talk about it.[4]

We noted a moment ago that about 40 percent of consumers claimed to discourage the eating of fried chicken and french fries. It is interesting, though, that while fried chicken sales actually fell 9 percent from 1985 to 1990, the sales of french fries rose 8 percent in the same period. Consumers are not necessarily consistent in following their convictions regarding nutrition. In fact, less than half of homemakers indicate they are careful to plan nutritious

[2] George D. Rice, "Leveraging Resources in a Mature Market," *Proceedings of the 18th Annual Chain Operators Exchange* (Chicago: International Foodservice Manufacturers Association, 1991).

[3] *Restaurants and Institutions,* May 29, 1985, p. 76.

[4] *Restaurant Business,* May 20, 1985, p. 135.

meals. And, consumers' preference for "all you can eat" specials rose 23 percent (from 30 percent to 37 percent interested) while expressed interest in "dieters specials" fell over 10 percent (from 18 percent to 16 percent of respondents) during the 1980s.[5] "Taste," as one expert put it, "is by far a more critical determinant of food selection than nutrition. However, to offer both is a home run."[6]

Industry Response

Restaurant marketers and managers have seen consumers' growing interest in nutrition as an opportunity rather than a problem. Menus *have* been changing in response to consumers' positive nutritional concerns. Baked and broiled chicken have become readily available—and KFC changed its brand name from Kentucky Fried Chicken to KFC, apparently to get the word *fried* out of its name. Chains featuring baked and broiled chicken have prospered, and even KFC has experimented with a skinless chicken entrée, Skinfree Crispy, with 20 percent less fat and calories, 39 percent less sodium, and 32 percent less cholesterol.[7] After an unusually short test market, McDonald's rolled out a low-fat hamburger, the McLean, which reduces fat content from 20 percent to 9 percent. To maintain flavor, fat is replaced with an additive derived from seaweed called carrageenin. Other hamburger chains are also introducing similar lean products. When Disneyland used a similar product in an unannounced test, it was eaten by 2,000 guests a day without any comment being registered.[8] Long John Silver's, long known for its fried fish, introduced baked fish which now accounts for 10 percent of its sales.[9] Dunkin' Donuts has developed a donut that is cholesterol free.[10] Hotel restaurants such as Hilton feature healthy items on all menus; and at the luxury hotel chain Four Seasons, one third of the items on the menu are "alternative cuisine" that features light, nutritious foods.[11] On the other hand, dessert chains continue to grow, and desserts sell well in all segments of the market. Donut chains prosper, too, serving lots of donuts and other goodies that *aren't* fat free. Thus, it seems that consumers are concerned about nutrition and health but want to reward themselves from time to time or have the best of both worlds: a salad with lots of rich dressing; a feeling of virtue *and* a full stomach. The industry, quite naturally, is responding to both sides of the consumer's personality.

[5] *American Demographics,* April 1988, p. 10.

[6] The facts in this paragraph, unless otherwise noted, as well as the passage quoted, are from Rice, "Leveraging Resources in a Mature Market."

[7] *Nations Restaurant News,* February 4, 1991, pp. 3–4.

[8] *The New York Times,* April 21, 1991, pp. 1, 17.

[9] *Nations Restaurant News,* November 19, 1990, p. 3.

[10] *TRA Foodservice Digest, Adweek,* February 11, 1991.

[11] *Restaurant Business,* September 1, 1989, p. 96.

CONSUMERISM

Many of the concerns of individual consumers, such as health, fitness, and nutrition, are shared by lots of consumers. On the other hand, some of these concerns have been selected by organized interest groups as important to consumer education, to raise the consumer's consciousness: this is *consumerism*. One authority pointed out that although some industry leaders regard the consumer movement as a fad, many others "believe that it is here to stay and that, if unheeded, it may lead to consequences which the hospitality industry will not be happy to accept." American consumerism has been around since the mid-nineteenth century, and can be defined as follows:

> Consumerism is, first of all, a social movement. It is a movement by which society, through representative groups and individuals, seeks social change. Consumerism has as its specific objective to achieve a balance of power between buyers and sellers. It is an effort to equalize the rights of buyers with the rights of sellers.[12]

In view of its increasing size and visibility, the hospitality industry has begun to attract the attention of consumer groups. A sampling of hospitality issues typically raised by consumers may lead to a better understanding of how consumerism can affect the food service field. Our discussion will include complaints about junk food, labeling, truth in dining, problems related to sanitation, and alcohol abuse.

JUNK FOOD AND A HECTIC PACE

One of the principal indictments by consumerists against food service (and especially against fast food and vending) is that it purveys nutritionless "junk food." Although fast food does pose some nutritional problems, the junk-food charge is just not true. Regarding mechanical vendors, the charge may say more about American food habits than about the nutritional adequacy of the food itself.

A typical meal at McDonald's—a hamburger, french fries, and a milk-shake—provides nearly one third of the recommended dietary allowance (RDA), or the equivalent of what a standard school lunch provides, with, however, a deficiency in vitamins A and C. The deficiency in these two vitamins can be remedied somewhat if the customer switches from a hamburger to a Big Mac, which contains the necessary lettuce and tomato slices. If the customer chooses to have a salad, of course, the dietary deficiency is no longer a problem.

Some critics just don't seem to like fast food at all. They charge that "fast foods, with their abundance of useless calories and sugar" (the junk-food

---

[12] Robert L. Blomstrom, "The Hospitality Industry and the Consumer Movement," *The Institute Journal,* April 1973, p. 9.

charge) are really a part of the problem of Americans' poor diet. Their prescription:

> Meals should be taken in a leisurely way, with personal interaction. . . .
> [People who opt for fast foods are being] dehumanized—they are becoming more like automobiles driving up to a gas station and being refilled. . . . The ubiquitous multimillion dollar advertising campaigns, particularly the millions spent on television advertising, has greatly influenced the public in the direction of fast foods.[13]

Two problems here go beyond the junk-food issue. These critics believe they know what is good for people (which, in a medical sense, they may), and they resent the fact that people choose to disregard their expert advice. The main criticism, however, is really of Americans' poor eating habits, notably "the quick pace inherent in our society."

Whatever else is true, the duty of the American restaurant business in a market economy is to serve consumers, not to reform them. But it is difficult for the hospitality industry to deal with this kind of criticism, in which the industry becomes a scapegoat for the annoyance that some feel at a simple economic reality: The food service within the reach of most pocketbooks uses food service systems that are not (and cannot be) labor intensive.

The second problem raised is that of the effect of advertising on consumer behavior. This issue reflects an old and complex debate in the general field of marketing. From our earlier explanation of the procedure for introducing a new product, perhaps you remember that restaurants are interested in offering only what the guests want, not in forcing something on them. For example, notice that the decor and atmosphere in specialty restaurants have been growing warmer and friendlier to meet earlier criticisms of coldness and austerity. And salad bars and packaged salads were added because that is what consumers wanted. That is, the weight of consumer opinion is usually felt in the marketplace. Change in business institutions comes, of course, more slowly than consumerists would like; but particularly in competitive industries such as food service, change comes only when it is clear that the consumer wants it. To some degree, the consumerists' demands for quick change reflect an antibusiness bias which some consumerists seem to have. Their background is often in government or academic life, and maybe they don't understand how businesses really operate. Many seem to prefer a command economy (with *their* preferences ruling) to a market economy where, in the long run, consumers' preferences rule.

The junk-food criticism will not just go away, however. Field studies suggest that many guests do not follow the Big Mac-fries-milkshake meal profile referred to earlier. For instance, to save money or suit their tastes, many customers replace the milkshake with a soft drink, and the result is a

---

[13] *Nations Restaurant News,* November 10, 1974, p. 4.

meal with less than one third the recommended dietary allowance. And salads, while they appeal to a minority of customers, are clearly not the number one seller in fast food. Moreover, a number of chains are under fire from consumerists for continuing to use beef fat (which is rich in saturated fat) for some products, especially french fries. We should note, however, that in response to consumers' concerns, most chains have shifted to vegetable shortening for most frying.

NUTRITIONAL LABELING

For many years the restaurant business has faced the possibility of legally mandated nutritional labeling. In the southwestern United States, a number of QSR chains voluntarily agreed to nutritional labeling to avoid having different requirements in each of several states.[14] McDonald's uses wall placards to list the nutritional content of every menu item sold, and this information is also printed on their tray liners. Burger King, Wendy's, Hardee's, and KFC provide this information to guests in a booklet available in the unit on request.[15]

In 1990, the influential National Academy of Sciences recommended that full-service restaurants be required to provide guests with a computer analysis of each *standard* menu item. (Specials would be exempt.) Fast-food restaurants would be *required* to provide nutritional information either on food containers or wrappers or to post it at the point of purchase.[16] While the details of how the information is to be provided and how much detail will be mandated are not yet clear, it seems likely that fuller nutritional information will be required from most food service units.

TRUTH IN MENU

The increasing use of convenience foods, frozen prepared foods, and foods prepared in remote commissaries has created an issue closely related to the nutritional labeling issue. The food service industry, in fact, has long advocated honest dealings with consumers, but individual operators have frequently strayed from full candor.[17] Included in one's "right to know," consumer groups insist, is a right to know where and how restaurant food was prepared. Laws requiring menus to state who prepared the food and when, where, and how have already been proposed.

The use of frozen food is certainly widespread. *Restaurants and Institutions* indicated that 90 percent of all operations use frozen food. Many operators feel it is their special method of preparation rather than the food's

---

[14] *Nations Restaurant News,* September 1, 1986, p. 1.

[15] *Nations Restaurant News,* October 8, 1990, p. 57.

[16] *Nations Restaurant News,* October 8, 1990, p. 57.

[17] John J. Bilan, "Taking Another Look at Accuracy in Menus," *Cornell Hotel and Restaurant Administration Quarterly,* November 1979, p. 8.

state before cooking that imparts quality. Most operators would like to think that "fresh" means prepared to order, whether or not the raw products are frozen, and that "natural" means unadulterated and not necessarily anything more. The fact is that frozen products, because of "field-side" or "on-board" freezing, are often of higher quality—that is, possessing more of the characteristics of the fresh—than a "fresh" product that has worked its way through the channels of distribution, deteriorating gradually in unfrozen storage. For example, several fast-food companies that purchase Icelandic cod deal with packers who have on-board processing capabilities so that the fish are frozen almost as soon as they come out of the ocean. Similarly, large frozen vegetable processors have equipment that follows the harvesters, processing the vegetables and freezing them at field side immediately after they are picked. The term *fresh frozen,* then, is not really a contradiction in terms.

It is, of course, possible to cook top-quality food in one place, freeze or chill it, transport it, reconstitute it, and serve a tasty, attractive product in another place. The problem is not the technology but a culture that changes more slowly than does its own technical capacities. Someday, commissaries and other centralized production systems may make genuine haute cuisine available to the mass market at prices that that market can afford. Before this happens, food service marketing techniques will be needed to complement (that is, to fulfill) the technology that already exists. Finally, when such a feat becomes possible, a consumer willing to accept gourmet food reconstituted from the chilled or frozen state will have to be waiting for it—and that is a marketing problem.

In the meantime, if the industry resists truth in menu because of the disruptions it clearly will cause, it might study the experience of grocery chains and retailers, who have learned not only to accept reasonable consumer demands but also to incorporate them in their marketing programs and to turn compliance to their advantage as well, as indeed McDonald's has done.

Some segments of the restaurant business have already become *service-intensive* retail establishments that give the final processing to products prepared elsewhere. The first person to show guests an advantage in choosing to accept remotely prepared food will have made an important marketing breakthrough. In the meantime, there are some signs that consumers are gradually beginning to accept remotely prepared foods.

Peter Drucker called consumerism "the shame of marketing." Consumerism, he feels, reflects business's almost exclusive emphasis on selling (which begins with "our product" and how to sell it) instead of on "marketing," which begins with the consumers' needs and expectations and moves toward supplying products that meet those needs.

> Consumerism is also the opportunity of marketing. It will force businesses to become market focused in their actions as well as their pronouncements. Developing a positive response to consumerist sentiment is probably more

effective than resentment and resistance. There is truth in the old adage, "If you can't fight 'em, join 'em."[18]

SANITATION

As with so many consumer issues, sanitation involves government regulations—in this case, as embodied in public health officers and inspectors. With the increasing use of off-premise, prepared foods, the incidence of food poisoning in public accommodations has been rising steeply. The kinds of sanitary precautions associated with traditional food service operations are inadequate for food service systems that prepare food, freeze or chill it, and then transport it elsewhere. First, the risks of thawing and spoilage are high. Second, the food is handled by more people. Some operators resist the increased emphasis on sanitation, but most have accepted—many enthusiastically—the need to upgrade sanitation practices and to establish and enforce high sanitation standards. The Educational Foundation of the National Restaurant Association has pioneered in the development of sanitation educational materials and programs. It is quite clear that for the most part, the industry and those calling for the highest standards of sanitation are, in principle, in the same camp.

ALCOHOL AND DINING

The many fatal accidents that have been attributed to driving under the influence of alcohol have handed to the hospitality industry a wide-ranging set of problems. On the one hand, in many jurisdictions, restaurants and bars that sell drinks to people who are later involved in accidents are now being held legally responsible for damages. The result has been, among other things, a great rise in liability insurance rates. Laws have been proposed—and in many jurisdictions passed—making illegal the "happy hours" and other advertised price reductions on the sale of drinks. In addition, in a less strictly legal sense, operators have been concerned about the image of their operations and the industry in general.

The industry's response has generally been swift and positive. One idea is "designated driver" programs. Designated drivers agree not to drink and to drive for the whole group they are with. Many operators recognize designated drivers with a button and reward them with free soft drinks—and a certificate good for a free drink at their next visit. Alcohol-awareness training—teaching bartenders and servers how to tell when people have had too much to drink and how to deal with them—is also becoming more common. If you work in an operation that serves alcohol, be sure to find out what the establishment's

[18] Peter F. Drucker, *Management Tasks, Responsibilities, Practices* (New York: Harper & Row, 1974), p. 64.

policy is regarding service to intoxicated guests—or those who *might* be intoxicated. You should do this not only because you will want to follow the house policy but because it will help you to understand better the industry's response to a complicated problem.

Consumers *are* drinking less, and this has posed problems for many operators. Because sales of alcoholic beverages usually carry a much higher profit than food sales, reduction in alcohol consumption has seriously affected profitability. The marketing response that has helped many operators is the development of a whole line of colorful and tasty "mocktails," which are made without alcohol. Featuring "lite" beers and wines also caters to the guest's desire to hold down caloric and alcohol intake while helping maintain sales.

FOOD SERVICE AND THE ENVIRONMENT

"Saving the environment" generates a great deal of concern and enthusiasm— and rightly so. Our purpose here, however, is to think about the impact of the environmental movement on food service. The view we will adopt, not surprisingly, is that of the business community, which looks at environmental proposals in terms of costs and benefits.

It can be difficult to discuss the environment because the concept is so broadly defined. An environmental awareness program at one hotel included, for instance, water conservation measures, elimination of aerosols (which damage the earth's atmosphere), use of guest amenities that had not been tested on animals, and a "tree planting excursion for all employees at a public park."[19] Hard Rock Cafes undertake to serve foods that are naturally fertilized and free of pesticide as often as possible and to serve only line-caught tuna because nets also kill dolphins.[20] All of this may be meritorious and praiseworthy, but it supports a notion of the environment that is so broad and diffuse that it makes it difficult to focus on the problems where food service can make a really strong contribution to the struggle to save the environment.

We certainly cannot afford to be indifferent to the problems of the environment as it is more globally defined. In fact, in the final chapter of this book we will consider a number of these issues, such as the greenhouse effect and the potential for a future energy shortage, as they relate to the outlook for hospitality. In this chapter, however, we want to examine and understand problems that are a threat and need to be dealt with at the unit level.

Restaurants and food service in general are basically a clean industry rather than a polluting one. It is true that in some settings restaurants are faulted for creating traffic or noise problems. A few neighborhoods have

[19] *Ontario Restaurant News,* November 1990, p. 8.
[20] *Nations Restaurant News,* February 19, 1990, p. 19.

The Fresh Kills Landfill is the largest manmade "structure" on the Eastern Seaboard. It takes New York City's trash—and is almost full. (Courtesy of AP/Wide World)

objected to cooking odors coming from kitchen exhausts. These, however, are exceptional rather than everyday concerns. There are areas, though, in which food service faces, at the unit level, a serious environmental problem. Along with other businesses and every household in America, solid-waste disposal— otherwise called garbage—is a problem whose time has come. As it turns out, garbage is not only an environmental problem but an operational problem as well. The cost of conventional waste disposal is going up by astronomical rates.

THINKING ABOUT GARBAGE: FROM DUMP TO WASTE STREAM

Not very long ago, garbage was taken to the dump—and dumped—and nobody thought much about the management issues involved. As the pressure of population, an ever richer economy, and a "throwaway society" interacted, however, problems of groundwater contamination, rodent infestation, toxic substances, and smell, to name a few, gave rise to a concern over the safety of what we now call a sanitary landfill. A first-class dump—that is, a sanitary landfill—costs close to $500,000 an acre to build. Specialized facilities designed to handle toxic substances such as ash from incinerators cost even more. To prevent groundwater contamination, a sanitary landfill is lined with clay or a synthetic liner and is equipped with a groundwater monitoring system. Because rotting garbage produces an explosive gas, landfills have methane-collection systems. To keep down the smell as well as the insects and rats, the day's garbage is covered with a layer of dirt each night.[21]

Sanitary landfills are expensive to build and maintain. More important, it is now hard to find any new dump sites because communities really don't want them in their own backyard. In fact, in just a little over 10 years, the number of landfill sites has dropped dramatically as Table 5.2 shows.

Americans generate about $3\frac{1}{2}$ pounds of garbage per person every day (from 50 to 100 percent more than other countries with similar living standards). That is about 100 pounds a week for a family of four, or $2\frac{1}{2}$ tons per year. The pressure not only from businesses but from households puts an increasing load on a declining number of landfills. In fact, it is estimated that 80 percent of today's landfills will be closed to use by the year 2000.[22] In the last few years, garbage disposal costs have been increasing by 32 percent annually.[23] The "tipping cost" (the cost to tip the contents of a garbage truck into a landfill) for New York City doubled in one year (1990),[24] and the Fresh Kills landfill, at 2.8 billion cubic feet of waste, has become the highest point of "land" on the East Coast and threatens to displace the Great Wall of China (3.6 billion cubic feet) as the world's largest structure.

Just at the point where the demand for landfill space is rising and the supply of such space is declining, another element of complication is added—

[21] *The Wall Street Journal,* May 1, 1990, p. A4.

[22] Leland L. Nicholls, "The 1990's Solid Waste: Costs and Benefits of Abandonment vs. Management." Presentation to the Foodservice Consultants Society International, New York, November 8, 1990.

[23] *Nations Restaurant News,* February 18, 1991, p. 38.

[24] Nicholls, "The 1990's Solid Waste."

TABLE 5.2 Landfill Sites

Year	Sites
1979	18,000
1987	9,000
1990	4,500 Est.
1991	3,300 Est.

Source: Environmental Issues (Norwalk, Conn.: James River Corporation, Dixie Products Business, September 1990).

public attitudes. The American public views environmental issues as one of the key public issues of the day. As the *Economist* put it, "Business has found that what green groups demand today, legislators enforce tomorrow."[25] It is more than a regulatory issue, of course. The environmentally concerned citizens are also food service customers, and their strong views need to be taken into account. In fact, opinion surveys show that environmentally concerned people make up about half the population—and they are both the highest in income and the best educated. Restaurants' interest in the solid-waste problem, then, is driven by a concern to be responsible citizens, by the concerns of their best customers, and by exploding waste-removal costs. As a result, we have replaced the concept of the dump, where things are dropped and forgotten, with that of a waste stream, which needs to be managed.

MANAGING THE WASTE STREAM

A study conducted at the University of Wisconsin-Stout gives us a good idea of the composition of the food service waste stream. Institutional food service and table-service restaurants generate about 1 pound of waste per meal served, while fast food generates roughly 1⅓ pounds per meal.[26] Table 5.3 shows the types and proportions of waste generated by the major categories of food service.[27]

[25] *Economist,* October 20, 1990, p. 93.

[26] Peter A. D'Souza and Leland L. Nicholls, *Waste Management: The Priority for the 1990's.* Technical Paper, University of Wisconsin-Stout, n.d. Only the figure for institutions is given in the report. The fast-food figure can readily be derived, using the check average given and a waste per 1,000 pound figure. The table-service figure, however, was estimated assuming an average of four chair turns per day for a seven-day week against an average of 25 pounds for family restaurants and 30 pounds for fine-dining operations.

[27] The report uses the term *fine dining* where I have used *table service.* The category found in the report for fine dining has a check average of $4 to $13. For the sake of consistency of usage in this text, I have changed this table. The authors note that the study was undertaken in a midwestern city and may differ somewhat from other regions.

TABLE 5.3 Contents of the Food Service Waste System by Food Service Type

Type of Waste	Proportion of Waste Stream for		
	Institutional	Table Service	Fast Food
Paper	40%	44%	65%
Plastic	23	16	17
Food	23	21	5
Glass	5	12	4
Tin	8	3	6
Aluminum	1	4	3

Source: Data adapted from Peter A. D'Souza and Leland L. Nicholls, *Waste Management: The Priority for the 1990's.* Technical Paper, University of Wisconsin-Stout, n.d.

As we set out to consider how the waste stream is to be managed, a word of caution is in order. The public perception of environmentally effective action is not necessarily consistent from year to year. In some cases, popular environmental views don't always make physical sense. "In 1976, when McDonald's switched from paper to polystyrene packaging for its burgers," for instance, "it was hailed as an environmentally wise decision. The public was worried about cutting trees and the energy that paper production consumed."[28] When McDonald's switched back to paper 15 years later, it was hailed as an environmental victory; but the case for this being so is, as we will see, at least open to question. Public perception, then, as well as scientific fact need to be taken into consideration.

The techniques available to deal with the waste stream can be summarized in three words: *reduce, reuse,* and *recycle.* These are the ideal solutions, but the facts of life require our list to be expanded to include composting, incineration, and the use of landfills. Figure 5.1 summarizes these techniques, and we will examine each of them briefly below.

Reduction of Waste

The most obvious first step is to avoid products and practices that give rise to waste and to encourage your customers to do so as well. A Burger King franchise in Michigan, for instance, offers customers the option of receiving their sandwich with or *without* wrapping. Wendy's, to cite another example, has switched from cardboard boxes to biodegradable paper bags for its children's meals. It has also switched the form of packaging in which it purchases food products.[29]

---

[28]*Fortune,* February 1990, quoted in *Foodservice and Hospitality,* October 1990, p. 30.
[29]*Nations Restaurant News,* November 19, 1990, p. 2.

---

1. Reduce
2. Reuse
3. Recycle
4. Compost
5. Incinerate
6. Landfill

FIGURE 5.1 Techniques for managing the waste stream.

McDonald's switch back to paper in 1991 was undertaken largely to reduce the total amount of waste coming out of their restaurants. Because of the bulkiness of "clam shells" and other plastic packages, the switch to paper will reduce the volume of packaging waste coming out of their units by 90 percent, according to *Nations Restaurant News.* The move, however, set off considerable controversy and illustrates the complexity of environmental decisions. McDonald's argued that the facilities and markets to recycle plastic were not available.[30] The fact is, however, that while plastics recycling is in its infancy, there is every evidence that recycling's capabilities *are* developing rapidly. Support has come not only from governments but from plastic manufacturers who are not interested in seeing their product "reduced out of business."

Set against the problems posed by plastics are those created by paper. A great deal of energy is used to grow, harvest, and process trees into paper. The process results in serious pollution of both air and water. While paper itself may be biodegradable, when it has plastic laminated to it, as does McDonald's sandwich-wrap paper, its degradability is seriously hampered if not eliminated. Moreover, if paper is simply dumped in a landfill, it will almost certainly not decay.

The way a landfill is managed results in only very slow and incomplete decay. The design of the landfill "results in insufficient amounts of water near the top of the landfill and insufficient amounts of oxygen in the depths to support the aerobic bacteria that are normally associated with biodegradation of garbage and paper." What decay does take place is the result of anaerobic bacteria (bacteria that live in the absence of oxygen), which act much more slowly than oxygen-breathing (aerobic) bacteria.[31] Thus, while a reduction in bulk is realized by McDonald's decision, it is at least open to question whether the overall environmental impact — including paper manufacturing pollution — is positive or not. In fact, Ed Rensi, president of McDonald's USA, indicated

---

[30] *Nations Restaurant News,* November 19, 1990, p. 4.

[31] Moira Marx Nir, "Implications of Post-Consumer Plastic Waste," *Plastics Engineering,* September-October 1990, p. 3.

the switch took place not because the plastic form of packaging was an inferior material but because customers "don't feel good about it."[32]

Reuse

Another seemingly appealing strategy for many operations is a switch from disposables to permanent ware (reusable china or plastic dinnerware). This would reduce dramatically paper and plastic waste. The problems this "solution" would create, however, suggest once again how important it is not to oversimplify. Restaurants built to rely on disposables have no space to locate a dishroom or china storage. If they remodeled to put it in, the cost would be exorbitant, and the space would probably have to come from customer seating — with reduced sales as the result. A heavy expenditure resulting in *reduced* sales would bankrupt many restaurants. Even if we assume, implausibly, that such a development could take place, the result of all the additional water discharged would cause the city sewage system, quite literally, to explode. A dishwasher, after all, requires from 70 to 500 gallons of water *per hour* to operate.[33] Such an increase in dishwashing would also result in thermal pollution of rivers from the hot water and chemical pollution from the very strong soaps used in dishwashing.

Other forms of reuse are more practical. Products can be bought in containers that can be returned to the manufacturer for reuse or reused in the operation. Instead of discarding skids in a warehouse or commissary, most are now being built to stand up to reuse.

The major opportunities available from a strategy of *reducing* and *reusing* appear to lie with changes in the way products are purchased. Minimizing unnecessary packaging, eliminating the use of toxic dyes or other substances that make a package hard to recycle, and using recycled products or recycling containers all contribute to a reduction in the total waste stream. McDonald's requires all of its suppliers, for instance, to use corrugated boxes that are made from at least 35 percent recycled content. The company is also testing "reusable salad lids and shipping pallets, pump-style bulk dispensers for condiments, and refillable coffee mugs."[34]

Recycling

A substantial amount of recycling, as Table 5.4 suggests, is already going on in food service. It is noticeable that metal, paper, cardboard, and glass are already established as recyclables. We should note that in recycling, all metals are not equal. Steel cans can be and are usefully recycled, but the advantages are nowhere near as great as they are for aluminum cans. The scale on which aluminum recycling is already operating can be inferred from results at one

---

[32] *Nations Restaurant News,* November 19, 1990, p. 4.

[33] *Foodservice and Hospitality,* October 1990, p. 28.

[34] *Nations Restaurant News,* November 19, 1990, p. 4.

TABLE 5.4 Proportion of Units Recycling in Tableservice Restaurants

	Sales Volume		
Product	Less than $500,000	$500,000 to $999,000	$1 million and More
Cans	45%	29%	23%
Paper	34	19	22
Glass	33	24	28
Plastic	16	11	13

Source: Data from *Nations Restaurant News,* March 18, 1991, p. 14.

company. Alcoa reports that can recycling, at 17 billion cans or 712 million pounds, grew nearly one fifth in 1990 over the previous year. In terms of environmental impact, Alcoa's 1990 output from scrap was the equivalent of the production of two large smelters and represented a reduction in energy use of 95 percent over a like output from ore. In fact, it's now cheaper to recycle aluminum than it is to mine bauxite, the ore it comes from.

Plastics, however, are so far the slowest performer in the recycling parade. The channels for recycling it are only now being widely established. Moreover, plastic recycling has its own special complications, which we will discuss later in this section.

The key factor in recycling is its economics. True, the materials in the waste stream have some value. But the basic driving force is the rise in landfill costs. While some communities still have adequate landfill space, the evidence is that waste trucked in from distant cities will in time fill these. Overall, landfill costs, as we noted earlier, are rising rapidly; and for large metropolitan areas, landfill availability is literally disappearing. As a result, the driving economic force in recycling is avoiding *skyrocketing landfill fees.*

Recycling requires considerable effort. Think about the case of fast-food waste as it is presently handled. Customers bus their own waste to a common receptacle. All of the contents of the receptacle is ultimately emptied into a single dumpster. Waste is picked up by the hauler quite frequently because it will otherwise develop odor and pest problems. The pickup is usually accomplished by a front-end loader, that is, a truck that lifts the garbage over the top of the truck and dumps it into the receptacle on the back of the truck. This type of truck makes between 50 and 60 stops a day to a variety of customers who have a variety of waste. Sorting the variety of waste found in that dump truck at the end of the day so it could be recycled would be prohibitively expensive if not impossible at this point. At the end of the line, the truck will simply have to dump into a landfill. We should now consider what it takes to accomplish this process so that recycling *is* possible.

First of all, how much sorting can we ask the customer to do? Some operators, particularly institutions, are using consumer sorting. Consumers

Source separation is critical to obtain only clean polystyrene. (Courtesy of Mobil Chemical Corp.)

Material can then be baled and sent to a recycling facility. (Courtesy of Mobil Chemical Corp.)

may be asked to use different bins for glass, paper, plastic, and food waste. In the home, where recycling has been undertaken in some cities, people are asked to sort glass into clear and colored; metal into aluminum and steel; paper into newsprint, corrugated (cardboard), fine (writing paper), and glossy. Wet, organic matter is also sorted separately.

Let us assume that we decide to persuade our customers to sort paper, plastic, and food waste into separate containers. New bins—taking up additional floor space—must be installed and a suitable "training program" set up for our guests. This educational effort would almost certainly include special signage showing the guest what was expected, and tray liners and posters explaining *why* we're undertaking this effort. At least during the start-up period, some personal "assistance" to explain the process—and solicit people's support—would probably be required.

In the back of the house, sorted trash removed from the front of the house will probably need to be resorted. If we don't do it, the recycler will almost certainly need to for several reasons. First, some people will resist sorting. Moreover, pranksters will think it funny to put things in the wrong bins, and lots of honest mistakes will be made. Somebody, therefore, will need to check the trash.

The storage we presently have is probably a dumpster with perhaps a second container for corrugated boxes. But under the new regimen we will need separate containers for several categories of waste. They certainly won't fit into the present back of the house so they will almost certainly have to be crowded into the loading dock area, which may require some redesign to make everything fit and still have room for delivery trucks. To save in storage space and make more economical use of hauling and landfill capacity, we will probably need to buy a compactor to compress the waste, reducing its bulk and the space required to handle it. Depending on the nature of the waste and the location and layout of our back-of-the-house area, we may even decide to invest in an enclosed, refrigerated conveyor belt to move garbage to the pickup area.

This is not the end of the complications. We probably at present have only one hauler—"the garbage truck." That company does everything for us with one truck. Under the new arrangements, different haulers might be required: one for paper, another for metal, and so forth. Even assuming one company can do all of the work, the truck that does the hauling will have to have multiple compartments, and most probably the hauler will have to use more than one truck, each designed for different parts of the waste stream.

The full cost of recycling doesn't end when the truck or trucks leave the door. More than likely the level of sorting undertaken at the restaurant, even after checking, is not as extensive as is required for final processing. Plastics, for instance, are made with different kinds of resins. Different resin-based products need ultimately to be sorted separately. The codes shown in Figure 5.2 were developed to make this further sorting possible. While mixed resin recycling is possible, it produces material that is not as useful as that made

The SPI plastic coding system is a method of labeling all plastic containers with a code which identifies their primary resin. The purpose of the code system is to help in sorting plastic products by resin for recycling. Not all plastics are the same, so for recycling of plastic to be successful, they must be sorted by resin in order to be reused in the manufacture of products. The plastic codes most often will be located on the bottom of the product. There are seven different resin codes.

PLASTIC MATERIAL CODE SYSTEM

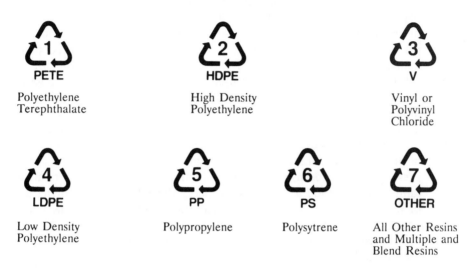

PETE

Polyethylene
Terephthalate

HDPE

High Density
Polyethylene

V

Vinyl or
Polyvinyl
Chloride

LDPE

Low Density
Polyethylene

PP

Polypropylene

PS

Polysytrene

OTHER

All Other Resins
and Multiple and
Blend Resins

The SPI coding is a national system which is necessary to maintain consistency throughout both the plastics manufacturing and plastics recycling industries. Regional recyclers must have the confidence that the coding symbol on the bottom of a container always means the same thing.

FIGURE 5.2 Society of the Plastics Industry (SPI) coding system. [*Source: Environmental Issues* (Norwalk, Conn.: James River Corporation, Dixie Product Business, September 1990).]

from pure resins. The most profitable recycling system, therefore, will separate plastics according to the base resins.

Because the technology of sorting garbage is changing rapidly, it may be that much more of the sorting will be done at recycling centers in future years. This could significantly reduce the restaurant's labor cost in sorting and make recycling more attractive. As we have noted, the advantage to the restaurant of recycling is financial—the hauling fees for recycling are less than the "tipping fee" at the landfill. A further major advantage is that of public relations. Customers are concerned about the environment and are likely to react favorably to firms that are leaders or solid performers in the environmental arena.

Composting

Composting refers to the collection and processing of food trimmings, scraps, and leftovers. Small-scale composting has been going on in rural areas (and backyards) for centuries. But, as a large-scale movement affecting all of society, it is still in its infancy.

Because of the wet, dense nature of food waste, it must be combined for composting with a bulking agent such as leaves, wood chips, or shredded paper to allow for air circulation. The material is placed in rows and, in most present-day applications, a front-end loader is used to turn the material periodically to maintain exposure to the air. More mechanized plants to manage the composting process will undoubtedly become common in the future. Finished compost can be used as potting soil or to enrich a garden or the soil around trees or bushes. Thus, the revenues derived are likely to be modest. Nevertheless, test programs report reduction in garbage removal cost of 50 percent and more because of costs saved by avoiding landfill fees.[35]

We should note an alternative method of disposing of food waste by using it as feed for animals, particularly pigs. Food waste should be steamed or pressure-cooked to ensure no contamination. There is, however, an uncertainty in this method because hog farmers reduce their herds as prices decline, or even go out of business. Some restaurants, too, have become concerned about any potential liability if contamination does occur in spite of every effort to avoid it. Nevertheless, where this method of disposal is available and economically feasible, it seems clearly desirable.

Incineration: Waste to Energy

In 1990, there were 100 municipal waste-incineration plants which processed 10 percent of the municipal solid waste in the United States. Two thirds of these had heat-recovery processes that enabled them to use the heat to generate electricity or steam. Thirty additional plants were under construction and there were plans for construction of 200 more. On the other hand, an additional 60 incinerator construction projects were on hold or canceled because of environmental concerns. One principal concern is air pollution; however, it does appear that technical advances in scrubber systems and combustion control make it possible to overcome these problems in *properly managed* systems.[36] There is, of course, no real protection from scrubber breakdowns or poor management except by careful monitoring. That is to say, given the fact that managements often perform poorly and that any highly complex system will have failures, the problem of air pollution from incinerators could be more severe than the present technology would suggest. Because the air pollutants

---

[35] Tom Watson, "Food Waste Composting: Institutions Get a Taste," *Resource Recycling,* November 1990, pp. 45–47.

[36] Nir, "Implications of Post-Consumer Plastic Waste," pp. 8–10.

can include heavy metals, acid that leads to acid rain, and poisonous dioxins, this is no small issue.

A second problem with incineration is that it reduces the trash by only 75 percent. The 25 percent that remains as ash is often dumped in landfills. Since the ash contains the same kinds of pollutants that can poison the air, as we discussed above, the danger of eventual leaching into groundwater is a serious one.[37] Specialized landfill sites with extra protection against leaching are needed.

Introduction of a major incineration facility can serve to disrupt a local recycling program. The incinerator cannot run only on what nobody else will take. Building an incinerator plant requires the commitment of a large amount of recyclables such as paper, cardboard, and plastic to incineration. These will be required as fuel to make it possible to burn everything else. Diverting these materials from the recycling stream can upset the economics of the community's recycling program.

A further concern put forward by environmentalists is the contribution that incineration can make to the greenhouse effect. Where the only alternative to incineration is dumping in a landfill, this concern is misplaced. Landfills generate methane, which traps heat radiation, and hence contributes more to the greenhouse effect than would the gases given off by incineration. If, however, the alternative to incineration is recycling, recycling would be preferred both because of its environmental impact (air quality and elimination of ash) and because of its significantly lower cost to the community and to individual businesses.[38]

Landfills

The least preferred method of disposal is the landfill. They are costly to construct and maintain and are potentially long-term environmental hazards because they hide rather than dispose of the trash, which decays only very slowly and imperfectly under the conditions of lack of oxygen and moisture discussed earlier. As noted, too, they can contribute to a worsening of the greenhouse effect. It appears that the scarcity of landfills will drive the cost of this method of disposal beyond what most operations can afford in the very near future.

Fortunately for food service operators, residential recycling programs being set up by municipalities and other governmental agencies are creating the channels of collection, redistribution, and processing necessary to make large-scale recycling work. Our discussion makes clear that moving toward recycling will be no simple matter, but it seems highly probable that restaurants will have "plugged into" the recycling channels for virtually all their trash disposal

[37] Nir, "Implications of Post-Consumer Plastic Waste," p. 10.
[38] Nir, "Implications of Post-Consumer Plastic Waste," p. 10.

by the end of the 1990s. Managing the waste stream will almost certainly be a concern that touches your career, so it is good to have a broad understanding of it.

TECHNOLOGY

Some years ago, a researcher looked into the future of food service, and this is what he saw:

> The restaurant of the future will be automated. One individual will be capable of running a 10,000-meal-a-day commissary. Computer-controlled, automated equipment will run the food processing operation from storeroom to cleanup as well as take care of inventory control and the reordering process. In addition, the computer will handle all records, write all necessary business reports (including the annual report), forecast requirements, and perform all cost accounting duties.
>
> Customers will dine in a computer-manipulated environment of aromatic and visual stimuli. They will stand before lighted menus picturing various entrees and punch out selections at order stations. Within 2½ minutes, they will be served the meal via conveyor belt running with the wall and stopping at the proper table. Dish busing commences upon the customer arising from the seat. Dirty dishes move onto a conveyor belt within an adjacent wall. The dishwashing process is completely automated. A 200-seat restaurant will require four employees and a manager.[39]

If technology can put an astronaut on the moon, it can surely bus tables. But it's not what is technically possible that counts; it's what makes economic sense. In the foreseeable future, even in the face of steeply rising wages, the 10,000-meal-a-day commissaries that come into use will require a good many more people than four or five, because it will make economic sense. Although a computer-operated food production, storage, and cleanup system is theoretically possible, it would be like using a computer just to add up a grocery bill. Less-expensive methods are available.

We hear reports of "6-armed robots" being designed for use in food service; but even if this six-armed fellow replaced three full-time workers, it would take five years for the savings to pay for the investment — if the repair bills were not too high. Moreover, how will people feel about giving their order to a robot out of a science fiction film, taking their food from it, and having it clean up after them? As a novelty, it sounds interesting — but for a steady diet, people may need quite a lot of time to get used to it, much less like it.

While the computerized environment referred to above or a fully automated food production system are unlikely to emerge in the foreseeable future, the labor shortage *is* giving mechanization and automation an even greater

[39] *Institutions/Volume Feeding,* October 1975, p. 47.

appeal to operators. Much of the change in equipment is incremental, that is, small improvements that make the kind of equipment we presently use even better at what we now use it for. These applications of technology include better energy control and more mechanization of existing equipment to make control of the production process easier. Examples include timers on friers and moving belts in ovens. In addition, in almost every area of food service the potentially revolutionary elements of technological change loom larger than they did just a few years ago. In the next few pages we will look briefly at developments in customer ordering and payment systems, food production, alternative unit designs, and information systems.

ENHANCING CUSTOMER SERVICE

Guest Ordering

While we are not likely to see customers being waited on by anything that looks like a robot, *people's ability to serve people* is being enhanced by electronics and computerization. Hand-held computer terminals used by waitresses and waiters to take orders at tableside automatically and instantly convey the order to the kitchen. Computers speed service, give servers more time to spend with the guests, or permit servers to serve more guests. Computer terminals are especially helpful where the service area is remote from the kitchen.[40] Whatever kind of ordering terminal is used, whether hand-held or a stationary one used by several servers, they generate legible guest checks, avoid errors in addition, speed service, and improve productivity.

In fast food, touch-screen terminals speed the order-taking process where they are used by servers. Arby's has found that transaction times are reduced 30 percent, and that touch screens improve service and shorten waiting lines while reducing staffing needs in the front of the unit. They also found, however, that a human alternative to ordering must be available because some people don't like mechanization. Based on banks' experience with automatic tellers, nonusers will make up about one third of the customers. While the technology for either hand-held or stationary computer terminals and touch screens is expensive, it does result in increased productivity and lower costs, and its use is clearly cost-effective in high-volume units.[41]

Another application of technology to the customer-restaurant interface is a video-equipped, drive-through, order-taking system that permits a more personal interaction between order taker and guest. Evidence is that the system also improves the transaction speed.[42] Moving diner information even further afield, Dine Out Inc., a New Jersey firm, offers people with a computer a

[40] *Restaurants USA,* January 1991, pp. 20–23.

[41] *Nations Restaurant News,* March 11, 1991, p. 7.

[42] *Nations Restaurant News,* November 12, 1990, p. 3.

Hand-held computer terminals speed service by instantaneously transmitting the guest's order to the kitchen. (Courtesy of NCR)

listing of more than 8,000 restaurants and entertainment spots in the Middle Atlantic states.[43] Single telephone numbers for delivery firms also enhance customer convenience for take out and delivery and offer economies of scale as well as insight into customer ordering patterns through guest history computer files.[44]

The fax machine has proved a boon to take-out and delivery operations. When one New York operation advertised its new fax ordering service, orders initially tripled but then settled down at a level two-thirds higher than they had been before.[45]

Guest Payment

Electronics is also simplifying the spread of the use of credit cards in fast food. Arby's, which has pioneered credit card use in fast food, uses a satellite broadcast system that can receive a credit card authorization within three seconds.[46] A study at Arby's showed that credit card customers spent between $6.00 and $7.00 compared with $3.80 for cash customers, and that 40 percent

---

[43] *TRA Foodservice Digest/Venture,* February 1989, p. 9.

[44] *Restaurants USA,* January 1991, pp. 20–23.

[45] *TRA Foodservice Digest/Food Costs,* September 9, 1989, p. 78.

[46] *Marketing News,* November 12, 1990, p. 1.

of the card customers came because the chain accepted credit cards. Other operators have found even greater sales volume increases from credit card use.[47]

Bank debit cards are also being used in some restaurants. Eighty percent of automatic teller machine (ATM) transactions are made in California, so it is not surprising to find a regional chain headquartered in California, Carl's Jr., pioneering the use of bank cards. Customers can charge their purchases on their bank card at Carl's. The customer can also use the in-store ATM at Carl's to take cash from their checking account.[48]

The credit card represents an important social technology supported in a number of ways by electronics. Credit cards are widely used in table-service restaurants. Their increasing use in fast food is an important service improvement that offers greater convenience to the customer and improvements in sales and efficiency to the operator.

From order to payment, the customer interaction is being facilitated by technology. We can turn our attention now to how the production process is being improved.

TECHNOLOGY IN THE BACK OF THE HOUSE

Food Production

Individual pieces of equipment are being improved by enhancing their energy efficiency both in terms of cooking and their effect on ventilation requirements. The technologies that underlie these developments are impressive, but the impacts are in marginal improvements in cost and operation. Some new equipment, such as the combination steamer/oven, add flexibility to the kitchen because that equipment can be used in more than one process. Another innovation, the two-sided griddle, reduces cooking times by one third to one half or more and also reduces shrinkage in the product.

The use of conveyors in ovens speeds cooking but, more importantly, improves control over the process. Setting the belt speed correctly ensures that the product will not be over- or undercooked because an employee's timing was off. One pizza operator uses a gas-fired conveyor oven to cook 350 eight-inch pizzas an hour—with a fresh-cooked pizza ready in 60 seconds.[49]

Refrigeration

In the 1950s, frozen *prepared* foods were introduced into restaurants. Frozen entrées simplified delivery and inventory problems and reduced skill levels while broadening the range of menu items that could be used in a kitchen lacking skilled cooks. The freezing process, however, has adverse effects on quality. Ice crystals that form at the time of freezing cut tissue in the product.

[47] *TRA Foodservice Digest/RBI Executive Report,* September 24, 1990, p. 1.

[48] *Restaurants USA,* March 1991, pp. 14–16.

[49] *Nations Restaurant News,* November 20, 1989, p. 1.

This changes the consistency of some products. Also, when products are reconstituted, they lose flavor-filled juices.

The next advance in the use of refrigeration was the development of chilled prepared foods. Foods are held in the latent temperature zone, from 28 to 30 degrees Fahrenheit or −1 to −2 degrees Celsius. In this temperature range, holding characteristics, in terms of both flavor and microbiological quality, remain at the level of the fresh product's quality. It appears possible that holding times may be extended to three weeks or more without loss of quality for some prepared products, and at a lower energy cost. *Sous vide* products, which are chilled and vacuum packed in airtight pouches, are in use in a number of hotels, clubs, and restaurants in the United States and in seven of the world's 23 Michelin five-star restaurants.[50]

The value of this new storage technology is in the scheduling flexibility and productivity it gives the operation. Skilled cooks can be brought into a central facility to work from nine to five, Monday through Friday, producing a product to be held in inventory. Less-skilled employees can be used during all the hours of operation to reconstitute a varied menu of high-quality products that have not lost flavor through the freezing process. One restaurant chain, for instance, went from one cook preparing soup for 2 restaurants to the same cook preparing soup for an expanded chain of 18 restaurants, still served by the same single cook using, however, larger equipment.[51]

Reconstitution

Reconstitution technology is also advancing. "State of the art these days in microwave ovens is 'scanning' models. A wand is scanned over a food package that contains coded cooking instructions and they are instantly programmed into the microwave's computer controls, insuring uniform results every time."[52] Voice-recognition technology may soon play a role in restaurants according to *Restaurants USA*. Equipment being developed includes a voice-activated microwave. The equipment will open its door and slide out a tray on command and then, at a word, slide the tray back in and shut the door. It appears feasible to also program recipes into the system.

Other "smart equipment" is on the horizon. Arby's has a prototype self-programming oven that identifies the correct temperature and signals when cooking is completed. Arby's is also perfecting a slicer attached to point-of-sale (POS) equipment. It will automatically portion sliced meat according to the portion size indicated by the POS operator. A shake machine that automatically cycles through the pasteurization process, saving two hours of cleaning time each day, is also under development.[53]

---

[50] Ronald P. Kooser, "Food Production Techniques," *Proceedings of the 17th Annual Chain Operators Exchange* (Chicago: International Foodservice Manufacturers Association, 1990).

[51] Kooser, "Food Production Techniques."

[52] *Nations Restaurant News,* July 30, 1990, pp. 40–42.

[53] *Restaurants USA,* January 1991, p. 22.

The robots that *are* being developed for food service are highly specialized and functional. This one, a "pizzabot," takes orders and makes pizza. (Courtesy of Carnegie Mellon)

Robots

Robots in science fiction usually look like motorized people with arms and legs and a kind of dashboard face. The robots that are gradually moving into food service are much more specialized and functional. They look like the machinery they are. Examples include a drink-dispensing tower that drops the proper size cup into place, drops ice, pours the drink ordered, and moves the finished product down a conveyor line to the guest.[54] Another is a frier-operating robot that cooks different products for the correct amount of time and then moves them to the bagging area.[55] A voice-activated "pizzabot" will take orders and prepare pizzas.[56]

[54] *Nations Restaurant News,* September 17, 1990, p. 50.

[55] *TRA Foodservice Digest/Chicago Times,* June 4, 1989.

[56] *Nations Restaurant News,* February 11, 1991, p. 114.

A word of caution, however, is in order. It is obvious that the more complex equipment becomes, the more its initial cost and the higher its maintenance costs. Moreover, frequent breakdowns can disrupt operations, annoying customers, and demoralizing employees. The issue of cost-effectiveness that we talked of earlier is still very much with us. One equipment company spokesman summed up the situation this way:

> There's just not much being done in robotics. The long-term need is for labor savings but even at their worst, $5 an hour employees are often more flexible than expensive pieces of replacement equipment.[57]

Scaled Down and Mobile Units

The economics of operation do favor certain kinds of innovation that involve both redesign and menu change. These are not technology-based changes, for the most part, but marketing-based evolutions of fast-food systems. Scaled-down units that fit in locations that wouldn't have been considered a few years ago, such as shopping malls, have now proved themselves. Mobile units are also effective in delivering food to temporary sites where there is a short-term demand for a day or a season. Examples include a large construction site or a major sporting event. Mobile units often deliver as much in sales as a regular unit that costs 10 to 12 times as much to build.[58] The technology of smaller units is not as colorful as flashing order panels and six-armed robots, but it is more firmly grounded in consumers' needs and preferences and in economic reality.

TECHNOLOGY AND MULTIPLE-UNIT MANAGEMENT

Chain management is highly dependent on computer and communication technology. Most large chains "poll" their units at least daily to get operating results—sales and key costs. Polling is done by having the headquarters computer call the unit computers over the telephone lines, usually after midnight when rates are lowest. Management reports and other information can also be "downloaded" from the headquarters computer to the unit computers or, increasingly, sent by fax. The heightened communication shortens management response times in both directions. Arby's proposes to use the satellite network mentioned earlier to achieve the same purpose.[59]

Food product ordering from unit to distributor is also being computerized. A direct software link to the distributor's ordering system—or to the company's commissary—reduces order-taking time and decreases mail, phone, and related clerical expenses.

Computerized systems are being used increasingly for communication *within* units, too, as well as with headquarters. The front counter and drive-

[57] *Nations Restaurant News,* February 11, 1991, p. 114.

[58] *Nations Restaurant News,* February 10, 1985, p. 80.

[59] *Marketing News,* November 12, 1990, p. 1.

Mobile fast-food units are an equipment innovation that broadens the market for fast food by providing greater location convenience for consumers. (Courtesy of Burger King Corp.)

through cash register are linked, for instance, to the kitchen. In turn, this system can be linked by a dedicated phone line to the home office, putting the unit continuously on-line with the company's central computer facility.[60]

Finally, reporting systems are being designed that save managers' time in the operating unit. These simplified management systems depend on computers to free managers from filling out reports and forms so they can spend that time with employees and guests.

ENERGY COSTS AND FOOD SERVICE

Utility costs in food service range from 3 to 5 percent and could go as high as 7 percent in an energy crisis. Thirty-five percent of this is used for food-production equipment, that is, to cook the food. Another 28 percent is used for heating, ventilating, and air-conditioning.[61] We have noted that more energy-efficient equipment has been coming to the marketplace, and continu-

[60] *TRA Foodservice Digest/RBI Executive Report,* June 5, 1991, p. 1.

[61] *Nations Restaurant News,* November 5, 1990, p. 45.

ing improvements are likely, especially if, as seems likely, energy prices rise. Still, cooking and air-conditioning are both processes so important that it is unlikely that energy prices could rise to a level where operators would curtail either of them. Moreover, the increase in the cost of labor, as well as its magnitude relative to energy cost, makes it likely that timesaving processing steps such as freezing and chilling will continue to be used as long as they result in significant labor savings, even though they do consume considerable energy. Labor is likely to remain the more important cost for the foreseeable future.

There are other impacts of energy cost and availability. We know from past experience that severe gasoline shortages result in dramatic reductions in travel. As a result, food sales fall. We will consider this issue again in the last chapter.

Considerable concern has been expressed over the use of nonrenewable petroleum resources in the manufacture of disposables. It is useful to put this concern in some proportion. About 2 percent of the total U.S. consumption of petroleum and natural gas is accounted for by *all* plastics manufacturing, and one half of 1 percent is consumed in *all* plastic packaging.[62] Any reasonable estimate of what proportion of that is fast-food packaging suggests such use has a negligible effect on energy availability. Under the circumstances, while rising energy costs may push the cost of plastic disposables up some, the use of disposables is not so crucial as to be curtailed in any but the most severe crises.

SUMMARY

Today's consumers' concerns with health, nutrition, and fitness have major consequences for food service, particularly in menu planning. Good taste and healthy food both need to be represented in menus. Consumerism is a force that heightens consumers' awareness of issues such as junk food, nutritional labeling, truth in menu, sanitation, food additives, and alcohol abuse.

Environmentalism is a consumer concern that presents major operating problems to food service. The key place where food service can make a difference is in managing the waste stream. The major opportunities available from *reducing* and *reusing* lie with changes in the kind of products that are purchased. *Recycling* has major advantages in reducing operating costs from landfill charges but is complicated to establish. *Composting* is a major potential means of disposing of organic wastes such as food products. *Incineration* is superior to landfilling but has adverse environmental impacts principally re-

---

[62] Nir, "Implications of Post-Consumer Plastic Waste," p. 12. Research by archeologist William Rathje in landfill sites suggest that fast-food packaging accounts for one quarter of 1 percent of municipal solid waste of all kinds.

lated to disposal of ashes. It can also disrupt a community's recycling program. *Landfills* are a last resort and because they retard decomposition are more of a means of storing waste than of disposing of it.

The major hindrance to the development of technological innovation in food service is cost in relation to benefit. The labor shortage, however, is spurring development of labor-saving and cost-reducing devices that enhance customer service. Technology also facilitates management in multi-unit companies through improved information management. While energy availability and cost must always be a concern of the hospitality industry, it is unlikely that energy costs will outweigh labor costs in the foreseeable future, or that it would eliminate air-conditioning or the use of disposables.

KEY WORDS AND CONCEPTS

To help you review this chapter, keep in mind the following:

Health, nutrition, and fitness
Dietary schizophrenia
Consumerism issues
Environmental issues
Waste stream
Sanitary landfill
Waste management
   Reduce
   Reuse
   Recycle
   Compost

Waste management (cont.)
   Incinerate
   Landfill
Technology
   Guest ordering
   Guest payment
   Food production
   Refrigeration
   Reconstitution
   Robots
Energy costs

REVIEW QUESTIONS

1. What is meant by dietary schizophrenia? What does it arise from? What do you think of the way the industry is responding to it?

2. Which of the consumerist issues discussed in this chapter have you encountered as a customer or employee of food service? What are your views on these issues?

3. Do you view the typical QSR menu as junk food? How would you respond to a charge of junk food against fast food?

4. Should restaurants be required to identify foods that were not prepared on premise?

5.   What is the status of landfill availability and cost in your community? What is its outlook? What is the outlook for recycling and composting in your area?

6.   Using as an example an operation that you are familiar with, describe the steps necessary to make recycling possible in that unit.

7.   What problems hinder the use of technology? What technological innovations do you think operations should be seeking? What problems do you think might arise from those innovations?

C H A P T E R 6

Courtesy of Sky Chefs, Inc.

INSTITUTIONS AND
INSTITUTIONAL FOOD SERVICE

THE PURPOSE OF THIS CHAPTER

This chapter provides you with information and a perspective on these growing markets which, taken together, account for nearly a quarter of the food service sales. The characteristics of this component of hospitality are unique, and yet the increasing emphasis on marketing and use of brand names makes it clear that institutions participate in the mainstream of food service. Moreover, this is a segment of food service that offers excellent compensation, good opportunities for advancement, and often more stable working hours. Because many companies operate in both the commercial hospitality industry and in the institutional or noncommercial sector, it is an area that you may come into contact with even if your plans now are to work in hotels or restaurants. It is, in short, an area of the industry that deserves careful examination.

THIS CHAPTER SHOULD HELP YOU

1. Understand the important distinction between client and guest.

2. Become familiar with the four major segments of institutional operations and the kinds of opportunities each offers.

3. Identify the major government food service programs and the clients they serve.

4. Explore the growing retirement housing community market and the involvement of hotel companies in it.

5. Recognize the importance of other institutional segments in which contract companies and other firms have a large stake, such as recreation, airline, and military food service.

6. Understand the important functions of vending in serving guest and client needs.

7. Explore the advantages of institutional operations and of contract companies in meeting an institution's food service needs.

COMPARING INSTITUTIONAL AND COMMERCIAL FOOD SERVICES

Dividing food service into commercial and institutional segments is somewhat artificial and misleading, as some of the same firms that profit from providing institutions with food services also operate in other areas of the hospitality industry. ARA Services, for instance, operates hotels in national parks, and Marriott, one of the largest contract food service companies, is also a major hotel company and operates restaurants on expressways and in airports.

There is, however, a difference between restaurant and institutional food service. Institutional food service was once a "captive market," in contrast with restaurants, where guests have a choice of facilities and menus. This distinction still exists, but its force has been greatly reduced. Companies such as ARA and Marriott have found that a marketing approach that begins with guest preferences and the assumption that patients, inmates, soldiers, and students are, in fact, *guests* wins more friends than the old "eat it and like it" institutional attitude. The institutional guest *does* have a choice in the long run. College students who don't like the food withdraw from board plans; patients who have a choice of hospitals often choose the institution with superior food service; and even inmates find ways to assert their food preferences. In an age of consumerism, moreover, even guests who can't "vote with their feet" and go someplace else, don't hesitate to complain. Therefore, competition among the various food service contractors is often decided on the basis of marketing techniques and management skills.

Even though many companies provide both restaurant and institutional food services and use similar marketing and managerial techniques in both areas, the major difference between the two markets is that the food service in institutions is a small part of a large operation with a larger purpose of overriding importance—health care, education, or manufacturing, for instance. In the restaurant, the challenge is to please the guest. In the institution it is necessary to meet the needs of both the guests and the client (that is, the institution itself).

The distinction between client and guest is important. The client is the institution and its managers and policymakers. These are the people who award the contract or, when the institution operates its own food service, hire

A marketing orientation that offers the guests the services *they* want is important to today's institutional market. (Courtesy of Marriott Corp.)

and fire the food service manager. Pleasing the guest (that is, the individual diner, patient, student, resident, or inmate) is important, but the client must be pleased as well. The president of ARA Services put it this way, "Today, you take a blank yellow pad, find out what the client wants, and try to institute a formula that works. It's really the client's operation, not the contractor's."[1]

A commercial restaurant makes a profit by pleasing its guests. There may be a substantial difference in an institutional setting between the needs and wants of the guest and those of the client. In school food service, for instance, the client's (that is, the school's) goals are providing not only adequate meals but also nutrition education by showing the students what a nutritionally balanced meal is like.

If the institution's food service is operated by a contract company, that company must arrange its contract with the client so as to provide its own profit. Contracts sometimes call for a fee paid by the institution to the contractor, usually based on the volume of sales. In that case, operating costs, sometimes including a subsidy to the operation, are the responsibility of the client institution. On the other hand, many contracts require the contractor to carry all costs *and* pay a percentage of sales to the client institution. Some institutions that operate their own food service also subsidize their operations while others operate to break even or to meet specified profit targets. Whether

[1] *Nations Restaurant News,* December 17, 1990, p. 48.

the operation is subsidized, break-even, or for-profit, however, there is always some budgeted performance target that must be met regardless of who operates the service.

An important point to stress is that the presence of a subsidy or the decision by an institution to operate at a break-even point does not remove pressure to achieve budgetary goals. Institutional food service operators are every bit as concerned as commercial restaurant operators to achieve budgetary goals. In fact, "making your costs"—that is, achieving a target cost ratio—can be more difficult in an institution with a low budget than in a commercial restaurant turning a profit.

The two segments also have different operating problems. For example, the number of meals and portion sizes are much easier to predict in institutional operations. Because of this greater predictability, institutional food service operations often operate in a less hurried atmosphere than that in restaurants, in which customer volume and menu popularity often fluctuate. And whereas management people tend to work long hours in commercial food service, the working hours in institutional food service are usually shorter, or at least more predictable.

On the other hand, although a guest may visit a restaurant frequently, few of them eat as regularly in their favorite restaurant as do the guests in institutional operations. Thus, varying the menu for a guest who must eat in the same place for weeks, months, or even years at a time can be a demanding task.

CONTRACT COMPANIES AND INSTITUTIONAL OPERATIONS

An important division within institutional food service is that between contract food service companies (hereafter, contract companies) and institutional organizations that operate their own food service (hereafter, institutional operations). The huge institutional market is still dominated by institutional operators, but the contract companies' share has been increasing. Table 6.1 shows that contract companies now provide one third of institutional food services. Health care is the area in which contract companies have the smallest market penetration, but it has been increasing, from only 8 percent in 1981 to 12 percent in 1991. Contract companies have also had success with public schools in recent years. The two areas in which the contract companies are well established are colleges and universities, and business and industry. Contract companies manage nearly one half of college and university food services and three quarters of business and industry.

TABLE 6.1   The Institutional Food Service Market, 1991

	Estimated Size of Total Market (millions of dollars)	Degree of Penetration by Contract Companies
Business and industry	$ 7,439	74%
Colleges and universities	7,208	44
Hospitals and nursing homes	15,444	12
Primary and secondary schools	5,049	25
Total	$35,140	33%

Source: Data from *Restaurants USA,* December 1990.

INSTITUTIONAL FOOD SERVICE OPERATIONS

Each of the four major divisions within institutional food services have unique characteristics. Moreover, the factors that affect the outlook for each vary. We should consider each of them briefly.

BUSINESS AND INDUSTRY FOOD SERVICE

Business and industry food service provides food for the convenience of both the guest (the worker) and the client (the employer). The client wants inexpensive food with enough variety and quality to satisfy the workers, as the client knows that food can directly affect the employees' morale. Quick service is also important, because the time for coffee breaks and lunch is limited.

The underlying forces that drive the B and I market (as the business and industry segment is called) are the size of the work force and the level of employment. The size of the work force affects the long-term outlook. When it was growing, the work force was a strong positive force, during the years when the baby boomers were leaving school and entering employment. Now that the surge is over, however, the Bureau of Labor Statistics estimates that the work force will increase at a more modest rate.

Within the work force, the trend toward more office and other white-collar employment is determining where the B and I volume will be. The volume of food service in commercial and office buildings is growing at a significantly faster pace than it is in manufacturing plants. In periods of low unemployment, B and I volume may rise but, on the other hand, B and I is especially sensitive to downturns in employment.

Aside from prisons, mental hospitals, and other custodial institutions, no part of the institutional food service market is insulated from competition with public restaurants. This is certainly true for the business and industry segment. As the chairman of ARA Services put it, ARA's competition is "fast food, dial a fax, the supermarkets, the vending truck and brown baggers."[2]

One of the ways that contract companies have found to meet competition from commercial operations is to develop food service concepts and brands of their own or use established commercial franchise brands. ARA's strategy has been to develop its own brands such as "Gretel's Bake Shop," "Itza Pizza," "El Pollo Grande," and "Leghorn." Brand-name units are themed much like any other chain operation, and the brand is promoted within the client's establishment. ARA finds a high level of consumer acceptance for these brands as evidenced by large increases in sales in units where they are established. The other advantage is that no franchise royalties are paid. This results in savings that can be passed on to both guest and client.

By way of contrast, Marriott makes extensive use of franchised brands such as "Pizza Hut" and "Nathan's Famous." Other brands in use at contract companies include "Wendy's," "Little Caesar's," "Dunkin Donuts," and "I Can't Believe It's Yogurt."

The advantages of the brand-name, specialty restaurant format, whether owned or franchised, are startlingly similar to the advantages that fast food has in the commercial restaurant business.

The operation has an identity that helps secure patronage from an increasingly brand-conscious food service customer.

The facility is simpler to build than is a full-menu concept, and the investment required is only about half as much.

Operating costs are lower, too, because of the simpler menu and because customers are accustomed to self-busing in fast food.

Fast food is fast—in-plant feeding at General Motors plants takes only 3 minutes, compared with 12 minutes under earlier formats.

The purpose of employee food service operations changes, however, with different employee levels. Many companies maintain executive dining rooms boasting fancy menus and elegant service. Such dining rooms are often used to entertain important business guests—customers, prospective employees, the press, and politicians. Executive dining room privileges can also be an important status symbol among managerial employees. Executive dining rooms receive more favorable tax treatment for business entertainment than does eating in a restaurant, which has been a significant factor in increased use of in-house facilities.[3]

[2] *Nations Restaurant News,* December 17, 1990, p. 58.
[3] *The Wall Street Journal,* January 10, 1991, p. B1.

COLLEGE AND UNIVERSITY FOOD SERVICE

To understand college food service, one must understand the "board plan." Students eating in residence halls may be required to contract for a minimum number of meals over a term or semester. The food service operation benefits from this arrangement in two ways. First, the absentee factor ensures that some students will miss some meals they contracted for, which permits the food service operation to price the total package below what all the meals would cost if every student ate every meal there. This makes the *package price* attractive.

Second, and more important, the board plan provides a predictable volume of sales over a fairly long period—a term, a semester, or a year. At the start of that period, the operator can closely estimate what the sales volume will be. Because attendance ratios and the popularity of various menu items are fairly predictable, the operator can also estimate how much food to prepare for each meal.

Although some colleges offer only a full board plan (three meals a day, seven days a week while school is in session), flexible board plans have become more and more popular on many campuses. For example, some plans exclude breakfast, whereas others drop the weekend meals. One food service company offers 91 different board plans on college campuses around the country.

In college food services, several different board plans may be available. Often, different styles of service—from fast food to formal dining—are offered to give a sense of variety. (Courtesy of Marriott Corp.)

With a flexible plan that invites students to contract for only the meals they expect to eat, the absentee rate goes down and the average price charged per meal goes up, because of the lower absentee rates. Nevertheless, in plans that drop a significant number of meals, the total price of the meal contract also drops. In any case, both the full board plan and partial plans generally charge students on the basis of the average number of meals they consume.

Another approach that is gaining ground is for students to contract for some minimum dollar value of food service and to receive a "cash card" with the amount they have paid credited to the card. As they use the card, the amount of each meal is electronically or manually deducted from the balance. Students usually receive the food purchased through their card at some discount from what competitive commercial operations charge, and so it is still a bargain. The contracts, on the other hand, give the operator a basis for projecting the demand for the school year for scheduling, purchasing, and general budgeting, and it also guarantees some minimum level of sales volume.

Flexible board plans represent one part of a marketing approach to college food service, an approach that adapts the services available to the guests' needs and preferences. Only 20 percent of college and university students, however, live on campus. Another 50 percent live off campus, and the remaining 30 percent live at home with their parents. The need to attract these students as customers heightens the competitive nature of college food service.[4]

The use of brand names and franchised concepts has taken hold in college and university food service and is by no means limited to contract companies. Institutions that operate their own food service have had success with that tactic too. When Michigan State University installed Burger King, Little Caesar's, Hobies, and Haagen Dazs in place of its more traditional grill operation in the student union, customer counts rose from 6,000 to 10,000 daily.[5]

College food service also uses special events and theme nights such as Hawaiian luaus or outdoor steak fries, just to give their customers a sense of variety and change of pace. A contract company has to sell the client (the institution) to obtain or keep an account. But it must also sell the guests (the students) every day with quality and variety. Otherwise, the students will unsell the client and demand a change in food service.

College students are generally pleasant to deal with, but they can be very demanding. They need to be consulted in planning, and patient attention to complaints is important, too. An unhappy *group* of college students—with a natural bent for boisterousness—can be a difficult group to deal with. College food service operators stress the need for a strong communications program between the food service staff and the students. All agree that, in addition to

---

[4] *Nations Restaurant News,* February 19, 1990, p. 27.

[5] *Restaurants and Institutions,* November 25, 1988, p. 76.

good food and tight cost controls, a successful college food service operation must have "people skills," that is, it must be able to deal effectively with the guests.

The college age segment of the population has been declining since the early 1980s, but college and university enrollments have had only a modest decline (about 1 percent) because of increasing numbers of older adults who have returned to college.[6] This adult segment is expected to continue to increase perhaps, in part, because of increased competition in the job market. In fact, the National Restaurant Association estimated a 7.4 percent compound growth rate for college food service from 1988 to 1991.[7] In 1995, the 18- to 24-year-old population group will begin a period of growth, which will last 15 years. As a result of increased participation rates *and* a growing population group, college and university food service seems likely to be a growth segment for nearly a generation to come.

HEALTH-CARE FOOD SERVICE

Health-care food service can be divided into three general categories: large hospitals (over 300 beds), small to medium hospitals, and nursing homes. In all three of these settings, health-care professionals—dietitians, along with such paraprofessionals as dietetic managers and dietetic technicians—play important roles.

The Dietetic Professional

"The dietitian," according to an authoritative study of the profession, "is a 'translator' of the science of nutrition into the skill of furnishing optimum nourishment. The word *translator* is used in its familiar context of 'translating ideas into action.' "[8]

The largest group within the profession is made up of clinical dietitians concerned principally with the problems of special diets and with educating patients who have health problems that require temporary or permanent diet changes. Administrative dietitians are concerned principally with the management of food service systems, for the most part in health care. (Dietitians also work in education and in non-health-care food services, and their commitment to community nutrition is growing rapidly as well.)

Dietitians who complete a bachelor's degree program and professional training (either in an internship program or in a coordinated undergraduate program that includes both academic classwork and professional experience) and who pass a registration examination are registered in the professional organization, the American Dietetic Association (ADA). Registered dietitians (RDs) are required by hospital accreditation standards and government regula-

---

[6] *American Demographics,* June 1990, p. 67.

[7] *Restaurants USA,* December 1990, p. 29.

[8] *The Profession of Dietetics: Report of the Study Commission on Dietetics* (Chicago: American Dietetic Association, 1972).

tions to supervise health-care food services either on a full-time basis or as consultants. In an increasing number of states, licensing is also mandatory.

The dietary department in a large hospital is headed by either an administrative dietitian or a hospital food service manager. A nondietitian who is employed as the hospital food service manager is supported by a chief of nutrition services, who is a registered dietitian. Large hospitals generally employ a number of clinical dietitians who spend considerable time with patients and prepare special diets. Once a special diet has been written, the clinical dietitian translates it into production orders for the cooks and tray assemblers and then makes certain that these orders are followed. An important part of the dietitian's work is interpreting the diet to patients, helping them understand the need for the diet, and preparing them to undertake their own specialized diet planning.

In a smaller hospital, the food service manager is somewhat less likely to be a registered dietitian. In such cases, however, a consulting registered dietitian will provide professional guidance.

The Dietetic Technician

A somewhat newer role in health care is that of the dietetic technician, who has completed an appropriate associate degree program. Technicians occupy key roles in medium and large hospitals, working under the direction of registered dietitians. Dietetic technicians screen and interview patients to determine their dietary needs or problems and, in large hospitals, often have supervisory responsibilities. In smaller hospitals, technicians may run dietary departments under the periodic supervision of consulting registered dietitians. One of the most important areas of opportunity for dietetic technicians is in extended-care facilities, such as nursing homes, where technicians serve as food service managers under the supervision of a consulting registered dietitian.

Technicians must take a registration exam, and fully qualified technicians are registered as DTRs, that is, dietetic technicians-registered. To reduce operating costs, many hospitals now employ fewer registered dietitians, and so are delegating more and more work to dietetic technicians.

The Dietary Manager

The dietary manager also has an important role in health-care food service. Dietary managers must have had a considerable amount of on-the-job experience and must also have completed a course of instruction covering subjects such as food service management, supervision, and basic nutrition. A separate organization, the Dietary Managers Association, provides for their education and certification as certified dietary managers (CDMs). Certified dietary managers are not members of the ADA.[9] Dietary managers are used principally in

---

[9] Ayres G.D. Carter and Ann L. Schrech, *The Role of the Dietary Manager: An Overview of the HIEFSS Role Delineation Study* (Hillside, Ill.: Hospital, Institution and Educational Food Service Society, 1983).

nursing homes. Some dietary managers have completed the dietetic technician's more extensive two-year course of instruction and may use either title.

Dietary Department Organization

The organization of the dietary department should be considered in the context of the overall health-care facility organization. Figure 6.1 depicts the organization of a medium-sized hospital. The work of the nursing division is, in general, self-explanatory. Other professional services include laboratories, X-ray services, and pharmacies. The dietary department is found in the general services division along with other support services, such as plant engineering and housekeeping. The fiscal services division includes functions such as accounting, receiving, and storage. Thus, in some hospitals, receiving and storage may be carried out for food service by another support unit. Administrative services include the personnel and purchasing functions. Here again, note that another division may assume these functions for the dietary department. This already-complex organization is further complicated by the medical and surgical staffs—the professionals on whose services the entire institution is centered.

Work in hospital food service is fast-paced, and many employees find the medical atmosphere exciting. The organizational complexity and need for *nutrition care* (the provision of special therapeutic diets) as a separate concern makes a career in health-care food service one of the most complex and demanding of the food service careers.

The organization of the dietary department will vary in its assignment and reporting relationships according to the size and function of the hospital. The main functions appear in Figure 6.2.

The same kitchen usually prepares the food for all the employees, house diet patients, and visitors. Some hospitals maintain a separate diet kitchen;

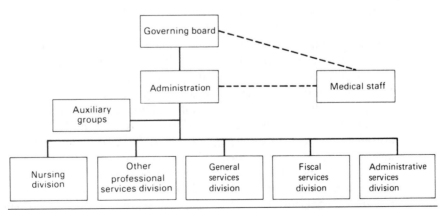

FIGURE 6.1 Functional organization of medium-sized hospital. (*Source:* American Hospital Association.)

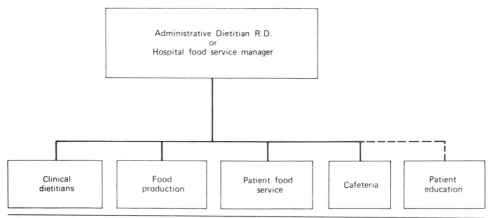

FIGURE 6.2 Functional organization of the dietary department.

others allow the same crew to prepare the special diets following appropriate recipes. Patient food service personnel deliver the food to the floors and return dishes and other equipment to the kitchen after the meals. The cafeteria serves the staff, visitors and, in some cases, ambulatory patients. Some large hospitals offer internships and other educational programs for dietetic professionals, just as they do for nursing and medical school graduates.

Nursing homes, extended-care facilities, and smaller hospitals perform these similar functions on a smaller scale. Thus, such an institution may employ only a consulting dietitian and may combine food production and patient food service. Or the cafeterias in some nursing homes may be expanded to serve all ambulatory patients, often in traditional dining rooms.

Trends in Health-Care Food Service

In the past, health care was a "recession-proof" food service with a strong growth potential. Although health care is still less sensitive to economic conditions than are many other food service segments, regulation by government agencies, which reimburse hospitals for many health-care expenditures, complicates administration. Regulators have capped costs by limiting the length of stay that is covered. Private health insurance plans quickly established similar limits. As a result, hospital occupancy and revenue were limited, too. Health care has consequently had to learn to live with less, which has had a dramatic impact on dietary departments. Because there are fewer patient meals to be served, the number of staff has often been reduced.

But, on the other hand, the lower hospital occupancy levels have led to greater competition for patients, and the dietary department often plays a key role in this competition by offering special services and frills. Hospitals have also found ways to reduce costs and boost revenue. These often include taking a marketing-oriented approach and building sales.

Lowering Costs.   With skyrocketing daily charges for hospital rooms and pressure from government and insurance companies for shorter hospital stays, hospitals have developed alternative arrangements for those patients needing less-intensive care. Hospitals have converted facilities to hotel-type accommodation or developed arrangements with nearby hotels to house discharged patients who still need to remain near the hospital.[10] These alternative accommodations are more affordable for the patient and, where in-house space is used, provide revenue to the hospital.

Another strategy for cost reduction involves consolidation of food-production facilities. One large unit takes on responsibility for basic production for several nearby facilities such as nursing homes and smaller hospitals.[11] Most hospitals that operate their own food service also purchase supplies, including food service products, through cooperative purchasing organizations. Pooled purchasing volumes, often in the hundreds of millions of dollars, secure lower unit costs.[12] In addition, hospital food service, like all other food service organizations, have carefully examined their employee scheduling practices and product use to ensure maximum efficiency. One hospital specializing in short-stay elective surgery, for instance, converted completely to frozen prepared foods, eliminating its kitchen entirely. The food service production activity is limited entirely to reconstituting frozen foods and portioning prepared salad greens for distribution to the floors.

Enhancing Revenue.   Most hospitals serve more nonpatient than patient meals. Not surprisingly, therefore, the nonpatient side of hospital food service has offered major scope for increasing sales. Hospitals have upgraded their public dining facilities to attract more business from staff and visitors in the hospital.[13] Like colleges and universities, some hospitals have added fast-food operations to their offerings. These not only have greater market appeal to customers but lower operating costs.[14]

Hospitals have also broadened their food service activities to target customers outside the hospital, such as senior citizens and people who have special diet needs. Promotion directed at people on special diets encourages people in the community to eat in the hospital or take out specially prepared food. One hospital in Minnesota offers a line of microwaveable frozen meals that is marketed in 20 states. Each meal contains soup, vegetable, starch, protein, and dessert.[15]

Some hospitals offer what is, in effect, commercial catering, handling weddings and other functions. Hospital bakeries offer fresh baked breads and

---

[10] *Lodging Hospitality,* November 1989, p. 28.

[11] *TRA Foodservice Digest/Foodservice Director,* July 15, 1988, p. 6.

[12] *TRA Foodservice Digest/Report on Institutional Foodservice,* September 1988, p. 1.

[13] *Nations Restaurant News,* February 4, 1991, pp. 29–31.

[14] *TRA Foodservice Digest/Food Institute Report,* June 16, 1990, p. 4.

[15] *American Demographics,* September 1988, p. 18.

pastries, including wedding cakes, to the public. Others offer regular take-out meals, delicatessens,[16] and even on-premise convenience stores. Hospitals also provide "Meals on Wheels" in many communities.

Some marketing efforts to increase revenues *are* aimed at patients, however. Two-tiered food service, for instance, offers upscale menus and services to patients who want that kind of attention. At one hospital, in addition to a special menu, patients—who pay a substantial extra fee—have a refrigerator stocked with beverages, fruit, and snacks placed in their room.[17]

Health-care institutions have been subject to cost pressures that result from both government regulation and from competitive pressures. Health-care institutions have responded with efforts to contain costs and to enhance revenues with a *better* mix of services aimed at a broader spectrum of customers, that is, with an improved marketing program. We should end this section by noting, in addition, that health care is expected to be one of the fastest growing areas in the economy well into the twenty-first century.

SCHOOL AND COMMUNITY FOOD SERVICE

The earliest government food service programs began around 1900 in Europe.[18] U.S. programs date from the Depression years of the 1930s, when the need to use surplus agricultural commodities was joined to concern for feeding the children of poor families. During and after World War II, the explosion in the number of women working fueled the need for a broader program. What was once the function of the family—providing lunch—was, in effect, shifted to the school food service system. From the end of World War II to the early 1980s, funding for school food service expanded steadily. With the coming of a more conservative climate under the Reagan administration, however, school food service (along with many other social service programs) was cut back drastically. Still, the basic functions of the program remain substantially the same.

The first function is to provide a nutritious lunch to all students; the second is to provide nutritious food at both breakfast and lunch to poor children. If anything, the role of school food service as a replacement for what were once family functions has been expanded.

U.S. Department of Agriculture regulations require that school lunches conform to a basic pattern and provide one third to one half of a student's minimum daily nutritional requirements. The following four elements must be present in prescribed quantities.

---

[16]*Nations Restaurant News,* February 4, 1991, pp. 29–34.

[17]*TRA Foodservice Digest/Foodservice Director,* October 15, 1988, p. 20.

[18]For an authoritative, extended treatment of the school food service program, see Gordon W. Gunderson, *The National School Lunch Program: Background and Development* (Washington, D.C.: Food and Nutrition Service, U.S. Department of Agriculture, n.d.).

1. Body-building foods, such as meat, fish, eggs, and cheese, that provide protein and iron. (Bread and butter are served with these foods to supply carbohydrates and fat.)

2. Vegetables or fruits high in vitamin A.

3. Vegetables or fruits high in vitamin C.

4. Milk, to provide calcium as well as protein.

The approved lunch pattern offers more than a nutritionally sound meal. It has become part of the educational program itself, teaching students what foods are necessary to health and growth.

A significant portion of the cost of school food service is met by subsidies in cash and kind provided by federal and state governments and the local school board. Children who qualify according to a means test receive a free lunch and breakfast. The majority of children participating in the school breakfast program qualify as disadvantaged.

Funding restrictions, however, have presented difficulties for school food service programs. The most obvious response to reduced government funding is to raise prices, but this often results in reduced participation rates. When the San Diego School District raised the lunch price 20 percent, to $1, participation rates fell 10 percent. Children from families just above the cutoff income for free and reduced prices are the ones who suffer most.[19]

School districts have reacted to reduced funding in much the same way that other institutions have, by increased marketing activity and, to a lesser degree, by diversification of activities to gain more revenues.

One of the problems with school food service programs has been a *requirement* of nutritious selections. The most successful response to this has been to develop menu offerings that closely resemble fast-food menus yet meet the Department of Agriculture guidelines. Pizza, Mexican foods, chicken nuggets, and popular sandwiches such as hamburgers and hot dogs play a major role in such menus. In effect, these menus give the consumers what they want. They are often criticized, however, for not doing the educational job of teaching students what they *should* eat. Nevertheless, given pressure to sell food at higher prices to maintain their economic viability, schools have had to embrace a marketing approach to survive.

School food service districts have also expanded their operation to outside customers. The Tulsa School District, for instance, sells both lunch and breakfast meals to other institutional customers, including parochial schools, a YWCA, and six Headstart programs.[20] Other efforts to build sales volume include catering and sale of take-out items, including fresh baked goods.

Marketing efforts are not limited to menu and format alterations. To meet the need to communicate with customers, student advisory councils are

---

[19] *Nations Restaurant News,* September 3, 1990, p. 25.

[20] *TRA Foodservice Digest/Foodservice Director,* February 15, 1991, p. 34.

formed in schools. School lunch dining areas are upgraded and remodeled to make them more attractive. Self-service speeds service while reducing cost and gives the customer a feeling of having a choice. An article on merchandising in the *School Food Service Journal* gives the kind of advice that might be heard from the home office of a company in the commercial sector, calling for some kind of promotional event at least once every two weeks, to compete with fast-food operations. Moreover, school lunch personnel must begin to function as sales people: "In the school food *service* industry, you're inviting paying customers into your lunch room to eat your good products. . . . Nonprofit does not mean no profit or no business sense. You're a business."[21]

The School Food Service Model

The accumulated experience of school food service suggests a model for public sector food service programs. The first element in that model is that it meet clearly defined social needs that attract broad public support. School food service provides nutritious meals to needy children who might otherwise go hungry, and it helps make well-balanced meals available to all students.

The second element in the school food service model is that it pools subsidies. The federal subsidy usually requires matching state or local funds. Because the subsidies from the various levels of government are pooled, the result constitutes a "bargain." The student's lunch, even if he or she paid the full price, is less expensive than it would be if purchased anywhere else—even if it were brought from home.

The attractiveness of this bargain encourages participation, and participation ensures the third element of the model, a high volume. This high volume makes the meal program more efficient, and it results in further economies. In short, it improves the bargain.

The pattern of administration is the fourth and final element. There is general monitoring of the fairly broad guidelines at the national and state levels, but most operational decisions are made entirely at a local level. Technical advice is, of course, always available. Thus, the model encourages adaptation to local tastes and conditions.

The "bargain" that school lunches offer to the young consumers and their families never has been completely dependent on the federal subsidies. Both state and local governments (and in some communities, charitable organizations) have contributed to the cost of school lunches in direct subsidies of varying amounts.

Increasingly, the school is being seen not just as an educational institution but as a social agency in the community that can use its physical plant— buildings, kitchens, dining areas—and its other resources, such as experienced administration, skilled cooks, and backup custodial staff, to serve a variety of population groups. In Independence, Missouri, for instance, the school dis-

[21] *School Food Service Journal,* June-July-August 1985, p. 26.

The first function of school food service is to provide nutritious food to students. (Courtesy of American School Food Service Association)

trict offers after-school care for elementary school students, day care for three- and four-year-olds, support programs and information networks for both parents of very young children and home day-care providers.[22] In fact, the need for day care will grow 21 percent in the period from 1989 to 1996. By 1995, 65 percent of new mothers will be working mothers.[23] We need not be surprised, then, if we see the school food service mandate begin to expand again in the 1990s.

Contract Companies in School Food Service

One of the fastest growing market segments for contract companies is the school market. Many school boards, facing tighter budgetary restrictions, are finding it advantageous to bring in a company with specialized food service expertise to take on what is, for them, an activity only indirectly related to education, which is the school system's principal mission and expertise. Because 75 percent of the market is "self-op" (that is, operated by the school system), there is a huge market for contract companies to pursue. Although its profit margin is not as high as for some other institutional sectors, school food

[22] *School Food Service Journal,* August 1990, p. 56.

[23] *American Demographics,* September 1989, pp. 20–21.

service is a logical addition to a contract company's operations. In many cases, the contract company finds it can serve a school board not only with food service but also in other areas, such as grounds maintenance and custodial services.

In an interview in which she discussed career opportunities with contract companies in the school food service area, Beth Tarter, human resource manager for Marriott's contract food services, pointed out that there are a number of advantages to this area. Because it is growing rapidly, there are numerous opportunities for advancement. The excitement of a very large account—$5 or $6 million—is more likely to come at an earlier stage than in other areas of food service. School food service also has quality-of-life advantages. This is an area that offers a professional career in food service with a five-day week. Night and weekend work occurs occasionally, usually in connection with a special event at a school, but such an event is the exception. Moreover, many people in school food service have 10½-month contracts that give them their summers off. One manager whose main joy in life is sailing pointed out that he could find no better job to match his professional expertise and his leisure interest. He spends his summers on a sailboat.

SERVICE PROGRAMS FOR THE AGING

In this section we will focus on the institutional service needs of the elderly. As we noted in Chapter 4, one of the fastest growing segments of our population for the foreseeable future will be people over the age of 65. Although many people in this age bracket are healthy and active, not all of them are. Similarly, many but not all of the people over the age of 65 are comfortable financially. While retirement incomes for most are not as high as for younger people, neither are financial needs. Many live in homes already paid for and have significant savings to draw on. On the other hand, not all elderly are affluent. Many must live on Social Security checks and limited savings. People over 75 are more likely to fall in this category. They are more likely to be financially needy and to require assistance to survive. The rapid growth of this group is one reason for the increasing demand for government supportive services for the elderly.

People over 65 commonly have disabilities related to their age. One third, for instance, experience some difficulty in lifting and carrying, climbing stairs, and walking more than a short distance (i.e., one-quarter mile or more), and one in five or six has *severe* difficulty with these tasks. Fifteen to 20 percent have some impairment of sight and hearing and experience difficulty getting around inside.[24] Disabilities such as these tend to be concentrated among those who are the oldest in the group. The Bureau of the Census predicts continuing growth in the number of people over age 85, predicting that by 2050 they will constitute 5 percent of the population. Demographers

---

[24]*American Demographics,* September 1989, p. 34.

The congregate meals program offers older Americans not only sound nutrition but also a chance to continue their participation in community activities and to combine food and friendship. (Courtesy of the U.S. Department of Health and Human Services, Administration on Aging)

and gerontologists, however, believe this segment may rise to 10 percent of the population by that time.[25] Clearly, this is a population group that will be growing for the foreseeable future and one with particular needs. We will look briefly at programs to meet needs for food service at the community level. We will also examine the growing life-care institutional segment in which hotel companies such as Marriott and Hyatt figure prominently.

Community-Based Services

The ideal arrangement for the elderly is to live independently in their own homes. As their physical and mental abilities deteriorate, however, they begin to require assistance. Seven million Americans provide help to elderly friends or family members without pay. (Three quarters of those providing the help are women, half of whom are employed outside the home.) Community

[25] *The Wall Street Journal,* November 28, 1989, p. B1.

agencies have come into being to provide help to people living independently and to families who are helping an elderly relative or friend.

Approximately 145 million congregate meals were provided to nearly 3 million elderly in 1990, while another 100 million meals were delivered through Meals on Wheels.[26] According to the Administration on Aging (AOA),

> The national nutrition program for the elderly is designed to provide older Americans, particularly those with low income, with low cost, nutritionally sound meals. Emphasis is given to providing these meals in group settings. The nutritional projects provide at least one hot meal a day (meeting one third of the daily nutritional requirements) five days a week to older citizens (60+) and their spouses of any age.

Although participants would be given an opportunity to pay for their meals, "no means test will be made and no one will be turned away on the basis of their inability to pay for a meal." Congregate meals are funded by the U.S. Administration on Aging and by state and local agencies.

Meals on Wheels and similar programs also receive direct and indirect support from all levels of government and from local private agencies as well. The programs deliver meals to people living in their homes who have difficulty getting out. In addition to funding from governmental and private agencies, these programs often rely on local volunteers for a significant portion of their manpower.

Entrepreneurial Opportunities

The difficulties of living at home that the elderly experience have created a significant set of business opportunities. To meet the needs of people who cannot care for themselves, a number of home-care services have sprung up. Some offer simply housekeeping services but others provide "sitter" service and limited nursing care. In addition, nutritional support companies offer nutritional care such as special diets. These home-assistance companies offer people with adequate training an interesting opportunity to go into business for themselves with a minimum of investment beyond their own skills and knowledge.

Retirement Housing Communities

A number of firms, including hotel companies like Marriott and Hyatt, have become active in providing a mix of services to affluent senior citizens. These people want to live in a community that can provide the independence of apartment living along with the security of having health-care and professional services available without having to move to another facility. Senior Living Services Division, Marriott's division title, suggests the priority of firms in this sector. It is to provide as full a life in retirement as an individual's abilities will

[26] Henry Posman, Administration on Aging, personal communication to author, June 7, 1991.

Classic Residences by Hyatt provide a pleasing upscale ambiance for affluent retirees. (Courtesy of Hyatt Hotels Corporation; Photo by Rion Rizzo)

permit. Marriott describes the four levels of service offered in its 12 communities in operation or under construction in 1991:

Independent Living.   Private apartment living where residents enjoy an independent life-style, with the security of knowing that whatever services or professional assistance they may need are readily available. Residents select a limited or full-service meal plan.

Assisted Living.   Private apartment living for residents who can maintain an independent lifestyle, but need limited assistance with day-to-day activities such as dressing, grooming, bathing, or monitoring of medication.

Personal Care.   Personal care takes assisted living a step further by providing a greater level of hands-on assistance in performing daily activities, while allowing residents to maintain as much independence as possible.

Licensed Nursing Facility.   A limited number of private and semi-private rooms are available for residents who need long-term or short-term intermediate and/or skilled nursing care and supervision. The facility is primarily for the use of residents of the retirement community.

In smaller communities operated by Marriott under the Brighton Gardens name, the independent living option is not offered.

Hyatt Corporation, another hotel company active in this field, operated six residences in 1991 and negotiations were in progress for a major expansion, indicating a major corporate commitment to the field. Penny Pritzger, president of Classic Residence by Hyatt, points out that residences such as these are principally a *need-driven* service business catering to people 75 years of age and older. Most people, she notes, would prefer to stay in their own home, but events such as the death of a spouse or problems of health that make going up stairs or driving a car difficult or impossible require them to choose a life-style that provides more assistance.

According to Ms. Pritzger, retirement housing is a marketing-intensive business in which referrals based on success with your present residents are crucial. "The business," she said, "is psychology as much as service." The successful operator combines the ability to deal professionally with the resident with an ability to deal compassionately and to recognize that your operation is your resident's *home.*[27]

As with so many other hospitality operations, food service is a key operating variable. Ms. Pritzger notes that meals are *the* principal social events of the resident's day. A survey by Marriott Senior Living Services notes that 91

---

[27]Penny Pritzger, Remarks made during a panel discussion on "Hospitals and Congregate Living Centers," at the 12th Annual Hospitality Industry Investment Conference, New York City, June 3–5, 1990.

percent of seniors responding said food quality was an important factor in choosing a retirement center.[28]

Perhaps because this sector of hospitality is so new, it has been characterized by high business-failure rates. In 1990, for instance, half the developers who had been in the field had left the market. Some of the problems experienced by operators included lack of operating know-how suited to the specific market, poor location choices, overrapid expansion, a nursing shortage, and increasing regulation.

OTHER INSTITUTIONAL FOOD SERVICE SEGMENTS

We will consider three additional institutional areas of operation: recreation, transportation, and military. As evidenced by the large size of the organizations in these sectors, each of them is an important element in the food service industry.

Recreation

ARA's Leisure Services Group presents a profile of a company with involvement in a variety of recreational activities. In 1990, that company operated food service at 21 convention centers, 34 stadiums and arenas, 14 state and national parks, and 12 racetracks. In addition, ARA has been responsible for the food service at virtually all Olympic and Pan American games since 1968. The characteristic of operating in this kind of environment is suggested by this comment by one stadium manager: "We're competing with Disneyland, the beach and the mountains along with the Dodgers, the Lakers and, everyone else."[29]

It seems that entertainment is nearly as important to stadium operators as a winning team, so we see more and more of a Disneyland kind of format that emphasizes enjoying the experience of coming to a ball game as much as the sport itself.[30] Hospitality service, particularly food service, has an important role to play in delivering the experience. In fact, *Restaurant and Institutions* 400, a list of the 400 largest hospitality firms, lists 5 firms in the recreation category, including 4 theme or amusement park companies.[31] As in other institutions, brand names are important. Marriott, for instance, is a franchisee of Carl's Jr. and McDonald's in its stadium operations,[32] as is ARA of Popeye's.

Military

Military and related food service falls into four categories: military food service; post and base exchange food service organizations; military officers',

[28] *Restaurants and Institutions Alert,* October 17, 1990.

[29] *Nations Restaurant News,* December 17, 1990, p. 63.

[30] *American Demographics,* June 1990, p. 22.

[31] *Restaurants and Institutions,* July 25, p. 32.

[32] *Nations Restaurant News,* October 22, 1990, p. 2.

noncommissioned officers', and enlisted personnel's clubs; and military health-care units. All four groups employ both civilians and military commissioned and noncommissioned personnel.

Food service ranks as a major activity in the military and 13 of *Restaurants and Institutions* 400 largest food service organizations are military units or military support groups. Like so many other institutional operations dependent on federal funding, the military has felt the sting of budget cuts and has responded with increased marketing efforts. Military food service operations are broadening the services offered to include take out and delivery, and tailoring menu offerings to fit ethnic interests and nutritional concerns common in this as in other segments of our population. Brand names are in use here, too. Exchange systems have become franchisees of major food service concepts such as Burger King, and the navy club system has developed its own brand, a pizza and pasta restaurant called Parcheezi's.[33]

For information on careers in these areas, of course, you need to go no farther than your local armed forces recruiter.

Transportation

Three airlines who operate their own food service, United, TWA, and Northwest, and one railroad, Amtrak, were among the 400 largest hospitality firms in 1990. In addition, three airline catering companies (who act as suppliers to several airlines) made that list.[34] A number of other companies also have in-flight food service divisions.

The airline food service business is fast paced and requires people who work well under pressure. The uncertain number of passengers on an outbound flight, sudden cancelations or additions to the airlines' schedule of flights, and the various equipment configurations used in different aircraft make in-flight food service a challenging field. And some carriers offer free or reduced-price travel as a fringe benefit.

VENDING

Vending is not really a segment of institutional food service but a method of delivering food service that is used in all segments. While vending is used in institutions, much of vending is not counted as food service. For instance, *Restaurants USA* estimated "vending and nonstore retailers" sales at $4.9 billion in 1989 but, according to *Vending Times,* sales of drinks, snacks, pastries, and other foods accounted for sales of $20 billion and total vending sales volume for that year was $25 billion.[35] Much of this should probably be

---

[33] *Restaurants and Institutions,* July 25, 1990, p. 171.

[34] *Restaurants and Institutions,* July 25, 1990, p. 44.

[35] *Vending Times: Census of the Industry 1990.*

Centralized preparation of food in many school systems permits significant economies of scale. (Courtesy of Sky Chefs, Inc.)

thought of as retailing competition to food service, but it is important to see the overall aggregate size of vending, which is summarized in Table 6.2. Moreover, we need to consider vending here briefly to understand its function for clients and the advantages (and disadvantages) it presents to guests.

Most vended food falls in the snack and beverage categories. A significant portion, however, constitutes main meal service, particularly breakfast and, to a lesser degree, lunch. In addition, the snacks and beverages are commonly used to supplement main meals brought from home. Vending, therefore, plays an important role in the overall food service business. The impact of vending in the workplace is suggested in the following brief case studies.

An office building housing some 2,500 employees was built in the heart of a large city. The designers refused to incorporate a restaurant because kitchen facilities and storerooms would take up space destined for other uses. Dishrooms and the necessary plumbing and air ducts required for a kitchen would also have added to the cost of the building.

In addition, the building's management did not feel qualified to operate its own food service and had heard that leased restaurants often took up much of the building manager's time. Finally, management felt that a restaurant would also create traffic problems at the loading dock, with the numerous deliveries and garbage and trash removal.

TABLE 6.2 Vending Sales, 1989

Product	Percent Share	Dollar Volume
Hot drinks	8.5%	$ 2,090,000,000
Cup cold drinks	7.7	1,888,000,000
Can cold drinks	29.2	7,140,000,000
Bottled cold drinks	9.1	2,238,000,000
Juice (through dedicated vendors)*	0.6	148,000,000
Packaged confections/snacks	18.9	4,626,000,000
Bulk vending	1.0	237,000,000
Milk	1.9	469,000,000
Ice cream	0.5	126,000,000
Pastries	1.6	402,000,000
Hot canned foods	0.6	150,000,000
All-purpose vendor foods	4.4	1,068,000,000
Cigarettes	12.7	3,120,000,000
Cigars	0.1	13,000,000
All other	3.1	765,000,000
Totals	100%	$24,480,000,000

Source: Vending Times, "Census of the Industry," 1990.
*Juice is also sold through can cold drink, bottle cold drink, and all-purpose equipment.

Although capital expense and operating complications argued against a restaurant, the designers wanted food service available in the building as a convenience to the occupants. Consequently, they designed vending restaurants that would provide an ample menu selection, including not only sandwiches but also scrambled eggs, sausage, and pancakes for breakfast, and fried chicken, french fried potatoes, Salisbury steak, and other traditional entrées for lunch and dinner. Although entrées such as these currently account for only a small percent of food service vending sales, their presence constitutes an important service for the guest.

The food (including sandwiches, which make up some three-quarters of the vended food service sales) is prepared at the vendor's commissary. The food is delivered before the building's regular operating hours, to avoid congestion.

In another city, a professional building accommodating about 500 people opened a small table-service restaurant just off the lobby. The occupants of the building were unhappy with the quality of the operation, however, and the operator finally went out of business. Its eight employees were replaced by a vending restaurant that offered a variety of specialty sandwiches prepared in the vendor's commissary and heated by the customer in an on-site microwave oven. The operation required one attendant on duty from 8:00 A.M. to 4:30 P.M. on weekdays.

On the positive side, vending restaurants are convenient, can solve economic and operational problems for building and plant managers, and can increase food service variety. Most food service vending operations are found in public buildings, plants, factories, and offices in which the clientele is too small to justify a full-fledged food service operation and too far from other restaurant facilities for the employees to reach them easily on their lunch hours.

Guests are rarely enthusiastic about vending restaurants, but their impersonality can be reduced by "attended vending," which provides a specially trained hostess who makes change, gives refunds, and handles complaints. Still, vending remains primarily a mechanical, self-service process.

The variety of products that vendors sell is growing and improving. Nearly one-half of the companies offering vended food services have their own commissaries, and their vending outlets usually are equipped with microwave ovens.

Vending has clearly become part of the "eating" market, as defined in Chapter 2, rather than the dining market. Vending companies have found that if they offer *manual vending* (that is, a cafeteria staffed by "real, live" people) during some of their hours of service, all of their products are more likely to be accepted. One vendor speculated that this is true because the personal touch allows the guests to associate the vended food with the people who provide food services in the more traditional cafeterias.

Vending offers the hospitality industry a means of extending food service hours to meet the convenience of guests, and to provide acceptable service where it would be economically impossible to provide full manual food service.

WHO OPERATES AN INSTITUTION'S FOOD SERVICE?

Now that we have discussed the clientele served by institutional food services, we can examine the arguments for and against the use of contract companies or institutional in-house food services. The principal arguments involve (1) economies of scale, (2) control of operations, and (3) management expertise.

RESPONSIBILITY FOR INSTITUTIONAL OPERATIONS

Institutional Operators

Many institutions see no need to pay the overhead and profits of a contract company. Operating on the assumption that their own employees can manage as efficiently as a contract company can, these institutions choose to keep the overhead and profit they otherwise would have to pay to an outside company. These institutions can control their operations, and to some extent they can

Centralized production systems permit close control not only of costs but of quality. (Courtesy of Sky Chefs, Inc.)

limit the staff turnover traditionally associated with contract companies, who frequently promote or transfer their employees. "If we like a person," said one university official, "we might lose him to a contract company. In our own operation, if we treat him right we have a good chance of keeping him—of maintaining staff stability."

Contract Companies

Contract companies feel that their method of operation offers advantages to operators of all sizes. True, unit managers may be transferred. We should note, however, that a contract company provides the client with two kinds of managers: the unit manager and the regional and district managers who train, evaluate, and supervise the unit manager's work and ensure management continuity. That continuity is an important offset to the possibility of transfer. Perhaps even more important, the transfer is a part of a process of career progression. People who want to advance are drawn to that kind of opportunity. Thus, a contract company is likely to attract aggressive managers. Managers who choose to stay with institutional operators are likely to have less opportunity for advancement although they will have other advantages, such as stability in where they live.

Another area in which contract companies offer advantages is that of purchasing. Selection of the best, most cost-effective purveyor offers major potential for savings. So does knowledgeable negotiation on the client's behalf by national buyers with broad experience. Contract companies conduct audits of cost-plus suppliers' books to ensure accurate billing, an expenditure of effort and money that might not be practical for an individual client. Finally, because contract companies buy on a regional or national scale, they can consolidate purchasing for several clients, thus achieving significant economies.

Contract companies also offer to their clients, at cost, extensive facilities planning services. These services include operational design (equipment), interior design, procurement, supervision of construction, and equipment installation. Specialized accounting and market-planning services may also be offered to clients.

Finally, contract companies offer the collective experience of management and marketing in many markets. Marketing programs can be tailored to individual clients, for instance, yet also draw on national marketing programs developed by the contractor. This has proved especially helpful in areas such as nutritionally oriented marketing programs.

Pros and Cons

To all of this, the large institutional operator will likely respond that a large institution — a medical center, university, or school district — is large enough to achieve most or all of these advantages on its own. A smaller institution might add that voluntary buying co-ops and judicious use of consultants can also achieve a good part of these effects. Both would emphasize that the institution retains full *control* over the operation, which reports directly to the institution's top management.

No doubt, contract companies would make responses to each of these points. Our purpose is not to settle the issue in any final way. There really is no *one* answer to the debate. What we want is to suggest the outlines of the competition between institutional operator and contract company for consideration by the reader.

SUMMARY

While the institution has a greater hold on its market because of convenience, restaurants provide a lively alternative and plenty of competition for most institutions. In addition, institutional food service must serve the needs of both the client institution and the individual guest. Contract companies have the largest market share in business and industry and nearly half of college and university food service. Institutional operators have the dominant role in health-care and school food service, although contract companies' share of those markets has been increasing. Brand-name concepts and aggressive marketing are important in all sectors of institutional food service.

The largest public sector (i.e., government) food service program is school food service. Its long experience in serving young people and their families suggests a model for other public sector activities. That model is based on acknowledged social need, pooling of subsidies, concentration of activity to achieve high volume, and flexible administration that permits local initiatives. Other programs that may or have emerged in the public sector include child-care food service and congregate meals for the elderly. Retirement housing communities provide affluent older people with as much independence as they can manage but also afford them support, such as health care, without requiring them to move to another place. Other areas of institutional food service discussed were recreation, military, and transportation (mainly airline) food service.

Vending is an important method of delivering food service, particularly in places that are not large enough to support a full food service operation or where the investment in facilities and operating support needed by food service cannot be made.

The principal arguments regarding the choice between an institutional operation and a contract company involve questions of scale, control of operations, and management expertise.

KEY WORDS AND CONCEPTS

To help you review this chapter, keep in mind the following:

Client
Guest
Contract company
Institutional operator
Business and industry (B and I)
College and university
Health-care food service
Brands in institutional food
    service

Basic pattern of school lunch
    menu
The school food service model
New leisure class
Congregate meals
Home-care services
Retirement housing
    communities
Senior living services

Dietitian

Dietetic technician

Dietary manager

Recreation, airline, and military food service

Impact of vending

REVIEW QUESTIONS

1. What do institutional and commercial food services have in common? How are they different?

2. How do guest and client interests differ? What interests do they have in common?

3. What characteristics are important to each of the four major divisions of institutional food service?

4. What opportunities do you see for extending hospitality services to the elderly? What facilities are available in your community for independent living for the aging?

5. What are the advantages and drawbacks of vending for the client? For the guest?

6. Who operates the food service in your institution? Do you think an institutional operator or a contract company will do the best job of providing for the needs of the guest? Of the client? Why?

P A R T 3

LODGING

CHAPTER 7

Courtesy of Sonesta Hotels

LODGING: MEETING GUEST NEEDS

THE PURPOSE OF THIS CHAPTER

Early lodging systems were shaped by transportation systems and patterns of destinations. In our increasingly affluent civilization, however, guest needs and preferences play an increasing part in shaping the way lodging is segmented. In this chapter we look at how consumer needs and community needs as well as transportation and destination patterns have shaped today's segmented lodging industry. Since franchise systems have played so large a part in developing lodging segmentation, they are considered here, too.

THIS CHAPTER SHOULD HELP YOU

1. Trace the development of basic location-oriented properties.

2. Relate the importance of guest need in the organization of lodging.

3. Identify and describe the function of the principal types of lodging.

4. Explain how lodging functions as a community institution.

5. Distinguish the functions of franchise systems for both hotel and guest.

6. Recognize the forces that are changing the way reservations systems function and the impact of those changes on franchise systems.

Professional lodging has always followed the patterns of transportation of its time: caravansaries, inns along Roman roads, posthouses, and so forth. It has responded, too, to changes in destination patterns. Toward the end of the nineteenth century, North American hotels grew up to serve the rail traveler. Often the hotel was physically connected to the railroad station. A few of these hotels still survive, and some, such as Toronto's Royal York, remain thriving centers. Of the hotels built during the first half of this century, those not physically connected to the railroad station were usually convenient to it and to the major destinations in the downtown sections of cities. Indeed, a revival of this pattern may follow a revival of rail travel, if the high-speed rail corridors proposed for the late 1990s are implemented.

In the past, while differences in quality and price existed, most hotels provided products and services for the entire market served. In present years, however, lodging has responded not only to changing transportation patterns but also to the varying specialized needs of travelers, producing distinct segments such as the all-suite and limited-service hotels.

THE EVOLUTION OF LODGING

The two principal determinants of hotel location, transportation system and destination, changed in the period of great economic expansion that followed World War II. As a result, several waves of hotel and motel building have changed the face of American innkeeping.

THE MOTEL

Although a few "Mo Hotels," or motels, were to be found in the Southwest even in the late 1920s, and "tourist courts" began to appear in the 1930s, the big wave of motel building followed World War II.

The end of the war released a pent-up demand for automobiles. During the 1930s, depressed economic conditions prevented many people from buying a car; then during the war, automotive production concentrated on military needs. The explosive growth in auto travel that followed the end of the war brought people into the travel market, as both buyers and sellers.

The first motels were small, simple affairs, commonly with under 20 units (or guest rooms). These properties lacked the complex facilities of a hotel and were generally managed by resident owners with a few paid employees.

They were built at the edge of town, where land costs were substantially lower than those downtown. The single-story construction that typified motels until the late 1950s (and even the two-story pattern of later motor hotels) offered significant construction economies, compared with the downtown high-rise properties built on prime real estate. Capital costs represent the largest single cost in many lodging establishments, and so the lower land and building costs and the lower capital costs that resulted gave motels significant advantages. These savings could be, and generally were, passed on to the guests in the form of lower rates.

Probably more important, motels offered a location convenient to the highway. Because the typical guest traveled by car, he or she could drive to any local destination during the day, returning to the accommodations in the evening. Meanwhile, inexperienced travelers, who had always been put off by the formality of hotels, with their dressy room clerks, bellhops who had to be tipped, and ornate lobbies, preferred the informal atmosphere of the motel, a "come as you are" atmosphere in terms of both dress and social preferences. In the motel they might be greeted by the owner working the front desk. Motel operators were proud of their informality. The personal touch they offered guests and the motel's convenience and lower prices were their stock in trade. Few motel operators had formal training, and many would gladly tell one and all that their lack of professional training was the very secret of their success.

THE MOTOR HOTEL

For a few years, it appeared that hotels (in general, the relatively large downtown properties) and motels (usually the small properties located at the edge of town) would battle for the new mobile tourist market. Unhappily for both the hotel and the mom-and-pop motel, the situation was not that simple.

In 1952, Kemmons Wilson, a Memphis home-building and real estate developer, took his family on a vacation trip. He was depressed by the dearth of accommodations to meet his family's and the business traveler's needs. He returned to Memphis with a vision of a new kind of motel property that combined the advantage of a hotel's broad range of services with a motel's convenience to the auto traveler. That insight revolutionized the lodging industry.

Motels became larger and began to offer a wider range of services. Dining rooms or coffee shops, cocktail lounges, and meeting rooms appealed to the business traveler. Swimming pools became essential to the touring family. Room telephones, usually present in hotels but generally absent in motels, became the rule in motor hotels, thus requiring a switchboard and someone to operate it. Whereas hotels and motels had offered coin-operated radios and television sets, free television and then free color television became the rule.

Although there were experiments with smaller inns, having 50 to 75 rooms, most lodging companies determined that generally a 100-unit facility was the smallest that made economic sense. That size permitted full utilization of the minimum operating staff and provided a sufficient sales size to amortize the investment in such supportive services as pools and restaurants. However, with the coming of the limited-service hotel, which does not include a restaurant, experimentation with smaller properties in smaller cities is again the order of the day.

THE AIRPORT MOTOR HOTEL

In the 1950s and 1960s, as air travel became more and more common, a new kind of property appeared, designed especially to accommodate air travelers. Even though these travelers arrive by air, they rent cars often enough to justify a lodging design similar to that of the motor hotel. Thus, the principal distinction of the airport property is its location. Airport motor hotels tend to emphasize their small- to medium-sized meeting-room capacities, because of the preponderance of business meetings at these properties. An important "extra" service provided by almost all airport hotels is the courtesy van which offers guests transportation between the property and the airport if they haven't rented a car.

THE DOWNTOWN HOTEL

Although the older downtown hotels faced new competition on the edge of town, they had little competition from the downtown market areas because new properties there were fairly scarce. At about the same time that U.S. cities began their urban renewal, however, the interstate highway system began to penetrate the downtown areas. The downtown renewal area, with its new office and shopping complexes, often revived interest in hotel construction designed to serve these new destinations. Urban renewal, coupled with the limited-access interstate highways, opened up the city to the nation's highway travelers.

Downtown properties have many advantages. They are near the large office complexes and retail stores; by day, they are near business destinations; and by night, they are close to many of a large city's entertainment centers. Although the downtown property generally depends less on "off-the-road" travelers than do the motor hotels, their guests arrive often enough by automobile (and use rented cars often enough) to justify ample facilities for automobiles. These facilities commonly include a motor entrance, a waiting area often called the motor lobby, and on-premise parking accessible to a guest without assistance from (and tips for) the hotel staff. In fact, many older downtown properties have been remodeled to include most of these facilities. Although on-premise parking has not always been feasible, reasonably convenient off-premise parking with valet service to pick up and drive the car is common. Thus, although not all downtown properties include the title *motor hotel* in their name, nearly all first-class downtown properties offer the services associated with them.

SERVING THE GUEST

In the past, one could speak in terms of a few hotel types related mainly to location and style of construction, as we have just done. Today, however, this *product* orientation has been fundamentally altered by the logic of marketing.

Properties such as the Stouffer Riviere Hotel mark the resurgence of the downtown hotel. (Courtesy of Stouffer Hotels)

While product and location still matter, putting the customers' needs and preferences first has resulted in a segmented hotel market made up of several quite different kinds of lodging. Before we can understand hotels, therefore, we must review the principal customer types.

These can be divided into business and personal. Each of these two can be divided further according to demographic characteristics such as age, sex, income level, and family status or life-cycle stage. Business travelers can also be divided into individual and group business. While we won't go into that

TABLE 7.1 Important Features in a Hotel for Business Travelers

Features	Percentage Indicating Extremely or Quite Important
Convenient location*	97%
Safety and security	95
Attention/service	91
Price/value	90
Facilities for business	81
In-room amenities	79
Large guest room	79
Excellent restaurants	70
Elegant atmosphere	60
Nonsmoking rooms	59
Health club/pool	51
Cultural attractions	29
Good entertainment	25
Prestigious name	18

Source: Hotels, September 1990, p. 19.
*For business purposes.

level of detail in every case, the way these different customer needs affect demand for lodging should be clear from our discussion.

BUSINESS TRAVEL

Fifty-six percent of travelers are leisure travelers or are traveling for some other personal reason, while 44 percent are on business. Because the average length of stay is longer for business travelers than for personal travelers, however, business travelers account for somewhat more than half of room nights spent in North American hotels. (One room rented for one night equals one room night.) Couples account for 46 percent of travelers, while men traveling alone account for 32 percent and women traveling alone for 22 percent.[1] This last group has been growing in size rapidly and will probably continue to do so for some years to come.

Table 7.1 reminds us of the advice of pioneering hotelman Elsworth Statler, who said that the three most important things about a hotel are "location, location and location." Clearly, however, Table 7.1 raises questions about Statler's priorities, since it shows a number of additional, basic consid-

[1] *Lodging,* April 1991, p. 11.

Lobbies in upscale hotels such as the Loew's Hotel in Santa Monica offer an impressive atmosphere to the arriving guest as well as a place to lounge or meet people. (Courtesy of Loew's, Santa Monica)

erations. Most important to business travelers, besides location, is to feel secure away from home, to be well served, and to feel they have received fair value for money. All of these characteristics received an "important" rating with 90 percent of guests, according to a Swiss hotel survey. The next most important group of factors involve hotel facilities and received high importance ratings from roughly 80 percent of guests.

Grand hotels, such as Loew's Anatole Hotel in Dallas pictured here, provide a ceremonial setting that helps symbolize the importance of convention events. (Courtesy of Loew's Hotels)

To meet the needs of business travelers, business centers in hotels offer such services as photocopying and fax machines, desktop publishing software, computer work stations, laser printers, dictaphones, and clerical staff on call 24 hours a day.[2] Such special targeting of business travelers is not limited to upscale properties. Super 8, a major budget chain, offers "work processors" to its business guests, including free faxes and photocopies (up to 10 of each),

---

[2] *Hotel and Motel Management,* May 27, 1991, p. 51.

assistance with pickup and delivery of overnight packages, and help finding clerical assistance around the clock.[3]

Meetings and conventions are a major and growing source of the travel dollar, having increased fivefold between 1972 and 1989 and by 37 percent just from 1987 to 1989. *Meetings and Conventions* magazine estimates that 57 percent of total meeting expenditures of nearly $44 billion are spent in hotels. The meeting customer has distinctly different needs and interests than the individual traveler, with availability of meeting facilities and a good banquet department at the head of the list. People booking conventions generally need larger hotels and meeting facilities. Many smaller properties, however, compete successfully for small meetings on the basis of personalized service.

Business travelers, not surprisingly, operate on dramatically different budgets. Some are quite cost-conscious while others have more generous expense accounts. Accordingly, business travelers are found in all price levels of the hotel business.

We should note, too, that the same people make different uses of lodging, depending on what they are doing. For instance, all-suites serve mainly the business traveler during the week. The same person may return for a weekend, but this time probably as a pleasure traveler with the rest of the family, and probably at a room rate discounted as much as 50 percent from weekday levels. The suite makes a nice place to do business during the week— and, if the price is right, is ideal to give parents and kids each their own privacy for family travel on the weekend. The rate is a critical consideration on weekends since travelers use their own money on the weekend but, generally, are reimbursed for business travel during the week.

Today there are two thirds as many women traveling alone as men, but Juergen Bartels, president of Carlson Hospitality (Radisson Hotels) Group, points out that 52 percent of all managers under the age of 35 are women. Referring to them as "an entire class of business traveler that didn't exist 20 years ago," he sees women as the fastest growing business travel market.[4] Women travelers have distinct needs and preferences. Those who can afford the higher rate, prefer suite hotels because they have a room separate from their bedroom to conduct business; and Embassy Suites, most of whose hotels have atriums, argue that women find the open hallway areas more secure. Some chains offer makeup mirrors, Woolite, iron and ironing boards, hair dryers,[5] and even separate floors for women. Others, however, argue that women want the same basic hotel services that men do and resent being treated differently. No doubt, as women traveling alone grow to be an even larger part

---

[3] *Lodging,* March 1991, p. 34.

[4] Juergen Bartels, Address to the Carlson Travel Network Convention, Phoenix, Ariz., May 3, 1991.

[5] *Lodging,* May 1991, p. 33.

Large function rooms like this one are necessary to serve the general sessions of large organizations. The Grand Ballroom at the Mayflower Hotel in Washington, D.C., offers a sumptuous setting for organizations to honor their top brass and impress their members. (Courtesy of the Mayflower Hotel)

of the business travel market, the industry's attention will continue to seek effective means of marketing to them.

LEISURE AND PERSONAL TRAVEL

While less than half the industry's room nights are accounted for by leisure and personal travel, Michael D. Rose, chairman of the Promus Companies (Embassy Suites, Hampton Inns, and Harrah's Casino Hotels), expects family *room* nights to increase 50 percent in the decade of the 1990s. Some of these families will be staying in hotels, we should note, because of the tendency for families with two working spouses to combine business trips with a weekend minivacation. In fact, weekend vacations increased 28 percent from 1984 to

Las Vegas is famous for the luxury of its suites, which are often provided at no charge to the "high roller" gamblers. (Courtesy of the Mirage Hotel & Casino)

1989.[6] Still, it is reasonable to assume that most family travel is principally personal travel, and virtually all of it reflects at least a strong element of the personal needs, wants, and desires of the traveler.

With the aging of the baby boomers, the middle-aged share of the lodging market is expected to increase from 54 percent in 1988 to 62 percent by 2000.[7] Two thirds of all dual-income households have children at home. These people are likely to be interested in shorter vacations, given the difficulty of arranging time off for two working spouses.[8] In the last half of the decade of the nineties, more of the children of the boomers became teenagers. This may well change the needs of family travelers and threaten somewhat the growth of family travel[9]—as teenagers decide they don't want to join in a family vacation.

Another growing travel segment is made up of senior citizens. Hotel chains are offering discounts to attract this market. While more cost-conscious, senior travelers are more likely to travel during off-peak seasons, when

[6] *American Demographics,* February 1990, p. 2.

[7] *American Demographics,* June 1991, p. 6.

[8] *American Demographics,* August 1988, p. 41.

[9] *American Demographics,* November 1990, p. 36.

hotels need the business. Fall travelers, for instance, are older and less family-oriented travelers.[10]

Much of the leisure travel budget is spent at destination hotels, so the aging of the baby boomers is good news for resort destinations because of the higher average incomes of middle-age travelers. Of course, the increasing senior population also offers major opportunities to hotels and tourism, generally.

TYPES OF LODGING

In looking at the major types of lodging in the marketplace today, we will adopt the system of classification put forward by the firm of hotel accountants and consultants, Pannel Kerr Forster. These major types are full-service, economy properties, resort, all-suites, conference centers, and convention hotels.[11] As we consider each of these, however, we will see that many need to be divided even further. One of the major separations is rate, while another is service level.

FULL SERVICE

A full-service hotel "provides a wide variety of facilities and amenities including food and beverage outlets, meeting rooms, and recreational activities." Full-service hotels are further classified as basic, upscale, and luxury.[12] The basic property offers all the services but minimal frills or extra services. Examples of a basic full-service property are a Holiday Inn, Ramada Inn, or Quality Inn. Upscale properties might include Hilton, Sheraton Hotels (although Sheraton *Inns* would generally be classified as basic), as well as Westin or Hyatt Hotels. Two of the best-known luxury chains are Four Seasons and Ritz Carlton. Some hotels in the chains described as full service or upscale also qualify as luxury, such as Hilton's Waldorf Astoria, Sheraton's St. Regis, or the Grand Hyatt.

The *basic* full-service hotel is likely to continue to play a major role in smaller communities, where such a property is the city's premier hotel. In other locations, however, such as in suburban communities around large cities, many of these properties are in trouble. In fact, Holiday Inn appears to be deploying a strategy of moving some of its U.S. properties either upscale into the Crown Plaza group or downscale into the new, limited-service Holiday Inn Express brand. Basic full-service properties, many of which are 15 to 30 years old or more, are threatened in particular by competition from newer limited-service properties. Basic properties that are upgraded (as, for instance, into the

---

[10] *American Demographics,* October 1990, p. 4.

[11] *Trends in the Hotel Industry,* USA ed. (Houston: Pannel Kerr Forster, 1990), p. 1. The definitions in quotes at the beginning of each section are taken from this source unless otherwise noted. PKF does not use the term "economy properties" as a classification (see note 16 on p. 227).

[12] The full-service categories are those used by Smith Travel Research in *Lodging Outlook.*

Crown Plaza group at Holiday Inn) add competition to the already crowded upscale segment.

In fact, all three levels of full-service properties in most cities are regarded as overbuilt by most industry commentators. This excess capacity depresses occupancy, room rates, and thus the wherewithal to operate the hotel to meet guest expectations of full service and to maintain the physical plant in good condition, These deficiencies only make the plight of the full-service hotel more difficult.

Newer basic full-service concepts such as Marriott's highly successful Courtyard hotels provide full-size luxury hotel rooms but severely limit the size of the lobby and the food and beverage facility (and services), and provide only one or two very small meeting rooms. These limitations reduce investment and hence capital costs. They also result in significantly lower operating costs. Thus the Courtyard and similar properties are able to maintain rates at or below the conventional basic full-service property and not a lot higher than the upper end of the economy market. As a result, these new properties are positioned to be effective competitors with older full-service basic properties and with limited-service properties, as well.

ECONOMY PROPERTIES

Days Inns advertises "We don't have it because you don't want it,"[13] making explicitly clear the segment to which the economy properties address their appeal: guests who want a comfortable, clean room but will quite willingly trade off extra services to obtain a lower rate.

Budget chains have been a factor in lodging since the early 1970s. In 1981, there were 30 budget chains with 1,600 properties and an estimated 160,000 rooms. By 1990, that number had grown to 75 chains with 72,000 properties and 670,000 rooms.[14] Twenty-six percent of customers stayed in economy properties in 1987, but that proportion had risen to 30 percent by 1990. This 4-point increase in demand in the economy segment compares with a 4½-point decline in demand for basic and upscale full-service rooms.[15] Economy properties can be divided into two general groups, limited service and hard budget.[16]

---

[13] *Lodging,* September 1990, p. 10. In practice, we should note, that Day's Inns has properties in a number of market segments but is most closely identified with the limited-service segment.

[14] Smith Travel Research, *Lodging Outlook,* December 1990. Smith Travel Research reports trends in occupancy, average rates, construction, and other industry developments based on reports from a sample of approximately 12,000 hotels.

[15] Smith Travel Research, *Lodging Outlook,* April 1991.

[16] In *Trends in the Hotel Industry,* Pannel Kerr Forster uses the term "limited service" for the entire economy group, without distinguishing between upper and lower price and service sectors. The appeals of the two sectors are clearly distinctive, however, and warrant a departure from the PKF terminology.

Limited service properties have only a small lobby area and, usually, little or no food service. The rooms, however, are often of a very high standard. (Courtesy of Choice Hotels International)

Limited Service

Limited-service properties such as the pioneer in this segment, La Quinta, Promus's Hampton Inns, Marriott's Fairfield, and Choice's Comfort Inns, maintain that the facilities and services they *do* offer are as good or better than those offered by full-service properties. These properties *limit* their service offering, providing little or no food and beverage service, and only very limited meeting facilities. Most, however, have a policy of either colocating with a known brand-name restaurant such as Denny's or McDonald's or building only in areas well served by other restaurants. Thus, while they offer no food service themselves, they make certain that it will be easily available to their guests.

While limited-service properties have experienced continuing increases in demand, supply has also continued to grow. Even in 1991, a year of economic

Luxury hotels offer not just comfort but also elegance in every appointment. Pictured (opposite) are a guest room and a mirrored bathroom from the Park Hyatt on Water Tower Square in Chicago. (Courtesy of Hyatt Hotels)

recession and of staggering losses for the lodging industry for the eighth year in a row, a number of the major lodging companies are building new limited-service properties, adding to a supply that has been growing very rapidly for some time. Moreover, conversion programs—that is, converting a property from one brand to another—threaten to simply move oversupply from one segment to another. Basic full-service properties are being converted to upper level, limited-service properties in increasing numbers; as we noted above, the Holiday Inn Express brand was created, in part, for this very purpose. Holiday Inn Express aims to have 400 properties by 1996.[17] Days Inns, even in bankruptcy, continued to grow in 1991 by both "new builds" and conversions of basic full-service properties to its limited-service brand. Comfort Inns, too, continues aggressive expansion of its successful limited-service product. Thus, although the limited-service segment has been much favored by consumers, it appears to be only a question of time before it is overbuilt. The limited-service sector reported an occupancy of 62.5 percent in 1990 and an average daily rate of $42.43.[18]

The economic logic of the limited-service sector has, until now, been reasonably straightforward. These properties feature full-sized rooms virtually identical to the higher priced full-service competition. There is no restaurant or bar, and only very limited small meeting space. Most properties offer a limited breakfast without charge. The fact is, it is easier and more cost-effective to give away food on this limited scale than to operate a full restaurant and sell food from early morning until late at night. The lower investment and reduced operating cost make the property profitable at the lower rates charged. By the mid-1990s, however, the booming overcapacity we just discussed may create problems in this sector.

Limited-service properties, we have noted, pride themselves on their good, if limited, service. Hampton Inns has introduced an unconditional guarantee that permits any employee to give customers their money back if they are not satisfied. The result has been a higher retention of customers and a more enthusiastic work force. Significantly, "give-backs" amount to less than one half of 1 percent of room sales; and for every dollar returned to customers, the company has calculated that they get back $8 in repeat sales.[19] The evidence is that Hampton's efforts are paying off in consumer satisfaction. A study in *Consumer Reports* magazine found that 92 percent of consumers give Hampton an A or B in quality ratings and indicate an intent to

---

[17] Bryan Langdon, Address to the 13th Annual Hospitality Industry Investment Conference, New York City, June 3, 1991.

[18] *Hotel Motel Management,* April 29, 1991, p. 35.

[19] Raymond E. Schultz, Remarks made during a panel discussion, Hospitality Industry Investment Conference, New York City, June 1991.

Sleep Inns and a number of other hard budget chains offer compact but very attractive rooms. Sleep Inns saves on operating expenses through a high degree of automation. (Courtesy of Choice Hotels International)

return.[20] Marriott's Fairfield Inns has taken a different tack but is no less concerned about service quality. That company computes employees' bonuses on the basis of the guests' assessments of the quality of the operation.[21]

Limited-service properties are expanding into smaller cities. Fairfield Inns has announced a 63-room prototype for smaller cities,[22] and Hampton also has designed a smaller property for cities of 75,000 or less.[23] This should help these chains not only to provide lodging in smaller communities but to secure reservation volume from these towns as well.

Expert industry observers predict that the limited-service segment will, in time, become as large as the basic, full-service segment.[24] Full-service basic conversions, then, as we have just noted, may be simply moving the oversupply from one segment to another.

---

[20]Michael Meeks, Remarks made during a panel discussion, Hospitality Industry Investment Conference, New York City, June 1991.

[21]Todd Clist, Remarks made during a panel discussion, Hospitality Industry Investment Conference, New York City, June 1991.

[22]*Lodging,* June 1991, p. 8.

[23]*Hotel Motel Management,* January 14, 1991, p. 1.

[24]Smith Travel Research, *Lodging Outlook,* February 1991.

Hard Budget

The market leader in this lower priced category, Motel 6, offers rates as low as $19 for single occupancy in some markets, but the average daily rate for hard-budget properties was $28.56 in 1990.[25] Typical of newer properties in this segment is Microtel, which offers a smaller room (30 percent less space) and built-in furniture for greater speed in room cleaning. Microtel also offers a number of deluxe features such as remote-control TV, touch-tone phones, and plush carpeting. Sleep Inns offers these features plus a VCR, minibar, and phone jacks that permit moving the phone from bed to table and back. A computer system keeps track of all transactions at Sleep Inns,[26] and it is the first operation in North America to provide automated registration during off-hours and to make use of the guest's credit card as a room key.

While many hard-budget chains such as Sleep Inns are franchised, the largest chain in the segment, Motel 6, owns and operates all its own properties. The company has no computerized reservation system and no 800 telephone number. Half of its guests, in fact, don't have reservations, and those who do must make their own and pay for any long-distance phone calls themselves. Guests prepay at registration. Motel 6 offers clean but somewhat Spartan accommodations in properties managed by husband-and-wife teams that live on site.[27] Clearly, the major appeal of Motel 6 is price. The company was acquired in 1990 by France's Group Accor and is committed to expanding at the rate of about 75 properties per year.[28]

Hard-budget properties expanded their share of rooms supply from 12.3 percent of hotel properties in 1987 to 16.3 percent in 1990. Their share of rooms sold, however, rose by a much smaller percentage, from 16.4 percent to 16.9 percent in the same period. The segment's relatively healthy occupancy of 70.6 percent, however, suggests that overbuilding is less of a threat in this segment, as yet, than in any of the others discussed so far in this chapter.

Table 7.2 summarizes the service level segments in lodging that we have been discussing.

ALL-SUITES

Suite properties report significantly higher occupancies than do other hotel properties.[29] As Table 7.3 suggests, average rates vary significantly from one

---

[25] *Hotel Motel Management,* April 29, 1991, p. 35.

[26] *Cornell Hotel and Restaurant Administration Quarterly,* May 1989, p. 5.

[27] *Lodging,* July-August 1990, p. 101.

[28] *Hotel Motel Management,* May 27, 1991, p. 76.

[29] All suites achieved a 75.2 percent occupancy in 1989 compared with 67.2 percent for the industry as a whole, according to Pannel Kerr Forster's *Trends in the Hotel Business.* Laventhol and Horwath reported 71.1 percent compared with an industry average of about 67 percent, according to *Hotels,* June 1991, p. 6. While the two samples yield somewhat different results, it is clear that all-suites achieve significantly higher occupancies.

TABLE 7.2 Lodging Service Level Segments

Segment*	Example of Companies Serving Each Segment
Full Service	
Luxury	Four Seasons, Ritz Carlton
Upscale	Hilton, Hyatt, Sheraton, Westin, Radisson, Marriott, Stouffer
Basic	Holiday Inn, Ramada Inn, Quality Inn, Courtyard by Marriott
Economy	
Limited service	Hampton Inns, Fairfield, Comfort Inns, Days Inns, La Quinta, Holiday Inn Express
Hard budget	Motel 6, Sleep Inns, Microtel

*There are all-suite properties that fit into every segment except hard budget.

region to another but are generally higher for suite properties than for full-service competitors.[30] Some of the variation in rates shown may be the result of variations in the definition of an all-suite property. There are, for instance, "budget-suite" properties and, at the other end of the scale, ultradeluxe suite

TABLE 7.3 Comparison of All-Suite Properties with Industry Averages, 1990

Region	Occupancy		Average Daily Rate	
	All-Suites	All Hotels	All-Suites	All Hotels
New England/ Mid-Atlantic	68.5%	68.3%	$91.49	$106.41
South Atlantic	67.8	66.4	83.84	67.76
North Central	70.7	60.3	75.34	52.78
South Central	67.3	62.3	67.05	56.02
Mountain/Pacific	71.2	66.6	83.99	75.24
Total United States	69.7%	65.0%	$81.21	$ 72.83

Source: Adapted from *Trends in the Hotel Industry,* special ed. (Houston: Pannel Kerr Forster, June 1991), pp. 4, 39.

[30] *Trends in the Hotel Industry.*

All suites offer guests spacious accommodations for work, entertainment, and relaxation. (Courtesy of Promus Companies)

properties. We will, however, confine ourselves to distinguishing between two categories that serve quite different traveler needs: the transient all-suite units such as those offered by the largest chain in the sector, Embassy Suites, and long-stay properties such as Marriott's Residence Inns.

Transient All-Suite Market

Embassy Suites offers guest accommodations about 20 percent larger in total square feet than a conventional hotel room. This space, however, is divided into two rooms, separated by the bathroom and a kitchenette. The properties (excepting a few conversions) are built around an atrium. The living room of the suite overlooks the corridor and atrium while the bedroom has an outside view.

The target customer for weekday business is an upper level executive, while families are good weekend customers. The living room couch pulls out to make a double bed, allowing children and parents to both have some privacy on a weekend minivacation. Figure 7.1 shows a floor plan of a typical Embassy Suite guest unit. Embassy Suites include a telephone and remote-control TV in *both* rooms, a minirefrigerator, electric coffee maker with a complimentary supply of regular and decaf coffee, a microwave oven, and a wet bar. The rooms do not, however, include a full kitchen.

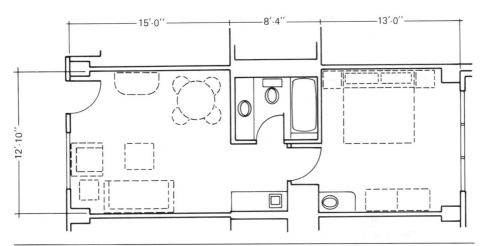

FIGURE 7.1 A typical guest unit at Embassy Suites. (*Source:* Embassy Suites.)

Some all-suite properties have restaurants and bars as well as limited meeting space, but it is common to limit food and beverage service to a complimentary breakfast and complimentary cocktails served in the late afternoon and early evening. Embassy Suites usually offer more extensive restaurant service but generally lease the restaurant operation to another company. The emphasis in the all-suite property is on the guest room. Food and beverage, where available, are provided as a supporting service, generally with restricted hours of operation.

Extended and Long-Stay Markets

Extended and long-stay properties cater to guests whose stay is 5 days or more. Extended-stay (5–29 days) guests make up the largest segment, and long-stay guests (30 days or more) are the next largest segment. Stays shorter than 5 days account for less than a third of the guests in these properties. Rates drop the longer the guest stays. The typical guest is a middle-aged, upper-middle-income professional or manager. A smaller proportion are employed in technical capacities. The vast majority are employed by a large company. Homewood Suites reports that nearly half of their customers are attending meetings and seminars while a third are on field assignments or projects. Five percent are being relocated and 16 percent are traveling for other reasons.

The extended-stay suite provides full-kitchen facilities, and many properties offer a shopping service that will accept a shopping list from the guest and pick up groceries at nearby shopping centers. Homewood Suites offers an on-premise convenience store. Extended-stay properties generally have a lobby building where guest registration takes place. A complimentary breakfast is served as well as complimentary cocktails in the evening. A lounge in this area

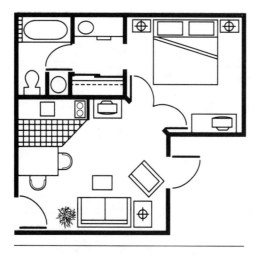

FIGURE 7.2 A typical extended long-stay suite. (*Source:* Promus Companies.)

provides space for guests to socialize with one another. An executive center provides copying and fax service, a typewriter, and a personal computer and printer. Most properties also have exercise and sports facilities such as basketball and tennis courts, a swimming pool, and an exercise room. Figure 7.2 shows a drawing of a typical guest unit at Homewood Suites.

The demand outlook for the extended-stay market is among the brightest in the lodging business. Homewood Suites estimates that over a third of the hotel rooms in the United States are booked to extended-stay travelers. Promus President Michael Rose notes that his company's research indicates that by the year 2000 the average worker will need to be retrained every five years, or up to eight times in his or her working career.[31] You may recall that nearly half of Homewood's present guests are attending meetings and seminars. Clearly the demand for long-stay accommodations will be supported by the trend toward frequent attendance at training programs.

The Outlook for Suite Hotels

Suite hotels have stirred a great deal of controversy in the industry. Proponents point to high occupancies and rates as evidence of strong consumer demand while critics note that the higher construction costs mean higher capital costs. The critics charge that capital costs are large enough that the advantage of rate and occupancy is offset by higher depreciation. Industry statistics are not as yet much help because they report results *before* capital

[31] Michael Rose, Address to Hospitality Industry Investment Conference, New York City, June 1991.

Residence Inns, a leader in the long-stay market, offers an all-suite property especially designed to meet the needs of guests who will be staying for more than a few days. The exterior courtyard view shown here resembles a low-rise condominium development. The guest facilities are designed for business entertaining. (Courtesy of Residence Inns)

costs.[32] Darryl Hartley-Leonard, president of Hyatt Hotels, has called suite hotels "one of the worst economic propositions this industry has ever seen."[33] On the other hand, Severyn Ashkenazy, president of *L'Ermitage,* one of the earliest and most luxurious of the all suite properties, suggests that the all-suite hotel represents the next step in the development of the luxury hotel.[34] Randall A. Smith, president of Smith Travel Research, notes that the original promise of the all-suite facility was two rooms for the price of one. This turns out, however, not to be realistic. All-suites hotels *need* to charge more to recover their heavier investment in those two rooms, and the key to this segment will be their ability to earn and keep the higher rate.[35]

THE RESORT HOTEL

The hotel accounting firm of Pannel Kerr Forster defines a resort hotel as one that is "usually located in a suburban or isolated rural location, with special recreational facilities to attract pleasure seeking guests." Resorts are destinations for travel that invite a guest to spend as much as a week or more and provide the extensive leisure facilities a vacationer expects. Accordingly, most resort guests are willing to pay higher rates for these services.

Some destination resorts offer a mix of activities suited to the sports enthusiast. The Homestead in Hot Springs, Virginia, for instance, offers in its advertising

> horseback riding, woodland walking, trout fishing, mineral spa, swimming, three 18-hole championship golf courses, tennis, buckboard and surrey driving, skeet and trap shooting, ten pin and lawn bowling, loafing, and skiing.

And the Greenbrier in White Sulphur Springs, West Virginia, describes itself as "a 6,500-acre estate secluded in the beautiful Alleghenies." In addition to sports, the Greenbrier, like most such "adult resorts," offers extensive meeting and convention facilities.

> The new conference center includes ballrooms, auditoriums, theatre, exhibit hall and 25 meeting rooms fully equipped with the latest audiovisual equipment. Capable of serving groups of 10 to 1,100.

---

[32] *Trends in the Hotel Industry* reported income before other fixed charges that ranged from a low of 3 percent to a high of 38 percent compared with just over 20.5 percent for all hotels. The variability in the suite hotel resorts suggests that a small sample size of 50 properties in five regions, or an average of only 10 properties per region, may be a problem, making the reported figures somewhat difficult to interpret.

[33] *Hotels,* January 1990, p. 34.

[34] Severyn Ashkenazy, Remarks made during a panel discussion, Hospitality Industry Investment Conference, New York City, June 1990.

[35] Randall A. Smith, Personal communication to author, June 20, 1991.

A quite different kind of "adult destination" (where, as in the Homestead and the Greenbrier, children are always welcome) is found in Las Vegas, the number one hotel city in terms of hotel sales. Las Vegas is famous for its gambling, but its resort hotels offer much more (including, sometimes, features for the whole family). For example, the Las Vegas Hilton advertises itself as the place

> where the real superstars play in Las Vegas. Now the largest, most complete resort in the world. Incredible dining in eight unsurpassed restaurants, including the spectacular Japanese Fantasyland, Benihana Village! Plus an 8½-acre outdoor recreation deck and even a unique "youth hotel" for the youngsters alone.

These adult-centered resort hotels do, of course, welcome children, but other destination complexes are designed primarily with the family, and especially children, in mind. The most famous of these is Walt Disney World (WDW). Although the resorts we described include many other activities, we can

The Mirage in Las Vegas sets a new standard for destination resort hotels not only with a waterfall and volcano out front but a domed rain forest garden and a special reserve for white tigers used in the hotel's floor show. (Courtesy of the Mirage Hotel & Casino)

accurately say that at WDW several hotels are integrated within a larger entertainment center. That center includes not only the three theme parks for which WDW is best known but also all varieties of water sports on a large lake, a sophisticated campground sporting its own entertainment centers, three golf courses, and the customary amenities and luxuries available at each hotel.

THE MEETING AND CONVENTION MARKET

Two quite different types of properties serve the group market. *Conference centers* serve smaller meetings and are often used by companies for specialized training classes. *Convention hotels,* on the other hand, serve larger groups such as conventions and trade shows.

Conference Centers

A conference center is "a lodging facility where 60 percent or more of total occupancy is generated by conferences and which offers a full-package plan including guest rooms, meals, and full-service conference rooms as well as skilled staff trained to serve meeting planners and attendees." Conference centers are operated by some very large corporations, such as General Motors and the Bell Telephone companies, to provide facilities for training their own employees. Other centers are operated by universities. Finally, private companies operate conference centers that offer a resort-like atmosphere to companies, associations, and other groups for extended seminars and training sessions. A typical cost per day at a university conference center would be from $100 to $150, while a private conference center such as those operated by International Conference Resorts of America, which offers a complete meeting package (CMP), would cost from $200 to $300 per day.[36] The CMP covers not only rooms but meals, meeting facilities, expert assistance in planning the details of the meeting, and a professional staff to ensure that the execution goes smoothly. Facilities include meeting rooms that are designed to be comfortable places to spend long hours of concentrated effort and that provide state-of-the-art audio and visual support. Outside the meeting, these resort properties include spacious lobbies and dining areas, golf courses, tennis courts, as well as health club facilities and swimming pools. While the cost of these facilities is high, the argument in favor of a conference center for a meeting is that *any* meeting represents a major outlay and the object must be to achieve productivity from the expenditure. Conference centers, then, argue that they may cost more but they offer more bang for the buck.

Convention Hotels

These larger properties "provide facilities and services geared to meet the needs of large group and association meetings and trade shows. Typically these

---

[36]Stanley E. Cox, Remarks made during a panel discussion, Hospitality Industry Investment Conference, New York City, June 1991.

hotels have in excess of 400 guest rooms and contain substantial amounts of function and banquet space flexibly designed for use by large meeting groups. They often work in concert with other convention hotels and convention centers to provide facilities for citywide conventions and trade shows."

Morris Lapidus, an architect who has designed convention hotels, provides an interesting and colorful description of the convention hotel and its function:

> The convention hotel is a new form of American hybrid. All of us are familiar with the great American convention, where an organization or corporation gathers as many members as it can in one particular place and fills up a horrendous agenda with lectures, meetings, group discussions, film shows, workshops and lots of drinking. The main reason for all this endeavor is to conduct a forum for ideas, to keep members apprised of what the parent organization has been doing, and to get everybody's idea of where they are going and how they should get there. It is also a nifty tax write-off.

> The convention hotel should be a ceremonial hotel, so far as meeting areas are concerned. This is the place where the "tribe" honors the chiefs, hands out the awards to diligent warriors, and welcomes the initiates. The organization's brass must look and sound good on the platform at meetings and banquets. The warriors—and the warriors' wives when present—should be equally seated and treated. And the novitiates, for whom it is an honor just to be there, must have an opportunity to feel part of the inner circle.

> The convention hotel must also have supersuites for the chiefs and many comfortable but similar rooms for the warriors. The novitiates may be housed more economically although this is seldom the case. They may share rooms and not be permitted to bring along their wives until they're full-fledged warriors.[37]

Lapidus also observed that the guest rooms at conventions are often social centers where friends or business associates come for a drink or an informal meeting. These rooms thus should be spacious and should separate the dressing area from the living quarters. The best arrangement, Lapidus declared, is to provide one double bed and a couch that can become a second double bed in larger rooms. Of course, there is a need for more modest single rooms for "warriors and novitiates," to use his analogy.

OTHER SPECIALIZED SEGMENTS

Condominiums

Condominiums, or "condos" as they are often called, generally offer the features of an apartment building—multiroom apartments with full kitchens,

---

[37]Morris Lapidus, "How Architects Design Rooms Differently," *Cornell Hotel and Restaurant Administration Quarterly,* May 1974, p. 69.

sometimes combined with those of a hotel, such as on-premise food and beverage service. The units, however, are usually sold to individual owners, but the overall property is operated by a management company. Condos that service the vacation market are most commonly located in resort areas.

Two kinds of condo ownership are available. Some condos are sold outright, and their owners have the right to year-round occupancy. Another, increasingly common practice is to sell "time-shares," the right to occupy the condo permanently and as an owner for a limited and specific time, with others having that right for other time periods. The price of a time-share usually depends on the desirability of the particular time period, with less attractive time periods costing substantially less than peak periods do. On the other hand, some time-sharing arrangements require the owners to buy shares in high, middle, and off seasons. Thus, for instance, a time-share package might be offered for one week each in the months of July, October, January, and April. Time-share-swapping networks enable the owners to swap with one another a week they own in Miami for, say, the same week or even a different week in Aspen.

Condos are competitive with hotels in two ways. First, they represent a form of interindustry competition in the same way that a second home or a camper does. That is, the owner of a condo in a resort location is much less likely to be a hotel customer because his or her funds are already invested in a vacation property.

Besides being an alternative to a hotel for their owner, condos—both those sold outright and those marketed as time-shares—are often rented out by the management company when the owner does not want to use the property. On a day-to-day basis, this makes them very real competitors with the hotels in their market. Some condo properties, particularly those offering many services, are operated by hotel companies and are marketed as resorts. Indeed, some companies have sold significant portions of a resort as condos or have built a condo component into their plan for the development and financing of a new resort. In effect, the sale of condominiums has become an important source of financing for the owners of the resort.

Bed and Breakfast

With the escalation of transient rates at hotels, an opportunity has been created to serve a more price-sensitive market. One response is the economy lodging segment we discussed earlier. Another is the provision of accommodations in a private home or the conversion of a residential property to accommodate transient guests. In a study of bed-and-breakfast (B&B) establishments in New York state,[38] nearly three quarters fit the first category, offering 4 or less rooms. Only 10 percent of the B&Bs in the state had more than 10 rooms.

---

[38] Chad P. Davison and Tommy L. Brown, *Cornell Hotel and Restaurant Administration Quarterly,* May 1988, pp. 17–21.

B&Bs, in total, account for about 2 percent of the overnight accommodations in that state but account for less than one half of one percent of room sales. B&Bs usually operate with low occupancies but, with very limited capital or operating costs, this is not a serious problem. Most B&B owners provide all the labor themselves, but one in four employs full- or part-time help. Most B&Bs, it would seem, are operated as a sideline, a source of "extra" income rather than as a principal occupation. There are about 20,000 B&Bs in the United States.[39] The business has become well enough established that a firm that cares for other people's B&Bs has sprung up to give owners a chance for a vacation.[40] B&Bs are also beginning to cut into the business travel market, offering people traveling on business not only an attractive rate but a home away from home. The highly personal style of the B&B—being a guest in someone's home—appeals to many travelers, both business and leisure.

LODGING AS A COMMUNITY INSTITUTION

You may have seen the following slogan behind the counter in some business:

This is a nonprofit business. We didn't plan it that way; it just happened!

To a greater degree than in many other industries, that not-so-funny joke applies to hotels and motor hotels, except that the meager profits may not be all that unexpected. To see why, we need to shift our attention from the purposes of the individual guest to those of the community.

In many small towns, the hotel or motel is more or less a public institution. It is a gathering place for local leaders and provides hospitality for visitors to the city's principal businesses. Because of these community benefits, some small-town hotels have been built more or less as nonprofit operations, with both ownership and even capital loaned without any real expectations of much profit. The benefits to the community—and to its principal institutions—are seen as sufficient to offset a lack of profit. Such resignation as this may not be the rule, but it is far from uncommon.

In practice, however, most hotel operators discover that an unprofitable hotel is also an unsuccessful hotel. Over the long haul, the need for operating subsidies, or the simple absence of sufficient financial return, makes the property lose its luster and then become downright unattractive. Eventually the owners grow reluctant to pay adequate executive salaries and to spend the funds necessary to maintain the physical plant. Gradually the plant decays, the organization loses its enthusiasm, and eventually the hotel closes its doors.

---

[39] *Lodging,* September 1990, p. 66.
[40] *TRA Foodservice Digest/John Naisbitt's Newsletter,* October 25, 1990, p. 8.

The community need for hotel services, however, often leads real estate developers to promote hotels as a part of real estate developments in large cities. A developer acquires the rights to a large tract of land and plans a complex of office buildings, department stores, and other retail establishments. The development may be situated downtown; it may work with urban redevelopment; or it may settle at the edge of the city as part of an office park or an industrial park consisting of offices, light manufacturing, or warehousing and distribution centers. Although the development's overt purpose is suggested by its title (urban redevelopment, office park, industrial park), one of the first buildings to go up will probably be a hotel or motor hotel. The developers hope, of course, that it will earn a profit, but they build it mainly because of its importance to the overall development.

The developer may not be particularly interested in entering the hotel field, but the development surely needs the hotel. Visitors with business in the area need a place to stay. Headquarters units need space for sales meetings and other technical conferences. Those with offices or who are otherwise working in the area need a place to eat lunch, get a snack, meet for a drink, and perhaps entertain out-of-town guests at dinner at the end of the day.

Most development projects are preceded by a feasibility study of the project's economics. Two extracts from such feasibility studies, conducted in a medium-sized city (Middleton) in a basically rural area and a large metropolitan center (Bigton), suggest some of the developer's underlying motives. (Because these are confidential documents, the identity of the cities has been disguised.)

> [This is] one of a series of studies dealing with the proposed Middleton Square developments in the Washington Street Urban Renewal Project area in Middleton.
>
> The urban renewal area covers six city blocks between the existing downtown area and the shore of Lake Washington. The proposed Middleton Square development contemplates a comprehensive, integrated development of new office structures (one of which is already under construction), adequate automobile parking, a full range of retail facilities including a major full-line department store, and the 300-room hotel which is the subject of this analysis. All of these facilities are expected to upgrade and modernize Downtown Middleton.

In a study conducted in a Bigton hotel development under consideration, the following information came under the heading of "Impact and Location":

> A new, large, and spectacularly designed hotel in Downtown Bigton would have a significant impact on Bigton. Properly promoted, the proposed hotel would not only focus more attention on Bigton as one of the nation's great metropolitan centers, but the hotel would also substantially improve the inventory of transient lodging accommodations in the downtown area, and thereby strengthen that area's competitive position in the lodging market. If

the hotel is as successful as predicted in this analysis, it will attract comparable competition to the downtown area—further reinforcing that area's position in the local lodging market.

The function of a hotel property, then, sometimes involves what economists call *externalities*—benefits external to the hotel itself, such as community development, the enhancement of property values in the area in general, and service to people who need food and lodging and would not visit the area without them. It's hardly surprising, then, that many new hotel properties have financial difficulties. This is particularly true for properties built during waves of real estate speculation such as those that occurred in the late 1920s, the early 1970s, and the 1980s. For sophisticated hotel operators, however, this kind of situation creates real opportunities.

FRANCHISE SYSTEMS

The word *franchise* comes from the language of political science and refers to a right bestowed by some authority. For example, when Kemmons Wilson created a successful operating format for a motor hotel, he began to *enfranchise* others with the right to use Holiday Inn's name. To do this, he adopted a practice similar to the *referral groups* already in existence and operated mainly by Quality Courts and Best Western Motels[41] (now Quality Inns and Best Western).

The general structure of a lodging franchise is the same as that of the business format franchise described in Chapter 3. The services to new and continuing franchises offered by hotel franchisors are also similar to those described in Chapter 3, and you may wish to refer to that section. We will confine ourselves here to a brief discussion of three important values provided to hotels by franchise organizations: a national identity, a referral system, and quality assurance. We will also look briefly at costs in franchising and some possible impacts of recent developments on franchise systems.

A NATIONAL IDENTITY AND BRAND NAME

In a market of national travelers, the identity of an independent property has little meaning except to the local townspeople and its frequent visitors. On the other hand, Motel 6, Holiday Inn or Hilton Inn convey meaning to travelers

---

[41] There is an important technical difference between a *franchise system* (in which the franchising company grants a right) and a *referral system* (in which a property and its ownership become members). There is not a great deal of difference, however, in how they operate, although the referral group is sometimes characterized by greater owner autonomy. For our purpose, the word *system* will denote either kind of operation.

One of the major benefits that a franchise company offers is a nationally advertised brand name. (Courtesy of Sheraton Hotels and Days Inns)

from any part of the nation. To these travelers, the mere mention of these names suggests the kind, degree, and probable cost of the services available.

National franchising companies spend portions of their own budgets on advertising in appropriate regional markets and in the national market. Most franchise systems also levy an advertising fee on each franchisee and pool these funds. Thus, the collective advertising fund makes it possible to purchase ads too expensive for an individual property. These include such media efforts as commercials on national radio and television and layouts in national magazines.

Franchise hotel-motel companies also print national directories showing the location of each of the system's properties. They provide national sales representation to trade and travel organizations and prepare specialized directories targeting those markets. Perhaps the most important services that franchisers offer the guest — and therefore, the operator — are referral systems and quality assurance programs.

RESERVATION SYSTEMS

When a guest wants to make a reservation, he or she can call a single number and either have a reservation at a distant point confirmed immediately or obtain help in locating alternative accommodations. Once the guest begins a trip, accommodations for subsequent nights' stops are only as far away as the room telephone. Thus, once a hotel system has a guest's patronage for a single night, it is in a favored position to sell the guest all subsequent accommodations. Most referral or reservations systems are either computer based or use a WATS (Wide Area Telephone System) line. WATS systems permit leasing of telephone lines, which drastically reduces the cost per call for high-volume use.

Some reservation systems rely on the local innkeeper to "deposit" a certain number of rooms of each type available. The computer acts as a kind of "bank" or clearinghouse for all units. The computer sells all rooms "on deposit" for the day in question without consulting the hotel in which the reservation is made. As each room is sold, the hotel is notified of the guest's name, the type of room wanted, and other information (arrival time and so on). This information is then used to block rooms for the arriving guests.

Increasingly, however, central reservation systems (CRS) are interfaced with the individual company's computerized reservation system. This eliminates the need to "deposit" rooms, and to update those deposits. It also gives the CRS "last-room availability"—that is, the ability to sell every available room.

Smaller chains may use an 800 number that is provided—under the hotel group's own name—by another company, such as GE Information Services or J.C. Penny Telemarketing.[42] These companies make reservations and transmit them to the local innkeeper's front desk by phone or interface directly with the property's in-house computer and reservation system. A recent development in reservation technology is leading more and more properties to adopt computerized reservation systems that can interface directly with a CRS. This development is the "universal interchange," that is, the interfacing of many different travel business computer reservation systems.

During the 1970s, a number of efforts were made to interconnect hotel reservation systems but these were not financially successful. In the mid-1980s, however, airlines began to handle hotel and car rental reservations in addition to their own traffic. Since then, according to Laurence Chervenak, a leading expert on hotel technology, the pace of change has quickened, with travel companies investing $3 billion between 1988 and 1990 in hardware and software to support interactive reservation networks. In 1985, 2 percent of hotel reservations were made by airline CRS systems. By 1991, that volume had grown to 20 percent and is still growing rapidly. CRSs are providing 60 to 70 percent of total volume in some hotels. Since not only airlines but most travel agencies and car companies, as well as hotel chains, are connected to one of the three major CRSs, the potential for access to travelers is tremendous.

The worldwide toll-free reservation systems that are now emerging are likely to be a major force for change in lodging. As fiber-optic communica-

---

[42] The discussion of the CRS that follows draws extensively on the article, "CRS, the Past, the Present, and the Future" by Laurence Chervenak, *Lodging*, June 1991, pp. 25–30.

tions, with their enormous carrying capacity, come into play later in this decade, the amount of information that computer systems will have available about a property is likely to rise and the cost to drop. Michael Rose, president of Promus, suggests that the importance of interconnection will be such that flexibility rather than cost will be the major consideration in reservation systems.[43]

There clearly will be room for independents to play in the interconnect game. A system established by Accommodations British Columbia, which is available to all members of the British Columbia and Yukon Hotel Association as well as motels and campgrounds in that province, proposes to provide all its members direct access to a system served by an 800 number and manned by reservations agents. That system, in turn, would also be linked to the airline megasystems.[44]

INSPECTION SYSTEMS: QUALITY ASSURANCE

Almost all franchise and referral groups specify a minimum level of physical plant and service requirements before admitting a new operation to the system. These requirements generally include a restaurant, a swimming pool, certain types of furniture and fixtures, and such operating services as room service and a 24-hour front desk.

In addition to specifying operating standards, a system usually enforces the maintenance of these standards through regular inspections made by either the systems inspection department or an established member of the system. The detail and care devoted to quality assurance by the modern motor hotel system provides assurance to the traveler of quality accommodations. It also maintains a level of quality among all operations that protects the integrity of the brand and helps secure repeat patronage.

COST OF A HOTEL FRANCHISE

An introductory fee in the order of $50,000 to $100,000 covers application cost, review of site and market potential, evaluation of plans, inspection during construction, and preopening service.[45] Continuing costs range from just over 1 percent of sales to over 8 percent and include the franchisor's royalty (3 to 6.5 percent), a marketing fee (1 to 3 percent), and the charges for the reservation system (1 to 2.5 percent). Interestingly, the lowest total affiliation cost is an association or referral organization, Best Western (1.2 percent).

---

[43] Rose, Address to Hospitality Industry Investment Conference.

[44] Chervenak, "CRS, the Past, the Present, and the Future," p. 43.

[45] Data in this section are taken from *Rushmore on Valuation* (Mineola, N.Y.: Rushmore Valuation Services, Winter 1989).

OUTLOOK FOR FRANCHISING IN LODGING

The forces that argue most strongly for affiliation are the importance of the brand name, the value of the central reservation system, and the ability to join in a national and international marketing effort. On the other hand, there are a number of factors that may, in time, undermine the power of lodging franchise systems.[46]

In franchising's early days, there was a significant stability to the franchise relationship. The practice of treating a franchise system as a financial asset to be bought or sold, as has happened with Holiday Inn, Ramada, and Howard Johnson franchises as well as with other companies, however, may have undermined that stability for some franchisees. Moreover, the practice of conversion franchising—that is, of soliciting properties away from other franchise systems—has led many franchisees to switch brands. Some properties have had two, three, or more franchises. Moreover, the advent of interconnected reservations systems that accept not only chains but properties that belong to voluntary associations that have arranged an interconnection may reduce somewhat the unique value of chains' reservation systems. Finally, the relatively solid performance and consumer acceptance of referral organizations such as Best Western (rated the top moderate-priced hotel chain by *Consumer's Reports*) may raise questions in the minds of some franchisees about the need to pay five or six times as much for an affiliation. If such questioning becomes rampant, we may see more referral organizations emerging in competition with franchising companies.

Clearly, no one would argue that franchise systems will disappear. We will need to watch, however, to see whether developments in the financial and technological dimensions of the industry begin to reduce the unique importance of franchise networks from their present high level.

SUMMARY

We began by looking at an earlier lodging industry, which was shaped principally by transportation and destination patterns. We saw, however, that in a marketing-oriented lodging industry, guest needs and preferences require closer consideration. These *are* still shaped by transportation and destinations but also by purpose of travel. Personal and business travelers have different needs, just as group business makes a different demand on the hotel than does the individual traveler. We saw, too, that demographic factors such as age, sex, income level, and family status or life-cycle stage also affect demand for lodging and preferences for lodging types.

[46] For a fuller discussion of these issues, see Thomas F. Powers, "The Lodging Industry: Dominance by Giants? A Contrarion View," *Hospitality Research Journal,* forthcoming.

We reviewed categories of lodging. Full-service hotels, which can be divided into luxury, upscale, and basic, provide the widest variety of facilities and amenities. All categories of full-service hotels are likely to be affected by oversupply for some time to come, with basic full-service properties most severely affected. The economy lodging business has a limited service segment that emphasizes rooms that are competitive with full-service properties. Food service and meeting facilities are severely limited but companies emphasize high quality in those services that are provided. The hard-budget segment within the economy lodging business emphasizes low price and smaller guest rooms and/or very simple accommodations.

All-suite properties serve the transient market but also have a segment that serves the long-stay market. The all-suite property offers separate sleeping and living areas. Long-stay all-suites offer larger suites and more extensive facilities in the guest unit. Emphasis in all-suite properties is on the rooms side of the house, but some food service is usually provided.

Resort hotels are in themselves destinations for travel and must offer a wide variety of amusements and activities. The conference center is often constructed in a resort-like setting, offering extensive activities, but it places special emphasis on meeting facilities and expert meeting service. Convention hotels meet the needs of large groups such as associations and trade shows. As such, they are larger hotels with extensive meeting space. Condominiums and bed-and-breakfast properties are specialized lodging facilities but compete only marginally with hotels. Lodging serves important community functions, but those functions, in the long run, will not be served successfully unless the hotel can operate profitably.

Franchise systems in lodging provide a national identity, a reservations network, and quality assurance. Franchise organizations and memberships are no longer as stable as they once were. The development of travel industrywide reservation networks may reduce the value of franchise organizations' proprietary networks. While franchise systems will continue to be important to operators, the emerging reservations network, involving all travel industry elements, may have a major impact on how hotel rooms are sold and on affiliation choices of individual properties.

KEY WORDS AND CONCEPTS

To help you review this chapter, keep in mind the following:

Transportation system   Motel
Destination   Motor Hotel

Airport and downtown hotel
Business traveler
Individual traveler
Meeting and convention
    guests
Leisure and personal travel
Full-service hotel
   Luxury
   Upscale
   Basic
Economy lodging
   Limited service
   Hard budget
All-suites
   Transient
   Extended and long stay
   Construction costs

Resort hotels
Meeting and conference
   market
   Conference centers
   Convention hotels
Condominiums
Bed and breakfast (B&B)
Community institutions
Franchise systems
National identity
Central reservation system
   (CRS)
   800 number
   Interface
Inspection systems
Quality assurance

REVIEW QUESTIONS

1. Do transportation systems and destination patterns still have an impact on lodging? If so, how?

2. Discuss which business and personal travel customers are likely to be attracted to each of the lodging types identified.

3. Which of the full-service properties are likely to experience the most competition? Why?

4. How do the travel motives related to the two segments of economy lodging differ? Describe the typical customer for each.

5. What is your assessment of the prospects of the all-suite hotel? Does it represent one of the worst economic propositions, the next step in the development of the luxury hotel, or something else?

6. How are resort hotels, conference centers, and convention hotels alike? How are they different?

7. Do you expect franchise systems to become more or less important?

Courtesy of Days Inn, Atlanta, Georgia

HOTEL AND MOTEL OPERATIONS

THE PURPOSE OF THIS CHAPTER

It is impossible to teach someone how to ''run a hotel'' from a book. Only practical experience can teach a subject so complex. This chapter is intended, however, to help you learn more quickly from experience by making you familiar with: (1) the major operating and staff departments in a hotel, (2) the information flows that tie a hotel together and how they are handled, and (3) the patterns of income and cost that affect hotel operations. Finally, this chapter outlines the major hospitality career entry points and the paths available for advancement.

THIS CHAPTER SHOULD HELP YOU

1. Name the major functional departments in a hotel and explain how they relate to one another.

2. Trace the general flow of work accomplished in the major departments and their key subunits.

3. Explain why the food and beverage department, though not the principal source of profit, is so important to a hotel's success.

4. Relate the principal sources of income and expense to the appropriate department according to the Uniform System of Accounts for Hotels.

5. Define the role of yield management in hotel industry pricing.

6. Explain how accounting statements can be used to measure the performance of key executives and department heads in the hotel.

7. Define and use the key operating ratios and terms that describe an operation.

8. Explain the relationship of the financial structure of a hotel to its cost of operations.

Hotel properties range from tiny to huge in size. Although large properties such as Chicago's Hilton and Towers or the Excalibur in Las Vegas catch the public's imagination, the majority of properties offer between 100 and 200 units. Because most students will encounter these kinds of properties in their work, the examples in this chapter will assume a motor hotel in the 100- to 125-unit range.

Surprisingly enough, most properties perform basically the same functions, but the way in which they accomplish them varies with the property size. When there are significant variations in routine practices in larger properties, we will note them. Our emphasis, however, will be on the similarities found throughout the hotel business rather than on the variations.

MAJOR FUNCTIONAL DEPARTMENTS

Figure 8.1 shows the basic functional areas of any hotel or motor hotel. This figure includes elements not found in some motels, however, as some motels lack food and beverage departments, and many do not have a gift shop or garage. Our purpose, however, is not to draw a chart that represents all properties inclusively; that would be impossible. Rather, we have outlined the major activities usually present in most properties.

A large property may employ a general manager under whom an executive assistant manager assumes responsibility for day-to-day operations. There is often a resident manager who supervises several departments on his or her side of the house, as Figure 8.2 shows, and a food and beverage manager who reports to the "exec."

On the other hand, in the 100-unit inn diagrammed in Figure 8.3, the general manager may be responsible—with an executive housekeeper and perhaps a front-office manager or chief clerk—for running the rooms and for supervising an assistant manager responsible for food and beverage. Thus, the executive staff may vary from two or three persons supported by a few department heads and key employees in a small property, to a substantial bureaucratic organization made of the many layers of authority necessary to operate a large complex property.

It is important to note that a smaller property may have functional areas (food production, bar, dining room, dish, pot, receiving, and cleanup, for instance, in the food and beverage area) but no true department heads. The

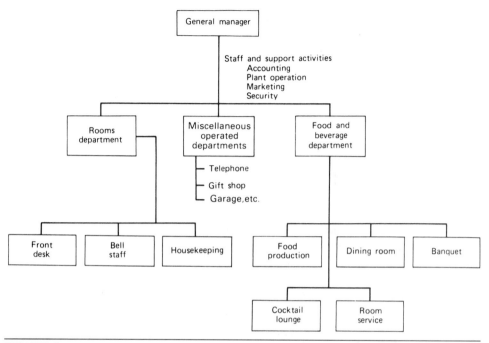

FIGURE 8.1 Major functional areas found in hotels and motor hotels.

restaurant in a small inn may be run by a restaurant manager who directly supervises all the employees with help from *lead employees* in each functional area on each shift. For instance, the hostesses for the day and evening shifts may provide leadership to the dining room staff during their shifts; a head cook on each shift does the same for the kitchen staff. The manager may be responsible for hiring and discipline on both shifts, usually along with someone designated as an assistant when the manager is off duty. This arrangement is economical and convenient in small properties as long as the restaurant manager delegates enough responsibility to avoid becoming overcommitted.

THE ROOMS SIDE OF THE HOUSE

Room rental is a hotel's main business and its major source of profit. The day-to-day operations of the typical rooms department yield a *departmental income* (the revenue remaining after the direct operating costs of the department are taken out) of about 70 percent, compared with 15 to 20 percent for the food and beverage department. Thus, the people on the rooms side of the house are crucial to the operation's financial success.

THE FRONT OFFICE

More than any other group, the desk clerks represent the hotel to its guests. They greet the guests on their arrival and make them welcome (or not,

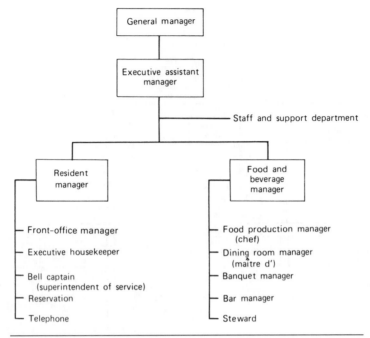

FIGURE 8.2 Simplified organizational chart for large hotel.

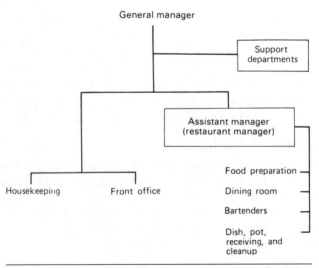

FIGURE 8.3 Functional organizational chart for small motor hotel.

The front desk is the nerve center of the hotel and the point of maximum guest contact for the rooms side of the house. (Courtesy of Country Hospitality Corp.)

depending on their manners). If something goes wrong, most guests will complain first to the front desk. And when the guests leave, the desk clerk checks them out. If anything has gone wrong, this will be a good time to catch it. ("I hope you enjoyed your stay, sir"—and then *listen* to the answer.) Although the duties of the desk overlap, they will differ with the work shift.

In the following discussion, a small inn serves as a model. The functions in a larger property may be broken down into specialties (reception desk, cashier, mail, and key clerk) performed by different persons. Our purpose is to describe the work and the functions. Your own observations will illustrate for you the variety of ways in which the work is organized.

The *morning clerk* works from 6:45 A.M. to 3:15 P.M. With a half-hour meal break, this is an eight-hour day. Because the evening crew comes in at 2:45 P.M. and the night auditor goes off duty at 7:15 A.M., all shifts overlap so as to ensure a smooth transition from one shift to the next. Some properties maintain a logbook in which information or events with which later shifts should be familiar are noted. The new shift's first task on coming on duty is to check the logbook to make sure they're fully briefed.

The morning shift's work is concentrated in the early hours (from around 7:30 A.M. until midmorning) on checking out guests. At the same time, of course, the employees on this shift answer the guests' questions and perform other routine tasks. But their main responsibility is checking out guests.

When a guest is ready to leave, the clerk verifies the final amount of the bill, posts any recent charges, and assists the guest in settling with cash, check, or credit card, according to the house credit policy. This credit policy, which lays down guidelines for accepting checks and specifies the acceptable credit cards, is an important part of any clerk's training.

Although the technical aspects of the clerk's work are important, the courtesy a clerk accords a guest is at least as important. A departing guest must have an opportunity to register complaints if he or she has had problems. The morning clerk's work thus includes a special responsibility for ensuring that guests leave with the intention of returning to the hotel on their next visit to town.

As guests check out and their rooms become vacant, housekeeping is notified. This permits housekeeping to make up the rooms promptly so that they will be ready when new guests check in later that day. As the rooms are made up, housekeeping notifies the desk so that early arrivals can be accommodated in rooms that are ready to rent. Alternatively, the room status can be changed to *ready to rent* at housekeeping's computer terminal later, when the room is made up.

Most properties now have computerized reservation systems that keep track of the balance between rooms available and reservation requests. The morning clerk and her or his supervisor, the guest services manager (or front office manager), monitor this process and block any special reservation requests. In a property that does not have a computerized reservation system, they will block the day's reservations.

The *afternoon clerk's* work is shaped by the fact that the heaviest arrival time begins, in most transient houses, a little after 4:00 P.M. The afternoon clerk, therefore, takes over the reservation planning begun by the morning clerk and greets the guests as they arrive.

First impressions are crucial, and the desk clerk's warm welcome often sets the tone for the guest's entire stay. By remembering the names of repeat visitors, meeting special demands when possible (such as for a ground-floor room), and bearing in mind that the guest has probably had a hard, tiring day of work and travel, the desk clerk can convey the feeling that the guest is among friends at last. The clerk checks in the guest, and that process establishes the accounting and other records necessary for the stay.

The *night auditor* is a desk clerk with special accounting responsibilities. When things quiet down (usually by 1:00 A.M.), the auditor posts those charges

If guests voice any complaints at checkout, the morning clerk should deal with them tactfully so that the guests will return. (Courtesy of La Quinta Inn)

not posted by the earlier shifts, including (most especially) the room charge. He or she then audits the day's guest transactions and verifies the balance due the hotel from guests as of the close of the day's operations. The auditing process can be quite complicated, but simply stated, the auditor compares the balance owed to the hotel at the end of yesterday with today's balance. He or she verifies that the balance is the correct result of deducting all payments from yesterday's balance and adding all of today's charges. This process, summarized graphically in Figure 8.4, not only verifies today's closing balance of guest accounts owed to the hotel but also systematically reviews all transactions when an error in the balance is found. For this reason, the night auditor's job is important, requiring intelligence, training, and integrity.

"Yesterday's" Closing Balance of Accounts Owed the Hotel by Guests

<u>MINUS</u>	all payments received today
<u>PLUS</u>	all charges guests made today
<u>EQUALS</u>	"Today's" closing balance

FIGURE 8.4 The night audit: a schematic view.

Automation of the Front Office

While the main elements of personal service—a smile, a friendly greeting, and generally courteous treatment of the guest—cannot readily be automated, much of the clerical work has been greatly simplified in most hotels by the installation of a Property Management System (PMS). The PMS improves operational efficiency by eliminating repetitive tasks and improves service by providing information more quickly and accurately. At the same time, the PMS improves operational control.[1] We need to understand the PMS in order to see how the front office functions.

The computer program (or programs) that embody the PMS prompt the clerk to follow an appropriate work sequence for every task. For instance, when a guest checks into the hotel, the clerk indicates if the guest has a reservation or not. If the guest has a reservation, the clerk need only type in the name and the computer will retrieve the reservation and automatically print out the necessary records. In most cases, the guest is simply asked to sign his or her name. If the guest doesn't have a reservation, the clerk gets the necessary information, following the format on the front-desk computer screen (depicted in Figure 8.5).

When the guest checks out, the computer once again presents a screen with prompts (note the menu at the bottom of the screen) that help the clerk to move through the appropriate sequence, verifying the balance with the guest, posting any late charges, and accepting payment by credit card or cash or billing the account directly if prior arrangements have been made. Figure 8.6 shows the screen the clerk sees when checking out Mr. Worthington.

Where the front-desk computer is interfaced (that is, electronically interconnected) to other systems, such as restaurant and bar point-of-sales (POS) terminals and a housekeeping-department terminal, front-office clerical rou-

[1] Douglas Engel and Joseph Marko, "Property Management System," *Lodging,* February 1986, pp. 17–20.

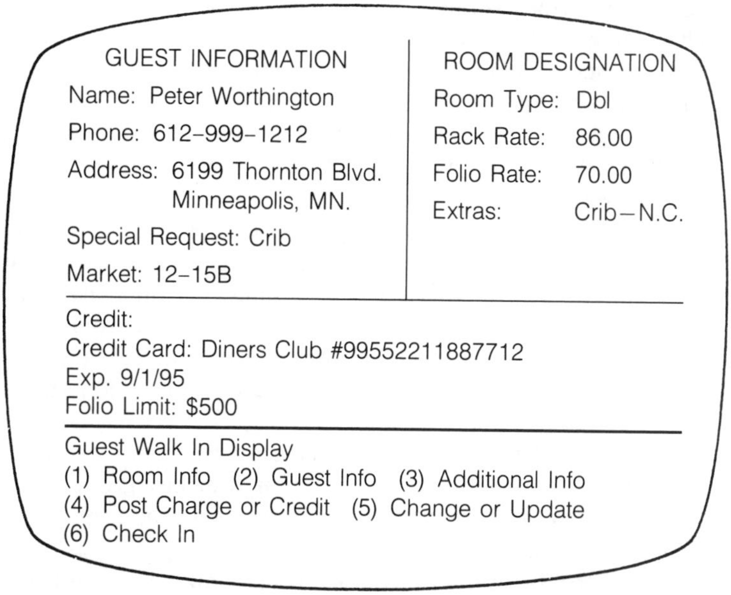

GUEST INFORMATION

Name: Peter Worthington

Phone: 612-999-1212

Address: 6199 Thornton Blvd.
Minneapolis, MN.

Special Request: Crib

Market: 12-15B

ROOM DESIGNATION

Room Type: Dbl

Rack Rate: 86.00

Folio Rate: 70.00

Extras: Crib - N.C.

Credit:
Credit Card: Diners Club #99552211887712
Exp. 9/1/95
Folio Limit: $500

Guest Walk In Display
(1) Room Info (2) Guest Info (3) Additional Info
(4) Post Charge or Credit (5) Change or Update
(6) Check In

FIGURE 8.5 The walk-in registration screen. Note the "menu" across the bottom of the screen that prompts the clerk as to the choices of activity appropriate to dealing with a walk-in.

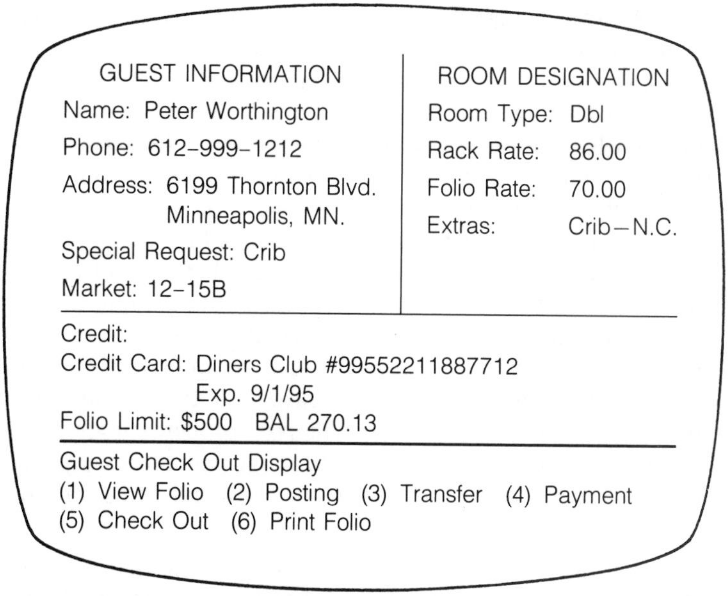

GUEST INFORMATION

Name: Peter Worthington

Phone: 612-999-1212

Address: 6199 Thornton Blvd.
Minneapolis, MN.

Special Request: Crib

Market: 12-15B

ROOM DESIGNATION

Room Type: Dbl

Rack Rate: 86.00

Folio Rate: 70.00

Extras: Crib - N.C.

Credit:
Credit Card: Diners Club #99552211887712
Exp. 9/1/95
Folio Limit: $500   BAL 270.13

Guest Check Out Display
(1) View Folio (2) Posting (3) Transfer (4) Payment
(5) Check Out (6) Print Folio

FIGURE 8.6 The check-out screen.

tines are further simplified. When guests settle a dinner or bar check by charging it to their room number, the cashier in the food or beverage (F&B) outlet posts this entry on their POS, and that posting is automatically entered on the guest's bill at the front-office terminal. Manual posting is required for any charges that are not automatically handled by the system, such as a guest paid out. Where F&B is not interfaced, the F&B charges are posted manually at the front office.

In much the same way, when housekeeping is interfaced, at the time the guest checks out the room shows up as vacant and ready to make up on the housekeeping terminal. When housekeeping personnel have cleaned the room, they make the appropriate entry and the room is automatically added to the ready-to-rent total in the front-office terminal. Where housekeeping is not interfaced, lists of "on change" and "ready-to-rent" rooms are usually communicated back and forth by phone.

More and more properties interface their front office not only with other departments but also with their chain or franchise group's central reservation system (CRS). This permits the CRS to determine room availability directly and automatically from the individual property. This is an important time-saver for front-office staff and helps maximize the usefulness of the CRS to the individual property. The PMS can also be used to automate a number of other functions in the hotel, as shown in Figure 8.7.

Reservations and Yield Management

Traditionally the hotel industry has looked at occupancy as a measure of success. Another indicator of operational success that we have always consulted is the average rate per rented room (the average daily rate, or ADR). Yield management puts these two together and, using forecasting based on the history of past sales, sets out to get the best *combination* of occupancy and ADR.[2] Yield management, then, involves varying room rates according to the demand for rooms in any given time period. The argument is that when the hotel is going to be full, it makes no sense to sell any rooms at special discount rates. On the other hand, on a night when the hotel is definitely not going to fill, selling a room at a discounted price is better than not selling it at all.

In practice, there are many situations between a full house and very low occupancy that need decisions about rates. In addition, there is the decision to overbook, that is, to take more reservations than there are rooms available based on a "no-show" factor that can be built into the yield management system on a seasonal and daily basis. While the staff at some properties operates its own yield management system, increasingly companies use computer programs specially designed to take account of a property's history of demand for rooms and to forecast demand and adjust rates as demand shifts

---

[2] Yield management is described more fully by one of its originators in lodging, Eric Orkin, in his article, "Boosting Revenues Through Yield Management," *Cornell Hotel and Restaurant Administration Quarterly,* February 1988, pp. 52–58. The discussion below draws on Mr. Orkin's article.

Property Management Functions

Front-Office Functions

Core Features	Optional Features
Guest Accounting and Service	Guest history
• Check in and checkout	Travel agent accounting
• Folio accounting	Budgeting statistics
• Telephone information	Word processing
Operations	
• Guest reservations	
• Night audit	
• Group registration and folio accounting	
• Housekeeping: Room status	

Back-Office Functions

Core Features	Optional Features
Accounts payable	Inventory
Payroll	Purchasing
General ledger	Budgeting
	Forecasting
	Purchasing

Other Service Functions

Sales and marketing analysis
Package and meal plans
Function-room scheduling
Banquet and catering sales
Word processing
Promotional mailings
Maintenance scheduling
Forecasting
Graphics: Menus

FIGURE 8.7 Property management functions. (*Source:* Adapted from Douglas Engel and Joseph Marko, "Property Management Systems," *Lodging,* February 1986, pp. 17–20.)

The front desk provides one of the first impressions that shape the guest's experience. The guest is unlikely to forget the front desk at Las Vegas's Mirage Hotel. It is situated in front of a wall-size coral reef aquarium. (Courtesy of Mirage Hotel & Casino)

from period to period. Increasingly central reservations systems will have yield management capabilities built into their program.[3]

Yield management does pose management problems. The first is the potential for guest confusion — and resentment — when confronted with different rates for the same services, depending on when a reservation is made. While customers are accustomed to variable rates on airfares, they may resent them with hotels. As Professor Sheryl Kimes of Cornell put it, "The airline industry comprises a small number of major competitors, and customers seldom have much choice. Hotels, on the other hand, have numerous competitors."[4]

Another problem is employee morale. To quote Kimes again,

> Yield management systems take the guesswork out of how many rooms to sell at what price but they also take some of the judgment responsibilities out of reservationists' and front desk workers' jobs. If a yield management system is not structured to allow workers some latitude to use their judgment, the people who have to use it might grow to resent the system.[5]

[3] *Hotel Motel Management,* October 22, 1990, pp. 85–86.

[4] Sheryl E. Kimes, "The Basics of Yield Management," *Cornell Hotel and Restaurant Administration Quarterly,* November 1989, p. 46.

[5] Kimes, "The Basics of Yield Management," p. 46.

As with so much in hotel operations, careful employee training is essential to secure an effective yield management system that is operated in a way that will not offend guests. To illustrate, an employee who is not well trained or who resents the system might say, "Sorry, we're going to fill that night so you'll have to pay the full rate." A properly trained employee might answer the same request, "I'm afraid we've sold out all of the rooms in that rate class, but we have some very nice poolside rooms available." Clearly the guest reaction to the two approaches would make quite a difference in future patronage.

While yield management is new to lodging, it can also be used in a number of other industries. Yield management is most widely used in the airline industry but can also be used in selling car rentals, theme park admissions, seats at sports events, cruises, hospital facilities, advertising time and freight shipments.[6]

TELEPHONE

Because the system of accounting for hotels recognizes the telephone activity as a separate department for revenue purposes, one often hears about the *telephone department*. But only in the largest hotels is there really a separate organizational unit to match this designation, and in such hotels, it is headed by a chief operator. The telephone service in many properties is handled by a person who also serves as a second desk clerk. Many properties, particularly those of approximately 100 units with automatic phone systems, require the desk clerks to operate the switchboard as part of their regular duties.

HOUSEKEEPING

Housekeeping, that less-than-glamorous but essential department, is as much a production department of a hotel as the front desk and bell staff are service departments. It is clear that without clean rooms to rent, a hotel would have to close. For this reason, the management should always pay close attention to morale factors such as pay and worker recognition in the housekeeping department.

The housekeeping department is usually headed by an executive housekeeper. In a smaller property, a linen room assistant may double as an assistant housekeeper and inspector. In larger properties, the executive housekeeper will have at least one assistant and several supervisors, generally known as inspectors, who supervise maids in a designated area.

In some hotels, housemen take responsibility for cleaning the halls and heavy work such as moving furniture. These employees often form a separate subdepartment. Hotels with their own laundries often assign the supervision of that area to the housekeeping departments. Generally a working laundry supervisor or lead worker handles routine supervision under the executive housekeeper's general direction.

---

[6]"Making Yield Management Work," *Travel and Tourism Bulletin,* June 1991.

THE BELL STAFF

Many motor hotels do without a bell staff because most of their guests prefer to "room" themselves. On the other hand, the bell staff plays an important role in the larger and more luxurious hotels. The process of rooming a guest includes more than just carrying luggage and showing a guest to a room. Rather, it begins when the clerk assigns a room. At this point the bellman takes charge, welcoming the guest in both word and manner and, on entering the room, demonstrating its operations and features. He or she shows the guest how to operate the air-conditioning and turn on room and bath lights. The bellman will usually turn on the television and run through the channels and networks available. He may also indicate when the food service is open and provide other information the guest may need.

In luxury hotels, the *concierge* offers the guests important services. He or she is expert in giving directions to local attractions, securing tickets to shows,

The bell captain or concierge plays a crucial role in making available the information about places and services the guest needs for a successful stay. (Courtesy of Sonesta Hotels)

and recommending tours and other entertainment. The concierge knows about local transportation, tour schedules, and nearly any other information a tourist might want. The concierge concept is unique to luxury hotels, or to luxury floors in larger hotels catering to a range of pocketbooks. In most hotels, the front desk and bell staff generally share the work that the concierge does in the luxury property, although the decreasing size of most bell staffs today restricts this service. Nevertheless, it is important to see that the guest (who is, after all, usually an outsider to the community) has some place in the hotel to turn for information. He or she is likely to need up-to-date information about airport limousine schedules; the hours of religious services and the locations of churches; and such entertainment possibilities as sporting events, movies, and the theater. Some hotels give employees special training in how to give directions and provide lists of local attractions.

FOOD AND BEVERAGE DEPARTMENT

Originally the hotel restaurant was designed to give a traveler in a strange city a place to eat where the food would be good or at least palatable—and safe to eat. In recent years, however, the restaurant industry has grown both in diversity of concepts and menus. Moreover, that growth has meant the spread of restaurants into more and more locations, making restaurant food service readily available. Many successful chain restaurants carry well-known brand names to which travelers are accustomed. In the face of stiffening restaurant competition for the hotel guest's food and beverage patronage, some hoteliers have developed hotels, such as the economy and all-suite properties discussed in Chapter 7, that offer only very limited food service—usually a complimentary breakfast and, in all-suite operations, complimentary cocktails in the evening.

On the other hand, in full-service hotels, the food service operation continues to be not only a vital service but a key competitive weapon.[7] Many full-service hotels have several quite different food outlets. This extends the services available to the guest—and helps keep the guest's food business in the hotel. While well-run restaurant and banquet departments are vital to full-service hotels, they are not by any means an easy thing to deliver. In fact, there's an old saying among hotel people that "if you can run the food, the hotel will run itself." Like most folklore, this exaggeration carries more than just a grain of truth. Perhaps a personal recollection will illustrate this point:

> My first job as an innkeeper was in a hotel with a leased food and beverage department. That is, the owners had leased the food and beverage department to a food service management company to "keep the food problems out of our hair," as they put it. This is sometimes a disastrous "solution," and it certainly was in my case.

---

[7] The student may wish to review the section of Chapter 2 regarding restaurant operating ratios, as they are also used in the industry in discussing hotel food and beverage operations.

> A banquet held in the hotel was fouled up, and I, as the innkeeper, was apologizing to a prominent automobile dealer for the problems he and others had had. I concluded my explanation by commenting that unfortunately, because the restaurant was leased, there was not much I could do about it. His reply has always stayed with me.
>
> "Tom," he said, "suppose you came down and bought a car from me and a few weeks later had mechanical trouble. Suppose my service department couldn't fix the trouble, and you came to me to complain and I told you, 'It's beyond my control. My service department is leased.' Would you ever buy another car from me? Your food and beverage department is *your* service department."
>
> I was genuinely hard put to give any adequate answer to his question— because there wasn't any.

Of course, the car dealer was right. Service in any part of the hotel is important. But nothing seems to enrage guests quite so much as slow breakfast service, cold soup, or tough steak.

Many hotels in recent years have emphasized the food and beverage department's role as a profit center, that is, a specifically identified, profitable part of the hotel's operation. The typical hotel food service department creates about half as much in dollar sales as does the rooms department but generally only provides between 10 and 20 percent as much profit as that generated by the rooms department.

Many hotelkeepers still regard the food and beverage department as a key marketing activity whose main purpose is to secure guest patronage for the hotel and only secondarily to generate profits. These operators don't throw money away. But they may price food and drink very reasonably and offer large portions or exceptionally good quality to attract patronage from the community. The reasoning is that this approach will attract guests to stay in their rooms.

Restaurants

Many motor hotels offer coffee-shop service, a more or less formal dining room, and a cocktail lounge. The hotel restaurant's hours of operation are related to the guests' needs rather than just to food and beverage profits. For example, many hotels open at least one food room at 6:00 A.M. to serve those who are early risers because they have come from another time zone, have an early plane to catch, or want to beat the morning traffic. The few guests who turn up before 7:30 in the morning hardly ever warrant the added payroll hours for cooks, waitresses, and the cashier. But if their schedules are accommodated, they are likely to return to the hotel and spend those rooms-department dollars that provide a 70 percent profit margin.

Similarly, the dining room's sales volume falls off dramatically in most properties between 8:30 and 9:00 P.M., but many hotel dining rooms stay open

The services available at most hotels include a cocktail lounge whose hours of operation are designed as much to accommodate the rooms guests as they are to make a profit on the bar itself. (Courtesy of Sheraton Hotels)

Food and beverage are, quite literally, the service department in a hotel or motel. (Courtesy of the New York Sheraton Hotel)

to accommodate the few late-arriving guests. The bar, too, may serve only a few guests in the midafternoon or after 9:00 P.M., but again, the full service a guest expects must be available.

Although management personnel need not always be present at opening or closing time, some lead employee, such as the cashier or first cook, must accept responsibility for unlocking and locking food storage areas, turning lights and equipment on at opening and off at closing, setting up the cash register or closing it out, and so forth.[8] Because of the long operating hours, one hostess is generally responsible for the day shift (from 7:00 A.M. to 3:00 P.M.), and a second is in charge of the evening shift (from 3:00 P.M. until closing). In smaller properties, one of these supervisors may be designated to act for management when the restaurant manager is not on duty.

Hotel menus, too, take on a special character related to the guests' needs. Breakfast and the evening meals are the most important to the transient hotel guest, who may not have arrived in time for lunch or may be away from the hotel for that meal. (Clearly, this statement does not apply to destination properties such as resorts.) Once again, personal experience furnishes a good illustration of this point:

> At breakfast, I always provided orange juice freshly squeezed in the dining room where the guests could see that it really was fresh. This was foolishly expensive from the restaurant's standpoint, but I received enough guest comment slips saying "I stay at this hotel because of the fresh orange juice" to convince me that we weren't really being extravagant.
>
> At the evening meal we offered, as a "Traveling Man's Special," one complete meal at a rock-bottom price featuring a low-cost appetizer, a wholesome but inexpensive entrée, salad, and dessert. In a freestanding restaurant, this would make no sense because it would reduce the check average, taking sales away from more expensive items on the menu. But many travelers are cost-conscious because they are paying their own expenses or, as with government employees (and professors!), they receive only limited reimbursement for their travel costs. A "bargain meal" thus attracts such customers to a hotel. Some guests told us they ate the inexpensive meal—but had a couple of cocktails before the meal and charged the whole amount on their expense accounts. The total cost was still within their company's travel allowance.

Banquets

Some large properties offer a catering department (or banquet department) headed by a catering manager who books and sells banquets. Smaller properties include this activity among the restaurant manager's duties. Larger proper-

---

[8] The responsibilities, tasks, roles and supervisory concerns described for restaurants in Chapter 3 are sufficiently similar that we need not repeat that information again here, except in a very general way.

ties have special full- and part-time banquet service staffs. Smaller properties draw banquet service personnel from their regular crew and often supplement them with part-time employees.

Banquets are often profitable but, once again, in many properties the banquet menus and banquet rooms are meant principally to serve the rooms department. Thus, a meeting may occupy one conference room all day. Perhaps the hotel supplies a coffee break and a luncheon in another room. It probably charges the business people little, if anything, over what those meals and snacks would cost in the dining room. Moreover, it may not charge extra for the meeting facilities. If such a meeting accounts for 20 or 30 guest-room rentals—or even only 10 or 15—the logic we have mentioned before clearly applies. The 70 percent profit on room sales makes desirable this use of banquet space.

Food Production

In most properties, the person in charge of food production is called the *executive chef*. A chef is a person who has completed, either formally or informally, the training that qualifies him or her to be a professional cook. The chef should also be an effective manager who can purchase food; hire, train, and discipline employees; and plan appetizing meals priced to yield a profit. All too often, however, the title of chef is bestowed on somebody who is, at best, a head cook. True chefs are still in relatively short supply and are expensive to hire. (On the other hand, a good chef will usually help the success of the operation, thus offsetting the cost.)

An increasingly common title in American food service is *food production manager*. Although these managers are almost invariably accomplished cooks, they emphasize kitchen management and rely on strict adherence to written recipes, rather than on their craft skills, to ensure quality. The type of management chosen by a property generally reflects the dollar volume of food sales. More sales may permit the expense of a chef or food production manager. Smaller properties may have to content themselves with a head or lead cook. In this case, the restaurant manager generally supervises the kitchen quite closely.

With the greater availability of quality frozen prepared foods as well as the growing acceptance of limited menus, an approach to food service that requires limited culinary skills is becoming more and more common in hotels that don't try to reach the luxury standard.

Large convention properties may support a separate subdepartment, often made up largely of part-time workers who just prepare banquet food. Some properties even use a separate banquet kitchen.

Because of the hours of operation, a manager should clearly designate early and late supervision hours. This supervision may require a lead cook—or perhaps the restaurant manager or an assistant—to work as a supervisor.

Modern hotels usually offer at least one informal dining room or coffee shop in which guests in informal attire will be comfortable. (Courtesy of Sheraton Hotels)

The Exceptional Case

As a student of food service, you should be aware that in a few hotels — usually older and smaller ones — the food department actually generates more profit than the rooms department does. In these cases, the innkeeper or owner is an unusually talented foods person and devotes the greatest portion of time to the food department. In these properties, as in all the others, however, the success of the food department invariably increases room sales.

Sanitation and Utility

Sanitation is so important that many hospitality programs offer entire courses on the subject. Our purpose here is simply to repeat the point made in Chapter 3 regarding the importance of dishwashers, pot washers, and the cleanup crew. In Chapter 3 we noted that many students find that the only summer jobs available are in these areas. They may not be the most interesting jobs but, as we said earlier, they provide an ideal observation point for learning about how a food service operation functions.

There is another reason for mastering these jobs while a student. The assistant restaurant manager job includes responsibility for this function in most hospitality operations — restaurants, hotels, and institutions. It is most commonly assigned to people just out of management training programs. Success in this job often launches a successful career, and a good working relationship with subordinates is helpful in this entry-level job. Few things will help you toward that goal more than the ability to roll up your sleeves and help out when one of your crew gets "stuck." (But always be careful not to turn yourself permanently into a manager-dishwasher just to win popularity contests.) Of course, you need not plan to spend your life in the dishroom, but never be afraid to say you started there!

STAFF AND SUPPORT DEPARTMENTS

Some departments or activities in the hotel offer no direct guest services. Instead, they maintain systems for the property as a whole, such as sales, marketing, and engineering. Some of these activities do, however, service the departments that deal directly with the guests: accounting and personnel immediately come to mind.

Sales and Marketing

Marketing means designing a hotel to suit the needs and tastes of potential guests—or shaping the operations of an existing property to its most likely guests. A second marketing function is encouraging the guests to choose your property by emphasizing all of those service activities that make the property pleasant and convenient. Finally, marketing is promoting the property among various potential guests and groups of guests. (This duty is often thought to be all there is to marketing, but it actually comes after the first two.)

Marketing is a general management function that involves all levels of the operation. One important day-to-day activity in this area is personal selling. In large properties, a sales manager and one or more sales persons are responsible for finding sales leads and following up on them with personal sales calls and booking functions. Some properties define the sales department's work as the national convention market. Others identify local firms as the principal place to concentrate their efforts. Determination of just which market to approach is a crucial top management decision usually made by the general manager, the sales manager, and even the ownership. In chains, corporate policy may dictate these decisions, but most often the precise market for a particular property must be specifically designated by the local management. (Some properties—in particular, resort hotels—hire outside sales firms called *hotel representatives* to represent them in key markets.)

In smaller hotels, the general manager is responsible for managing sales. He or she will commonly make the sales calls personally and entertain people from potential sales accounts in the hotel. In some properties, the general manager is assisted in this work by a full- or part-time sales representative.

Because marketing is essential, a major trade association, the Hotel Sales Marketing Association International (HSMAI), has developed to conduct educational and informational programs for both sales personnel and general management. This organization, which publishes excellent materials on sales and marketing, is a good one to join on graduation.

Engineering

The engineering function is so important that many programs have one or more courses devoted to the disciplines that support it. Once again, we will simply describe briefly the work of this area. Large- and medium-sized hotels usually employ a chief engineer who supervises an engineering staff. Together, they are responsible for operating the hotel's heating and air-conditioning; for maintaining its refrigeration, lighting, and transportation (elevator) systems; and for overseeing all of the hotel's mechanical equipment. Breakdowns in these areas seriously inconvenience guests. And of course, utility costs have always been significant and in recent years have been increasing at an alarming rate.

In small properties, the engineer is often little more than a handyman who carries out routine maintenance and minor repairs. Outside service people supply the more specialized maintenance skills. In these properties, the inn-keeper often supervises the engineering (or maintenance) function.

In any property, large or small, general management should at least

1. Determine what periodic maintenance of equipment is required (oiling, filter changing, making minor adjustments, and the like).
2. Establish a schedule for accomplishing that work.
3. Develop a reporting system and physical inspection system that assures management that this work is carried out properly and on time.

Accounting

Sometimes referred to as the *back office* (in contrast with the front office or front desk), accounting is charged with two quite different duties, accounts receivable and financial reporting and control. In large hotels, the accounting department may be headed by a comptroller and consist of several skilled clerical workers. Chains generally develop sophisticated corporate accounting departments that supervise work at the individual property. In a small property, on the other hand, the work is usually done by some combination of the innkeeper's secretary, a chief clerk, and an outside accountant.

When guests check out, they may pay their bills with cash, but they often charge this expense instead. The accounts receivable (bills owed by guests) in a hotel are divided into two parts. First, a *house ledger* (or tray ledger), kept at the front desk, is made up of bills owed by guests in the house. Charges by guests posted after they have checked out and charges by other persons, such as restaurant patrons not in the hotel, are kept in what is often called the *city ledger*. The name is derived from an earlier time when charging hotel bills was not common. Instead, guests paid cash when they checked out, and any charge not in the house ledger was a charge from some local customer, someone "in the city" rather than "in the house" who had a charge account at the hotel. Incidentally, the word *ledger* originally referred to a book on whose pages these records were kept. Today, records of charges are maintained "in memory" on a computer. The function, however, and even the terminology are the same.

The other, less routine accounting functions involve preparing operating statements, conducting special cost studies, and overseeing the hotel's cost control systems. In small properties, much of this work is done by an outside accountant, whereas the larger properties often have their own full-time accounting staff headed by a comptroller or chief auditor.

INCOME AND EXPENSE PATTERNS AND CONTROL

As with so many subjects discussed in this chapter, whole courses are often devoted to the topic of this section. Our purpose here, therefore, is to provide you with an understanding of the control structure of a hotel and a limited introduction to the vocabulary of control in hotels and restaurants.

THE UNIFORM SYSTEM OF ACCOUNTS

Hotel accounting is generally guided by the Uniform System of Accounts for Hotels, which identifies important profit centers in hotels as *revenue departments.* The uniform system first arranges the reporting of income and expense so that the relative efficiency of each major department can be measured by the *departmental income.* Table 8.1 shows a typical rooms-department schedule of income and expenses for a 120-room motor hotel, and Table 8.2 shows a food and beverage department schedule for such a property. The rooms-departmental income and the food and beverage departmental income figures help the manager evaluate the performance of key department heads working in those areas.

To determine the property's overall efficiency, we deduct four categories of *undistributed operating expenses* from the total of the various departmental incomes. These costs—administrative and general expense, marketing and guest entertainment, property operation, and maintenance and energy costs— are judged to be costs that pertain to all departments in a way that cannot be perfectly assigned to any one department.

The amount remaining after deducting these four categories of expense from the total of departmental income is called *total income before fixed charges.* (Until recently, this amount was called, somewhat more colorfully, *house profit.*) This figure is probably the best measure of the success not only of the total property but of the general manager as well.

TABLE 8.1 Rooms-Department Schedule of Income and Expenses

	In Dollars	In Percent
Room sales	$2,555,110	100.0%
Departmental expenses		
Salaries and wages	355,160	13.9
Employee meals	10,220	0.4
Payroll taxes and employee benefits	76,653	3.0
Laundry and dry cleaning	38,327	1.5
China, glass, silver, and linen	25,551	1.0
Commission	38,316	1.5
Reservation expenses	17,886	0.7
Contract cleaning	7,665	0.3
Other expenses	76,647	3.0
Total rooms expenses	$ 646,425	25.3%
Rooms-departmental income	$1,908,685	74.7%

For this reason, many managers receive bonuses based on their performance as measured by this figure. It is fair to evaluate the manager without regard to the remaining costs, which can best be described as capital costs. Almost all of these costs—rent, property taxes, insurance, interest, and depreciation—are a direct function of the cost of the building and its furnishings and fixtures. The responsibility for these costs lies with the owners who made the decisions when the property was first built and furnished. These costs, therefore, lie beyond the control of the manager. Table 8.3, a typical statement of income and expense for a 120-room property, shows how all of these figures relate to net profit.

KEY OPERATING RATIOS AND TERMS

In Chapter 3 we introduced some key ratios and food service terms, which are used in hotel food service as well. In addition, the hotel industry has other indicators of an operation's results:

Occupancy is generally indicated as a percentage.

$$\text{Occupancy percentage} = \frac{\text{Rooms sold}}{\text{Total rooms available}}$$

Average rate is an indication of the front desk's success in selling both the least expensive and the higher-priced rooms.

TABLE 8.2 Food and Beverage Department Schedule of Income and Expenses

	In Dollars	In Percent
Food sales	$1,031,382	72.9%
Beverage sales	381,993	27.1
Total food and beverage sales	$1,413,375	100.0%
Cost of sales		
Food cost (after credit for employee meals)	$ 347,544	33.6%*
Beverage cost	81,046	21.4%*
Total food and beverage cost	428,590	30.3%
Gross margin	984,785	69.7%
Public room rentals	25,440	1.8%
Other income	18,374	1.3
Gross margin and other income	$1,028,599	7.28%
Departmental expenses		
Salaries and wages	159,347	32.5%
Employee meals	21,201	1.5
Payroll taxes and employee benefits	101,763	7.2
Music and entertainment	40,988	2.9
Laundry and dry cleaning	12,720	0.9
Kitchen fuel	4,240	0.3
China, glass, silver, and linen	26,854	1.9
Contract cleaning	5,654	0.4
Licenses	2,826	0.2
All other expenses	70,669	5.0
Total food and beverage expenses	$ 746,262	52.8%
Food and beverage departmental income	$ 282,337	20.0%

*These two cost percentages apply respectively to food sales and beverage sales, whereas all other ratios are total sales.

$$\text{Average rate} = \frac{\text{Dollar sales}}{\text{Number of rooms sold}}$$

The average rate is also a mix of the double-occupancy rooms sold (rooms with two or more guests). This is reflected by the ratio

$$\text{Number of guests per occupied room} = \frac{\text{Number of guests}}{\text{Number of occupied rooms}}$$

TABLE 8.3 Highway Motor Hotel Statement of Income and Expenses for Year Ending December 31, 19XX

	In Dollars	In Percent
Revenues:		
Rooms	$2,555,110	60.2%
Food—including other income	1,031,382	24.3
Beverages	381,993	9.0
Telephone	101,865	2.4
Other operated departments	80,643	1.9
Rentals and other income	93,376	2.2
Total revenues	$4,244,369	100.0%
Departmental costs and expenses:		
Rooms	$ 646,425	15.2%
Food and beverages	1,131,038	26.6
Telephone	131,575	3.1
Other operated departments	55,177	1.3
Total costs and expenses	$1,964,215	46.2%
Total operated departments' income	$2,280,154	53.8%
Undistributed operating expenses:		
Administrative general	$ 415,948	9.8%
Marketing	195,241	4.6
Property operation and maintenance	241,929	5.7
Energy costs	199,485	4.7
Total undistributed expenses	$1,052,603	24.8%
Income before fixed charges	$1,227,551	29.0%
Property taxes and insurance:		
Property taxes and other municipal charges	$ 110,353	2.6%
Insurance on building and contents	21,222	0.5
Total property taxes and insurance	$ 131,575	3.1%
Income before other fixed charges	$1,095,976	25.9%
Capital costs:		
Depreciation and amortization	$ 331,060	7.8%
Interest	428,681	10.1
Total capital costs	$ 759,741	17.9%
Net income before income taxes	$ 336,235	6.4%

Because housekeeping is the largest and most controllable labor cost in the rooms department, many hotels compute the average number of rooms cleaned in the following ratio:

$$\frac{\text{Average rooms cleaned}}{\text{per maid day}} = \frac{\text{Number of rooms occupied}}{\text{Number of 8-hour maid shifts}}$$

All of these ratios are usually computed for the day, the month to date, and the year at year's end. Comparisons of these indicators with earlier operating results and with the budget provide important clues to an operation's problems or success.

CAPITAL STRUCTURE

We will discuss some of the financial dimensions of the hotel business further in Chapter 9. At this point, however, we need to describe briefly the capital costs found on the hotel's income statement because they are a significant part of a hotel's cost structure. *Capital costs* include rent, depreciation, and interest. A related cost, property taxes, can be included here because these taxes are dependent on the value of the land and the building.

Depreciation is a bookkeeping entry that reflects the assumption that the original cost of the hotel building, furniture, and fixtures should be gradually written off over their useful life. Interest, of course, is the charge paid to the lenders for the use of their funds.

The hotel industry is *capital intensive*. That is, it uses a large part of its revenue to pay for capital costs, including real estate taxes. Close to 20 cents of every sales dollar go to cover costs related to the hotel's capital structure.

Hotel development is attractive to some investors because it is highly *leveraged*. Leverage, as a financial term, refers to the fact that a small amount of an investor's capital can often call forth much larger amounts of money lent by banks or insurance companies on a mortgage. A fixed amount of interest is paid for this capital, and so if the hotel is profitable, the investor's earning power will be greatly magnified. But the investor's modest initial investment need not be increased. Earnings go up, but interest does not. Nor does investment—hence the word *leverage.*

Leverage, as developers have discovered repeatedly, can be a two-way device. Operating profits boom in good times and cover fixed interest payments many times over. When times turn bad or the effects of overbuilding begin to be felt, revenues fall, but interest rates (and required repayments on the principal of the loan) do not. The result can be a wave of bankruptcies.

ENTRY PORTS AND CAREERS

An old adage says that there are three routes to advancement in the hotel industry: sales and marketing, accounting, and food and beverage. According to this adage, sales and marketing is the best route to the top in good times, but accounting, with its mastery of cost control, is the surest route in bad times. These three routes do seem to lead to advancement, but they are by no means the only places to start.

FRONT OFFICE

Many people begin their careers in the lodging industry in the front office, the nerve center of the hotel and the place where its most important sales take place. Obviously, the front office is an important area. With the growing importance of the limited-service property, moreover, it increases in prominence because in those properties it is the most important area of technical knowledge. On the other hand, we should note that front-office techniques can be mastered fairly quickly. Moreover, this mastery still leaves a good many of the hotel's important operating functions outside the front office yet to be learned. Although some executives have risen to general manager from the front office, most of them are found in small properties. If your ambitions include advancement to general manager, you will want to think carefully about building on a successful front-office experience by adding experience in another area. In a limited-service property, this should probably be sales.

Many people find front-office work, with its constant change and frequent contact with guests, the most rewarding of careers. Moreover, improved pay scales in this area in recent years have upgraded the long-term attractiveness of this work, as has the increasingly sophisticated use of the computer in the front office. Another advantage of working in this area is a more-or-less fixed work schedule, although the afternoon shift's hours (from 3:00 P.M. to 11:00 P.M.) and those of the night auditor (from 11:00 P.M. to 7:00 A.M.) are viewed by many as drawbacks to those specific jobs.

ACCOUNTING

It is certainly true that during the Great Depression of the 1930s, many of the successful managers were accountants. Today, however, accounting has become a specialized field, and successful training in this area can be so time consuming that one can hardly expect to master the other areas of the operation. Although accounting may not offer as easy a route to the general manager's slot as it once did, it does offer interesting and prestigious work for those who like to work with numbers. Moreover, the hours in this area tend to be reasonably regular, and the pay is usually good.

Although accounting per se is not as common a route to general manager as it once was, a new offshoot of accounting, operations analysis, is quite a different story. Operations analysts conduct special cost studies either under the direction of the auditor or as a special assistant to the general manager. Some operation analysts work in corporate headquarters. The operations analyst's job is such a good training ground for young managers that a regular practice of rotation through this job for promising young managers has become, in some companies, a feature of management development.

SALES AND MARKETING

The key to the success of any property is sales. Thus it is not surprising that many successful hotel operators have a sales background. On the other hand, salespeople often find that a grounding in front-office procedure and in food and beverage operations (with special emphasis, respectively, on reservations procedure and banquet operations) leads to success in sales. Successful sales personnel are much in demand, and a career in sales offers interesting and financially rewarding work to the successful.

The importance of sales and marketing tends to increase when there is an oversupply of rooms in a market. Increasingly, the marketing manager for a hotel is asked to conduct market research or to analyze market research done by others. Indeed, a common requirement for senior positions in marketing is the ability to prepare a *marketing plan*. Such a plan evaluates the local environment and the competition, sets goals for the plan period (usually one to three years), and presents the strategy and tactics to fulfill the plan. A solid educational background is a great help to the modern hotel marketing manager.

FOOD AND BEVERAGE

Food and beverage is one of the most demanding areas of the hotel operation, and it is an area in which Murphy's law — "If anything can go wrong, it will!" — most often applies. Success calls for the ability to deal effectively with two separate groups of skilled employees — cooks and serving personnel. Along with mastering both product cost-control techniques (for both food and alcoholic beverages) and employee-scheduling techniques, the food and beverage manager must also work in sanitation and housekeeping and master the skills of menu writing. He or she must complete all these duties against at least three unyielding deadlines a day: breakfast, lunch, and dinner.

Many general managers brag that "I'm basically a foods person." Their success probably can be traced to the factors we discussed earlier in the chapter: the food and beverage department is the service department of the hotel and, in competitive markets, a successful food and beverage operation helps fill the hotel. Food and beverage managers may, however, find themselves stereotyped by firms as "foods people" and their advancement hindered because owners prefer to keep them in their specialty, in which qualified managers are so scarce. In cases in which advancement to general manager is blocked, however, qualified managers have not usually had trouble finding another job.

An advantage of careers in food and beverage is career-progression flexibility. Accomplished management and supervisory people in the food and beverage field almost always enjoy the option of moving to work outside the hotel in restaurants, clubs, or institutions. Although food and beverage probably requires longer hours than does any other area in the business, it is typically a well-paid position and offers not only career flexibility but unusually solid job security as well. Finally, it forms a sound basis for advancement into general management.

OWNING YOUR OWN HOTEL

Many students are attracted to the hospitality management field because they would like some day to own their own businesses. Whereas new hotels require large investments, existing operations can sometimes, under special circumstances of two different kinds, be purchased with little or no investment. First, after a wave of overbuilding and during economic recessions (and particularly when these two occur simultaneously), bankruptcies become common. And when banks must take over a hotel, they need someone to handle operations. They are often willing to give to a person with the know-how to take the property off their hands an opportunity for an ownership interest.

Some older hotels in smaller cities offer another kind of opportunity. They may have lost their competitiveness as hotels, while still occupying prime downtown real estate in a good food and beverage location. Because of this fact, together with an older hotel's extensive banquet facility and liquor license, the property may be revitalized by a well-run and imaginatively promoted food operation. The profits of that food operation may then be plowed back into improving the hotel facilities. The improved facilities *and* the property's improved reputation, earned by its newly successful food and beverage operation, often result in a greatly improved rooms business. Examples of such operations can be found in many parts of the country. Where they are found, they always share these three characteristics: excellence in the food operation; unusually effective promotion, generally enhanced by the manager's community involvement; and very, *very* hard work by that manager, who seems to live and breathe the hotel and restaurant business.

The hotel business offers many rewarding careers in front office, accounting, marketing and sales, and food and beverage. For those whose ambition and temperament makes them want to extend themselves, the top job is within reach and ownership is in sight.

SUMMARY

The first topic we discussed in this chapter was the major functional areas of a hotel and who runs them. Although big hotels have true departments and department managers, smaller hotels would designate these as areas, supervised by lead employees.

We next examined the rooms side of the hotel. The front office is particularly important, as it is the guests' first real contact with the hotel. The front office generally has a morning clerk, an afternoon clerk, and a night auditor, all with both different and overlapping duties. All help in making reservations, generally through a computerized reservation system.

The Property Management System (PMS) makes the operation of the front office more efficient and usually links it electronically to the hotel's other departments and, more often than not, to the hotel chain's central reservation service. Reservation systems often make use of yield management systems that are designed to get the best total dollar revenue possible through a mix of occupancy and average daily rate. Other rooms-side departments are the telephone department, the housekeeping department, and the bell staff.

The food and beverage department is very important to the full-service hotel, as it may determine whether guests return to the hotel (or come in the first place). We described the kinds of restaurants that various kinds of hotels offer, banquet facilities (if any), food production, and sanitation and utility.

We next looked at hotels' staff and support departments: sales and marketing, engineering, and accounting. The accounting department is sometimes referred to as the back office. We explained the hotel departmental income and expenses, operating ratios and terms, and, finally, capital costs.

We finished the chapter with a look at the best routes to advancement in the hotel industry—front office, sales and marketing, accounting, and food and beverage—and the advantages and disadvantages of each. We also discussed the possibility of owning your own hotel.

KEY WORDS AND CONCEPTS

To help you review this chapter, keep in mind the following:

Rooms department
Food and beverage
    department
Rooms-department income
Food and beverage
    department income
Front office: welcoming and
    complaints
Night audit
Overbooking
Telephone department
Housekeeping

City ledger
Total income before fixed
    charges
Undistributed operating
    expenses
Occupancy
Average rate
Property management systems
    (PMS)
Yield management
Number of guests per
    occupied room

Bell staff
Rooming the guest
Staff and support departments
HSMAI
Back office
House ledger

Average number of rooms
cleaned per maid day
Capital costs
Capital intensive
Leverage
Career paths

REVIEW QUESTIONS

1. How does the organizational structure differ in large hotels and small?

2. Describe some of the duties of the morning clerk, the afternoon clerk, and the night auditor.

3. What are the benefits of a property management system? How does it make the front office run more smoothly?

4. What is the purpose of yield management? What problems does it pose?

5. What does the saying "If you can run the food, the hotel will run itself" mean?

6. Describe the different kinds of restaurants that a large hotel might have.

7. What are the advantages of the sanitation and utility area for a summer job?

8. What are capital costs? How important are they in hotels?

CHAPTER

Courtesy of Stouffer Hotels

FORCES SHAPING THE
HOTEL BUSINESS

THE PURPOSE OF THIS CHAPTER

Fundamental to an understanding of the hotel business is an understanding of the complex economics of lodging. This helps us to comprehend the development of new hotel formats, which have burgeoned in the past few years. Competition within the hotel industry involves location and product but, in recent years especially, also operating decisions about facilities, service levels, and amenities. With these fundamental considerations in hand, you are in a better condition to assess and perhaps chart your career prospects in an industry in a state of rapid change.

THIS CHAPTER SHOULD HELP YOU

1. Discuss the economics of the hotel business.

2. Describe the forces that create hotel building cycles.

3. Discuss the dimensions of the hotel investment decision and its impact on operations.

4. Assess the advantages of management companies for owners—and for yourself as a prospective employee.

5. Identify individual entrepreneurial opportunities that may accompany reverses in the hotel business generally.

6. Assess the competitive value of services and amenities offered, or not offered, by various lodging segments and companies.

THE ECONOMICS OF THE HOTEL BUSINESS

Hotel developers build long-term assets on the basis of relatively short-term cycles. A hotel's lifetime is usually 30 or 40 years and often 100 years or more, but the cycle of hotel building is more like 10 to 20 years in length. The result, historically, has been periods of excess capacity followed sooner or later by periods of more or less frantic building.

In fact, the hotel business is cyclical, capital intensive, and highly competitive. Even though many competitors have expanded lodging capacity, it is a business whose real (inflation-adjusted) growth prospects need to be questioned. Finally, we should recognize that hotel companies have two kinds of customers: guests who want to rent a room and developers who want to build hotels.

A CYCLICAL BUSINESS

The hotel business is cyclical. First, the demand for hotel rooms rises and falls with the business cycle. Generally, the demand for hotel rooms changes direction three to six months after the economy does.[1] This is not surprising, as both business and pleasure travel are easy expenditures to cut out in a declining economy and to restore when it improves. In any local market, the hotel business is likely to have its own cycle, related to the supply of hotel rooms, as well as the demand for them. But the cycle generally starts with the demand for rooms, potential or actual. Perhaps the easiest way to see this cycle is to work through an imaginary, but quite realistic, example.

An Example of the Hotel Business Cycle

"Oldtown," a quiet city of 100,000, has been a stable community with a balanced economy for many years. Not long ago, during a period of general economic expansion, a large national company built a large factory complex in Oldtown. The ripple effect from this spread to the suppliers for the factory complex as well as to a number of other companies who, when they heard about the factory complex, learned what an attractive site Oldtown was. Employment soared: some people were transferred to Oldtown, and others moved there seeking jobs.

Our story now shifts to Major Hotels' corporate offices where in a meeting with the vice-presidents of operations and real estate, the vice-president for development suggests that Major ought to look into building a hotel in Oldtown. There is immediate agreement to do a preliminary study. Three months later the preliminary study shows encouraging results, and so several lines of activity are set in motion. A consulting firm is hired to do a formal feasibility study; an architect is hired to do preliminary design work; and

---

[1] John J. Rohs, *Lodging: Light at the End of the Tunnel* (New York: Wertheim Schroder & Co., 1991), p. 9.

informal conversations with Major's bankers begin. Six more months pass. The results of the consultant's feasibility study confirm Major's preliminary study; the preliminary design is a beauty, and everybody agrees this could be a great hotel; and the bankers, having looked at the studies and the design, decide to process quickly Major's loan application. (They have had a surge in deposits and need to get that money into interest-earning loans. They need to lend, just as Major needs to borrow.) Best of all, the ideal location has been found, and negotiations to acquire a site are going well.

At a meeting of Major's executive committee, a formal proposal to go ahead is presented. The discussion touches briefly on the competition, but everyone quickly agrees that Oldtown's existing hotels are tired and will be no match for the proposed property. When somebody asks, "Is anybody else going in there?" the answer is, "A few people have been nosing around, but there's nothing firm as far as we can tell." Everyone agrees that it is time to purchase the site and sign a design contract with the architect. Because this is a meeting, everybody's commitment is a public matter.

The same series of events is taking place at Magnificent Hotels, LowCost Lodges, Supersuites, and a couple of other companies. But because each company keeps things fairly quiet until everything is settled, there are only vague rumors that others are also interested in Oldtown.

Finally, 18 months after the first vice-presidential meeting at Major, the company announces that a 300-room hotel will be built in Oldtown, and the ground breaking is set two weeks hence. The story is front-page news. Over the next six months, similar announcements from Magnificent, LowCost, and Supersuites make the front page, too.

At Major, these other companies' announcements make quite a stir. At a meeting of the executive committee, they all shake their heads and agree that those other companies are crazy; they have no sense at all in overbuilding like this. One very junior vice-president who is sitting in raises the possibility that Major should abandon the project, but he is quickly shouted down. Thousands of dollars have already been spent on feasibility studies and architectural work; a site has been purchased; and contracts have been signed for construction. "Besides," says the financial vice-president, "what would our banks say if we pulled out now? Do you think we'd get another loan commitment as easily next time?" Because *everybody* has agreed to the project publicly, for any to admit that he or she was wrong would also be publicly embarrassing.

Eighteen months later, Major's beautiful new property opens, and the general manager hands the following situation report to the vice-president of operations:

> Within four blocks of my office, there are a thousand rooms under construction. Every place my sales staff goes, they trip over our competitors' people. Magnificent is slashing its convention rates for next year; LowCost has announced a salespersons' discount when its hotel opens next month; and Supersuites is offering free cocktail parties every evening.

I think we will do all right after the first couple of years because our operation is going to be stronger and of better quality, but don't expect much for our first two or three years until we are established.

There are no further announcements of lodging construction in Oldtown.

We have spent quite a bit of time looking at this cycle of events to illustrate the significance of factors such as the complexity of the decision to build a hotel, the lead time required, the preliminary expenditures, and the public corporate and individual commitment to the decision. This cycle shows that an increase in demand can set off a series of events that usually cannot be stopped even when it becomes clear that the market is or will be overbuilt.

In some markets, the demand keeps increasing, and in three to five years another round of building starts, this time fueled by all the old faces plus — for those who didn't get in the first time — a need to be represented in the growth market. In other markets, it takes years for the demand to catch up with the overbuilding.

Our example was of a local market, but this is usually part of a larger, national market. Different local events related to a general national period of prosperity set off building booms in many local markets because demand for hotel rooms is closely related to general economic conditions. When the national economy turns down, so does the hotel business.

Hotel building tends to come in waves or cycles that end, much to everybody's surprise, in an overbuilt industry. Figure 9.1 shows the cycle of hotel construction between 1968 and 1985. As we will see, the cyclical pattern of construction was disrupted by the introduction of segmentation, which prolonged the construction boom until 1991, making the oversupply problem worse.

A CAPITAL-INTENSIVE BUSINESS

For the restaurant business, the biggest costs by far are food and payroll, followed by other direct operating expenses. Thus when sales fall precipitously, so do expenses. Hotels also have some large variable costs, most being in the food and beverage department. Lodging itself, however, is capital intensive; that is, it requires large investments of capital in fixed plant and equipment. And capital costs such as depreciation, interest, insurance, and property taxes are fixed costs. Moreover, a large portion of a hotel's operating expenses are fixed, too. Thus, even if there are many vacancies at Major's new hotel, its capital and other fixed costs will continue regardless of business and must be met. If the mortgage payments are not made, the mortgage lender will (generally) foreclose.

What may happen in this situation is complicated. The mortgage holder — let's say an insurance company — forecloses, and then it will own a hotel that it doesn't know how to operate. If it acquires a lot of hotels in this way, which sometimes happens, it may hire a management company or even

FIGURE 9.1 Hotel construction is cyclical. [*Source:* Randall C. Zisler and Robert A. Feldman, *The Real Estate Report* (New York: Goldman Sachs, April 1986).]

establish its own hotel-operating division. (In fact, Prudential Realty Group, an affiliate of one of the larger lodging mortgage holders, Prudential Insurance, is one of North America's larger hotel "chains.") Most mortgage holders, however, just want to find another company to take over the mortgage. They are in the business of lending money at interest, and they want a "performing loan" (one that is making payments on time) on their books rather than a hotel full of guests looking for an owner to complain to if their eggs aren't cooked right.

The original developers probably were able to borrow 60 to 70 percent of the total cost of the property and arranged to meet the rest of the investment through their own resources or by attracting other equity investors (owners rather than lenders). If the property's mortgage is foreclosed, the equity holders' stake (30 to 40 percent of the investment in this example) will be lost.

The property may then be sold by the mortgage holder at a "distressed price," at, let's say, 65 percent of its original cost (roughly, the amount of the mortgage). The new owners will receive a significant operating advantage because their capital costs will now be lower, reflecting the lower purchase price. This advantage can and frequently does mean a lower rate structure for the recapitalized property.

To see why, we need to recognize that room rates are closely related to the cost per room incurred in building or buying the hotel. The rule of thumb is that the average room rate must reflect one dollar for every thousand dollars in cost per room. This rule of thumb is useful only as an estimate and is not actually used in setting the final rate, which will relate to the local rate structure, operating costs, the interest rate on the mortgage, and other factors. Still, it provides a surprisingly good estimate of what the final rate will be in most cases and we can use the rule of thumb in this illustrative case. Assume a hotel costs $75,000 a room to build and later is sold in bankruptcy for 65 percent of its original cost. The original owner would need to charge an average rate of about $75, while the owners who acquired the hotel in bankruptcy could make an adequate return with an average rate of under $50.

Other properties in that community find it difficult to meet this new lower rate if they have not been "through the wringer" (that is, bankrupted and sold at a discount to reflect the owners' equity being "washed out"). Indeed, a recapitalized property with lower fixed costs can destabilize the market and, in bad times, set off a wave of financial crises in that market through rate reductions that can't be matched by the existing capital costs at other properties.

We will argue later that this is a problem but it also presents major windows of opportunity for qualified management people in the hotel business.

A COMPETITIVE BUSINESS

This is not the place for an extended theoretical discussion of monopoly, oligopoly, monopolistic competition, and so forth. We do need to note, though, that some businesses like automobile and aluminum manufacturers are dominated by a few sellers. In these industries, competition may be fierce but prices tend to remain stable; some economists speak of administered prices—prices set by company decisions rather than market forces.

Room rates in lodging *tend* to be fairly stable because most properties do have a high fixed-cost structure. (Hotel payrolls have a large fixed rather than variable element related to the minimum crew needed to stay open. This combines with capital costs, as we just noted, to make for a high overall fixed cost.) The lodging business is much more competitive than an oligopoly such as the automobile industry. There are "many buyers and many sellers." Thus, no one company exercises control over the market. Moreover, everybody can easily find out what rates are being charged. (In the language of economists, these conditions describe good, if not perfect, competition.) In these competitive conditions, every tactic tends to be met by a counterattack, and lower rates in one property put immediate price pressure on other properties in the same market segment and often, indirectly, on properties in other sectors as well.

The highly competitive structure of the industry makes local or regional oversupply of rooms a very serious proposition. Competition means that at the bottom end of the cycle, some companies can get bruised. Older and outmoded properties may be "withdrawn from the market," that is, torn down or converted to another use, often sooner than expected.

A GROWTH BUSINESS?

A growth industry is one that grows more rapidly than the economy as a whole. Since 1985, the growth in *supply* has been at or below the rate of the economy as a whole (i.e., gross national product).[2] A better measure is the growth in *demand,* which has been at about that same rate since 1985 although the evidence available indicates a lower long-term growth rate than the economy. In fact, the hotel business is not a growth industry.[3]

We should note that this is neither a good nor a bad thing, simply a fact of life. The hotel business *does* suffer from a shortage of qualified managers, and there are certainly many opportunities at all levels for people who are interested in the business. Moreover, although there may not be growth in the national market, many regional markets offer growth opportunities, as do market segments such as economy and all-suite properties. From an economic perspective, however, the lack of a strong growth trend in total demand should be understood, particularly in the light of our discussion of product segmentation in Chapter 7.

Lodging demand, that is, the number of rooms occupied, did grow very slowly in the last half of the 1980s, but occupancy remained at a depressed level—somewhere around 60 percent—and was projected to be only 62.5 percent in 1991.[4] The industry experienced, in 1991, its seventh consecutive year of losses, with 60 percent of all hotels operating at a loss.[5] In the five years ending in 1991, industry authorities estimate 10,000 hotel properties will be taken over by mortgage holders.[6] The reason for lodging's poor occupancy and financial performance deserves our consideration.

In the first half of the 1980s, tax laws encouraged investors to build hotels. In some cases the demand for accommodation did not warrant a new

[2] Rohs, *Lodging: Light at the End of the Tunnel,* p. 8. Rohs cites Smith Travel Research.

[3] When I first made such a statement in 1974, in an article in *The Institute Journal* published by the American Hotel Motel Association Educational Institute, it caused considerable irritation in some quarters in the hotel business, presumably because "growth" was good, and so nongrowth must be bad. I am happy therefore, to note that I have since found plenty of company among the experts. For instance, Daniel Lee, then a security analyst at Drexel Burnham Lambert, who stated, "Although cyclical, the lodging business is not a 'growth' industry" (Daniel R. Lee, "A Forecast of Lodging Supply and Demand," *Cornell Hotel and Restaurant Administration Quarterly,* August 1984, p. 37); and Glenn Withian, managing editor of the *Cornell Quarterly,* stated, on the basis of Laventhol & Horwath data, "The number of hotel rooms occupied per day has remained relatively flat for more than three decades." (Glenn Withian, "Hotel Companies Aim for Multiple Markets," *Cornell Hotel and Restaurant Administration Quarterly,* November 1985, p. 51.)

[4] Rohs, *Lodging: Light at the End of the Tunnel,* p. 8.

[5] *Hotel Motel Management,* May 27, 1991, p. 79.

[6] Robert C. Hazard, Address to the 13th Annual Hospitality Industry Conference, New York, June 4, 1991. Mr. Hazard quoted Bjorn Hanson of Coopers Lybrand.

property, but the tax benefits made the hotel profitable for the investor anyway. Under these circumstances, the hotel industry caught the fancy of real estate developers, and hotel chain and franchise companies began putting more emphasis on the real estate development part of their business. The low occupancy level in 1986, then, was the result of a building spree induced by then current tax laws. When the tax laws were changed, we might have expected the building boom to stop. Instead, nearly 100,000 rooms were added for each of the next five years.[7] Much of the building in 1986 and 1987 can be explained as projects still in the developmental pipeline when the tax code was changed that were subsequently finished. The other factor, however, and one that continued to operate throughout the 1980s, was the development of new lodging concepts, particularly in the limited-service and all-suite categories. As chains and franchise groups sought entry into every viable market for their *new* concepts, already established hotel properties were badly hurt.

The picture is further clouded by a number of factors that have held back growth in the demand for lodging in recent years. First, travel patterns and consumer preferences have changed. With faster travel, executives can fly into a city, do their business, and fly home on the same day. Shorter trips have become the rule. In addition, long-distance telephone calls substitute more and more for face-to-face meetings, and videoconferencing could have a similar, though smaller, impact. In pleasure travel, campers and trailers, or even second homes, are often used instead of transient lodging. People who spend their vacation in their summer cottage are obviously not hotel customers at that moment.

The lodging industry's pricing practices have almost certainly contributed to these trends. Throughout the early 1970s, hotel prices increased at about the same rate as did other prices. From 1972 until quite recently, however, room rates increased substantially faster than did the costs of other goods and services, as illustrated in Figure 9.2. As early as 1984, the president of Quality Courts (now called Choice International), charged that hotels were frightening guests away because of their "excessive product pricing and a decrease in the perceived price-value relationship."[8]

Room-rate growth slowed somewhat in 1987 and even more from 1988 to 1991. With five years of slower price increases, the hotel industry as a whole is likely to be perceived in the mid-1990s as offering a somewhat better buy to consumers and business people than it did just a few years ago. Moreover, as financing has dried up for new hotel construction, the wave of construction has slowed substantially. Finally, most of the new growth is in the more popular all-suites, limited-service, and hard-budget categories that have clearly found favor with the consumer. Accordingly, the industry should enter the mid-1990s with a stronger outlook than it has seen since the early 1980s.

---

[7] Rohs, *Lodging: Light at the End of the Tunnel,* p. 8.
[8] *Nations Restaurant News,* December 7, 1984, p. 93.

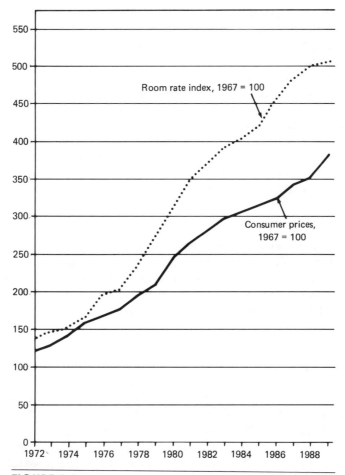

FIGURE 9.2 Consumer price index versus average daily rate. (*Source:* Pannell Kerr Forster & Co., *Trend of Business* —1990.)

DIMENSIONS OF THE
HOTEL INVESTMENT DECISION

In the early 1990s, the hotel industry has largely gone out of fashion with lenders. In the face of industrywide losses extending back several years, it is not surprising that it is very difficult to borrow money for new construction. It is important, however, to realize that this is far from the first time this has happened. Hotel development generally passes through periods when it is not popular, following the peak in development activity in each cycle. We can almost certainly look forward to renewed interest in hotels as the oversupply is worked out by lessened construction; as economic conditions improve, which seems probable; and as prosperous consumers with more free time are attracted to the currently retarded growth in room rates as well as by the growing stock of popular new concepts. In a word, we can confidently expect that we have not seen the last up cycle in hotel construction. It is useful, therefore, to explore the decision to invest in a hotel, recognizing three dimensions: financial, real estate, and operations. Two additional financial dimensions, exchange-rate fluctuations and differing national standards for investment practice, affect international transactions.

FINANCIAL

Many hotels have been built in the past principally for reasons related to the financing of the project rather than to the hotel's operating success. Some of the factors that enter into such decisions include interest rates and taxes. We will consider below, too, the international financial dimensions of exchange rate and differing perceptions of investment value.

Taxes

As we noted earlier, the U.S. tax laws of the early 1980s encouraged the construction of hotels by offering special tax credits that meant investors could sometimes make money on the project even if the hotel was not profitable. While those artificial inducements to construction are gone, interest rates on loans are still tax deductible. Take, for example, one corporation that paid interest of 9.2 percent on its debt; after paying taxes of about 40 percent, the cost of the loan, after taxes, was only 5.6 percent.[9] The "tax saving" arises because, while all of the interest must be paid, some 40 percent of it in this example is balanced by a reduction in income tax.

Another tax aspect is introduced by the increased globalization of the lodging industry. The purchase of Holiday Inns by Bass, Ltd., an English firm, for instance, was facilitated by differences in British tax laws, which created a tax advantage for Bass that was not available to the American seller. Japanese investors find advantages in the tax deductibility of foreign-exchange "losses" that can be created by accelerating payments of debt between U.S. subsidiaries of Japanese companies and the Japanese parent when exchange rates favor this tactic.[10]

---

[9] Avner Arbel and Robert H. Woods, "Debt Hitchhiking: How Hotels Found Low-Cost Capital," *Cornell Hotel and Restaurant Administration Quarterly,* November 1990, pp. 105–110.

[10] Tadayuki Hara and James J. Eyster, "Japanese Hotel Investment: A Matter of Tradition and Reality," *Cornell Hotel and Restaurant Administration Quarterly,* November 1990, pp. 98–104.

Exchange Rates

Indeed, exchange-rate fluctuations have made U.S. assets attractive to foreign buyers from time to time. Assets purchased when the yen, mark, franc, or pound has a favorable rate of exchange appear cheaper when viewed from the advantage of the higher currency. To illustrate, let us assume two currencies, the dollar and the "bazoola," each worth 1 unit of the other. Now let us assume that, for any of a number of reasons, the bazoola rises over an 18-month period to the point where it is worth $2. At this point, $1 is worth only one half of a bazoola. From the point of view of the holder of bazoolas, a $1 million asset, which would have cost a like amount of bazoolas 18 months ago, can now be purchased for only 500,000 bazoolas. For such a purchaser, the change in cost is about the same as if the price had gone from $1 million to half that. In actual fact, a hotel whose value remained at $100 million in the United States from 1984 to 1988 would have cost a Japanese buyer 24 billion yen in 1984 but only 13 billion yen in 1988.[11]

Perception of Investment Values

Another international dimension is that the *perception* of investment values differs from country to country. American investors tend to focus on short-term returns while Japanese investors take a significantly longer view. Japanese investors are motivated to acquire real estate by the scarcity of prime real estate in their home country while U.S. investors are principally interested in cash flow. Thus the U.S. investor is more interested in the annual return on the investment while the Japanese investor is more interested in the appreciation, over time, in the value of the asset. Nearly 30 percent of Japanese investment in real estate in the United States is made in hotels and resorts, and hospitality is the largest single area of Japanese investment here. While their investment in U.S. real estate has declined, it amounted to $13 billion in 1990 and is reliably estimated to be in the range of $6 to $10 billion in 1991.[12]

REAL ESTATE

Hotels also may be built because a community or area development needs the property; that is, the hotel may be necessary to a larger project. The underlying value of the real estate and its appreciation may be a more important consideration to some investors than is the profitability of the hotel. For example, a number of foreign investors in North America have apparently been willing to invest money in hotel properties for their longer-term appreciation and as a safe haven for their funds.

Hotels are also generally considered a good inflation hedge and they have actually performed well on that score. Since hotels have usually been able to raise their rates and thus keep up with inflation, the income stream of a hotel is

---

[11] Hara and Eyster, "Japanese Hotel Investment."

[12] *Real Estate Newsline* (Los Angeles: Kenneth Leventhal and Co., April 1991).

likely to rise over the long run by at least enough to offset inflation. In fact, between 1975 and 1990, room-rate increases exceeded inflation in all but five years.[13] The ability to increase revenues is much less in other real estate projects in which rents are generally fixed by long-term leases. As a result, hotels, although they have a higher risk than other real estate, find favor with investors, especially during the optimistic, growth phase of the hotel industry cycle.

Hotel companies have become highly active not only as operators and franchisors of hotels but as real estate developers. Promus, for instance, describes itself as a "merchant developer of land." That is, Promus sees itself as maintaining "growth . . . at a rapid pace," in significant part, by buying, developing, and then reselling land and hotel properties.[14] As of early 1991, Promus had some $350 million worth of hotel assets that were for sale. Similarly, Marriott Corp. had hotels for sale that were built or scheduled to open in 1991 with a value of over $2 billion.[15] Indeed, such companies have a real interest in continuing expansion of their brands to gain a greater share of the market and to ensure that their brand has a presence in the widest number of markets as well as to gain the profits from development. Promus announced in 1990, amid much talk in the industry of serious oversupply and continuing losses on an industrywide basis, the formation, with a Japanese investment group, of Hospitality Capital Corp. to help the company's franchisees to secure financing for new properties. The motives of franchisors to expand, however sensible they may be from the individual company's vantage point, are motives that lead to the "overbuilding" that was so much talked of in the industry in the early 1990s.

The attractiveness of North American real estate to offshore buyers, especially those in Asia and the Middle East, contributed to the growth in hotel development in the 1980s and is likely to do so again in the next building cycle. "The Japanese," as Hara and Eyster put it, "are not investing in the hospitality industry *per se* but rather in hotels as value-added real estate."

An Operating Business

The hotel's operation is often the first investment dimension that students of hotel management automatically think of. As we have just noted, however, hotel companies—and other developers—have significant business interests outside of operations in both development and franchising of hotels. This does not mean they are uninterested in operations, however. In fact, both Promus and Marriott require the buyer to sign a management contract on hotels they

---

[13] Arbel and Woods, "Debt Hitchhiking," p. 106. I have adjusted their statement to include 1989 and 1990 data based on Rohs, *Lodging,* p. 8.

[14] Michael D. Rose, "A Message from the Chairman," *Promus Companies,* March 1990.

[15] Daniel R. Lee, *Marriott versus Promus* (New York: First Boston Co., February 20, 1991).

The "downstairs" market is willing to pay the higher price a full-service hotel must charge because services such as meeting rooms are important to them. (Courtesy of Stouffer Hotels)

develop so that they retain the right to expand their chain and manage the property as well.

Segmentation: For Guests or Developers?

Much of the development of new product segments — economy, all-suite, executive floors, superluxury — can be related to specific market segments. For example, economy segments are aimed at rate-conscious consumer groups such as retirees. (Days Inns reports that a significant proportion of its rooms are occupied by seniors.) Residence Inns has a clearly targeted segment in mind, and full-service hotels' upscale range of products, from executive floors to superluxury, is for the expense-account market. Transient all-suite hotels target upper level executives on weekdays and upper-middle-income families on weekends. Segmentation certainly meets guest needs.

On the other hand, we have noted that many hotel companies are real estate developers, and a strategy of segmentation has also met their business needs as developers. Having several brands that appeal to different final consumers permits hotel companies to put more than one hotel in a market. Thus, if Promus had an Embassy Suite in a city, it could still quite legitimately

Guest rooms at Courtyard by Marriott are designed with distinct functional areas for relaxing, working, sleeping, and dressing. King-sized beds are a feature in 70 percent of the rooms. (Courtesy of Marriott Corp.)

develop its other brands for *their* segments—a Hampton Inn for the limited-service market and a Homewood Suite for extended-stay guests. This helps sell hotels and franchises to investors as well as rooms to guests. As the editor of the *Cornell Hotel and Restaurant Administration Quarterly* put it,

> Most hotel companies are largely service companies that sell a product—a specific kind of hotel—to developers. . . . Today, hotel companies are offering developers a range of hotels so the company can match the hotel product to the site. Having multiple brands or chains allows hotel companies to provide a product to meet developer needs.[16]

As a result, hotel companies may be developing more than one property in the same city—a Hampton Inn and an Embassy Suite, or perhaps a Marriott Courtyard and Fairfield. While the company's brands are not generally competitive with each other, there is, inevitably, a degree of overlap. It is not as

[16] Glenn Withian, "Hotel Companies Aim for Multiple Markets," *Cornell Hotel and Restaurant Administration Quarterly,* November 1985, pp. 39–51. In the argument cited here, Withian is quoting industry analyst Daniel Lee.

clear, however, whether the seven brands of Choice Hotels International are noncompetitive. The company makes the claim, based on an extensive study, that there are advantages "to locating competing brands in a company's portfolio close to each other," and that this practice is more likely to have "a positive than a negative effect on all the brands at a location."[17] From an ethical point of view, there is nothing even faintly questionable about a company's developing two hotels that will compete with each other. The franchisor is in the business of selling franchises; the franchisee wants to invest in a property; and a developer needs a property to round out a project. Each pursues his or her own interest in an informed way. The resulting increase in competition is a business risk that should surprise no one.

Nevertheless, the interests of hotel companies, franchisees, and developers heighten the possibility that markets will be overbuilt, that the cycle we discussed at the beginning of this chapter will be more pronounced than if the players limit their attention to just consumer demand.

Solutions to Oversupply

One solution to an oversupply of rooms in the market is time and a continuing growth in demand. The other solution is to withdraw rooms from the market or to convert the property to other uses. It is estimated that 1.1 percent of hotel rooms are withdrawn each year.[18] Although the closing of a hotel is usually a sad day, especially for its owners, staff, and frequent guests, most properties do eventually reach a point where the continued investment to maintain and refurbish a property is not warranted. Indeed, inherent in the notion of depreciation is the fact that properties wear out.

On the other hand, the emergence of brands that are deliberately designed to prolong the economic life of older properties complicates this process more than a little. What has happened is that most lodging companies in the midprice market have gradually raised their standards over the years. As older properties reach the end of their initial franchise period, some are just not acceptable *to the franchisor* for refranchising. Others are acceptable but only with a level of investment that the *franchisee* feels is not economically viable. The result has been a growing number of properties that are still quite *usable* but which need an affiliation to replace the brand they have left.

A number of brands have emerged as conversion brands. Park Inns was established by people formerly associated with Holiday Inns with the avowed intention of serving midscale franchisees not happy with their current franchising. Rodeway, acquired by Choice as one of its seven brands in 1990, will be

[17] Frederick W. Mosser, "Impact—Not a Four Letter Word" [advertisement], *Cornell Hotel and Restaurant Administration Quarterly,* February 1991, p. 9. Mosser is reporting on a study by Prof. Ken W. McCleary at Virginia Polytechnic Institute commissioned by Choice Hotels International.

[18] Daniel R. Lee, *Lodging* (New York: Drexel Burnham Lambert, 1984), p. 23.

mostly a conversion brand according to *Hotel Motel Management*.[19] Holiday Inn Express expects to have 400 properties by 1996, many of them conversions from Holiday Inns.[20] Hospitality Franchise Systems announced HoJo Inns, also largely a conversion brand for older Howard Johnson properties.[21]

For the most part, conversions move older hotels from midmarket brands to brands that are competing in the upper end of the economy market. This is clearly a useful tactic for the owners of these properties but, in prolonging the economic life of these hotels, conversion brands contribute to the industry's oversupply problem.

MANAGEMENT COMPANIES

The arrangement between the management company and the hotel owner, a *management contract,* is described by Professor James Eyster of the Cornell Hotel School:

> A management contract is a written agreement between a hotel motor inn owner and operator in which the owner employs the operator as an agent (employee) to assume full operational responsibility for the property and to manage the property in a professional manner. As an agent, the operator pays in the name of the owner, all property operating expenses from the cash flow generated from the operation; it retains its management fees, and remits the remaining cash flow, if any, to the owner. The owner provides the hotel or motor inn property to include land, building, furniture and fixtures, equipment, and working capital and assumes full legal and financial responsibility for the project.[22]

The first management company may have been the Cesar Ritz Group. Before the turn of the century, Ritz, with his famous chef, Escoffier, was "paid a retainer to appoint and oversee the managers of separately owned hotels. That arrangement allowed the hotel to advertise itself as a Ritz hotel."[23] The first U.S. "hotel management company" was the Treadway Hotel Company, which began operating small college inns in the 1920s.[24] During the 1930s, the American Hotel Corporation managed bankrupt hotels, but as late as 1970 there were only three or four management companies in operation in the United States.

---

[19] *Hotel Motel Management,* August 20, 1990, p. 82.

[20] Brian Langdon, Address to the 13th Annual Hospitality Industry Investment Conference, New York, June 4, 1991.

[21] *Hotel Motel Management,* September 24, 1990, p. 15.

[22] James J. Eyster, *The Negotiation and Administration of Hotel Management Contracts,* quoted in Robert M. James, "Management Companies," *Lodging,* June 1985, p. 105.

[23] Lee, *Lodging,* p. 23.

[24] Robert M. James, "Management Companies," p. 105.

In the 1970s and 1980s, the number of hotels expanded rapidly, with much of the development being undertaken by people whose abilities and experience lay in finance and real estate rather than in hotel operations. To manage the hotels developed by these nonowner operators, the number of hotel management companies expanded rapidly. By 1985, there were about 125 such companies.[25] With the wave of financial difficulties and distressed properties that accompanied the industry's reversals in the last half of the 1980s, the number of management companies grew in five years by 60 percent, to about 200 in 1990.[26]

There are two kinds of management companies. First, most chain organizations such as Hilton, Holiday Inns, or Sheraton serve as management companies for hotels under their franchises. Chains dominate the management contract field, Professor Eyster tells us, for properties with more than 300 rooms. Chains require a substantial minimum fee just to defray their central office overhead. They have difficulty in working with smaller properties that don't generate enough revenue to cover the minimum fee. Accordingly, smaller management companies dominate in the under-300-room category.[27] Independent management companies have several advantages, according to Robert M. Jones, chairman of the American Hotel and Motel Association's International Council in Hotel-Motel Management Companies. They are able to operate properties under several franchises and offer owners more control over daily operations and more flexibility in contract terms.

The independent management companies also offer several advantages to those starting a career in the hotel business. The company with a successful track record will have experienced and knowledgeable people in its senior ranks. Working with and under such well-qualified and broadly experienced managers can be an education in itself. Moreover, a larger company will probably have properties of varying sizes and franchise affiliations and thus offer both opportunities for career progression from smaller to larger properties and a broad variety of experiences. The largest independent management company in terms of number of guest rooms in 1990 was Prime Management, which managed 17,400 rooms in 115 properties. Sage Development Resources, with 5,637 rooms and 40 properties, ranked number 25 in number of rooms under management.[28]

Naturally, as with any company you are considering working with, it is a good idea to inquire about the company's reputation before signing on in a responsible position. And, again, as with any company, a good way to get to know a prospective long-term employer is through employment in the summer or part time during the school year.

---

[25] James, "Management Companies," p. 105.

[26] *Lodging* November 1990, p. 31. The source for the estimate is, once again, Mr. James.

[27] James J. Eyster, "Management Contracts," *Cornell Hotel and Restaurant Administration Quarterly,* May 1988, pp. 43–55.

[28] *Hotel Motel Management,* May 27, 1991, p. 39.

Entrepreneurial Opportunities

We should pause here to note the significance of the management company's function for those who want to have ownership interest in a hotel. Management companies serve a need for mortgage holders and developers that can also be filled by individuals. Those individuals, who, through education and experience, prepare themselves to manage a hotel, can regard a time of economic reverses for the industry as a time of opportunity for themselves. Particularly with locally financed (that is, mortgaged) properties that get into trouble, there is a real opportunity from time to time to get into an ownership position in return for assuming an existing mortgage. This kind of opportunity is more likely to come up with older properties, and so the importance of a good food background—in order to merchandise the property—is clear.

COMPETITIVE TACTICS: SERVICES AND FACILITIES

"We don't have it because you don't want it" is the headline in the Days Inn advertisement we mentioned earlier. A company spokesperson said of the ad, "Most consumers are not interested in such amenities as health clubs, day-care centers, or presidential suites. The customer wants value for his dollar and he wants a clean, comfortable room and he doesn't need an exercise instructor."[29] On the other hand, at about the same time a Radisson official said, "We're not cutting back on services and amenities. That is to cut what we offer and that's not what our customers expect."[30] Which one is right? Obviously, in the segmented lodging market of today both of them can be right but for different target customers.

Services and amenities are crafted to meet the needs and preferences of particular target markets. At a very basic level, the industry is dividing into properties that serve the "upstairs" guest and those that serve the "downstairs" guest.[31] "Upstairs" guests are interested in what you find upstairs in a hotel, that is, guest rooms. They want comfortable, clean accommodations. This market is willing to give up "extra" services—that is, services that they don't want—for a lower price. The success of Motel 6 clearly indicates that there is a large upstairs market that focuses on *just* the basics in the guest room.

The downstairs market, on the other hand, either needs the more extensive services of a full-service hotel or finds them desirable. "Downstairs" guests want the traditional main floor attractions of full-service hotels: dining rooms, cocktail lounges, meeting and banquet facilities, and the like. Downstairs guests are willing to pay for the additional services because they are necessary

---

[29] *Lodging,* September 1990, p. 10.

[30] *Lodging,* November 1990, p. 92.

[31] The upstairs-downstairs guest dichotomy originated, I believe, with the Marriott organization.

The guest in the "upstairs" market is willing to trade off lobbies, banquet rooms, and food service in return for a very comfortable room at a reasonable price. (Courtesy of Red Roof Inns)

or because they can readily afford them. Generally we would include not only full-service transient hotels but also convention hotels, conference centers, and resort properties in the service-intensive downstairs segment. One of the most basic service decisions involves food service. Another involves tailoring the level and kind of other services and amenities to guest requirements and preferences. We should note again that downstairs guests traveling on business during the week on an expense account may be upstairs guests seeking basic accommodations and a lower price when traveling at their own expense on the weekend.

HOTEL FOOD SERVICE

Hotels serving the upstairs market have chosen to eliminate or reduce drastically the food service available in the property. It is important, however, to realize that they have not ignored food service because off-premise food service is almost invariably available nearby.

Bed and Breakfast—Plus

The practice of giving away a continental breakfast is certainly not new but has been common in small motels for some years. But the advertised, standardized availability of a "free breakfast," that is, one covered by the price of the room, has a special appeal. In the economy market, for instance, a continental breakfast of juice, pastry, and coffee is generally all that is provided. In some all-suite properties, as well, a continental breakfast is the standard, but a number offer a full, cooked-to-order breakfast. All-suite properties also commonly provide a free cocktail party, typically from 5 to 7 P.M.

Many all-suite properties also provide a scaled-down, on-premise restaurant, but very few offer substantial meeting and banquet facilities. Residence Inns has a grocery shopping service available without cost to their guests, and Homewood Suites provide an on-premise convenience store. Because long-stay suites provide a full kitchen, they do not offer any food service beyond a complimentary breakfast. Among all-suite properties, then, there is not the uniformity in curtailment of food service that is found among most budget properties. In general, however, elimination or at least simplification is the rule.

Leased Food Service

Leasing the hotel's food service is more common in medium-priced hotels of 300 rooms or less.[32] As well, over 90 percent of Embassy Suites restaurants are leased. Embassy argues that this permits them to focus all of their attention and effort on their high-profit guest rooms business. We should note, too, that it greatly simplifies staffing at the general management level. Managers with food service competence are required where the hotel operates rather than leases its food service. Because Embassy operates its own complimentary breakfast and evening cocktail hour, basic services *are* assured for the room guest.

On the other hand, *Nations Restaurant News* reports that the practice of leasing restaurants peaked in 1987 and 1988 and has slumped markedly since then. They quote a consulting company expert as saying, "There were just some dismal failures." Experience in the industry seems to be that leased operations do fine while business is good but when sales volume falls disputes multiply.[33]

When business falls off, the hotel is most in need of a good food operation as a competitive weapon in a tight market. On the other hand, the restaurant leasing company gains no benefit from increased rooms-department revenue and, as you will recall, a restaurant has a much lower operating profit level than does a hotel. The problem is that each company has its own business objectives. In good times the clash of interests is not apparent. When business turns down, however, the restaurant *has to* cut costs—and services—to survive. The guest suffers—and will almost surely go elsewhere in the highly competitive hotel business.

[32] *Lodging Hospitality,* October 1990, p. 175.
[33] *Nations Restaurant News,* February 18, 1991, p. 42.

Brand Name Restaurants

Availability of some kind of food service in the immediate area *is* essential for most hotels that do not operate their own food service facilities. As Carlson Hospitality expands its economy brand, Country Lodging, for instance, it locates one of its Country Kitchen family restaurants on the same piece of real estate.[34]

Probably the best-known company to rely on the on-site franchised restaurant is La Quinta Motor Inns. This economy motel chain offers a build-to-suit leased restaurant on the motel site. It has used this arrangement with several restaurant companies, including Denny's, Cracker Barrel, Bob Evans Farms, Waffle House, and Shoney's. Since fast food has become so expert in breakfast service, La Quinta has also begun to work with companies such as McDonald's and Wendy's who offer the fast breakfast service their rooms customers want. Generally the lease specifies the minimum number of hours of operation and allows the guests to charge their food to their room.

Full-service hotels have begun to lease out restaurants not just to an operating company but to franchisees of major food service chains. Alternatively, some hotel operators have become franchisees of these chains themselves. The names of chains now operating within a hotel, such as Denny's, Bennigan's, Bobby McGee's, Steak and Ale, and Restaurants Associates, are well known to the traveling public and, as such, serve as a draw for the hotel. In addition, as franchisees these operations receive field support and advice from the franchise organization that can help smooth out some of the rough spots.

Conventional Hotel Restaurants

A single direction for hotels' food services is by no means clear. Some hotel operators are finding that they can't compete successfully with local top-quality food service restaurants in attracting local trade and so are building smaller restaurants and reducing the number of the food service outlets in the hotel from two or three to one. Even some luxury hotels are opting for more casual outlets rather than formal dining rooms.

Upscale hotel companies such as Marriott and Hyatt as well as luxury properties such as Four Seasons continue to meet guest expectations for *full* service with a variety of restaurants in their properties, and these almost always include a top-of-the-line, luxury restaurant. As the president of one hotel company put it, "Strong, community oriented restaurants and lounges add 7 to 8 points to our occupancy rates." In a similar vein, the president of Royce Hotels explained, "If you call secretaries in West Palm Beach and ask them where to stay, they probably say Royce because they eat in the restaurant

---

[34] *Hotel Motel Management,* March 25, 1991, p. 3.

and visit the lounge. Eighty percent of our business is generated through local referrals."[35]

Restaurants as a Competitive Strategy

Hotel restaurants do not generally make money after all costs are considered. One hospitality consultant has estimated that after allocation of all overhead, a hotel restaurant actually loses about 5 percent on sales.[36] This difficulty arises because food service is the hotel's "service department." The argument for devoting all the time and effort to food service, however, is made fairly well by the executives quoted in the previous paragraph. Food service in many markets adds points to occupancy and secures local referrals. The resulting higher occupancies more than offset the poor profit performance of food service.

Whereas limited-service hotels such as Hampton Inns or Fairfield Inns minimize food service at the present time, these properties currently have the advantage of being brand new. When they have several look-alike competitors, all offering the same advantages, the competitive situation may prove more complex, particularly as their facilities age.

At the point when the lodging market becomes highly competitive, the chances are that the importance of a good-quality food and beverage operation will be "rediscovered" by more and more operations. On the other hand, it is quite clear that there is and, for the foreseeable future will be, an important segment of lodging customers that is willing to trade off a reduction in "downstairs" services in return for a lower price.

OTHER SERVICES AND AMENITIES

A wide range of services, distinctive physical plant features, and products outside the food and beverage department are used by hotels to differentiate a property from its competitors.

The Concierge and Superfloors

The basic function of the concierge is to provide guest service and information. The cross keys, symbol of the concierge, is intended to convey a degree of expertise and knowledge significantly above that of the bell staff. The concierge knows the right restaurants, the best shows, and can probably get reservations or tickets if they are required. In many ways, the concierge acts as a friend to the stranger out of town, giving service and rendering that "extra" in service that makes a stay a distinctive experience in hospitality.

Many hotels are adding a concierge to the lobby staff, and a number of companies associate the concierge closely or exclusively with their superfloors,

---

[35] *Nations Restaurant News,* March 10, 1986, p. F29.

[36] Bjorn Hansen, "Hotel Food Service: Where's the Profit?" *Cornell Hotel and Restaurant Administration Quarterly,* August 1984, p. 96.

that is, special areas such as executive floors and tower suites. On these floors special lounges and other services are commonly provided. Although there are many variations, perhaps the easiest way to examine the practice is to look at one hotel company.

At CP Hotels' Toronto property, L'Hotel, three classes of service are available: standard, business class, and entrée gold. The word *service* is emphasized because the basic product, the rooms and their furnishings, while somewhat differentiated, are fundamentally similar because all rooms are in the luxury class throughout the hotel. The business class and entrée gold are a part of a strategy of meeting the particular service tastes and needs of upscale, frequent travelers.

Guests entering the hotel intending to register for a standard room (about 65 percent of the hotel) register at the front desk and are shown to their room by a bellman. The concierge in the lobby provides them with standard services such as information, reservations, and tickets.

Guests entering the hotel intending to go to the business class floors register in a special express line, using a special express registration procedure. Other services include complimentary cable television with remote control, and evening turndown service. Special personal amenities include hair dryers, plush bathrobes, extraplush towels, and freshly cut flowers. Business class rooms cost about 25 percent more than standard rooms.

Entrée gold guests are generally recognized by the doorman because they are repeat guests. They are sent directly to the entrée gold floor, where they are met by the concierge and shown to their room after the very brief registration formalities are concluded in the gold lounge. In the center of the gold lounge, consisting of several rooms furnished in the style of a private club, is the office of the concierge and his or her staff. Prompt, personal service is emphasized in the lounge. A complimentary deluxe continental breakfast is served to entrée gold guests in the gold lounge. In addition, each room is supplied with a small box of fine chocolates. Other services include complimentary local phone calls, an honor bar in the gold lounge with complimentary canapes from 4 to 7 P.M., and coffee or tea served without charge with the guest's wake-up call. Entrée gold guests receive, in addition, all the services and amenities that business class guests receive. The gold lounge offers an honor bar, secretarial services, and a "boardroom" for small meetings. The full dining-room menu is available from room service. Both business class and entrée gold guests are offered complimentary limousine service to the center of downtown. Rates on the gold floor are about 45 percent higher than are those on the premiere floors.

Before concluding this discussion, we should comment again on the wide variety of practice. Luxury hotels, such as the Four Seasons or Dallas's Turtle Creek, offer substantially the same services as those available on the gold floor, but to *all* their guests. On the other hand, many motor hotels and virtually all economy properties have completely eliminated the bell staff, on the theory that today most people prefer not to be bothered with a bellman.

Fitness Facilities

According to *The Washington Post,* 2,000 hotels—10 times as many as just a few years earlier—list some kind of health and fitness facility in their advertising. Health-club memberships have been growing at a 20-percent rate; company fitness programs are becoming common; and more than half of all U.S. firms are expected to start programs within the next decade. Thus, all these people who have committed themselves to a fitness program quite naturally don't want to break their routine when they travel, and so it is not surprising that hotels and motels are adding fitness programs. Resort and convention hotels invest in more elaborate facilities, whereas economy and midscale properties tend toward more modest arrangements. The basic equipment required are exercise bikes, treadmills, rowing machines, weight-training equipment, and floor mats.

The notable fact about fitness centers is the speed with which they are—and can be—added to a property. This kind of service can be expensive to add, but it is also a fairly easy service to add—and easy for competitors to copy, as well.

Business Centers

Two thirds of business travelers surveyed indicated a business center was an important service in a hotel, and 40 percent of them indicated it was very important.[37] In another survey conducted by Swissotel, "facilities for business was one of the top five features ranked as important or very important by 8 out of 10 guests responding."[38] And, as we noted earlier, even economy motels make business services available. Business travelers are on the road frequently and are potentially repeat guests. It makes sense to cater to their needs in order to gain their regular patronage.

ASSESSING SERVICES AND AMENITIES

As a competitive tactic, what stands out is the ease with which many of the services and amenities we have been discussing can be copied. The first hotel or motel in a city that put in a television set undoubtedly had an advantage—but not for long. And shampoo—once rarely seen in a hotel room—has now become commonplace. Indeed, in regard to personal-care amenities, it is becoming necessary to have them just to avoid damaging the property's reputation, but it is difficult to see them as offering any lasting competitive advantage. Similarly, exercise facilities are an easily duplicated service. But finding or training a good concierge is almost as difficult as providing memorable food service. Again, food service is very difficult to do well, and its very complexity ensures that it will not be easy to copy. Although some property types may be able to dispense with food service and rely on restaurants in their

---

[37] *Hotel Motel Management,* May 27, 1991, p. 51.

[38] *Lodging,* March 1991, p. 34.

neighborhood, it seems likely that they will have greater difficulty in differentiating themselves from their competitors, especially as the properties age. Soap, shampoo, or a weight room probably won't help either. As the ultimate differentiating service, food service's role seems secure.

THE OUTLOOK FOR THE LODGING BUSINESS

Perhaps the easiest way to introduce our discussion of the outlook for the lodging business is with a personal recollection:

> The first job I had in the hotel business was in my father's hotel, the Fargoan, in the year I graduated from high school, 1949. The hotel advertised that every room had access to a bath—which was true, as there were two of them on each floor. Our least expensive room was a "plain court room," which rented for $1.40 per night. These were tiny rooms that looked out on a small air shaft. The "plain outside room" was not much larger, but it did have an outside window. It rented for $1.65. Both rooms had access to a bath—down the hall.
>
> Of course we had rooms with "connecting bath," too. As I recall, a single-with-bath rented for the princely sum of $2.50, and a double was somewhere above $3.00. The rooms were clean but small and had no radio and, of course, no TV.
>
> Lest anyone think poorly of that hotel, let me tell you that it was AAA-approved and that, in his day, my father had a reputation as a leader in the industry. In fact, this book is dedicated to him out of respect for his achievements.

UPGRADING

The fine little hotel in which I worked in high school couldn't even compete in today's market. The story of the hotel industry since that time is one of continuous upgrading: radios, televisions, swimming pools, larger rooms, bigger beds, plushier rooms. And that story line seems unlikely to change. The industry is highly competitive, and so improvements are quickly matched. Hotel guests have consistently opted for the improved property with the higher rates, until rates escalated to a point where a place was created at the lower end of the market for economy properties. It is interesting that the first Holiday Inns in the early 1950s were, in many ways, the economy chain of *their* day, and that gradually the upgrading process has moved them into a midscale position.

Today's economy properties resemble closely the Holiday Inn rooms of a few years ago, and we see limited-service properties competing on the excellence of the facilities and services that they *do* offer. The potential for upgrading—at whatever level—is hard to resist.

Some services such as a swimming pool or exercise room are fairly easy for other properties to match. They don't offer a strong basis for differentiation. (Courtesy of Days Inns)

CYCLES

Rather than a growth industry, the hotel business is a cyclical one in a fairly static market. This makes competition even fiercer, and the most successful competitive tactic in the long run has been to improve the product even if the rate increases. As the upgrading proceeds, the rates must follow to preserve profits. Although the hotel industry's rates rose very slowly from 1989 through 1991, they will quite likely begin to escalate again as supply and demand come into better balance.

Although overbuilding at one end of each cycle seems to be a chronic problem, that is not necessarily bad news for aspiring hotel management people. The opportunities that failing properties have provided in the past have been the basis for some of the most successful hotel careers. Conrad Hilton, as Hilton Hotels President Carl Mottek recently pointed out, bought the Waldorf Astoria for 4.5 cents on the dollar and made it successful because he and his organization knew how to run it. Not everyone can buy on that scale, but there are many other entrepreneurs whose history is the same on a smaller scale. A cyclical business presents opportunities to those who know how to operate a business.

The intensity of the cycle that ends in overbuilding appears, if anything, to be heightened by the increasingly prominent role played by developers. The real estate developer's need for a hotel to complete a project and give it appeal has encouraged the development of oversupply in some markets, but as we've argued, that has meant opportunities for many. In 1970, there were only 3 or 4 management companies; today there are 200, large and small. These management companies came into being because a hotel belonging to somebody else was an opportunity for them.

FOOD SERVICE

The new hotel formats increasingly emphasize the guest room and rely on outside restaurants — or smaller on-premise restaurants — to provide an essential service. In doing so, they may have given up a key competitive tool, but there doesn't seem to be any question but that food service will play a secondary role in the economy sector of the lodging business. The consumer has accepted that and come to expect it in return for holding down room rates.

Some lodging concepts have eliminated or de-emphasized food service, concentrating their efforts on the guest room. (Courtesy of Choice Hotels International)

Still, we will probably see a resurgence in food and beverage above the strictly economy properties. Accordingly, anyone entering the field would still do well to seek a solid grounding in restaurant operations.

The demand for improved service—and all the difficulties of attracting and keeping good service employees that we discussed earlier—apply to hotels as well. "People" skills to deal with demanding guests and scarce employees will be at a premium.

GROWING MARKETS

Certainly, the demographics we discussed in Chapter 4 suggest a growing leisure travel market. Middle-aged people have the highest propensity to travel of any age segment. The exploding leisure class of retirees beckons the industry nearly as strongly as does the arrival in middle age of the baby boomers. The future looks bright—but competitive.

SUMMARY

The hotel business is highly competitive, characterized by periodic increases in the number of rooms available. Accordingly, we say it is cyclical. Because it requires such a large investment in fixed assets, it is capital intensive. Often hotels are built to meet not only the guests' needs but also investors' needs. The growth in the number of management companies running hotels under contract is, in large part, the result of real estate developers' building new properties to meet *their* own needs. Segmentation, too, has contributed to the growth in rooms supply as each company seeks to be represented with each of its products in all major markets.

Hotel companies are competing through market segmentation, by developing specialized products for particular markets and by curtailing investment and services in some areas, principally food service, so as to permit competitive rates even with upgraded guest rooms. Other competitive tactics include offering (or not offering) various special services and amenities. Even though food service is being eliminated or deemphasized in some segments, superior food service remains an important competitive point of difference for many properties. The greatest problem in the hotel business is developing new ways of balancing room rates and lodging value to meet consumers' current needs and preferences.

KEY WORDS AND CONCEPTS

To help you review this chapter, keep in mind the following:

Cyclical business
Capital intensive
Competitive conditions
Growth industry
Hotel investment decision
   Financial dimension
   Exchange rate effect
   Real estate dimension
   Operations dimension
Segmentation
   For guests
   For developers
Oversupply

Conversion franchising
Management companies
Upstairs-oriented guests
Downstairs-oriented guests
Function of hotel food service
Leased food service
Concierge
Superfloors
Lodging outlook
   Upscaling
   Cycles
   Food service
   Growth

REVIEW QUESTIONS

1. How does the hotel business react to the business cycle and to the local market?

2. What are capital costs? Why is the hotel business a capital-intensive business?

3. How have travel patterns and consumer preferences changed in regard to the demand for lodging?

4. What are the main elements of a hotel investment decision?

5. Why did management companies come into being?

6. How do independent and chain management companies differ?

7. What is the difference between the preferences of the "upstairs" and "downstairs" guests?

8. What does the decision to refranchise entail? What will a conversion do for an older property?

9. In what areas are hotels best differentiated from one another? What area is least likely to be copied? Why?

P A R T 4

**TRAVEL,
TOURISM,
AND THE
HOSPITALITY
INDUSTRY**

C H A P T E R 10

Courtesy of Loew's Hotels

TOURISM: FRONT AND CENTER

THE PURPOSE OF THIS CHAPTER

Travel and tourism at the local, state, and even national levels are vital to the health of our economy, as well as to the hospitality industry. Indeed, tourism is big business and growing rapidly in North America and worldwide. Because the economic and social impacts of tourism are so significant, no hospitality manager can afford to overlook the subject. This chapter discusses the economic dimensions of tourism as well as the social and cultural impacts.

THIS CHAPTER SHOULD HELP YOU

1. See the importance of tourism in the economy as a whole.

2. Understand the factors that are supporting the growth of travel and tourism.

3. Become familiar with current travel trends.

4. Know the significance of the travel multiplier in assessing the economic significance of tourism.

5. Recognize the importance of tourism in providing employment.

6. Recognize the significance of tourism as a part of international trade and as a source of strength in America's balance of payments.

7. Assess the noneconomic positive and negative impacts of tourism.

Tourism's importance to the hospitality industry is obvious. Some parts of the industry, such as hotels, derive almost all of their sales from travelers. Even food service attributes roughly 25 percent of its sales to travelers. And many leisure-oriented businesses with a major food service and hospitality component, such as theme parks, are also dependent on travelers.

In the economy as a whole, the importance of tourism and the hospitality industry is increasing each year. Indeed, as employment in "smokestack" industries—that is, manufacturing—falls, the service industries, especially those businesses serving travelers, must take up the slack by providing new jobs. Tourism, then, is central not only to the health of the hospitality industry but also to the economy as a whole.

Tourism is the collection of productive businesses and governmental organizations that serve the traveler away from home. According to the U.S. Travel Data Center, these organizations include restaurants, hotels, motels, and resorts; all facets of transportation, including rental cars, travel agents, and gasoline service stations; national and state parks or recreation areas; and various private attractions. The industry also includes those organizations that support these firms' retail activities, including advertising companies, publications, transportation equipment manufacturers, and travel research and development agencies.

TRAVEL AND TOURISM

Travel and tourism are as American as baseball, hot dogs, apple pie, and the interstate highway system. Three quarters of all Americans aged 16 and over take at least one pleasure trip in the course of a year.[1] In 1990, Americans took nearly 1.3 billion such "person trips."[2] (A person trip, as you may gather, is one person taking one trip. If two persons go on that trip, that equals two person trips. A trip is any travel 100 miles or more away from home.) Moreover, tourism is growing rapidly, fueled by more leisure time, rising family incomes, and the more favorable demographic trends we have discussed in earlier chapters. We can look briefly at each of these factors.

GROWING LEISURE

There are several reasons for the increase in leisure time. People at work now have more time off. Most companies' vacation policies have become more liberal. And the number of legal, paid holidays has increased and, significantly for tourism, more of these are timed so as to provide three-day weekends.

---

[1] *The Personal Travel Market in the United States* (New York: Newspaper Advertising Bureau, Inc., October 1987), p. 7.

[2] *The 1990 Travel Market Report* (Washington D.C.: U.S. Travel Data Center, August 1991), p. 6.

Leisure travel is judged by many experts to be the biggest source of growth in travel in years to come. (Courtesy of Busch Gardens Tampa)

Although the typical workweek has stayed at 40 hours for many years, flex time and other flexible scheduling arrangements are giving more people more leisure time. In Europe, some manufacturing industries have even broken with the 40-hour workweek norm; and in Sweden, the average workweek is under 30 hours.[3] In the United States as well, we may see pressure for shortening the workweek.

INCOME TRENDS

The two-income family has become a major factor in travel. The majority of women today expect to work outside the home. A two-income family not only increases total family income but adds to the family's security. If one spouse is laid off, that does not eliminate all of the family's income because one spouse continues to work.

Very commonly women leave the work force for a period at the time of the birth of a child, and many women return to work only on a part-time basis while young children are still at home. For those committed to a career outside the home, however, the ultimate intention is to return to full-time work. A further element of stability to family incomes today, we might note, is the fact

[3] Kenneth E. Hornback, "Social Trends and Leisure Behavior." Paper delivered at the 1985 National Outdoor Recreation Trends Symposium, Myrtle Beach, S.C., February 24–27, 1985.

that if a husband loses his job or otherwise suffers an economic reversal, young mothers can and will expand their working commitment outside the home earlier than they may have originally intended.

There are two motives for women to work outside the home after marriage. One relates to a preference to be in the work force for professional and career reasons, and for the challenge, stimulation, and variety that working provides. Another reason, for many women, however, is to maintain the family income at a level that affords the family a comfortable and satisfying life. Income growth after inflation in most occupations has been slow in recent years, and in some cases family members have shifted from highly paid manufacturing work to less well-paid occupations, often in the service sector. Thus, some women work at least in part because they have to maintain their family income.

Two-income families, then, are not all well-to-do "yuppies" (young urban professionals). Many families pool two modest incomes to support a comfortable life-style. Because they are working to maintain a comfortable life, it is not surprising that they are disposed to spend their money on the goods and services they want. They are good customers—and even in bad times, they can usually maintain at least one income, making the stability of families' spending in bad times greater today than it was a generation ago.

Almost all two-income families have time pressures. When both parents work, the household chores still need to be done and children must be cared for. This means that many people may have to sacrifice leisure time for household and family maintenance chores. Therefore, when they *do* get away, time is at a premium, and they seek "quality time." Though sensitive to price/value comparisons, these travelers generally seek good value for their money rather than low-cost recreational experiences.

DEMOGRAPHICS

Our discussion of the "middle-aging of America" in Chapter 4 suggested the impact of demographic changes on tourism. Middle age generally means higher income and a greater propensity to travel. In fact, people in the latter half of middle age, from age 50 to 64, dominate the luxury travel market.[4] These travelers are typically "empty nesters," whose children have left home. At the same time, they are at or near their peak earnings.

Another significant demographic development for tourism is the increasing number of senior citizens. Indeed, authoritative estimates indicate that well over a quarter of households headed by a person aged 65 or older have enough discretionary income to do some leisure traveling. Although this group, made up largely of retirees, is generally not as prosperous as are people with employment income, they have much more leisure time. Accordingly, elderly

---

[4] Jeffrey P. Rosenfeld, "Demographics on Vacation," *American Demographics,* January 1986, p. 40.

Camping serves the needs of American travelers of all ages, including the growing number of retired Americans for whom leisure is a full-time way of life. (Courtesy of the National Park Service)

travelers often choose group travel at off-peak times and seasons and tend to be more price conscious. The travel industry has responded with numerous special price arrangements aimed at senior travelers.[5]

TRAVEL TRENDS

The most frequent reason for travel is to visit family and friends. Other pleasure travel, for outdoor recreation and entertainment, is just behind that, and business and convention travel is in third place. Figure 10.1 summarizes purpose of travel. While business travel dipped slightly in the face of a recession in 1990, personal travel increases more than offset that drop. As Figure 10.2 indicates, total travel has continued to grow for several years.

[5] Rosenfeld, "Demographics on Vacation."

Outdoor recreation is one of the major motivations for travel in North America. (Courtesy of Kampgrounds of America)

MODE OF TRAVEL

After automobiles, airlines are the second most common means of transportation. Following deregulation of air travel by the federal government, airfares fell significantly. The increase of air travel's proportionate share of passenger miles since 1979 probably reflects this fact. It is interesting to note, however, that when airline prices reversed their trend in 1988, the airline's share declined moderately. Common carriers (air, rail, and bus) have had a larger share of passenger miles during the 1980s, however, as a result of air travel's overall increase, as shown in Table 10.1. Bus travel actually declined 16 percent in the last decade. Rail travel, although still the smallest in share of travel, has a considerable potential for the future.[6]

TRIP DURATION

As two working spouses in a family becomes more common, vacations have become shorter. As Figure 10.3 illustrates, the typical vacation of the 1950s and 1960s was an annual event lasting 10 to 14 days. During the 1970s and 1980s, vacations, on average, were shortened to 5 to 7 days, and taken twice a year. Kenneth Hornback, chief of socioeconomic studies for the National

[6] *The 1989–90 Economic Review of Travel in America* (Washington, D.C.: U.S. Travel Data Center, 1990), pp. 7–27 and A-3.

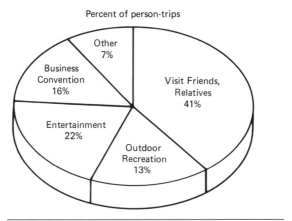

FIGURE 10.1   Purpose of trip. (*Source:* U.S. Travel Data Center's National Travel Survey—1990.)

Park Service and a perceptive student of changing leisure patterns, tells us that the typical vacation of the 1990s is a 2- to 3-day "minivacation" which, although concentrated in the warmer months, offers people a break in fall and winter, too.[7] In fact, the length of the average pleasure trip declined from about 5.5 nights in 1985 to 4.3 nights in 1990.

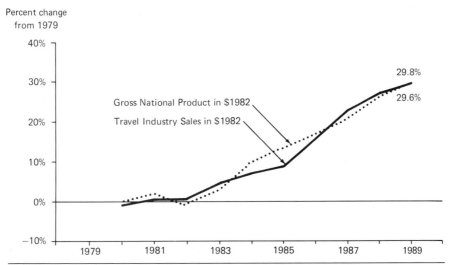

FIGURE 10.2   The travel industry has grown as fast as real GNP over the last decade. (*Source:* U.S. Travel Data Center.)

[7]Kenneth E. Hornback, "Distributing Demand: Notes on a Space/Time Solution for the Outdoor Recreation Demand/Supply Problem." Paper delivered at the Southeastern Recreation Research Symposium, Asheville, N.C., February 14–15, 1991.

TABLE 10.1 Intercity Transportation in the United States, 1979 and 1990

Mode of Transport	1979*		1990*	
	Billions of Passenger Miles	% of Passenger Miles	Billions of Passenger Miles	% of Passenger Miles
Common carriers				
Air	212.7	18.6	345.1	22.7
Bus	27.7	2.5	23.3	1.5
Rail	5.0	0.4	6.2	0.4
Total	245.5	21.5	374.6	24.6
Auto, truck, and recreational vehicle	895.7	78.5	1,146.1	75.4
Total, all modes	1,141.1	100.0	1,520.7	100.0

Source: Data from U.S. Travel Data Center.
*USTDC estimate.

The popularity of weekend vacations and shorter trips combining pleasure and business seems to be more prevalent among younger travelers. Affluent travelers with an average age of 50 or more, on the other hand, prefer vacations of a week or more.[8]

Era	Timing	Duration (Days)	Frequency
1950–60	———	10–14	Annual
1970–80	— —	5–7	Biannual
1990	– – – – –	2–3	Bimonthly
	J'''F''''M'''A''''M'''J'''J'''A''''S'''O''''N'''D		

FIGURE 10.3 Vacation style changes. (*Source:* Kenneth E. Hornback, "Distributing Demand: Notes on a Space/Time Solution for the Outdoor Recreation Demand/Supply Problem," Southeastern Recreation Research Symposium, Ashville, N.C., February 1991.)

[8] *Travel Trends,* Better Homes and Gardens, vol. 5, no. 1.

PRICE SENSITIVITY

The trends in auto and air travel support the notion that travel is price sensitive. As we noted earlier, when air fares fell following deregulation, air travel grew rapidly. When fares began to rise, however, air travel declined somewhat (see Figure 10.4). Likewise, when gas prices escalate sharply, auto travel declines. Further evidence of price sensitivity: as the cost of owning and operating a car has increased, people have tended to buy smaller cars and to keep them longer.[9] While travel by personal vehicle is still the most common form of travel, consumers do change their behavior to moderate the impact of rising costs.

THE ECONOMIC SIGNIFICANCE OF TOURISM

In total business receipts, tourism has consistently ranked second or third among all retail businesses. Only grocery stores—and in some years, auto-

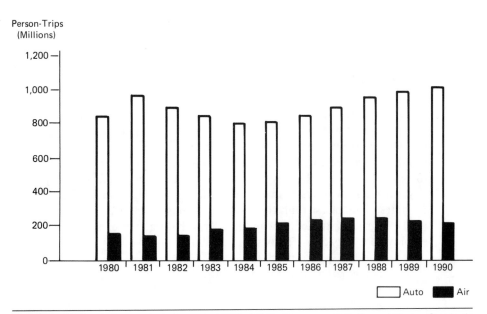

FIGURE 10.4 Auto and air travel, 1980–1990. (*Source:* U.S. Travel Data Center's National Travel Survey.)

[9] Hornback, "Social Trends and Leisure Behavior."

mobile dealers—have greater sales. Measuring the industry in terms of employment, tourism provides more jobs than does any other industry except the health services.[10]

Although tourism currently accounts for $350 billion in receipts in the U.S. economy, that is only a superficial, first-order measurement of travel importance. You may recall the term *multiplier* from your economics courses. A multiplier measures the effect of initial spending together with the chain of expenditures that result. (For example, when a traveler spends a dollar in a hotel, some portion of it goes to employees, suppliers, and owners, who in turn respend it—and so it goes.) Although the precise computation of the *travel multiplier* need not concern us, some experts estimate that the final impact of tourism is 3 to 3½ times greater than is that of the initial expenditures of the tourists themselves. Figure 10.5 illustrates how the multiplier works in practice. Figure 10.6 indicates the annual impact of an additional 100 visitors a day on an average U.S. community, including the impact of the multiplier.

Travel has become a mature industry, growing at about the same rate as the economy as a whole. In recession years, however, tourism usually holds up better than does the rest of the economy. Hence, tourism is an important source of both growth and stability in the local, state, and national economies.

As Figure 10.2 indicated, the growth in receipts in the travel industry has been at about the same level as the gross national product (GNP) over the last decade.

TOURISM AND EMPLOYMENT

Approximately 1 in every 20 civilian employees is employed in an activity supported by travel expenditures. That is nearly 5 million people. The travel industry contributes to job growth far in excess of its size. Employment in the last decade, as indicated in Figure 10.7, has grown 43 percent, more than twice the growth rate for all industries. Travel and tourism generate more jobs than any other private industry in 13 states and is one of the top three employers in 37 states. The lowest rank the industry attains in *any* state is 11th out of 69 industry groups studied.[11] The U.S. Travel Data Center sums up tourism's employment impact as follows:

> Over the past several decades, travel activity in the U.S. has continually demonstrated the ability to create new jobs faster than the rest of the economy to provide a disproportionate number of jobs to traditionally disadvantaged, and to produce new employment opportunities during

---

[10] *The 1989–90 Economic Review of Travel in America*, p. 13.
[11] *The 1989–90 Economic Review of Travel in America*, p. 66.

Tourist Spending for		Tourist Industry Expenses		Secondary Business Beneficiaries

Tourist Spending for	Tourist Industry Expenses	Secondary Business Beneficiaries
Hotels	Wage, salaries, and tips	Employees
Restaurants	Payroll taxes	Government agencies
Entertainment and recreation	Food, beverages, and house- keeping sup- plies	Food industry
Clothing		Beverage industry
Personal care		Custodial industry
Retail	Construction and maintenance	Architectural firms
Gifts and crafts		Construction firms
Transportation	Advertising	Repair firms
Tours	Utilities	Advertising firms
Museums and his- torical	Insurance	News media
	Interest and prin- cipal	Water, gas, and electric
	Legal and ac- counting	Telephone com- panies
	Transportation	Insurance indus- try
	Taxes and licen- ses	Bank and inves- tors
	Equipment and furniture	Legal and ac- counting firms
		Air, bus, auto, and gas
		Taxi companies
		Government com- panies
		Wholesale sup- pliers
		Health care

FIGURE 10.5 The tourist dollar multiplier effect: tourist dollar flow into the economy. [*Source:* Michael Evans, *Tourism: Always a People Business* (Knoxville: University of Tennessee, 1984).]

economic recessions. In 1989, travel's job creating powers waned relative to the overall economy but still provided a healthy boost to U.S. employment.[12]

Although only about one-quarter of food service employment can be traced to tourism, a much larger proportion of hotel and motel employment serves travelers away from home.

PUBLICITY AS AN ECONOMIC BENEFIT

Communities often spend large sums of money to advertise their virtues to visitors and investors. They establish economic development bureaus to bring

---

[12] *The 1989–90 Economic Review of Travel in America,* p. 37.

Direct Impact	*Total Impact**
$1,570,000 in retail and service industry sales to visitors	$2,990,000 in business receipts
$327,000 in wages and salaries	$757,000 in wages and salaries
29 new travel industry jobs providing additional income for 23 households with 60 residents	66 new jobs providing additional income for 53 househololds with 139 residents
$134,000 in state and local tax revenue, enough to support 33 school children	$217,000 in state and local tax revenue, enough to support 53 school children
Two more retail or service establishments	Five more retail or service establishments

*Includes direct, indirect, and induced impact

FIGURE 10.6 Annual impact of 100 additional visitors a day on the average U.S. community, 1989 preliminary. (*Source:* U.S. Travel Data Center.)

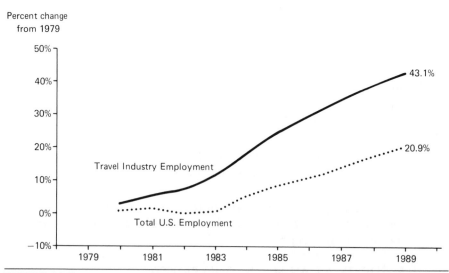

FIGURE 10.7 Travel industry employment has grown faster than total U.S. industry employment. (*Source:* U.S. Travel Data Center.)

employers to town and even offer tax rebates and low-cost financing. Aside from its direct economic impact, tourism also offers a chance to achieve many of these same benefits. That is, a tourist attraction brings visitors to a city or area, and they can then judge for themselves the community's suitability as a place to live and work. A major tourist event in a city or region attracts huge numbers of visitors, often for their first visit to the area. Assuming the region has natural charms and man-made attractions, some visitors are likely to become interested in relocating there—or at least in making a return visit.

THE UNITED STATES AS AN INTERNATIONAL TOURIST ATTRACTION

International tourism spending at home and abroad by all the world's peoples is the world's largest "industry," accounting for 5.5 percent of total economic activity (as measured by GNP) and for about 6.6 percent of world employment, or some 130,000,000 people, making tourism the largest employer in most countries.[13] Tourism spending was $2.1 trillion in 1988 and is projected to grow by over 60 percent to $3.4 trillion in 1998, a compound growth of 5 percent.[14] *International* tourism—that is, spending by travelers outside their home country—was estimated at $209 billion in 1989, and international arrivals, in total, were about 1½ times the population of the United States, or 404 million people.[15] Such numbers boggle the mind, perhaps, as much as they enlighten it, but they are cited to help us grasp an important fact: International tourism is, indeed, a huge set of businesses whose effects are worth taking the time to understand.

MEASURING THE VOLUME

There are two different ways to measure the volume of international tourism. *Arrivals and departures* measures the volume of people traveling; *receipts and payments* measures money spent. Dollar figures have the disadvantage of being distorted by fluctuating currency values; but to measure the *economic impact,* currency measures must be used. The best measure of *activity,* on the other hand, is the physical measure, arrivals and departures.

U.S. Arrivals and Departures

In the six years from 1985 to 1991, total arrivals in the United States rose to about 44 million in 1991, an increase of 74 percent, as shown in Figure 10.8. Figure 10.9 shows that U.S. departures over the same period also increased, but more slowly—by only 29 percent. Figure 10.10 shows that nearly two

---

[13] World Travel and Tourism Council report quoted in *Hotel Motel Management,* May 13, 1991, p. 1.

[14] *Travel Industry World Yearbook,* quoted in *Hotels,* January 1991, p. 40.

[15] *Hotels,* January 1991, p. 6.

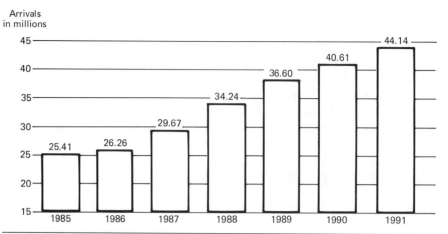

FIGURE 10.8 Total foreign tourism to the United States. (*Source:* U.S. Travel and Tourism Administration.)

thirds of the total foreign arrivals are from Canada and Mexico.[16] A large portion of these are very short stays, many less than a day. To focus on the richer long-stay market, Figure 10.11 shows the increase in travel by visitors from *overseas* to the United States. The number of overseas visitors has more

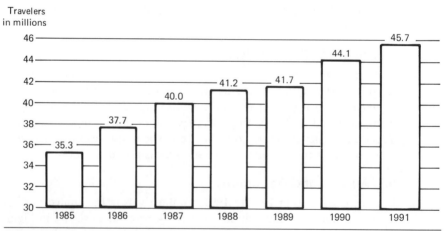

FIGURE 10.9 Outbound travel by Americans. (*Source:* U.S. Travel and Tourism Administration.)

[16] Nearly two thirds (64 percent) of departures are also to Mexico (34 percent) and Canada (30 percent).

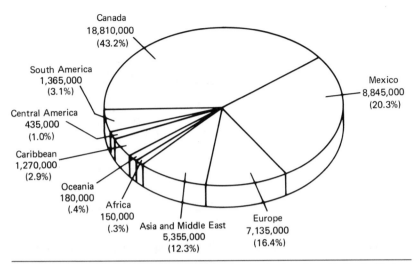

FIGURE 10.10 International tourist arrivals in the United States, 1991. Total arrivals: 43,545,000. (*Source:* U.S. Travel and Tourism Administration.)

than doubled since 1985. As Figure 10.12 shows, the United States had roughly 10 million more departures than arrivals in 1985. By 1991, however, the number of arrivals and departures was projected to be more nearly equal, with a difference of only 1.5 million.

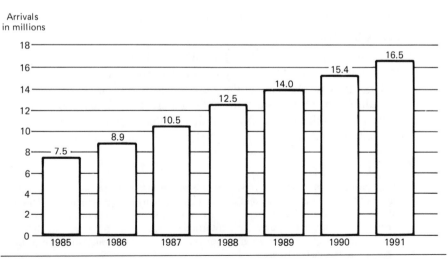

FIGURE 10.11 Overseas visitors to the United States. (*Source:* U.S. Travel and Tourism Administration.)

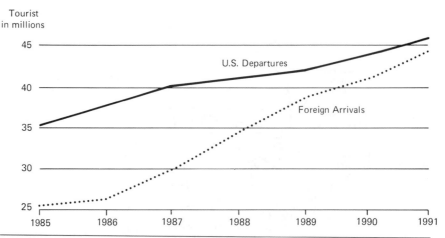

FIGURE 10.12 The traveler gap is rapidly closing. (*Source:* U.S. Travel and Tourism Administration.)

U.S. Receipts and Payments

Since 1985, the growth in U.S. receipts has increased at a rate nearly three times as fast as the growth in spending by U.S. citizens abroad, as shown in Figures 10.13 and 10.14. In 1989, U.S. receipts exceeded payments by Americans traveling abroad for the first time. As Figure 10.15 indicates, the tourism surplus is projected to continue to grow.[17] Figure 10.16 identifies the United States's principal sources of international receipts.

REASONS FOR GROWTH OF UNITED STATES AS A DESTINATION

The growth of the United States as an international travel destination, according to the United States Travel and Tourism Administration (USTTA), "is due in large part to the U.S. dollar's continued weakness that made the U.S. a bargain for many foreign tourists."[18] Figure 10.17 illustrates graphically the impact of a falling dollar. As the dollar's value in deutsch marks, pounds, and yen fell, thus effectively lowering prices to visitors who held those currencies,

---

[17] The payments, receipts, and travel balance shown in the figures include payments by U.S. nationals to foreign carriers as outflows and payments by foreign nationals to U.S. carriers as inflows. The limited evidence suggests that something like 85 percent of payments to carriers are spent in the country of the payer. This distortion is a minor one, however, since the difference in the balance of payments to carriers is on the order of $2 billion. The basic picture shown, therefore, is reasonably accurate.

[18] *Recap of International Travel To and From the United States in 1989* (Washington, D.C.: Office of Research, U.S. Travel Service, August 1990), p. 1.

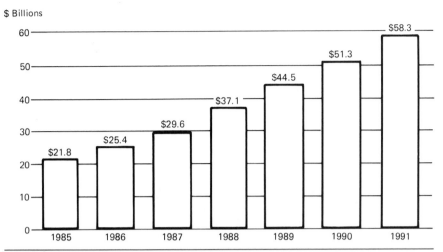

FIGURE 10.13 Receipts from foreign visitor spending. (*Source:* U.S. Travel and Tourism Administration.)

the number of visitors increased. The reverse, of course, is also true. As the U.S. dollar fell, although many more Americans traveled abroad, the rate of increase for overseas travelers in the U.S. declined.

There are reasons other than changing currency values for the increase in foreign visitation. A principal one is the world's rising standard of living, particularly in Western Europe and Asia. As well, the political changes in Eastern Europe led to a large percentage growth in travel, although from a

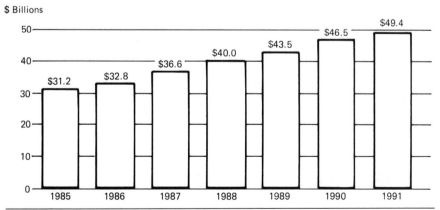

FIGURE 10.14 Payments by outbound U.S. travelers 1991/1985. (*Source:* U.S. Travel and Tourism Administration.)

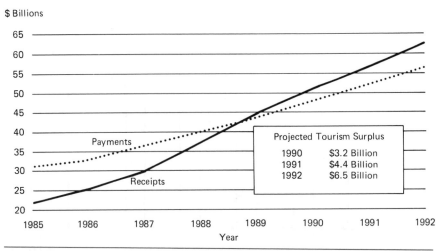

FIGURE 10.15   U.S. international travel receipts and payments. (*Source:* U.S. Travel and Tourism Administration.)

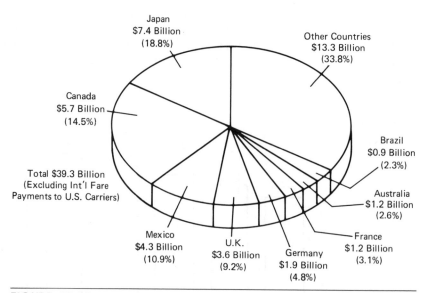

FIGURE 10.16   Sources of U.S. international travel receipts, 1990 estimates. (*Source:* U.S. Travel and Tourism Administration.)

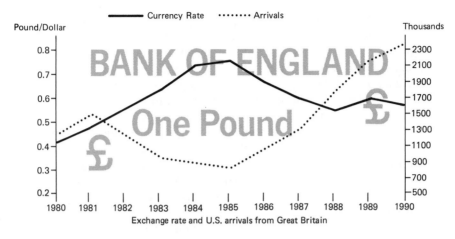

Exchange rate and U.S. arrivals from Great Britain

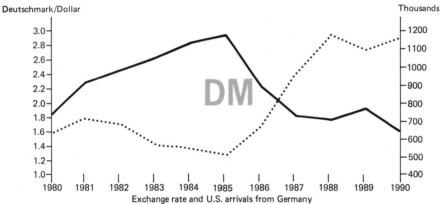

Exchange rate and U.S. arrivals from Germany

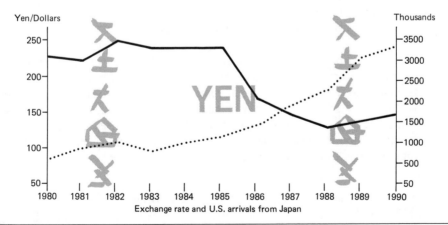

Exchange rate and U.S. arrivals from Japan

FIGURE 10.17 Effect of changing exchange rates on U.S. arrivals, 1980–1990: from Great Britain (top), from Germany (center), and from Japan (bottom). (*Source:* U.S. Travel and Tourism Administration.)

very low starting point. Another factor appears to be increasing competition among international air carriers, which has held fares down. In addition, as more people travel, more people want to travel. People hear about places from friends and want to go there. International travel is seen less as a venture into the unknown and more as something everybody's doing.

The North American industry has begun to recognize weaknesses in the "packaging" of North American travel experiences, and major improvements in the marketing of North America are under way. Finally, the United States has been "discovered" as a tourist destination. American attractions fascinate. Walt Disney World is the most popular destination with overseas visitors, but others as varied as the Grand Canyon, New York City, the Mississippi Valley, and Las Vegas all offer the visitor something new and different from what they can see at home.

As John Norlander, president of Radisson Hotels has pointed out, the United States is a good travel buy. The overcapacity built by the hotel industry in the 1980s gives the United States the best physical plant available to compete in the world market for tourism in the 1990s.[19] Robert Hazard of Choice Hotels International has pointed out that many European countries have an annual visitation equal to their total population.[20] The United States, with visitation of only 45 million and a population of over 250 million (and space to match), has a long way to go to catch up with that.

The stake the American travel industry has in international travelers is illustrated in Figure 10.18. The proportion of tourism receipts accounted for by foreign visitors has grown from 7 percent in 1985 to over 11 percent in 1991. That is a 60 percent proportionate increase in a short period of time. As Hazard put it in a recent address,

> If we could double the number of international visitors, we would add another $52 billion in travel sales, create 700,000 new jobs and, best of all, occupancies in the U.S. hotel industry would rise by 11 points.[21]

In the hotel industry, some properties in large cities with large numbers of foreign tourists attribute one third or more of their occupancy to visitors from outside the country. And many hotels, responding to the needs of foreign visitors, are anxious to hire multilingual managers, clerks, and service personnel. Some hotels have also begun actively to promote foreign business through representation at travel trade fairs abroad and through solicitation of foreign tour business from travel agents.

---

[19] John A. Norlander, Remarks to the Travel Industry National Conference, Pittsburg, Pa., October 7, 1990.

[20] *Lodging,* October 1990, p. 26.

[21] Robert Hazard, "International Chains; Expansion Philosophies for the Next Five Years." Address to the 13th Annual Hospitality Industry Investment Conference, New York City, June 3, 1991.

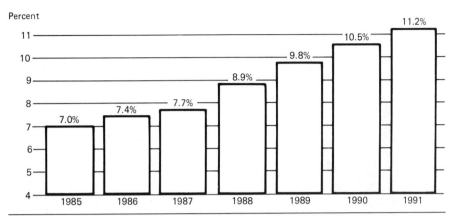

FIGURE 10.18 Foreign visitor spending as a percent of U.S. travel receipts. (*Source:* U.S. Travel and Tourism Administration.)

IS TOURISM AN INDUSTRY?

Let us pause here for a moment to review the concept of the hospitality industry we developed in Chapter 1. We concluded that such an industry could be characterized by a common heritage, by the similarity of operating problems shared by the various components, and by the high mobility that managers and workers enjoy. For instance, a supervising manager might well move from a restaurant into hotel management and then to some form of institutional work such as club management or college housing and food service.

Although we constantly use the term *hospitality industry,* there is no such thing as a corresponding tourism industry. This is because tourism is a highly varied, though often interrelated, bundle of economic activities. Although these economic activities often court the same customer, the services rendered, and the operational problems encountered, are different enough to limit the mobility of a trained employee or manager from one activity to another. This is the principal difference between the hospitality industry and tourism.

It is true, of course, that some positions in one component of the hospitality industry cannot be transferred within the industry. A desk clerk, for instance, has skills peculiar to the hotel business, and a greenskeeper's knowledge is useful mainly in the club business. The heart of the hospitality industry, however, is food service, in which there is a great deal of intra-industry mobility for workers in food service; any manager qualified in food service operations can probably move with comparative ease to other parts of the industry. But the field of tourism lacks this kind of common thread.

Visitors enjoy treats while strolling through Rhinefeld, a replica of a German village in Busch Gardens, Williamsburg, Virginia. (Courtesy of Busch Gardens Williamsburg)

A few more examples will illustrate our point. An airline, a car rental agency, and a hotel may share the same customer, but the services they provide differ strikingly. The airline provides its transportation strictly from point to point on some predetermined schedule. The car rental agency also provides transportation and related support services, but it dictates neither a schedule nor a destination. Moreover, its customers travel alone or with companions of their own choosing. Hotels, in turn, provide a stationary shelter for some period specified by its guests.

Operational problems within tourism vary widely, too. For instance, aircraft maintenance, automobile maintenance, and hotel maintenance obviously require different facilities, skills, and planning. It is unlikely that the same person could, for instance, service the electrical system of an aircraft, an automobile, and a hotel.

Differences also appear in the structure of the firms. The airline and car rental fields are dominated by a few very large companies, but the hotel industry is a highly competitive field of which not even the most successful hotel chains can claim a corner.

Most importantly, as we said earlier, there is little ease of movement for employees among the tourism segments. Tourism is not one career field but many. Thus, the car rental agent seeking work at an airline ticket counter would have to be retrained. A skilled waitress works in tourism and might have learned a great deal that would be useful as a stewardess, but we don't hear much about waitress experience as a qualification for employment as a stewardess.

One factor that is bringing hospitality and tourism into a closer working relationship is the emergence of a worldwide information network. Computer linkages are tying central reservation systems (CRS) for hotel companies to the CRS of airline and car rental companies. Since almost all travel agents are linked to one of the airline CRS, this information network facilitates the sale of hotel rooms by many other travel firms. This network and its implications for the hotel industry are discussed further in the last chapter.

Hospitality managers do need to acquire a general understanding of tourism, as the two fields share many professional interests. Tourism constitutes an important market for many hospitality firms. For example, the success of the airlines in selling to travelers will directly affect the occupancy rates of the hotel industry, and the hotel guest may well want the service of a rental car. As time goes on, moreover, integrated travel firms, which bring a variety of travel services under one ownership, may become more common.

State, regional, and local travel promotion also is important to hospitality firms, and so such promotion deserves their support. In general, however, the relationships among the industries that serve the tourist, though complementary and interdependent, do not extend into the interindustry career ladders.

NONECONOMIC EFFECTS OF TOURISM

So far we have stressed the economic impact of tourism, for instance, its effect on the gross national product and employment. But tourism has other impacts, both unfavorable and favorable.

CROWDING

A successful tourist attraction may, in effect, self-destruct from its own success. One of the major potential problems of tourism is crowding: so many people want to see the attraction that its own success destroys its charm.

At successful theme parks, this problem is addressed by designing places where guests will be waiting in line in "staging areas," with interesting views and even live or mechanized entertainment to distract the visitors. Another theme park tactic is to have lots of cleanup help, so that paper, cigarettes, and other trash never accumulates, thus reducing or eliminating some of the evidence of crowding.

Another example can be found in areas of scenic beauty such as popular national parks where trails often become more and more difficult as they progress. Indeed, most people turn around and return to the parking lot once the pavement ends. And even fewer continue once the unpaved trail actually becomes difficult to follow. In effect, reducing the amenities is a subtle form of unstated rationing of which the ultimate example is the wilderness area, where entrance is only on foot or by horse. Difficulty of access can thus reduce crowding.

Along with crowding, tourism can result in noise, odors, and pollution. A special form of crowding is the traffic jam. Not surprisingly, people who live in a tourist attraction area may have mixed or hostile feelings about further development because of their concern for privacy, the environment, or just their ability to get safely to and from home on crowded highways.

Another possible impact of crowding is "crowding out." For example, a beach or other scenic area formerly used by local people may be bought and its use restricted to paying visitors. This has happened on several Caribbean islands and in some cases resulted in the local populace's becoming unfriendly or even hostile as they found their beaches becoming inaccessible to "natives." This led to sharp clashes between the local people and the visitors, an unfriendly environment, and then a drop in the number of visitors.

These potentially unfavorable developments related to tourism give rise to the notion of "carrying capacity," that is, that an area can accept only a certain number of visitors without being hampered as a desirable destination.

FAVORABLE NONECONOMIC EFFECTS

But not all noneconomic effects are necessarily unfavorable. Tourist success can often fuel local pride: Some tourist "events" such as festivals and fairs may be staged to celebrate some aspect of the local culture. Agricultural fairs, for instance, which draw thousands—and sometimes hundreds of thousands—of visitors, celebrate a region's agricultural heritage and its favored crops as well as provide for important educational activities such as 4H meetings and contests.

In other cases, a local tradition may be observed. In a Portuguese community, it may be a blessing of the fishing fleet; in an area where many of German descent live, it could be "Oktoberfest." In these cases, adults are reminded of their background, and the young see their heritage dramatized as visitors come to admire it. Indeed, much early travel was for the purpose of pilgrimage, and religion still plays an important part in travel in some areas.

Because of its important impact on the hospitality industry tourism is significant to students of hotel, restaurant, and institutional management. But even if this weren't your field of study, it would be important for you to know about it. This is because whatever problems tourism raises, its positive impacts not only economically but also culturally and socially make it an important phenomenon of contemporary mass society.

SUMMARY

This chapter opened with a definition of tourism and the reasons that it is important to the hospitality industry. We then explained why people are traveling more: more leisure time, rising family incomes, and more middle-aged people who have the time and money to travel.

The most common reason for traveling is pleasure, and then business. More people travel by car than by any other means. Travel by air increased over the last 10 years but fell somewhat when fares began to rise, illustrating that travel is price sensitive. The largest number of hotel guests are pleasure travelers, but business travelers consume more hotel nights because of longer average trips.

The economic significance of tourism is clear: Tourism ranks second or third in total business receipts. Moreover, about one in twenty people is employed in an activity supported by travel expenditures. Indeed, communities seeking potential employers may profitably use tourism as an attraction.

The United States is also an international tourist attraction, its popularity often based on the value of the U.S. dollar versus that of other currencies as well as a number of other factors. Foreign visitors to this country are an important means of improving the U.S. balance-of-payments as well as the U.S. employment outlook.

We discussed whether tourism is really an industry in the way that the hospitality business is. Finally, we closed the chapter by touching on the noneconomic effects of tourism, both unfavorable (such as crowding) and favorable (such as festivals, fairs, and the celebration of local traditions).

KEY WORDS AND CONCEPTS

To help you review this chapter, keep in mind the following:

Pleasure trip   Person trip
Price sensitivity   Two-income families

Factors affecting travel
   Leisure
   Income
   Demographics
Purposes of travel
Mode of travel
   Personal vehicle
   Common carrier

Business travel
Travel multiplier
Tourism and employment
Balance of payments
Travel balance
Employment mobility in tourism

REVIEW QUESTIONS

1. What is tourism, and what organizations does it include?

2. What factors have caused the increase in tourism?

3. What are the main reasons that people travel?

4. Which age groups travel most, and what kinds of trips does each group take?

5. What are the recent trends in automobile and airline travel, and what are their causes?

6. Is tourism important economically to the United States? Explain.

7. What factors account for the improvement in the U.S. travel balance? What could threaten the favorable balance?

8. What is the U.S. hospitality industry doing to attract foreign visitors?

9. Describe some of the noneconomic favorable and unfavorable effects of tourism.

C H A P T E R 11

Courtesy of American Airlines

DESTINATIONS: TOURISM GENERATORS

THE PURPOSE OF THIS CHAPTER

Travelers are going places! Destinations and attractions are magnets that set the whole process of tourism in motion. In this chapter we look at the motivations of travelers as well as the nature of mass-market travel destinations. Many of these are, to all intents and purposes, a part of the hospitality industry and offer attractive career prospects. Even if this were not the case, you would want to be familiar with the economic and operating characteristics of destinations to round out your understanding of tourism.

THIS CHAPTER SHOULD HELP YOU

1. See the relationships between travelers' motives and the attractions at destinations.

2. Distinguish between primary and secondary attractions.

3. Identify the characteristics that make the destinations of mass-market tourism different from those of the more aristocratic travel patterns of just a few years ago.

4. Know more about the kinds of activities theme parks offer to entice travelers.

5. Take advantage of the increasing significance of regional theme parks in planning your work experience.

6. Appreciate why the economics of casino gambling makes some communities consider legalizing them in new markets.

7. Become familiar with the significance of large- *and* small-scale urban play centers as a part of the tourism plant of any community.

8. Evaluate the importance of "temporary" attractions, such as fairs and festivals.

9. Assess the importance of natural attractions to tourism.

MOTIVES AND DESTINATIONS

If people had no place they wanted to go, tourism would be in trouble. In fact, people travel for many reasons, for instance, work and recreation. In this chapter we will be concerned almost exclusively with recreation, but even for this, the motives are varied because recreation is more than "just play." Webster tells us that recreation also means reviving, giving new vigor, refreshing, and reanimating as well as amusing, diverting, or gratifying.

Recreation has a function, then, in life. It is, in some ways, not just the opposite of work; it is its counterweight. Recreation relates to relaxation but also to stimulation, to gaining renewed energy, as well as to playing. As a necessary and vital part of life, not surprisingly the things that attract different people are highly varied. For instance, perhaps the earliest motive for travel was religion and the sense of renewal of commitment that was—and is—experienced by the pilgrim. Today's pilgrimage attractions include Lourdes in France and Fatima in Portugal and, in the New World, Guadelupe in Mexico and Ste. Anne de Beaupre in Quebec.

Health interests have also long been a major travel motive. In ancient times, the Romans were drawn to springs thought to have health-giving properties, which became fashionable again in the eighteenth century. Hot springs in the United States, such as Hot Springs, Arkansas, and French Lick Springs, Indiana, are less popular today than they were a few generations ago. In regard to another kind of health interest, the Mayo Clinic attracts so many people that its home in Rochester, Minnesota, has one of the highest ratios of hotel rooms per resident of any city in the United States.

Scenic beauty, especially the mountains and the seashore, have long been a major attraction. Scenic beauty is often coupled with *health-building activities*—hiking, skiing, and swimming, for instance—so that both body and mind are refreshed by vistas and activities. Today's state and national park systems are the most extensive response to these touring motives in history.

Sporting events, from the first Olympics in 776 B.C. to the Kentucky Derby and the Superbowl, have attracted thousands of serious sports enthusiasts as well as untutored onlookers. Indeed, sports arenas have become such

Much of North American recreation is family centered. (Courtesy of the Recreational Vehicle Industry Association)

big business that some institutional food service companies have created special divisions just to manage sports food service.

Culture, including history and art appreciation, are judged by some as not very interesting stuff—yet every year the battlefields of yesterday throng with thousands of visitors on guided tours, the Louvre is one of France's major cultural treasures, and the Art Institute of Chicago is one of that city's significant draws. Perhaps because work is so important to Americans, another major attraction in Chicago is its Museum of Science and Industry which celebrates the American heartland's industrial prominence. Music and theater festivals all across Europe and North America are used more or less consciously by many cities to enhance the cultural life of the area—and to attract visitors' spending to strengthen the local economy.

Theater and spectacle—whether Broadway's White Way or Walt Disney's theme parks—are currently among the most significant tourist attractions. And we should note that there are literally hundreds and thousands of less well known theaters and amusement parks that stimulate the local culture and local economy by catering to the interests of people close to home.

Mill and Morrison distinguish between what they call *primary or touring destinations* and *secondary or stopover destinations.*[1] Primary destinations

---

[1] Robert Christie Mill and Alastair M. Morrison, *The Tourism System* (Englewood Cliffs, N.J.: Prentice Hall, 1985), Chap. 8.

have a wide market and draw travelers from a great distance. These kinds of destinations, such as Walt Disney World, attract visitors from the entire North American continent and all over the world. Because such a high proportion of their visitors are away from home, these primary destinations create a heavy lodging demand. Orlando, Florida, for instance, is like Rochester, Minnesota, a city with a disproportionately high number of hotel rooms per capita. So is Las Vegas.

Secondary destinations draw people from nearby areas or induce people to stop "on their way by." Some secondary destinations may in fact have a higher number of visitors than primary destinations do. The Grand Canyon, for instance, attracts fewer than 3 million visitors a year, although they come from all over the world. In contrast, many regional theme parks draw that many visitors, and Atlantic City, which is mainly a regional casino gambling center, attracts well over 10 times that many. In general, we can say that a primary attraction requires more services per visitor, but this does not detract from the importance of successful secondary attractions. Indeed, even smaller secondary attractions make important contributions to their locale.

The balance of this chapter will be an examination of those destinations and attractions to which hospitality services are important enough that the attraction can usefully be thought of as part of the hospitality industry. We will consider destinations such as theme parks and casinos as well as significant secondary destinations in urban centers such as sports centers, zoos, museums, and universities. We will also look briefly at attractions in the natural environment such as national parks, seashores, monuments and the like. Finally, we will consider "temporary" destinations such as festivals and fairs. Our main interest will be in the impact of these kinds of destinations on opportunities in the hospitality industry, their significance for hospitality managers, and possible careers in such complexes.

MASS-MARKET TOURISM

Until quite recently, travel was the privileged pastime of the wealthy. The poor might migrate—to move their homes from one place to another in order to live better or just to survive—but only the affluent could afford travel for sightseeing, amusement, and business. That condition has not really changed; some affluence is still required for business and recreational travel. What has changed is the degree of affluence in our society. We have become what economists call the "affluent society."

When travel was reserved for the higher social classes, its model was the aristocracy. In hotels, for example, dress rules required a coat and tie in the dining room. But as travel came within the reach of the majority of Americans, the facilities serving travelers adapted and loosened their emphasis on class. Many of the new establishments have, in fact, become "mass" institutions.

In a conversation with the author, a Walt Disney World training official summed up this change. Speaking of the attitude of some college-educated employees (when first hired) toward the guests that the employees considered "hicks," he said, "We point out to them that we, at Disney World, are *performers, not reformers.* We're here to help people have a good time, not to improve their manners or to change them in any other way." Thus, Disney World has virtually no dress code for guests. People come as they are. All

At Walt Disney World and other theme parks, employees are "performers, not reformers." A relaxed, come-as-you-are atmosphere is intended to support the guests' fun, and dress codes, such as those in more traditional resorts, are the exception in the newer-style operations. (Courtesy of Walt Disney World)

comers are served and enjoy themselves as they see fit within the limits of reasonable decorum.

In Las Vegas casinos, mink-coated matrons play blackjack next to dungaree-clad cowboys. These are not "social clubs" that inquire who your parents are or which side of the tracks you live on. The color of your money is the only concern. Likewise, anybody with the money can buy a reserved seat in any of the country's new superdome sports centers. What we see developing are new "play environments"—places, institutions, and even cities designed almost exclusively for play.

These essentially democratic institutions supply a comfortable place for travelers from all kinds of social backgrounds. Accordingly, as the popularity of these facilities increases, we see a new, more egalitarian kind of lodging and food service institutions flourishing.

PLANNED PLAY ENVIRONMENTS

Recreation is as old as society. But a society that can afford to play on the scale that Americans do now is new. Some anthropologists and sociologists argue that "who you are" was once determined by your work, what you did for a living, but that these questions of personal identity are now answered by *how we entertain ourselves.* In his book *Future Shock,* Alvin Toffler spoke of the emerging importance of "sub cults" whose life-styles are built around nonwork activities. For these people, work exists as a secondary matter, as only a means to an end. Michael Rose, chairman of the Promus Companies, suggests that play will have an increasingly important role in our civilization. He sees a time not far off when many people's concerns will be centered around "the pursuit of pure leisure."

> To talk about a society in which leisure is the most important thing flies in the face of the work ethic and religious codes which have dominated our country, Japan, and many in Northern Europe for generations. But it is becoming increasingly clear that the new century will see (a society) dominated by leisure.[2]

Play environments, of course, are not newer than play itself. Fairs at which work (or trade) and play were mixed date back to the mid-1800s in the United States and to medieval times, or even earlier, in Europe. The first amusement park was Vauxhall Gardens in England, built in the 1600s, and the first U.S. amusement park, Coney Island, dates from 1895. What is new, however, is the sophistication that a television-educated public demands in its amusement centers today, and the scale on which these demands have been

---

[2]Michael D. Rose, "The Advent of the 21st Century from the Chrysalis of the 1990's." Address to the 13th Annual Hospitality Industry Investment Conference, New York City, June 3, 1991.

met since the first modern theme park opened at Disneyland some 25 years ago. Disneyland, in effect, showed the commercial world that there was a way to entice a television generation out of the house and into a clean carnival offering live fantasy and entertainment.

MAN-MADE ENVIRONMENTS

THEME PARKS

In the early 1970s, a number of old-style amusement parks closed their doors because they "offered little more than thrill rides and cotton candy and these days Americans want much more than that."[3] They fell in the face of more sophisticated competition from theme parks that catered more effectively to people's need for fun and fantasy.

According to industry sources, the United States has about 40 major themed attractions and 560 other, more traditional amusement parks.[4] Theme parks, which account for only 7 percent of all amusement parks, receive a much larger share of park receipts. These parks have clearly become an important part of both the national tourist market and the local entertainment market. The number of their visitors in 1990 was estimated at 253 million, the equivalent of roughly one visit for every person in the United States. In practice, though, about half the guests visit at least twice a year.

The New York Times described this new breed of park as follows:

> Most new amusement parks are variations on the basic Disney conglomeration of colorful animal characters, reproductions of historical buildings, ingenious thrill rides, and quality stage shows, all in a lavishly landscaped, spotlessly clean outdoor setting suitable for a day long family excursion.
>
> Gone are the rickety ferris wheel, the sawdust midways, the bingo barkers and the girly reviews that gave so many parks questionable reputations in the pre-Disney days.[5]

Themes

Just as restaurants are expected more and more to offer atmosphere as well as food, today's television-oriented traveler expects a park environment that stimulates and entertains in addition to offering rides and other amusements. One way to meet this demand is to build the park around one or more themes.

---

[3] *The Wall Street Journal,* August 2, 1972, p. 1.

[4] Ms. Pat Durickna, director of public relations, International Association of Amusement Parks and Attractions, personal communication to author, July 1991.

[5] *The New York Times,* May 30, 1976, p. 20.

Theme parks still offer many traditional rides such as this "Loch Ness Monster" roller coaster which reaches speeds of 709 miles per hour. (Courtesy of Busch Gardens Williamsburg)

Some of Walt Disney World's themed areas in its Magic Kingdom, for instance, are Main Street USA, Adventureland, and Frontierland.

Some parks, moreover, are built around one general theme. Busch Entertainment's "Olde Country," located near historic Williamsburg, Virginia, uses a seventeenth-century European theme for the park as a whole and within that general theme offers eight areas themed to specific countries or regions: Banbury Cross and Hastings (England); Aquitaine (France); Rhinefeld and Oktoberfest (Germany); Heatherdowns (Scotland); New France (early North America); and San Marco (Italy).

Whatever the theme, parks offer rides, one of the most popular being water rides. In fact, Busch has developed a separate theme park, adjacent to its Busch Gardens in Tampa, built around water and water rides. Adventure Island, as it is called, offers 13 acres of tropically themed lagoons and beaches featuring water slides and diving platforms, water games, a wave pool, a cable drop, and a rope gym.

Although some parks cater to nostalgia (a romantic longing for the past), others recreate the past in a more realistic way. The "Towne of Smithville," in New Jersey, for instance, has restored a mid-1800s crossroads community. It offers a Civil War museum and a theater as well.

Some parks take their themes from animal life. Busch Gardens in Florida offers "The Dark Continent," a 300-acre African themed park that includes the Serengeti Plain, home of one of the largest collections of African big game. It also serves as a breeding and survival center for many rare species. The animals roam freely on a veldtlike plain where visitors can see them by taking a monorail, steam locomotive, or skyride safari.

The natural environment, including live animals, reptiles, and birds, forms a vital part of the theme in many parks. (Courtesy of Busch Gardens Tampa)

Busch has also developed a park, Sesame Place in Langhorne, Pennsylvania, near Philadelphia, that blends physical and play activities with science experiments and computer games. In one experiment, called star lightning, the visitor can make gases, enclosed in a glass ball, interact with electromagnetic fields to create lightning and rainbow colors. Another experiment uses a laser and turning mirrors controlled by the guest to create a hands-on experience of the effects of reflection. Sesame Place also offers one-week computer camps, school field trips, and college-accredited computer courses for teachers.

Like virtually all modern theme parks, Sesame features full-sized cartoon characters, including Ernie and Bert from Sesame Street. And Big Bird and Oscar are featured in a video show in which the audience participates. Like other parks, too, Sesame Place offers rides and theater-style entertainment.

Busch does not limit its visitors to viewing animals. In other themed areas, it offers a wide variety of rides and shows. For instance, Timbuktu, a re-creation of an ancient desert trading center, features the Phoenix boat-swing ride, a Dolphin theater, 1,200-seat Festhaus dining and entertainment complex, the Scorpion coaster ride, a carousel, the Sandstorm thrill ride, a games arcade, and African crafts. Marrakesh, a simulation of a walled Moroccan village, offers Moroccan craft demonstrations, an "All That Music" song and

The performing whales are an integral part of the Marine World theme. (Courtesy of Marine World Africa USA)

Some theme parks include specialized education program formats for students from kindergarten through university age. (Courtesy of Sea World)

dance revue, shopping bazaars, belly dancers, snake charmers, and the Mystic Sheiks of Morocco, a brass-and-percussion marching band.

The sea offers other enticing themes. Marineland, in California, besides shows related to its ocean theme, offers to anyone who can swim a swim-through aquarium known as Baja Reef. For those who are certified scuba divers, a trip is available in a special stainless steel cage into a 560,000-gallon tank filled with over 60 sharks.

Sea World, with successful parks in Florida, Ohio, and southern California, features shows in a 3,000-seat stadium for viewing "Shamu, the three-ton Killer Whale." In a 5-million-gallon lagoon nearby, dolphins perform before a 2,500-seat stadium. Like many theme parks, Sea World offers organized educational tours featuring the work of Sea World's research organization. A liberal amount of education-as-fun is found in its regular, entertainment-oriented shows.

An official of the Disney organization summed up the theme parks' approach to education this way: "Before you can educate, you must entertain." Theme parks do, indeed, constitute a rich educational medium.

Scale

Theme parks are different from the traditional amusement parks not only because they are based on a theme or several themes but also because of their huge operating scale. As in nearly everything else, Disney leads the way in plant scale. The entire Walt Disney World (WDW) in Florida comprises 27,400 acres and offers three quite distinctly different theme parks, each with its own numerous food service and retail stores. The original Magic Kingdom offers seven different "lands" or distinctively themed areas such as Main Street, Adventureland and Frontierland. EPCOT offers "Future World," featuring high-tech pavilions, and the World Showcase, which boasts representative displays from nations around the world. Disney-MGM Studios gives visitors a firsthand look at backstage and the workings of a major film and video production facility. Several smaller themed areas include Pleasure Island, which offers after-dark excitement in its six nightclubs and five restaurants, mainly to young adults and couples without children. In addition, there are two water parks, Typhoon Lagoon and River Country, which is a part of the Fort Wilderness campground. There are 18 hotels on or adjacent to the parks that are operated or affiliated with WDW. The career significance of WDW and similar enterprises is suggested by the fact that WDW is one of the largest private employers in the state of Florida.

REGIONAL THEME PARKS

Theme parks catering to a regional rather than a national market have been growing at a rapid pace in recent years. This development seems to be based on the increasing cost of transportation and the pressure of inflation on many family incomes. Regional parks serve a smaller geographic area than, for instance, Disney World, and are often more targeted toward particular groups in their marketing.

For instance, Atlanta's Six Flags offers special parties for high school graduating classes and presents an annual Christian Music Festival featuring "top Christian talent" that might not be as popular in other regions of North America. In Pigeon Forge, Tennessee, near Knoxville, Dollywood recreates the Smoky Mountains of the late 1800s through crafts and country music as well as atmosphere, old-time "home-cooked" food, and rides. Country music is a regular part of the "Parton Back Porch Theatre," and during the National Mountain Music Festival in July, it features Dolly Parton, for whom the park is named. A crafts theme is featured during a month-long National Crafts Festival in October. Regional parks such as Dollywood are clearly major sources of tourism: Dollywood attracts over 1.5 million visitors each year.

Regional parks, though not as large as Walt Disney World, are not small. Six Flags over Georgia, for instance, is situated on 331 acres and offers over 100 rides, shows, and attractions. Rides in these parks are of impressive scale. Six Flags' Splashwater Falls, which rises five stories to fall into 250,000 gallons of water, has a carrying capacity of 1,800 passengers per hour and cost nearly

The forces of evil, dragons, and dragonettes stir up the lagoon of Walt Disney's Epcot Center in Florida in an effort to disrupt the good guys whose mission is to paint the sky with rainbow colors. (Copyright © The Walt Disney Company, 1986)

$2 million to build. Thunder River, a boat ride, cost $4 million to build, covers 7 acres, and moves 167,000 gallons of water per minute. It, too, has a carrying capacity of 1,800 per hour. Entertainment is on a large scale at Six Flags, too. The Southern Star Amphitheater has 4,000 fixed seats and can be expanded to seat 20,000.

Not surprisingly, regional parks have a significant commitment to food service. Knott's Berry Farm, for instance, in Buena Park, California, the nation's oldest themed park, has 35 eating places on its 150 acres and additional food service in the adjacent Knott's Market Place. Not far away, Marineland features a Burger Galley, International Cafe, Pacific Pizza, an Ice

The Butterfield stagecoach meets the iron horse in Knott's Berry Farm's Old West Ghost Town. Knott's stagecoaches are authentic antiques that date back as far as 1847. The locomotive, #41 out of the Baldwin works in Philadelphia, was made in 1881 and operated for many years pulling narrow-gauge passenger trains in the Rocky Mountains. Today's old-time adventurers can experience what travel was like on the American frontier a hundred years ago, with their journeys interrupted by "holdups" that are staged daily by masked outlaws from the staff of Knott's funfighters. (Courtesy of Knott's Berry Farm)

Cream Shoppe, Seaside Sandwich Shop, and Corby's Corner. Marineland also has outdoor catering locations that can handle company picnics and special groups of from 150 to 5,000.

Smaller recreational centers that service not a region but a city or part of one have grown most rapidly in recent years. One authority noted,

> We have seen a developing interest in what we are calling the tertiary market, those looking for less expensive, less time-consuming and more participatory type of amusement. Developers are creating smaller action parks, miniature golf facilities, family entertainment centers and combinations of these—either within malls and other commercial centers or as freestanding facilities.[6]

Employment and Training Opportunities

The growth of regional and even local theme parks and amusement centers is a favorable development for hospitality students because of the opportunities

[6] John R. Graff, executive director, International Association of Amusement Parks and Attractions, Address to the 1991 Travel Outlook Forum, Pittsburgh, Pa., October 16, 1990.

they offer for employment and management experience. Theme parks often operate year round, but on a reduced scale from their summer peak. During the months when school is out and, too, when outside weather conditions favor park visitation, attendance soars. To meet these peaks, the crew expands each summer. To supervise this expanded crew, college-age people are chosen, usually from last year's crew, as supervisors, assistant managers, and unit managers. These positions are often quite well paid, but more significantly they offer a chance to assume responsible roles beyond those that most organizations offer to people of this age. Generally these opportunities are accompanied by training and management development programs.

As a personal note: I have graded more summer field-experience papers that I care to recall, and consistently the best opportunities and training experiences I have encountered have been in regional theme parks. A word of advice, then, is to take a close look at the regional and local theme parks in your area as a possible summer employer.

CASINOS AND GAMING

To move from the innocent amusement of theme parks to casinos and gaming may seem a giant step, but they do have a good deal in common as tourism attractions. In a moment we will look briefly at two quite different markets: Las Vegas and Atlantic City. But first some discussion of gambling in the United States is in order.

Some might think that Las Vegas and Atlantic City are the only two centers of gambling in North America, but a moment's reflection on the variety of legal gambling activities around us quickly leads us to discard that notion. Gambling is fairly widespread in the United States. Casino gambling is legal in all of Nevada; in Atlantic City, New Jersey; in Deadwood, South Dakota; and in three historic districts in Colorado. As well, it is permitted on board excursion boats in Illinois, Indiana, and Mississippi, and approval of riverboat gambling seems likely in Missouri in the near future. Seven states permit slot machine gambling, 12 license card rooms, and 32 have state-run lotteries (33 counting the District of Columbia). All but 5 states permit betting on horse or dog races, or both, as well as charitable gambling. Only 2 states permit no form of legalized gambling—Hawaii and Utah.[7]

The question of gambling does raise serious moral and social issues, but it is clear that the practice, in one form or another, is quite widespread. Efforts to legalize casinos in several additional jurisdictions in both the United States and Canada, however, have failed repeatedly. Recent legalization of gambling on Indian reservations, however, may well reverse that trend. Gambling's profit potential for companies and the favorable economic impact for communities is so great that we are likely to see continuing pressure to allow it in other

---

[7] *Legalized Gambling in the United States* (Reno: Nevada Gaming Control Board, September 1990).

The town that casinos built! The top picture shows Las Vegas as an insignificant desert railroad town just after the turn of the century. Pictured below is the famous Las Vegas "strip" today. (Courtesy of the Las Vegas Convention and Visitors Authority)

mainland jurisdictions. Areas that have seen significant efforts to gain legalization of casinos in one form or another include Miami, New Orleans, Detroit, Michigan, and Galveston, Texas. There has also been considerable interest in casinos in the Pocono Mountains in Pennsylvania, the Catskills in New York, and in the province of Quebec. Given the importance of economic impact arguments, we should look at this aspect briefly at the same time that we examine the two existing continental North American casino centers.

Las Vegas

The first settlement in Las Vegas can be traced back to 1829, but the town's formation dates from 1905, when it was a small desert railroad town. Casino gambling was legalized in 1931. Following World War II, Las Vegas grew more rapidly as large hotels were built, and by the 1950s Las Vegas had become an established tourist destination combining casinos, superstar entertainment, and lavish hotel accommodations. Today the Las Vegas metropolitan area has a population of over three-quarters of a million people and over 57,000 hotel and motel rooms, nearly 1 for every 15 inhabitants. The city's annual occupancy rate ranges from the high seventies to the low eighties, as compared with a nationwide occupancy in the low sixties.

Las Vegas has a good deal more to offer than casinos. The city is also known for its incredible stage shows featuring such extravaganzas as "Siegfried & Roy" at the Mirage Hotel. "Siegfried & Roy" claims to be the most expensive spectacle ever created at a total cost of $50 million, including a $25 million, 1,500-seat theater built to the specifications of this extravaganza. The show features two dozen exotic wild animals, highlighted by the stars'

Casinos are becoming more widely accepted outside of Nevada and Atlantic City, and the indications are that this is a trend that will continue. (Courtesy of Resorts Casino & Hotel, Atlantic City)

collection of 19 rare white tigers, and a cast of some 70 humans, 60 of them dancers. Siegfried and Roy are large-scale "illusionists" who perform such high-tech feats of magic as turning a beautiful woman into a 600-pound white tiger and making an elephant disappear into thin air.

Hotel room rates in Las Vegas are among the most affordable in the resort industry, and eating inexpensively is no problem. Many hotels sell breakfast for as little as 99 cents and offer a buffet-style dinner for less than $5.00. Las Vegas also sports 12 championship golf courses and 19 tennis and 7 racquetball facilities. Obviously, entertainment and sports facilities as well as lodging and food service bargains are used to attract visitors to play in the casinos.

But there also are national attractions around Las Vegas that enhance the city as a destination. The famous Hoover Dam and Lake Mead, with its 500 miles of shoreline, are less than a half hour away. Death Valley is a half-day's drive away, and the Grand Canyon is an easy day's drive from Las Vegas. Less well known attractions within an hour's drive include the Valley of Fire, Red Rock Canyon, and a clutch of ghost towns.

Las Vegas is thus a fully developed tourist mecca, served by 19 major airlines. McCarron International Airport averages nearly 575 flights daily.

In addition to its recreational features, Las Vegas has a highly developed convention business, including a 13-million-square-foot convention center with another 1.5 million square feet available at major hotels in the area. More than 1.7 million conventioneers attend over 500 conventions held in the city annually, and another 20 million tourists pass through the city each year.

The fact is that there is not much else in Las Vegas other than tourism, the businesses that serve the tourist, and the businesses that serve those businesses and their employees. Las Vegas is the ultimate in destinations—the city that tourism built.

Of course, gambling is the mainstay of the Las Vegas economy. Casinos take in roughly $4 billion in Las Vegas each year. Tourists spend nearly $500 each per visit, while conventioners spend well over $600 and trade show attendees nearly a thousand dollars per visit—all in addition to the sums spent on gaming. In total, nongambling-visitor spending is over $10 billion a year. About 25 percent of the Nevada work force is employed directly in the gaming industry while 69 percent works in tourism.[8]

Laughlin

Las Vegas statistics cover all of Clark County, which includes another rapidly growing gambling center, Laughlin, Nevada. Casino gambling began there in a modest way in 1969. In 1984, Laughlin's population was only 95 people. By 1990, it had risen to 6,200 but, more significantly, the town had grown from

[8] Rob Powers, spokesman for the Las Vegas Convention and Visitors Authority, personal communication to author, July 29, 1991.

one small casino and restaurant to a city sporting nine major hotels along the Colorado River with 730 rooms and another 4,300 under construction.

This is a quite different market from Las Vegas. There are few high rollers in Laughlin. The major segments of the market are families, many with children, and retirees. The whole ambiance of Laughlin is different from that of Las Vegas. Las Vegas is dark. Casinos have no windows. Dealers wear neat uniforms, usually including ties, and pit bosses sport at least a suit and often a tux. In Laughlin, picture windows are all the rage; everything is brightly lighted and open, and most casino employees wear Western dress, even the pit bosses. Much of the volume of traffic comes from nearby prosperous cities in Arizona such as Phoenix, while most of the rest are from southern California. In the winter, however, there is a significant number of "snowbird" customers who fill parking lots with recreational vehicles. A location convenient to Arizona and California population centers, a more "laid back" atmosphere and, of course, the presence of casino gambling seem to account for the phenomenal growth of Laughlin.

Atlantic City

Atlantic City has a lot to teach us about tourism, both good and bad. Atlantic City has always been a tourist city since its founding in the mid-1850s, and it was once the premier resort city on the East Coast of the United States, famous for its boardwalk and its resort hotels, catering principally to prosperous upper-middle-class Americans. But with the coming of automobiles, motels, lower-cost travel, and changing tastes in leisure, Atlantic City began to deteriorate. From 1960 to 1975, the city's population declined by 15,000, the number of visitors fell to 2,000,000, the number of hotel rooms decreased by 40 percent, and Atlantic City became a case study in the difficulty of reviving a tourist center once it had gone downhill.

As one observer put it, Atlantic City was a tourist resort without any tourists.[9] From a peak tourist center for earlier generations, Atlantic City became virtually an abandoned hulk, rusting away at its moorings. Like many older, worn-out tourism centers, its plant was outmoded and in bad repair. Perhaps more serious, it no longer had any appeal in the market, and the revenue wasn't there to rebuild. Then in 1976, gambling was approved, and in 1978 the first casino hotel opened.

The city's turnaround has been remarkable. Since 1978, when the first casino opened, over $5 billion has been spent on new facilities, and nearly 80,000 casino and noncasino jobs were created. More than 30 million people visit Atlantic City each year, making it the number one tourist destination in the United States.

---

[9] David Gardner, executive vice-president, Atlantic City Casino Association, personal communication to author. Mr. Gardner was employed as a city planner in Atlantic City during the 1960s.

The casinos are required to reinvest 1.25 percent of their gaming revenues in the community and state—an estimated $1.6 billion in the first 25 years—through the state-run Casino Reinvestment Development Authority. Since casino gambling was approved, casino hotels have paid nearly $5 billion in taxes, regulatory fees, and required reinvestment.

Atlantic City is quite different from Las Vegas. Although there are two major cities within a day's drive of Las Vegas—Los Angeles and San Diego—Atlantic City has one-quarter of the U.S. population within a 300-mile range. New York City, Philadelphia, and Washington D.C. all are within 150 miles. Over half of Atlantic City's visitors arrive by car, and another 37 percent arrive by bus. Both air and rail travel are now on the increase, with the completion of an AMTRAK link to New York, Philadelphia, Baltimore, and Washington and an enlarged airport that is slated to grow even more. While these two modes of transport are growing rapidly, they accounted for only 2 percent of arrivals in 1990.

Atlantic City's skyline is a study in contrasts. Its 13 new or renewed casino hotels are the latest word in casino glitter, but between them are open spaces where old buildings have been razed, and in many places hulks remain, boarded up. Outside the boardwalk's immediate vicinity, much of the city is still dilapidated slum housing, though that is rapidly being replaced with public housing for lower income residents, private apartment developments aimed at the middle class and, on the ocean front, expensive condominiums.

In contrast with Las Vegas's 57,000 hotel and motel rooms, Atlantic City has only 11,000 rooms. With the large number of day trippers, of course, Atlantic City does not need as many accommodations. On the other hand, Atlantic City hotel operators and tourism officials have recognized that overnight guests have a greater impact on the economy. As a result, the agencies responsible for marketing Atlantic City and southern New Jersey have launched a collaborative effort to encourage longer stay guests. Visitors are encouraged by this new regional program to see the historic and scenic attractions that abound in the area. New Jersey is, after all, one of the original 13 colonies, rich in history. And its beaches that border the Atlantic Ocean have long been famous as vacation spots.

In 1990, Atlantic City had 5,000 conventions and trade shows that attracted 175,000 attendees, who spent over $400 million in the area. The city is committed to expanding existing convention facilities, and a $210 million convention center is planned in conjunction with the new rail terminal, the existing convention center, and a proposed 1,000-room noncasino hotel. As convention and exhibit space, as well as more hotel rooms, becomes available, along with greatly improved transportation facilities, the growth prospects for Atlantic City are bright indeed.

The economic impact of Atlantic City is also being felt outside this city of 36,000 people, in the 125,000-person Atlantic County, and in the wider South Jersey area. Atlantic City has led all other New Jersey labor markets in growth since 1980, according to the Governor's Economic Policy Council, and the New Jersey Department of Labor has identified Atlantic County as one of the fastest-growing areas in New Jersey.

Casino Markets and the Business of Casinos

The business of casinos, obviously, is gambling, at table games such as roulette, blackjack, and dice. In addition, a major and growing gambling pastime is the slot machine. From the casino's point of view, what matters in evaluating a customer is his or her volume of play, because the odds in every game clearly favor the house. Big winners are good news for the casino because of the publicity they bring. But in the long run, the casino wins.

Casino markets can be divided into four general groups: tourists, high rollers at the tables, high rollers at the slot machines, and the bus trade. Tourists are those who visit the city to take in the sights, see a show, and try their hand at "the action"—but with modest limits in mind as to how much they are prepared to wager and lose, usually up to $100 but often as much as $250 or $500.

The high roller, as one Atlantic City casino executive put it, is a person who plays with "black chips," that is, hundred-dollar chips. In Las Vegas, James Kilby, Boyd Professor of Casino Management and Operations at the University of Nevada at Las Vegas's College of Hotel Administration, indicates that a high roller's average bet would be in the $150 to $225 range and that he or she would be expected to have a line of credit of $15,000 during a typical three-day visit to Las Vegas. Although some properties operate with a lesser quality high roller, they are finding that the cost equals or exceeds the revenue.[10]

For high rollers, gambling is the major attraction, but they thrive also on the personal attention given to them by the casino and hotel staff and the "comps"—complimentary or no-charge services and gifts—provided by the casino. Some high rollers wager more than the average and, a few, much more. In general, the level of "comps" is based on the volume of play—with some casinos prepared to provide free transportation, luxurious hotel suites, meals, and show tickets, for instance. For those who are heavy gamblers, the hotel may provide a limousine or even a helicopter to bring them from their home and return them—and keep on file such information as the hat, shoe, or suit size of the gambler's spouse; and the player's preference in food, wines, flowers, chocolate; and the like.

Some casinos rate high rollers in terms of the "buy in," that is, the amount of chips they buy, but an increasingly common measure is the player's theoretical loss. This is based on the estimated average wager and the average time spent at the table. What is of interest, here, is the dollar volume of play, not whether the player wins or loses during any particular trip. But again, over the long run, the casino always wins. The theoretical loss is based on the dollar volume of play times the casino's average winning margin at the game. Some

---

[10] James Kilby, personal communication to author, August 1991.

casinos are prepared to provide as much as 35 to 50 percent of a player's theoretical loss in comps.

More modest but still significant is the high roller slot player. In Atlantic City, a $500 gambling budget qualifies as a "slot high roller," but Kilby suggested $2,000 as the requirement — in cash or line of credit — for Las Vegas. Kilby also noted in connection with this higher amount that Las Vegas has a large number of $5 and $25 slot machines.

Comps and special recognition are extended to these players, too, according to their level of play. Casinos issue cards with an electronic identification embedded in them. These cards are inserted into the machine to record the player's level of play, and comps based on the volume of play (not losses). In fact, a $1 slot player is worth more to the house, according to Kilby, than a player who bets $100 a hand. On average, if a player bets $100 a hand, he or she will lose $100 an hour but, after all expenses (including comps), the casino's profit on that win is only $20 to $25 an hour. The average $1 slot player, on the other hand, will make a $3 average play (put in $3 worth of coins) per "pull" and average 300 pulls per hour. In that hour, as you can see, $900 will be bet and the house's average win will be 5 to 8 percent, or between $45 and $72. Because there is very little labor associated with slot machines, the house earns an 80 percent operating profit, or between $36 and $57.60. The increasing proportion of casino space taken up by slot machines is explained in good part by a changing consumer base that includes a much wider spectrum of society than it did 20 or even 10 years ago. As you can see, however, the superior profit margins of slot machines probably enter into the calculation, too. Fifty-five percent of play today is in slots, with an 80 percent department profit; the remaining 45 percent of play is in *all* other games — with a 20 to 25 percent department profit.

A final category could be called the "low roller," the bus trade. These are generally lower income people, often retirees and, surprisingly, often people on unemployment compensation. They, too, come for the gambling but usually have a budget of only $35 to $70. They often are attracted by a bargain low price.

In Atlantic City, this bus trade still provides the backbone of the year-round volume of business. In fact, on a typical day in Atlantic City, somewhere between 1,000 and 1,500 charter buses arrive laden with day trippers, there for somewhere between 4 and 12 hours. These players, too, are attracted by relatively generous comps. A typical bus deal, costing $10 to $12, includes round-trip bus transportation, a $5 meal discount coupon, and a $10 roll of quarters ("coin," as it's called in Atlantic City) to get them started. A number of casinos, however, have begun to deemphasize the low-roller day trippers and bus tours. As a result, bus volume in Atlantic City fell by over 10 percent in 1990.

Casino Staffing.   The casino gaming staff is made up of dealers (and croupiers), a floor person (once called the floor man) who supervises several dealers, and a pit boss. (In craps, a boxman assists the dealer, handling the bank). In the pit—a group of similar games—the pit boss is assisted by a pit clerk who handles record keeping.

The pit boss is really a technician, expert from years of experience in the practice of the game. He or she generally supervises the play, approves "markers"—that is, approves the extension of credit (within house limits)—approves in-house food and beverage comps for known players, and generally provides personal attention to high rollers.

The floor person supervises between two and five dealers, depending on the game, and never more than four games. He or she is also responsible for closely watching repeat customers to estimate their average bet, a figure that is crucial to the casino's marketing intelligence.

Slot machine areas are staffed by change people working under a supervisor. Change people and supervisors also offer recognition and personal contact for frequent visitors and slot high rollers.

Comps above a certain dollar level are generally approved by the casino's senior management. Comp services for a "junket" group are approved by the casino's marketing staff. Junkets are similar to tours that might be sold by a travel agent except that the "sights" are generally the casino and its hotel environment, and there may be no charge for any of the services because of the expectation of casino play by the visitor. Junkets are put together by the casino or, more commonly, by junket brokers in distant cities.

Working in casinos is very difficult. It requires a quick mind and an ability to work with people who are under considerable pressure. Players sometimes become abusive and unreasonable, and staff are expected to avoid, whenever possible, a difficult scene and permanently alienating a player and his or her friends. Not surprisingly, the higher the roller is, the greater will be the patience that may be expected of the staff.

Dealers need to be alert to players' attempts at cheating, and they themselves are constantly scrutinized by supervisors and security personnel because of the temptation of dishonesty where so much cash is changing hands.

The author would be uncomfortable if he did not close this section with a personal observation:

Gambling does raise serious moral and social questions for many, including me. Often gamblers exceed the limit of what they can afford, damaging their ability to care for their families. My observation, moreover, is that gambling creates an environment that often degrades people and raises money and material things to a higher level than they deserve. A real and somewhat scary question, though, is whether this emphasis on money and things and the deemphasis on people are a result of gambling or whether gambling is a reflection of those traits at large in our society. Whatever my views on the moral and social aspects of casinos and gambling, however, I don't feel that I can be a serious student of the hospitality industry and ignore such a large and growing part of our industry that appears to have so much appeal to our customers.

URBAN ENTERTAINMENT CENTERS

Urban entertainment centers vary widely. Some are designed on a smaller scale as a draw for local traffic and an enhancement to the local environment. Others are on a scale nearly as grand as those we considered in regard to theme parks, and there are many in between.

Sports stadiums have been with us since the time of Rome's Colosseum, but the latest variety of such centers is the covered "superdome," such as those in Houston and New Orleans. Describing the New Orleans superdome opening, *The New York Times* spoke of the 9.7-acre, 27-story facility as the "second in what promises to be a continental string of mammoth sports emporiums. Cities are now vying to build the largest, most expensive stadiums.[11] The *Economist* described the publicly owned domed stadium as essential to gaining the status of a big league city. "The tenant teams not only draw in the fans and help pay off the stadium bonds and overheads, they also create jobs and general business."[12]

These facilities host not only sports events but entertainers and rock concerts as well. They provide gathering places that entertain residents or visitors to a city. Typically, they reach out to an area around the city—and sometimes to the entire nation—drawing in the visitors and tourists.

A similar facility, the convention center, mixes business and pleasure. The visitors to a convention or trade show are on business. But many of these gatherings are more social than professional, and even the most business-oriented meetings are, in large part, devoted to having a good time.

Convention, trade show, and sports centers were once largely the preserve of great metropolitan centers such as New York with its Coliseum and Chicago's McCormick Place. Increasingly, however, cities such as Seattle, San Jose in California, and New Orleans, large but of second rank in size, have developed urban entertainment centers as a means of challenging established travel patterns and increasing the travel business in their market.

In fact, the urban play (and business) centers now extend into cities of the third and fourth rank. Like many other cities of under a million population, San Jose, California, is using an urban entertainment center as the centerpiece of its $500 million program to revitalize the city's downtown. A $100 million sports center will be home for the San Jose Sharks, a National Hockey League team. The arena, to open in the fall of 1993, "will also accommodate a variety of events such as professional basketball, concerts and

---

[11] *The New York Times,* August 4, 1977, p. 40.

[12] *Economist,* June 16, 1984, p. 25.

family shows." A new convention center, opened in 1989, includes a civic auditorium complex, a 163,000-square-foot exhibit hall, and a theater and performing arts center. A Hilton Hotel and Towers will be constructed adjacent to the center and is expected to "draw 23,000 new convention delegates per year who will spend $7.9 million in the city annually."[13]

Although medium-sized cities cannot bid in the national convention market for the large conventions, they often can attract smaller national meetings and regional conferences. For this reason, many cities successfully sell bond issues to build civic meeting centers that improve a community's ability to compete for its share of the travel market. That travel market, more and more city leaders are learning, means more sales for local businesses, increased employment, and more tax revenues.

Whether the results of these civic efforts always justify such an investment is open to question. In any case, though, somebody must operate these centers, and the skills involved (dealing with various traveling publics, providing food service, and managing housekeeping and building operations, to name only a few) clearly fall within the hospitality management graduate's domain. The significance of this new area of hospitality management may be measured by the fact that ARA Services has established a special division to manage such centers.

Increasingly, urban planners are including in their developments plazas designed to accommodate amusements, dining, and other leisure activities. The prototype of this kind of plaza is Rockefeller Center in the heart of New York City, with its ice-skating rinks in winter, and horse shows, karate demonstrations, and model airplane contests in milder seasons.

Of the more recently constructed plazas, according to *The Wall Street Journal,* the First National Plaza in front of the First Chicago Building is a model for plazas to come. A computer controls the fountain, so that visitors won't get splashed on windy days. From May to October, the plaza features free noontime entertainment, late afternoon concerts, and an outdoor cafe. It also has, year-round, a restaurant, a bar, a legitimate theater, and retail shops.

City waterfront redevelopment projects, too, have become centers that attract visitors and enrich the lives of the local people. Baltimore's National Aquarium, for instance, is credited with contributing some $90 million to the state's economy. At the Monterey Bay Aquarium, 2.4 million visitors helped restaurants at Fisherman's Wharf weather their winter sales slump. In addition, there have been so many visitors to the Monterey site that it set off a local hotel construction boom, according to *The Wall Street Journal.*[14]

Restoration and revitalization of aging sections of a city require the involvement of hospitality industry operations. In Texas, Dallas Alley was

---

[13] Henry W. Cord, Presentation to the Hospitality Industry Investment Conference, New York, June 4, 1991. The quotations are from a document "Focus on San Jose" distributed by Mr. Cord.

[14] *The Wall Street Journal,* November 22, 1985, p. 27.

built in what "was just a half-forgotten place down by the tracks, the back door to Dallas, where freight cars lingered on sidings and dusty warehouses and small factories stood one after another."[15] In an old Sunshine Biscuit factory and an adjoining building that was once a Coca Cola bottling plant, a group of private investors built Dallas Alley, an aggregation of nine nightclubs. The center is located near a $25 million festival Marketplace housed in a former cracker and candy factory. Dallas Alley, alone, attracts over a million visitors annually.

Museums were once thought of as stuffy, but the *Economist* characterized the best-equipped science museums as "grown-up playpens. Interaction is the key word. Visitors can take a weather-reporting class, watch a fish spawning cycle, experiment with sounds and colors or bone up on elementary mathematics of chance. There are also plenty of satellites, laser guns and deep sea diving bells."[16]

Another kind of "living museum," a zoo, can be a major tourism generator. For instance, each year roughly 5 million visitors come to the San Diego Zoo. The zoo also operates an 1,800-acre wildlife preserve 30 miles north of San Diego. The zoo and preserve, like so many other tourist destinations, have a substantial educational mission. The preserve, for instance, is visited by 40,000 elementary and secondary schoolchildren each year. An important service provided to visitors, of course, is food service, and because the number of visitors to destinations such as aquariums and zoos—like so many other seasonal attractions—expands when school is out, these operations can offer summer experience opportunities to students, with a decent chance at getting into a supervisory position.

Shopping centers are usually thought of as catering principally to local shoppers. But even so, such centers can be more than a little ambitious. The new St. Louis Centre suggests the scale of a large, locally centered mall and the often close relationship of such centers to the hospitality industry. The centre was begun as an urban renewal project in 1972 and was completed 13 years later at a total cost of $17.5 million. Comprising a two-block stretch of downtown St. Louis, the centre serves about 10 million people each year, of whom nearly a million are out-of-towners. The centre has 17 fast-food restaurants and 13 sit-down restaurants whose combined annual food service volume is $12.5 million.[17]

Finally, we will look briefly at a mega-shopping center in Western Canada built on the grandest scale yet undertaken. In the case of the West Edmonton Mall, the aim from the very first was to attract tourists as well as local residents to the center, as Edmonton, Alberta, a city of 560,000, could not support a mall of this scale by itself.

[15] *Southern Living,* January 1988, pp. 62–63.

[16] *Economist,* June 14, 1986, p. 82.

[17] Ms. Patsy Baldwin, assistant general manager, St. Louis Centre, personal communication to author, July 1991.

A shopping center with a difference. Canada's West Edmonton Mall is both a mall and a theme park. Among its attractions are four submarines. (Courtesy of Triple 5 Corp.)

The scale quite literally boggles the mind. Consider its total indoor area of 5.2 million square feet, equivalent to 28 city blocks. The ceiling peaks at 16 stories with a mile-long, two-level main concourse, served by 15,000 employees. The interior plantings include $3 million worth of tropical plants—among which is a grove of 50-foot palm trees—and the 37 animal displays include Siberian tigers and a 300-pound grouper! The mall houses an amusement park and a water park with a 5-acre pool where you can surf on 6-foot waves, water-ski, ride the rapids, and get a suntan, even when the outside temperature is well below zero. The sights include an 80-foot-long Spanish galleon, an 18-hole miniature golf course, a 50,000-gallon aquarium, and four submarines. The 33-foot-long computer-controlled subs will seat 24 people. Built by a family of Iranian immigrants, the Ghemezians, the mall is dedicated to the idea that shopping is more than just a utilitarian chore and can be an

Getting a tan while swimming in a pool with 6-foot breakers when the ground is covered with snow is no longer a fantasy. Mega-malls in northern locations are making themselves into major tourist attractions by incorporating miniature theme parks. This mall is in Edmonton, Alberta. (Courtesy of Triple 5 Corporation)

opportunity for fun. The mall has its own tourism promotion budget of $5 million (roughly equivalent to the budget of the province of Alberta)[18] and its own tour-packaging travel agency.

About a third of the visitors to the mall are from Edmonton and its trading area. Nearly a fifth are from Alberta outside the 60-mile trading area. The other half come from the rest of Canada and the United States. Half of these Canadian visitors and 75 percent of the Americans come specifically to visit the Edmonton Mall. U.S. visitors average a four-day stay. Visitors, interestingly enough, spend as much or more money outside the mall as they do inside.

On average, 400,000 people visit the mall each week. Annually, the mall generates 6 million tourists (that is, people from outside Edmonton), of whom about a half-million come from the United States.[19] Naturally the mall has a

[18] *The Wall Street Journal,* October 7, 1985, p. 1.

[19] Ms. Deane Eldredge, director of public affairs, Triple 5 Corporation, personal communication to author, July 1991.

major impact on hospitality industry firms in Edmonton and is itself a significant part of the local hospitality industry, with 10 restaurants, numerous fast-food operations, and a 360-room luxury hotel. A similar center will open in early 1992 just outside Minneapolis, Minnesota.

TEMPORARY ATTRACTIONS: FAIRS AND FESTIVALS

Fairs date from the Middle Ages when they served as important centers for economic and cultural revival. Festivals also have their roots in early history and were originally religious events.

World's Fairs are year-long attractions, but even a local fair such as the agricultural fair in Duquoin, Illinois, which annually attracts a quarter of a million people to this town of 7,000, can have a major impact on a city. Some fairs celebrate local industry, whereas others have cultural and historical roots, as is the case with Mardi Gras in New Orleans. Tradition is not enough, however. A successful event must also have direction, purpose, and goals.[20] Indeed, a festival or fair is a quasi-business activity. Its success is measured by its ability to attract visitors, to cover its costs, and to maintain sufficient local support to keep it staffed, usually almost entirely with unpaid volunteers.

Winter festivals reposition the season of slush and rust as a community asset. The growing popularity of winter sports fits well with ice carnivals. The one in St. Paul, Minnesota, which dates all the way back to 1886, includes events such as "concerts, skiing, sleigh rides, ice sculptures, hot-air balloon rides, parades, a royal coronation, car racing, and a softball tournament — on ice." Quebec's ice carnival, begun in 1954 "to energize a stagnant economy, is now the city's third largest industry and generates revenues of $30 million a year."[21]

Events such as these clearly affect the economy of the cities and regions that sponsor them. Local patrons spend money from their family entertainment budget that might have left the community. Visitors "spend in food, lodging, souvenirs, gasoline, public transportation and the like. In some cases the event itself makes purchases which add to the dollar stream of the community."[22]

The economic effects of fairs and festivals have a major impact on the community and especially on its hospitality industry. For this reason, hospi-

[20]Marlene E. Boland, "The Dynamics of Community Festivals," Master's thesis, School of Rural Planning and Development, University of Guelph, 1985, p. 52.

[21]*American Demographics,* November 1988, pp. 45–47.

[22]Laurence S. Davidson and William A. Schaffer, "A Discussion of Methods Employed in Analyzing the Impact of Short-Term Entertainment Events," *Journal of Travel Research,* Winter 1980, p. 12.

tality industry managers are often prominent sponsors and backers of such events. We ought not lose sight of the fact, however, that, like so many other aspects of tourism, fairs and festivals also have important social and cultural benefits to their communities: They celebrate the local heritage and bring members from all parts of the community together to work as volunteers.

In some cases, a festival may even be used to help in the regeneration of a community. In New Haven, Connecticut, the Office of Housing and Neighborhood Development uses neighborhood festivals as a centerpiece in its Commercial Revitalization Program. The effect of a festival on a neighborhood's turnaround is described as follows:

> The signs of change are now visible to the community. The investment climate has improved substantially and outside interest has emerged. There may be a desire to "show off" improvement. Many new characters are involved and the character of the area is changing.[23]

Large or small, then, these kinds of events can be a vital part of the life of a community, city, or region.

MOVING ATTRACTIONS: CRUISES

Cruise ships[24] have all the features of a resort hotel, albeit with smaller rooms and an additional crew to run the ship. In 1990, 3.7 million Americans took a cruise. The industry has doubled since 1983 and is growing at a rate of over 10 percent a year. The cruise business, however, is still very small. The entire world cruise-ship capacity would equal about 65 percent of Orlando's 290 hotels, for instance. On the other hand, cruise-ship passengers are forecast to continue to grow at a rate of from 10 to 15 percent throughout the 1990s. One thing hindering growth, however, is that most of the *markets* are in North America, while the manufacture of cruise ships is limited almost entirely to Europe. Because the dollar has been falling relative to European currencies, the ships end up being more expensive than planned after the three years it takes to build one. Nevertheless large, cash-rich organizations such as Carnival Cruise Lines and the Carlson companies, which also owns Radisson Hotels, are committed to provide more capacity.

The cruise market can be divided into three basic segments. A younger market seeks the thrill and adventure of a luxury cruise, with a stop at a different port each day. A family-oriented segment combines a three- or four-day cruise with a three- or four-day visit to Orlando and such attractions as

---

[23] *A Promotion Guide to Commercial Revitalization* (New Haven, Conn.: Office of Housing and Neighborhood Development, n.d.), p. 9.

[24] Information in this section is taken from Daniel R. Lee, *Carnival Cruise Lines* (Boston: First Boston Corp., May 21, 1991).

Cruise ships such as this partially sail-powered vessel operated by Club Med can avoid off seasons by moving to waters where the weather is more favorable. (Courtesy of Club Med. Photo by Michel Verdure.)

Walt Disney World and other theme parks located there. A third, smaller, upscale segment favors luxury cruises on smaller vessels to out-of-the-way destinations. The all-inclusive pricing of cruises is an advantage with all three segments. One hotel industry official referred to cruise-ship competitors as one of the "winners" of the late twentieth century. They will appeal, he said, to leisure-oriented travelers who prefer the all-inclusive pricing and are "looking for value and convenience as well as certainty in their experience."[25]

The cruise-ship equivalent of a room is a two-berth cabin. Since cruise ships cost about $150,000 a berth, the "per room" investment is $300,000, higher than many resorts. On the other hand, the all-inclusive pricing also ensures a high sales per "room" because meals are included and the price also includes airfare to the port of embarkation. Cruise lines usually purchase airfares at a deep discount from air carriers and are able to make a substantial profit on their resale. Nevertheless, the large capital investment makes a strong marketing organization to secure full capacity utilization essential. While cruise ships are costly to build, they have the advantage over a hotel of moving from place to place. The Caribbean, for instance, is popular in the winter but cruises to Alaska blossom in the summer. As a result, there is much less discounting of cruise prices in their off seasons.

[25] Rose, "The Advent of the 21st Century from the Chrysalis of the 1990's."

Most on-board jobs are filled by foreign nationals who are paid relatively low wages but receive generous tips. For tax reasons, virtually all cruise ships are registered in a foreign country. Work in the land-based marketing organizations, however, is open to North Americans.

NATURAL ENVIRONMENTS

Not everything, by any means, that attracts tourism is man-made. In the public sector, national and state parks, forests, and waters should interest hospitality students just as much. These uniquely American recreation areas have been copied the world over. As far as hospitality innovation goes, they are, in fact, relatively new. The first park created by Congress, Yosemite, was established toward the end of the Civil War, in 1864.[26] The National Park Service itself was not established until 1916.

The number of visits to national parks grew rapidly in the 1950s and 1960s, expanding to roughly four times the 1950 total by 1965 and doubling again by 1980. As Figure 11.1 indicates, growth slowed during the first half of the 1980s and even showed a modest decline in 1985.[27] The early 1980s, you may recall, saw both a serious recession and an energy crisis. Because the largest number of parks and other reserved areas under National Park Service (NPS) administration are located in areas distant from population centers in the midwestern and eastern United States, national park visits are sensitive to economic conditions and to the price and availability of gasoline.

In 1990, there were 17.5 million overnight stays in national parks. Lodging in park concession hotels accounted for 22 percent of those stays, and recreational vehicle stays accounted for another 22 percent. Tent camping accounted for 38 percent. The balance of 19 percent is reported as "miscellaneous" but is largely accounted for by organizational group camping.[28]

The National Parks Service Act of 1916 established the National Parks System with the clear intention of providing recreation and, at the same time, preserving the parks intact for the enjoyment of future generations. The increased crowding of existing facilities has led those interested in preservation as well as recreation—including the National Park Service itself—to propose drastic limitations on use of private automobiles within parks. The National Parks and Conservation Association (NPCA), a private group that supports a

---

[26] The first national park was Yellowstone, established in 1872. Yosemite was originally a California state park created by the U.S. Congress. It became a national park in 1890.

[27] National Park Service (NPS) statistics have undergone a substantial revision. The *Statistical Abstract* published by the NPS shows figures adjusted to the revised basis only back to 1980, making direct comparisons to earlier periods difficult. The 1950–1980 results are based on unadjusted totals and should be regarded as an estimate.

[28] *Statistical Abstract* (Washington, D.C.: National Park Service, 1990).

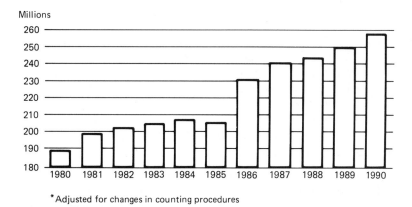

Millions

*Adjusted for changes in counting procedures

FIGURE 11.1 National Park Service recreation visits. (*Source:* National Park Service.)

conservationist view of natural parks, has suggested that such accommodations as hotels, cabins, and campgrounds be restricted or even reduced within these parks. Similar proposals have been advanced for such high-intensity recreation activities as downhill skiing (with its requirements for ski lifts), snowmobiling, hunting (particularly in the eastern states), and seashore activities.

The NPCA does not argue that hospitality facilities and services should be unavailable. Instead, it proposes that *staging areas* with lodgings and other services be established in nearby communities and that these staging areas be connected with parks by low-cost transportation. Proposals like this would reduce private auto use and help preserve the natural beauty, a park's principal attraction and reason for being. It might also create major new commercial recreation areas and opportunities for hospitality firms and graduates of hospitality management programs. Moreover, given the leadership of the national parks in the field of recreation, this pattern might well extend to state parks and forests in future years if it is accepted by Congress and the people.

This huge tourism activity has created many opportunities for tourism enterprises serving the areas that surround natural recreation sites. Although park management is a specialized field addressed in professional education programs in parks and recreation management at colleges and universities, the management of the auxiliary services in and around parks—particularly food services, hotels, and motels—lies within the hospitality management career area. Park lodging and food service concessions hire large numbers of students and, in fact, are staffed largely by students during peak periods. People who work for the same concessionaires for several summers have a good opportunity of gaining supervisory experience—and of seeing some beautiful country.

SUMMARY

In this chapter we discussed recreation, its motives and its destinations. After explaining why people travel, we divided their destinations into primary or touring, and secondary or stopover. Then we talked about planned play environments, such as national and regional theme parks, casinos (as exemplified by Las Vegas and Atlantic City), urban entertainment centers such as sports stadiums and mega-shopping centers, cruise ships, and, lastly, the natural environment, especially national parks.

Along the way, we pointed out the possible employment opportunities for both temporary jobs and permanent careers. Destination attractions are often big hospitality businesses in themselves and act as magnets that keep the flow of tourism not only going but also growing.

KEY WORDS AND CONCEPTS

To help you review this chapter, keep in mind the following:

Recreation	Bus trade
Primary and secondary attractions	Comps
	Fairs and festivals
Planned play environments	Cruise market
Theme parks	Urban entertainment centers
Casinos	Mega-shopping centers
Casino markets	Natural environments
High rollers	

REVIEW QUESTIONS

1. What are some of the reasons that people travel?

2. What is the difference between primary and secondary destinations?

3. Briefly describe a theme park that you have visited, and explain why you think it is popular.

4. How do national theme parks, such as Disney World, differ from regional theme parks, such as Six Flags?

5. Besides gambling, what advantages does Las Vegas offer?

6. What are "comps," and how do casinos decide to whom they will give them?

7. Do you think that mega-shopping centers will be successful? Why or why not?

8. What is a staging area, and why is it important?

CHAPTER 12

Courtesy of Kampgrounds of America

BUSINESSES SERVING THE TRAVELER

THE PURPOSE OF THIS CHAPTER

In Chapter 10 we looked at the economic, social, and cultural significance of tourism. In Chapter 11 we focused on destinations and attractions, the generators of tourism. Now we turn our attention briefly to businesses that serve the tourists and are closely allied to the hospitality industry: passenger transportation, travel agents, and travel wholesalers. These businesses are a vital part of the tourism system of which the hospitality industry is also a part.

We will also look at a business some would say is a competitor of the hospitality industry. Camping is clearly competitive with hotels, but it is probably more useful to look at campgrounds as a part of our hospitality universe.

Finally, in this last chapter on tourism, we need to direct our attention to what lies ahead for tourism. We will find that real promise for growth is the key factor.

THIS CHAPTER SHOULD HELP YOU

1. Identify major trends in the travel business and possible future developments in this allied industry.

2. Understand the role of the travel agent as a retailer and wholesaler.

3. Relate the services of the travel agent to the hospitality industry, and particularly to hotels.

4. Assess the campground industry's present situation and outlook.

5. Develop a picture of campground customers and their needs and of the economies of camping.

6. Appreciate the degree to which campgrounds and RVs are competitive with the hotel business.

PASSENGER TRANSPORTATION

In Chapter 10 we looked at travel trends as a part of tourism. Here, we'll briefly survey travel again, this time to gain a perspective on the travel business as an allied industry that works with hospitality firms in serving travelers. Tourist expenditures make up practically all of the sales of firms engaged in public intercity travel—*common carriers,* as they are called. Common carriers include the airlines, bus companies, and railroads.

In the past 10 years, travel between cities has continued to increase.[1] Table 12.1 shows that the 10-year increase was 36 percent, to a total of 1.5 *trillion* miles. The *share* of travel captured by common carriers has also risen from just over one fifth in 1980 to nearly a quarter by 1990. While the total *share* of travel by private vehicle declined (from 78.9 to 75.4 percent), the total number of miles Americans traveled in their own cars, trucks, or recreational vehicles (RVs) increased 30 percent, to a level of over 1 trillion miles. Clearly, the private motor vehicle is still the dominant mode of transportation in North America.

As Table 12.2 shows, bus travel has declined not only in its share of travel but in total passenger miles. (One passenger going one mile equals one passenger mile.) Rail travel, too, has seen a decline in share but that is somewhat deceptive. In the mid-1980s, the size of the passenger rail system was reduced significantly as a result of lower government subsidies. The modest increase in share since 1985, and the dramatic increase in total passenger miles reflect significant gains in volume for the reduced network AMTRAK currently operates. If fuel costs increase during the 1990s, there is a real possibility that rail travel will make an even greater comeback because of its superior fuel efficiency.

Airlines have been overwhelmingly the common carrier of choice. Total passenger miles have increased nearly 70 percent in 10 years. We noted in Chapter 10, however, that this increase occurred during a time when the cost of pleasure travel by air was generally falling.

---

[1] Data in this section are taken from the *1990 Travel Market Report (Full Year)* (Washington D.C.: U.S. Travel Data Center, 1991), and *The 1989-90 Economic Review of Travel in America* (Washington, D.C.: U.S. Travel Data Center, 1990).

TABLE 12.1 U.S. Intercity Transportation by Common Carriers and Private Vehicles (in billions of passenger miles)

Vehicles	1980		1985		1990*	
	Miles	Percent	Miles	Percent	Miles	Percent
Common carriers	236.3	21.1%	306.4	23.9%	374.6	24.6%
Autos, trucks, and RVs	881.3	78.9	975.3	76.1	1,146.1	75.4
Total	1,117.6	100.0%	1,281.7	100.0%	1,520.7	100.0%

Source: U.S. Travel Data Center.
*1990 data estimated.

Following deregulation in 1978, the number of airlines increased dramatically and competition was fierce on almost all routes. Gradually, however, as one carrier after another failed or merged with a competitor, the number of airlines in operation decreased and so did competition. The evidence is that, on routes served by only one carrier, fares have increased significantly. In a travel market dominated by a few carriers, the likelihood of fare cuts has decreased. Moreover, fuel costs are a very significant part of today's airline cost structure. After the energy crisis of the early 1980s, fuel costs moderated and this helped hold airfares down; but fuel costs seem likely to increase, and that will likely be reflected in higher prices.

There are literally hundreds of thousands of special fares—many available only for a short period of time, ranging from a few minutes to a few days. (Special fares generally appear on the computer network used by airlines and travel agents and can be discontinued at will by the carrier.) Almost all of these

TABLE 12.2 U.S. Intercity Transportation by Common Carriers (in billions of passenger miles)

Sector	1980		1985		1990*	
	Miles	Percent	Miles	Percent	Miles	Percent
Air	204.4	86.5%	277.8	90.7%	345.1	92.1%
Bus	27.4	11.6	23.8	7.8	23.3	6.2
Rail	4.5	1.9	4.8	1.5	6.2	1.7
Total common carriers	236.3	100.0%	306.4	100.0%	374.6	100.0%

Source: U.S. Travel Data Center.
*1990 data estimated.

special fares are discounted fares, and the impact of discounting, of course, has been to hold down the cost of travel. Most special fares, however, are structured so that they will not be attractive to the business traveler. Many, for instance, require travelers to stay over a Saturday night, a night when most business travelers would rather be home with their families. The effect of discounted fares, then, has been to keep personal travel costs down while business travel costs rise. As a result, personal travel by air has continued to increase. Business travel grew until 1990, when it declined slightly in the face of a recession, a war (and terrorism scare), and higher prices.

The probability is that airline fares will continue to rise. This recalls our earlier discussion about rail travel. There is a real possibility that rising airfares will fuel the growth in rail travel, particularly between major population centers.

CHANNELS OF DISTRIBUTION

Those who manufacture consumer goods talk about the several "layers of businesses" between the manufacturer and the final customer. Some of these intermediary businesses and agents are wholesalers, manufacturer's representatives, and brokers. Typically, these intermediaries move the product from the manufacturer to the retailer, who then sells to the final user, the retail customer. Although most hospitality firms provide goods and services directly to the customer without any intermediaries, the travel agent and tour operators represent important exceptions.

TRAVEL AGENTS

The U.S. Travel Data Center defines travel agents as follows:

> Travel agencies make travel reservations for the public and sell transportation, lodging and other travel services on behalf of the producers of the services. They are retailers: they sell travel services provided by others directly to the final customer.[2]

In 1989 there were 30,000 travel agencies operating in 35,000 locations, twice as many as were in operation nine years earlier. Travel agencies employed 175,000 people.

Large, multiunit travel agencies are highly visible and we sometimes have the impression that they dominate the travel field. In fact, however, two thirds of the agencies sold $2 million or less worth of travel, and 90 percent sell less than $5 million. Notice that the sales figures cited are gross travel sales from

[2] *The 1989–90 Economic Review of Travel in America,* (Washington, D.C.: U.S. Travel Data Center, 1990), p. 22.

Already an American institution, Walt Disney World's Cinderella
Castle symbolizes North America's most famous theme park.
(Courtesy of Walt Disney World)

which the agency receives a commission. Commissions on air travel within
North America are 10 percent, while international commissions are about 11
percent. Hotel and cruise commissions range from 10 to 15 percent. The
average agency sold $2.6 million in travel in 1989. Thus, the travel agent field
is one characterized by small businesses with average net commissions of less
than $300,000.

Travel agents' business is split just about evenly between business travel
(52 percent) and personal travel (48 percent). While agents book about 10
percent of all trips, they account for 20 percent of the dollar value of trips
booked. Not surprisingly, sales of domestic travel (70 percent) outweigh sales
of international travel, but the latter, at 30 percent, is clearly a significant

TABLE 12.3 Travel Agency
Sales by Category

Category	Proportion of Sales
Airlines	58%
Cruises	15
Hotel rooms	11
Car rentals	8
Rail	4
Miscellaneous	4

Source: "Travel Agent Study," Presentation to the 1991 Travel Outlook Forum, Pittsburgh, Pa., October 16, 1990.

factor. As Table 12.3 indicates, the lion's share of agency sales are airline tickets.

Travel agents not only make reservations and sell tickets but also sell packaged tours. In fact, 21 percent of their sales of leisure travel are packaged tours. It's clear that travel agents have considerable influence on the consumer and thus on the sales of other firms serving travelers. Two thirds of pleasure travelers, for instance, seek the advice of their travel agent on hotel selection, package tour choice, and car rental. About half ask for help in selecting a destination and in the choice of airline.

Business travel, as we noted, accounts for just over half of travel agents' sales, so it is not surprising that the overwhelming majority of agents (87 percent) provide their services to businesses as well as to individuals. Nearly two thirds handle convention (59 percent) and meeting arrangements (57 percent). Only 40 percent, however, handle incentive travel, such as sales contest awards. While business travelers are somewhat less likely than pleasure travelers to seek a travel agent's advice, nearly half do so regarding hotel choice (47 percent) and airline and car rental choices (44 percent).

Growth of travel agency locations was very rapid in the early 1980s (a rate of 14 percent) and, technically, the growth rate was still 8 percent by the end of the decade. This figure, however, includes satellite ticket printers (STPs), which have increased in significance in recent years. In fact, by 1989 STPs accounted for half of the growth in travel agent outlets and 10 percent of all travel agent units. A major use of STPs is to service larger business travel accounts. Still, after the fast growth of the first half of the 1980s, staffed travel agency locations were growing at a healthy rate of about 4 percent per year at the end of the decade, supporting the notion of a fast-growing travel field.

Travel wholesalers and tour brokers arrange to purchase space and services from all of the firms that serve travelers—carriers, hotels, restaurants, and attractions such as those we discussed in the last chapter. Then they sell the services of these firms to the consumer, often through retail travel agents in return for a commission on those sales. Travel wholesalers such as American Express often retail their own tours, but they also work with the retail travel agencies that sell the tour package to customers in their local markets. Carriers (such as airlines and bus and rail operators) also have their own tour operations and act as wholesalers of package tours. The tour wholesaler purchases services at deep discounts. They make their package attractive by offering a retail price that is still significantly less than the cost of all the package elements if the guest purchased them separately. Even after this discount, both the tour broker and the retail travel agent have a margin for their operating costs and profit.

Hotels (especially resort hotels) often profit handsomely from associations with travel agencies. In return for the commissions they pay these agencies, the hotels have their properties represented in many communities. The travel wholesaler, too, can be important to hotels, because a listing in a wholesale package guarantees a listing with all of the wholesaler's retail affiliates. Some hotels, however, avoid travel agent representation and the accompanying commissions if it produces, on balance, relatively little income.

RESERVATIONS NETWORKS

In the period 1988 to 1990, nearly $3 billion was spent on developing computerized central reservations systems (CRS) that serve various travel companies.[3] The leaders in this area have long been the airlines, but hotel companies and car rental companies have also developed similar systems. In the past, airline companies made airline reservations, and hotels and car companies made their own reservations. Travel agents called the appropriate reservation system to inquire about or reserve a seat, room, or automobile. The new and potentially revolutionary development in this area is the linkup of these systems so that they can communicate with one another on virtually a worldwide basis. Since 95 percent of travel agents have computer terminals linked to one of the airline systems, the emerging system has literally thousands of instantaneous selling points.

The airline systems, such as American's SABRE, are the backbone of the emerging worldwide CRS network. To hold down the cost of developing these systems, airlines have banded together so that three megasystems are emerging. The geographical scope of these systems is indicated by Figure 12.1. To understand the full complexity of interconnection that is now possible, however, it's important to note that travel agents, car rental companies, hotels, and even travel offices of businesses as well as individuals can all contact one another for information as well as to make reservations. THISCO (The Hotel

---

[3] The following discussion draws extensively on Lawrence Chervenak, "CRS The Past, the Present, The Future," in *Lodging,* June 1991, pp. 25–30 and 41, and on the newsletter published by Mr. Chervenak's firm, *CKC Report, The Hotel Technology Newsletter,* April 1991, pp. 5–10.

Major Reservation Systems Affiliated	Principle Location	Participating Airlines
Sabre	United States	American Airlines
Apollo	Europe	Alitalia British Airways KLM Swiss Air United Airlines U.S. Air
Gallileo	Europe	British Airways KLM Swiss Air
Gemini	Canada	Air Canada Canadian Air
Worldspan	United States	Delta Northwest TWA
Abacus	Singapore	Cathay Pacific Arina Airlines Malaysian Airlines Philippine Airlines Singapore Airlines
Amadeus	Europe	Air France Iberia Lufthansa SAS
System One	United States	Continental

FIGURE 12.1 Three emerging central reservation megasystems. (*Source: Lodging,* June 1991.)

Industry Switch Company) has been formed by 17 U.S. hotel companies to develop a "switch" to provide an effective link between airline CRS and hotel CRS. As a result of this interconnection, any terminal on the system can contact any other; that is, a travel agent, company travel office, or airline reservations agent can make a reservation with any hotel CRS connected to the system. A similar "switch" service, ResAccess, has also been developed by Avis' reservation system, Wizcom. Figure 12.2 portrays the complete system and illustrates all the potential interconnections.

The impact of the emerging interlinkages will be magnified when multinational networks of fiber-optic cable ringing the world are completed. Fiber-optic cable can carry much more information than existing cable and at a much lower cost. As a result, it will become possible to transmit pictures of a property, its rooms, and facilities as well as banquet menus, layouts, and other

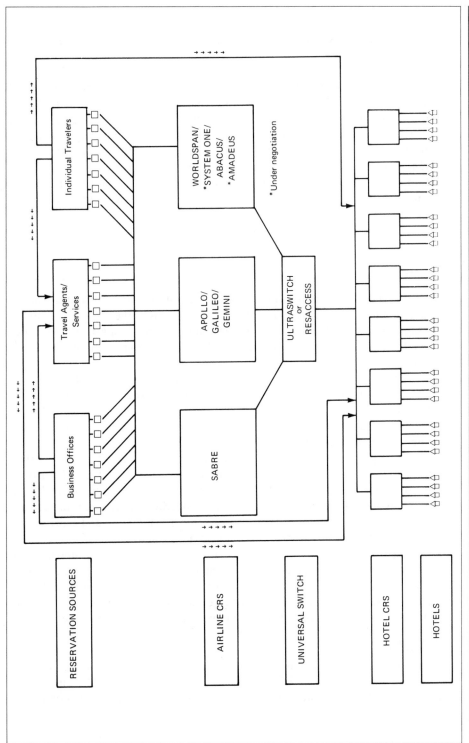

FIGURE 12.2 The emerging central reservation network. (*Source: CKC Report, the Hotel Technology Newsletter,* April 1991.) This figure has been modified according to later data supplied by Mr. Chervenak.

information to anyone—a travel agent or company travel office, for instance—and for reservation requests to flow to properties.

Even before the information-carrying capacity is expanded, the network-switching capability will make it possible for airline reservations agents and travel agents to book all the reservations needed for a trip—air, hotel, and auto—in a single consumer transaction. Lawrence Chervenak, an authority on the technology involved, points out, however, that many travel agents may be hurt by the easy availability "of alternative techniques for gaining information and making reservations which will become available to travelers." As a result, he notes, "For many travel agents, surviving will depend on their becoming more effective packagers and travel consultants, rather than just order takers."[4]

CAMPING

Much of the park visitation discussed in the last chapter constitutes what is called *day use:* the family piles into the car and visits the park for a day of hiking, picnicking, fishing, and so forth and returns home in the evening. Nevertheless, a significant portion of park use is overnight, and most of that use involves camping.

There are about 12,000 campgrounds in the United States. Although they range in size from very small to over 3,000 sites, the average campground has about 150 sites and covers 50 to 60 acres. There is a trend toward longer operating seasons, with somewhere between one third and one half of the campgrounds remaining open all year.

Campgrounds are increasing in size and are expanding the services they offer. The more profitable ones are often part of a chain or franchise group. Like other forms of the competitive lodging industry, campgrounds feel pressure to match the improvements of their competitors and so continually are upgrading their amenities. For instance, cable TV hookups and baby-sitting have become more popular, and there also are available more food services, sports instruction, guide services, and entertainment at campgrounds. Many campgrounds also offer some kind of shelter as well as the raw campsite, with the campgrounds renting trailers to campers. Other amenities such as hiking trails, stocked fish ponds, beach frontage, and marinas are likely to become more common as the trend toward competitive upgrading continues.

CAMPERS

Camping is a popular activity for families and is especially attractive to young families. The low cost of camping is advantageous to a family with young children, as housing and feeding four or five or more people in motels and

---

[4] *CKC Report,* p. 9.

Family camping is one of the most popular outdoor activities in North America. (Courtesy of Recreational Vehicle Industry Association)

restaurants can be costly. While tent camping is the least expensive approach, many campers prefer the convenience and comfort of a recreational vehicle. Most Americans have tried camping at one time or another, and the evidence indicates that roughly one third of Americans intend to camp again. A recreational activity that can boast a third of the population is a popular one indeed.[5]

Earlier we discussed camping in public parks. We should note, however, that there is also a very large private campground industry. In general, private campgrounds tend to be located along the main routes of travel rather than in specifically scenic areas. Because they are operated for profit, private campgrounds must locate near main arteries of traffic where, like hotels and motels, they are most convenient to the traveler and hence more likely to enjoy a favorable occupancy rate.[6] Campgrounds operated by parks and other public agencies, however, are generally located in a scenic area, often removed from

[5]Richard T. Curtin, "American Families Esteem the Camping Experience," *RV Dealer,* April 1982, p. 10.

[6]Of course, many private campgrounds are in scenic locations. Rather, our point here is that the major determinant of location for successful commercial campgrounds is accessibility to a large volume of traffic.

Commercial campgrounds such as KOA are an important part of the growing recreation industry. (Courtesy of Kampgrounds of America)

the main thoroughfares. Publicly operated campgrounds do not aim for a profit and these camps often experience lower occupancy rates in all but the peak season.

RECREATIONAL VEHICLES

Recreational vehicles bring a degree of creature comfort and even luxury into camping. In a way, they are self-service lodging. Sales of RVs depend on a number of factors, some of which vary from year to year. Since RVs require a

A wide variety of recreational vehicles is available to fit different family sizes, budgets, and tastes. (Courtesy of Recreational Vehicles Industry Association)

substantial investment, they sell better in good times than in bad. Because many buyers finance their purchase with a loan, RVs also sell better in years when interest rates are lower. Finally, high gas prices hurt sales, perhaps because of the perception consumers have of affordability as much as because of the real impact on the cost of ownership. Gas shocks, high interest rates, and recessions have had adverse impacts on RV sales in some years (see Figure 12.3). In spite of periodic factors such as these, however, it is also clear that large numbers of RVs sell, even in difficult times. In 1990, there were an estimated 8.5 million RVs in the United States.[7]

One factor that has a longer range impact on RV sales is changing demographics. The age group that makes the most frequent use of RVs is people 45 to 54 years old. Thus the middle-aging of the baby boomers is a strong plus for RV ownership and use. Indeed, in the 1990s people aged 45 to 54 will be moving into the high leisure group of over fifty-fivers with much if

[7] Philip Ingrossa, Recreational Vehicle Association, personal communication to author, September 3, 1991. The estimate is based on a 1988 study.

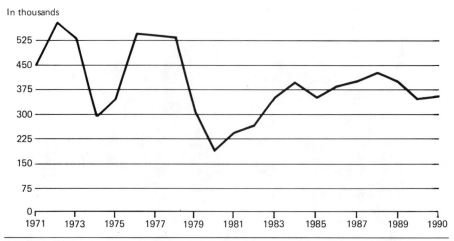

FIGURE 12.3 Recreational vehicle shipments, 1971–1990 (in thousands of units). (*Source:* Recreational Vehicle Industry Association.)

not all of their spending power intact. People over 55 have less debt and fewer calls on their income for the expenses of raising a family. Thus the continued growth of the active elderly, too, argues for solid underlying demand for RVs and accompanying travel service expenditures.

As Figure 12.4 shows, the cost of buying an RV can be tailored to suit the pocketbook. Not surprisingly, owners of folding camping trailers — sometimes called "pop-up trailers" — tend to be younger families. Truck campers, the next least expensive type, are used by people whose life-style (and usually occupation) indicate ownership of a pickup. Many converted vans are used for family or personal transportation and so the whole cost of the vehicle need not be seen as recreational. On the other hand, older and more prosperous families who can make a major capital commitment to leisure have a wide range of choice. One in 10 American households own an RV, and the Recreational Vehicle Industry Association estimates that 30 million RV trips are taken annually. Most are vacation trips of more than three days.

Buying a brand new RV is certainly not the only way to become an RV owner. Sale of used RVs are also a major factor. In fact, nearly half of the owners bought their first RV in the secondhand market. Two thirds of current RV owners have owned a used RV. It's interesting to note that over half of 15-year-old motor homes are still in use and that half of the travel trailers manufactured last more than 20 years. Rental of RVs has also had a major impact. Rentals increased substantially in the 1980s, and tax laws allow owners who make their vehicles available for rental most of the year to gain very substantial savings.

	Average Retail Price	Number Sold (thousands)	Percentage of Total
Conventional travel trailer	$12,661	52.5	14.8
Park trailer	$17,014	7.2	2.0
Fifth-wheel travel trailer	$19,901	27.9	7.9
Truck camper	$ 8,891	9.7	2.8
Folding camping trailer	$ 4,365	30.7	8.7
Conventional motor home (Type A)	$60,350	29.0	8.1
Van camper (Type B)	$32,650	5.9	1.7
Motor home (Type C - Mini)	$36,906	13.6	3.9
Motor home (Type C - low profile)	$35,771		
Motor home (Type C - compact)	$26,333	0.6	—
		3.2	1.0
Multiuse van conversion	$23,593	174.2	49.1
Total — all RVs		354.5	100.0

FIGURE 12.4 Summary of RV sales by type, 1990. (*Source:* Recreational Vehicle Industry Association.)

RV manufacturers have taken a number of steps to adapt their product to higher gasoline costs. First of all, efforts to pare size and weight have commonly reduced overall weight by 10 percent, and in some cases by as much as 25 to 50 percent. Changing the shape of the RV to reduce wind resistance can account for as much as a 15 percent savings in fuel. In fact, Winnebago, one of the largest RV manufacturers, claims a gas mileage rating of 15 miles to the gallon for some of its models. Finally, with more small cars on the highway, new-model towable vehicles have been designed that can be pulled by subcompacts.

It is useful to consider the impact of the RV as a *competitor* to hotels and motels. With an estimated average use of 23 days per year (see Figure 12.5),

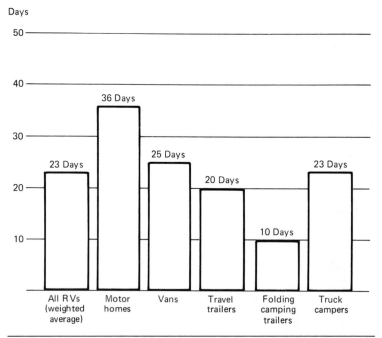

FIGURE 12.5 Average number of days used per vehicle. (*Source: Changing Times* magazine.)

the approximately 9 million RVs generate the equivalent of over 200 million room nights per year. That is enough to fill over 4,000 motor hotels, each with 200 rooms, to a 70 percent occupancy on a year-round basis.

While it is true that RVs are a significant competitor to lodging, those same 200 million nights away from home also yield a bountiful harvest of sales not only to campgrounds but to many other tourism businesses. The RV is a major factor in both tourism and hospitality today, and demographic projections suggest the RV's role may become even more significant as baby boomers age.

THE ECONOMICS OF CAMPING

From the standpoint of investment and operating costs, the campground is remarkably flexible. The cost per room for the construction of a budget motor hotel probably exceeds $25,000, and rooms in luxury downtown properties cost $100,000 or more. But campgrounds spend, on the average, between $1,500 and $3,500 per campsite. Obviously, the unit — a campsite with utility hookups—costs less than a hotel room. Moreover, the campground provides very little in the way of supporting services such as lobbies, restaurants, and cocktail lounges.

Although a motor hotel's staff may run as high as one employee per guest room (including all departments), a commercial campground may employ no full-time people other than the couple who owns or operates the camp. Rather, it probably will hire only part-time employees for seasonal peaks. In the absence of an owner, campgrounds operated by state and national parks and the like tend to employ only a small number of year-round people, but their duties—park management, maintenance, and security, for example—are often spread out over an entire park. In most public parks, there are no full-time, year-round employees whose duties are devoted solely to dealing with the campground. Neither private nor public campgrounds are labor intensive.

Although hotels may be said to be both capital intensive (requiring large amounts of capital for construction) and labor intensive (requiring many employees for operation), campgrounds are neither. Interestingly enough, however, camping itself is both labor and capital intensive.

If we estimate an average investment of $20,000 in an RV and an average life of 15 years, we would depreciate the RV at a rate of $1,335 a year. Assuming an average use of 23 nights, which is consistent with industry averages, we have a cost of $58. The average campground rental fee is about $12, so the average cost of a night in an RV is something like $70. In fact, these very rough estimates suggest that RV users spend as much or more per night than the average rate in a hotel, which was about $78 in 1989. What has happened is that the investment has been shifted from the operator (as in a hotel) to the guest. The capital investment is made by the guest, who accommodates his or her own tastes and pocketbook at the time the RV is purchased. An added economy for campers, of course, comes from preparing their own food when they want to instead of eating in restaurants.

Camping is, of course, labor intensive, and campers obviously supply their own labor. They cook the food, wash the dishes, and make the bed. Because it's all part of a "fun" outing, much of this drudgery is treated as recreation and, in any case, the work usually takes the form of chores that consume only a small part of the camper's time. Of course, if we added up all the minutes spent by all campers on campground chores, we would find that more work hours are consumed in a campground than in a hotel or motor hotel. But because nobody pays for these hours, they do not appear in the money rate charged. The shift is to that most egalitarian and uniquely American institution—self-service.

The campground offers some distinct advantages in flexibility. Most motor hotels have an occupancy percentage break-even point somewhere in the range of 60 to 70 percent. Depending on its original cost, a campground can show an acceptable profit with an annual occupancy of just above 30 percent. A seasonal campground is thus probably easier to operate profitably

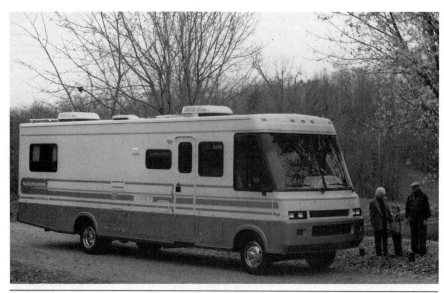

Campgrounds are not capital or labor intensive but camping is. Campers provide the capital at the level of expenditure that suits their needs and pocketbooks. (Courtesy of Winnebago Inc.)

than is a seasonal hotel or motor hotel. Furthermore, accommodations in campgrounds can be provided in seasonal areas when a short season or limited traffic would never support a hotel. A wider range of places to visit, therefore, becomes available to travelers, and this variety encourages tourism growth.

CAREERS IN CAMPING

According to Kampgrounds of America (KOA), a major chain, the best preparation for operating a campground is actual working experience. From a management standpoint, campgrounds are bare-bones operations. The essentials of campground management fall within the area of hospitality management: accounting, managing people, dealing with guests, and the like. Only a few year-round jobs exist in camping (except for ownership). Seasonal employment is widely available, and so students with an interest in campground management have ample opportunities to become acquainted with the working side of the business. Career opportunities in commercial camping are limited largely to campground owners. The construction cost of a typical commercial campground facility ranges between $250,000 to over $1,000,000. Of this total cost, 65 to 75 percent could be borrowed from a bank.

In addition to the option of operating as an independent, both KOA and Yogi Bear Jellystone Campgrounds, a chain owned by Leisure Systems Inc., are heavily committed to franchising, and a number of other smaller, regional chains and franchise groups are growing, too. Thus, a brand name, operating expertise, and management training are readily available to those with the necessary capital.

THE FUTURE OF TOURISM

We began this chapter by observing that travel and tourism are established and growing parts of the American scene. The energy crisis of the early 1970s and a recession in the early 1980s temporarily retarded the development of tourism and probably altered the kinds of services offered. Although petroleum prices have stabilized at lower levels than the peaks they reached in the early 1980s, gasoline now costs much more than it did before the first energy crisis. Consumers, however, have adjusted to these higher prices, and travel by personal vehicle remains the dominant mode of transportation.

Among common carriers (airline, bus, and rail companies), airline sales have shown considerable growth, probably as a result of deregulation. However, consumers have begun to curtail air travel in the face of rising airfares. Bus travel continues at a depressed level, but rail traffic has begun to show healthy growth.

Business and consumers are responsive to price fluctuations. In times of rapid travel-cost increases, they will use substitutes such as the telephone or switch to destinations closer to home. Changes in the price of petroleum—a major determinant of the cost of travel—are clearly a crucial consideration in looking at the future of tourism.

Because petroleum is both an economic resource and a political weapon, it is difficult to forecast its price at any point in the future. Barring a political catastrophe, however, it seems likely that although petroleum prices will fluctuate to some degree, they will not increase to anywhere near the dramatic degree they did during the energy crises of the 1970s and 1980s. Though many experts anticipate a moderate rise in petroleum price levels beginning around the early 1990s, the big new factor on the tourism horizon is demographic. The move of the baby boomers into those age groups that have the highest propensity to travel suggests that tourism will continue to grow and change.

The tourism plant that is in place has largely been built to accommodate the baby boomers while they were growing up and then as young adults. But as these people enter middle age, their tastes are clearly changing. We have already seen how the motel business is adapting itself to those tastes with the all-suite hotel, for instance.

Another likely possibility is the greater significance of rail passenger traffic in some high-population areas of the United States such as the North-

Personal service is very much part of allied tourist businesses as it is in the hospitality industry. (Courtesy of Delta Airlines)

east and the Upper Midwest, as well as between key population centers such as Seattle and Portland, San Francisco and Los Angeles, Dallas and Houston, and Miami and Tampa/Orlando. The era of the grand North American hotels began with the expansion of railroads in the mid-1800s. A major shift to high-speed rail transportation could bring equally fundamental changes in some regions to the tourism plant of the mid- or late-1990s.

The kinds of attractions that will draw visitors in a better educated, more affluent society are changing, too. Theme parks continue to be attractive, but educational and cultural interests are bringing North Americans back to the campus during summer sessions, and to museums and zoos. In the past, museums and classrooms were not seen as major tourist attractions, but that seems to be changing. Aspiring tourism entrepreneurs owe it to themselves to keep abreast — or, better, a little ahead — of developments on the local cultural and educational scene. On the other hand, to retain a balanced view, recall that the number one tourist attraction in North America is Atlantic City and its casinos.

Another factor shaping tourism's offerings is the labor shortage, which suggests that the most likely attractions will be those that are not labor intensive. That is, the acceleration of a trend toward less personal service, already well established by fast food, is a distinct possibility in all mass-market tourism.

In tourism, as with restaurants, the lure of the home entertainment center as an alternative "destination" can be expected to play a competitive role in tourism. Similarly, "big ticket" purchases—computers, video and VCR systems, sports cars, and boats—all constitute competitive alternatives for the potential tourist's dollar. The industry's growth, then, will not be automatic, but we can be reasonably sure that the folks who brought us Disneyland, John Portman's grand hotels, and Ronald McDonald—in a word, the very competitive tourism industry—will not rest on their laurels. Tourism will compete, and successfully, for the consumer's dollar.

SUMMARY

We began the chapter by discussing common carriers—airlines, bus companies, and railroads—and comparing their numbers of passenger miles traveled with that of private vehicles.

Next we turned to travel agents, both travel retailers and tour operators, and how they benefit travelers as well as the hospitality industry. We noted that a revolution in the accessibility of central reservations systems to all travel firms and to businesses and individuals will probably result in greater importance for intermediaries as a source of business for hotels.

We moved on to camping in parks and private campgrounds and the advantages and disadvantages. We also described the campers themselves: what kinds of people are most likely to camp and why. Then we considered the various kinds of camping vehicles, paying the most attention to recreational vehicles (RVs).

The business aspects of camping was our next topic. We compared campers with hotel guests and then running a campground with running a hotel. We found that camping may not always be much cheaper than staying in a hotel and that like running a hotel, camping itself may also be both capital and labor intensive.

We finished the chapter with a discussion about careers in camping and about the future of tourism in general.

KEY WORDS AND CONCEPTS

To help you review this chapter, keep in mind the following:

Common carriers
Passenger miles
Travel agents
Travel retailers
Tour operators

Central reservation systems
(CRS)
Campgrounds
Recreational vehicles (RVs)

REVIEW QUESTIONS

1. What are common carriers? Passenger miles?

2. What is the difference between travel retailers and travel wholesalers?

3. Who benefits more from using a travel agency—a traveler or a hotel? Why?

4. Why would a hotel choose not to be represented by a travel agency?

5. What is the profile of the family most likely to go camping? Explain why this family might choose to camp.

6. Is it cheaper to camp or to stay in a budget motel? Explain your choice.

7. Is camping itself labor intensive? Why?

PART 5

SPECIAL TOPICS IN HOSPITALITY MANAGEMENT

Courtesy of Benihana

THE ROLE OF SERVICE IN THE HOSPITALITY INDUSTRY

THE PURPOSE OF THIS CHAPTER

While details differ, the tangible side of the hospitality industry is surprisingly similar. Fast-food operations resemble one another within food categories; one budget motel offers pretty much the same as another; and so forth. Whether it's Big Mac vs. the Whopper, or Hampton Inns vs. Fairfield Inns, company offerings look a lot alike. Increasingly companies are realizing that *service* is the best way to achieve differentiation and is what can give an operation a competitive edge. This chapter examines service as a process, considers the work of rendering service as a personal experience and, finally, considers how companies manage service.

THIS CHAPTER SHOULD HELP YOU

1. Define service in terms of guest experience and the operation's performance.
2. Describe the principal characteristics of service.
3. Recognize service as having tasks and interpersonal aspects.
4. Understand that the "emotional labor" involved in giving service is part of the job in the hospitality industry.
5. Become familiar with the two views of managing the service process.
6. Learn how companies organize for service.
7. See service as a basis for successful competition.

"Dear Mr. Wilson," the letter from Mortimer Andrews to the company president began, "Yesterday I arrived at your hotel in Chicago with a confirmed reservation guaranteed by my credit card only to be told that no room was available. I was furious and let the desk clerk know how I felt in no uncertain terms. The clerk, John Boyles, handled the situation so well that I wanted to write and tell you about it.

"John responded to my very angry tirade about my reservation by admitting the mistake was the hotel's. He said that he had made reservations for me at a nearby Sheraton and that your hotel would take care of the difference in the room rate. When I reluctantly agreed, he called a cab—after letting me know your hotel would pay the cab fare, too.

"What struck me was John's real concern for my situation, his professional manner, and the fact that he didn't give me any excuses. 'It was our mistake and we're anxious to do everything we can to make it right.' John carried my bags out and put me in the cab, convincing me that somebody really cared about this weary traveler.

"I travel a lot and it's hard work without the extra hassles and foul-ups. On the other hand, everybody makes mistakes. John's concern and assistance make a big difference in the way it feels when one of them happens to you. I thought you should know about this young man's superior performance. He is a real asset to your company. He restored my faith in your hotel and I'll be back."

This incident may not seem like a major event, but consider for a moment just what the stakes are. Mr. Andrews is a frequent traveler. If we assume that he is on the road an average of two days a week, at the end of the year his business would be the equivalent of a meeting for 100 people. If we assume an average rate (in all cities he visits, large and small) of $65 per night, the room revenue involved is $6,500. Using industry averages, he is likely to spend an additional $3,250 on food and beverage. In other words, the receipts from this one guest amount to a $10,000 piece of business—and there is no shortage of other hotels he could stay at if he doesn't like yours.

The rule of thumb, moreover, is that a dissatisfied customer will tell the story of his or her problem to 10 others. The possibility for bad word of mouth and potential loss of other sales makes the problem of the dissatisfied guest even more serious.

In fact, a study of 2,600 business units in all kinds of industries, conducted by the Strategic Planning Institute, has been summarized in this way: "In all industries, when competitors are roughly matched, those that stress customer service will win."[1] If this is true in manufacturing and distribution, how much more true must it be for those of us whose business *is* service.

---

[1] William H. Davidow and Bro Uttal, *Total Customer Service: The Ultimate Weapon* (New York: Harper & Row, 1989), p. 40.

The population group that has dominated the hospitality industry (and most of the rest of the economy) are the baby boomers. Over the next 15 years, this group will continue to move into the relatively affluent middle years. They are the best-educated consumers, quite literally, in history. These relatively affluent, sophisticated consumers (as we have noted elsewhere in this text) can afford and will pay for good service. Moreover, competitive options give them plenty of other places to go if they don't receive the kind of service they seek. It is not too much to say that excellence in service will be a matter of survival by the year 2000.

The role that John Boyles played in keeping Mr. Andrews' business illustrates how important the service employee is in hospitality. That incident invites us to consider just what service is, how it is rendered in hospitality companies, and how companies can organize for and manage service. These are the subjects of this chapter.

WHAT IS SERVICE?

"Service," according to one authority, "is all actions and reactions that customers perceive they have purchased."[2] In hospitality, service is performed for the guest by people (a waitress serves a meal, for instance) or by systems such as the remote guest check-out operated through a hotel's television screen. The emphasis in our definition is on the guest's total *experience*. Indeed, from the guest's point of view, service is the *performance* of the organization and its staff.

The guest and the employee are personally involved in the service transaction. If a customer purchases a pair of shoes or a car, he or she takes the finished product away with no concern about who made it or how. On the other hand, in hospitality, to give one example, a lunch is served. The service is produced and consumed at the same time. The service *experience* is an essential element in the transaction. If the server is grumpy and heavy-handed, likely the guest is unhappy. A cheerful and efficient server enhances the guest experience.

Notice we say *enhances*. The tangible side of the transaction must be acceptable, too. All the cheerfulness in the world will not make up for a bad meal or a dirty guest room. At the same time, it is also true that a good meal can be ruined by a surly server, just as a chaotic front office or poor bell-staff service can ruin a stay in a hotel that is physically in excellent shape. The hospitality *product,* then, includes both tangible *goods* (meals, rooms) and *intangible services*. Both are essential to success.

The server's behavior is, in effect, a part of the product. Because servers are not the same every day—or for every guest—there is a necessary variability

[2]Christopher H. Lovelock, *Services Marketing* (Englewood Cliffs, N.J.: Prentice-Hall, 1984), p. 3.

Service means performance to the organization and an experience to the guest. In QSRs, the emphasis is on speed of performance, which accommodates a guest in a hurry. (Courtesy of Marriott Corp./Host International)

in this "product" that would not be encountered in a manufactured product. The guest is also a part of the service transaction. A guest who is not feeling well or who takes a dislike to a member of the staff may have a bad experience in spite of all efforts to please. Thus the quality of guests' experiences may vary in spite of every effort to control it, a point to which we will return later in this chapter.

Because service *happens to somebody,* there can be no recall of a "defective product." It is now a guest's experience. For this reason, there is general agreement that the only acceptable performance standard for a service organization is zero defects. *Defects,* however, should be defined in terms of the type of operation and the guest's expectations. At a McDonald's, waiting lines can be expected during the rush hour and will be accepted as long as they move with reasonable speed. But a dirty or cluttered McDonald's, even in a rush period, represents a "defect," an emergency that needs to be remedied right away. On the other hand, a waiting line at a restaurant in a Four Seasons Hotel is a defect, an emergency that needs to be remedied by a hostess or manager offering coffee or soft drinks and apologizing for the delay. Zero defects is the goal for which both organizations design their systems. While neither company is perfect, both have standards that dictate emergency action, such as management stepping in to help out until the defect is remedied, when a defect occurs.

Because the consumption of the service and its production occur simultaneously, there is no inventory. An unused room, as the old saw goes, can never be sold again. A dining room provides not only meals but the capacity of a certain number of seats. While unused food remains in inventory at the end of the day, unused *capacity*—an unused table—has no use tomorrow. This puts pressure on hospitality businesses to operate at as high a level of capacity as possible, offering special rates to quantity purchasers. A hotel's corporate rate structure is one example of such quantity pricing.[3]

Let us summarize the characteristics of service that we have identified to this point. Service is experience for the guest, performance for the server. In either case, it is intangible, and the guest and server are both a part of the transaction. This personal element makes service quality control difficult—and quite different from manufactured products. Because there is no recall of the guest's experience, the standard for service operations must be zero defects. Finally, production and consumption are simultaneous. Thus, there is no inventory.

TYPES OF SERVICE

There are three general types of service transaction: mechanical, indirect personal, and face-to-face transactions.[4]

Mechanical transactions in hospitality include vending machines and such services as remote check-out using a TV. Other examples are the in-room well-stocked refrigerator that takes over much of the room service department's work in a hotel—or a hotel's automatic-dial telephone system. Mechanical transactions are generally acceptable and sometimes even preferred by the guest where they eliminate inconvenience, such as waiting lines. On the other hand, as frequently vandalized vending machines eloquently testify, mechanical failures often infuriate people. There is a premium on correct stocking, maintenance, proper programming, and adequate capacity so that breakdowns in service will not occur when no *person* is there to speak personally for the operation.

---

[3]For a discussion of capacity management and the relationship of hospitality operations and marketing generally, see Thomas F. Powers, *Marketing Hospitality* (New York, John Wiley & Sons, 1989), especially Chap. 5.

[4]This discussion draws on G. Lynn Shostock, "Planning the Service Encounter," in John A. Czepiel, Michael R. Solomon, and Carol F. Surprenant, *The Service Encounter* (Lexington, Mass.: Lexington Books, 1985), p. 248. Shostock's terminology (*remote, indirect,* and *direct*) is slightly different.

Indirect personal transactions include telephone contacts such as hotel reservation services, the reservation desk at a restaurant, or the work of a room service order taker. Some indirect transactions such as those just mentioned are generally repetitious in nature and thus subject to careful "scripting." That is, because most of these interactions follow a few very similar patterns, the employee can be trained in considerable detail as to what to say and when to say it. Some indirect contacts, however, are nonstandard. For instance, a guest calls the maintenance or housekeeping department directly from his or her room with a problem. An individual response to the particular guest problem is necessary, but the general procedure in such cases can be clearly specified in advance. Training in telephone manners—and careful attention to just who answers the phone in departments that don't specialize in guest-contact work—is essential to maintaining the guest's perception of the property.

Face-to-face transactions have the most power to make an impression on the guest. Here the guest can take a fuller measure of people—their appearance and manner. People whose work involves frequent personal contact with guests must be both selected and trained to be conscious, effective representatives of the organization. Because an increasing part of the services in modern organizations are automated, the personal contact that *does* take place must be of a superior quality. It is also important that public-contact employees be prepared to deal sympathetically with complaints about automated services. As John Naisbitt has pointed out, the more people have to cope with "high tech," the more they require a sympathetic human response from the people in organizations. Naisbitt calls it "high touch."[5]

We must continue to be interested in all kinds of service transactions, whether personal or not. The work of designing computerized systems or scripting standardized indirect transactions, however, is generally specialized and done by experts. Virtually all of us, on the other hand, will have to deal with guests face to face. Accordingly, much of our attention in the balance of this chapter will focus on personal service. Figure 13.1 summarizes the characteristics, while Table 13.1 shows the three types of service interaction.

RENDERING PERSONAL SERVICE

Service involves, in the words of Webster's *Unabridged Dictionary,* "helpful, beneficial, or friendly action or conduct." As we have just noted, some of these actions are provided by mechanical or computerized devices or involve only indirect personal contact, usually by phone. The most challenging service area involves helping that is performed person to person.

---

[5] John Naisbitt, *Megatrends: Ten New Directions Transforming Our Lives* (New York: Warner Books, 1982).

Service is
- an experience that happens to the guest.
  No recall of defects is possible.
- performance for the organization.
  Zero defects is the service system design goal.
- a process whose production and consumption are simultaneous.
  Unsold "inventory" has no value.

Because the employee is so much a part of the guest's experience, the employee is part of the product.

FIGURE 13.1 Characteristics of service.

As Figure 13.2 suggests, there are two basic aspects to the personal service act: that of the task, which calls for technical competence, as well as that of the personal interaction between guest and server, which requires what we can sum up for now as a helpful or friendly attitude.

TASK

As recently as the late 1970s, the hospitality industry's ideas on personal service as expressed in training programs and waiter-waitress manuals focused principally on procedure.[6] The following is a representative sample from the classic, *Essentials of Good Table Service:*

TABLE 13.1 Three Types of Service Interaction

Type of Interaction	Example	Key Points
Mechanical	TV check-out	Acceptable if eliminates inconvenience. Failure unacceptable to guest. Plan to be error free.
Indirect	Telephone contacts room service housekeeping	Detailed scripting desirable for many transactions. General procedure specified.
Face-to-face	Guest registration	Person represents the organization to the guest.

[6]For a fuller discussion, see Thomas F. Powers, "Service: An Institution in Transition," *Cornell Hotel and Restaurant Administration Quarterly,* May 1979, pp. 61–69.

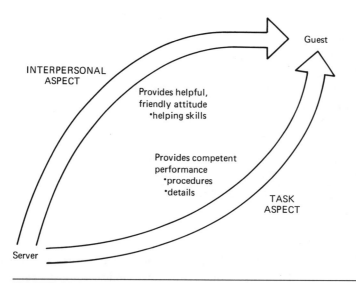

FIGURE 13.2 Two aspects of service.

The Correct Way to Hold Plates: Plates should be held with the thumb, index finger, and the middle finger. The upper part of the plate's rim should not be touched; this prevents fingers from getting into the soup or leaving marks on the plate.[7]

Clearly, functional task competence is still an essential element in any service action. Guests don't want a thumb in their soup any more than they want a bellman to get lost rooming them—or a front desk that has lost their reservation.

In modern service organizations, the task side of service is controlled by management through carefully developed systems that are supported by written *procedures*. Procedures of this kind control work—and results—in very much the same way that a carefully designed assembly line controls the way goods are manufactured.[8]

As one authority on the study of services put it, "In real estate, the three components of successful investing have always been *location, location and location*. In service encounter management, the components for success might be stated as *details, details, details*."[9] If a service organization is failing,

---

[7] *The Essentials of Good Table Service* (Ithaca, N.Y.: *The Cornell Hotel and Restaurant Administration Quarterly,* 1971), p. 22.

[8] Carol A. King "Service-Oriented Quality Control," *Cornell Hotel and Restaurant Administration Quarterly,* November 1984, p. 92–98.

[9] Shostock, "Planning the Service Encounter," p. 253.

Both technical competence and a helpful, friendly attitude toward the guest are important to personal service. (Courtesy of Stouffer Hotels)

blaming the employee is a "cop out." Getting the procedures right and a proper system functioning is the task of management.

While there is no substitute for accomplishing the task of service competently, that alone is seldom enough to secure repeat business in a highly competitive marketplace.

INTERPERSONAL SKILLS

The other aspect of personal service involves the way in which the server — waitress, bellman, or desk clerk — approaches and deals with the guest. Perhaps the best model for thinking about the kind of behavior that secures a favorable response from the guest is that of "helping skills." These were originally derived from studying the working techniques of psychotherapists. The helping skills have now been simplified into a technique for anyone whose work involves interacting with people. In fact, methods for its use have been developed for a wide variety of "people workers," ranging from police to college residence hall proctors to nurse's aides. All have in common that they are "people helpers" and provide services to people.

The core conditions of a friendly and helpful attitude can be spelled out more fully. Servers need to be able to put themselves in the other person's shoes; in a word, they need empathy. They need to present a friendly face to the guest and to do so in a way that is not going to be seen as just an act; they need to be (or at least appear) sincere.[10]

Trainers in the skills that underlie successful interpersonal behavior assume that things like eye contact, facial expression, hand movements, and body language, generally, are *learned skills,* hence readily teachable. For instance,

> Good eye contact consists of looking at another individual when he is talking to you or when you are talking to him. Eye contact should be spontaneous glances which express an interest and desire to communicate further.
>
> Poor eye contact consists of never looking at another individual; staring at him constantly and blankly; and looking away from him as soon as he looks at you.[11]

Thus, employees must learn not just to have an attitude that is helpful and friendly to the guest but to convey that attitude to the guest by their behavior. Excellent interpersonal behavior is characterized by warmth and friendliness, and a manner that imparts a sense of being "in control" to the guest — or the sense of being in charge of someone who knows very well what they are doing.[12]

THE PERSONAL COSTS OF PERSONAL SERVICE

Jane Wallace of *Restaurants and Institutions* writes:

> I was standing in a moderately long line at an airport auto-rental counter when an obviously upset man elbowed his way ahead of me and shouted at the young woman working there: "This car is a piece of s---! Exchange it for the white Cadillac in space 64." He flung the keys on the counter.
>
> With remarkable composure for one her age, she asked, "What seems to be the matter, sir? Is there a mechanical problem?"

---

[10] Two of the popularizers of interpersonal skill training put this more formally: "empathetic understanding, positive regard, and genuineness." See Steven J. Danish and A. L. Hauer, *Helping Skills: A Basic Training Program; Leader's Manual* (New York: Behavioral Publications, 1973), p. 1.

[11] Danish and Hauer, *Helping Skills.*

[12] King, "Service-Oriented Quality Control," p. 97. I have used a somewhat different choice of words.

"It smells like the inside of an ashtray, and the radio doesn't work. Exchange it right now," he yelled, literally throwing his rental agreement in her face.

"I'm sorry, sir," she replied. Then, with true Southern Californian pride, she added, "But I didn't do this to you. Remember, I'm a person, too."

The disgruntled customer continued to grumble at her while she completed the paperwork for the exchange. "Please don't be rude," she pleaded, "I'm working as fast as I can."

I could see that her eyes were very moist when she finally handed him the new contract and said, "Have a nice day."

As soon as he had left, she turned to the waiting customers and her co-workers. Trying to smile, she said, "I'm sorry," and burst into tears. I'm sure she worried about the incident all day.

It is hard for a young adult not to take such criticism and anger personally. Giving service requires emotional as well as physical stamina.[13]

There are many pleasant interchanges in personal service but the kind of situation Jane Wallace described here could as easily have taken place in a restaurant or at a front desk. Coping with unpleasant guest behavior, however, is one of the tasks of the hospitality service worker at any level of the organization. It is worth considering the options the young lady in Jane Wallace's story might have considered.

- She could have made some very colorful suggestions about what the irate customer could do. That would have gotten an embarrassed laugh from the others waiting in line — *and made the situation worse.*

- She could have suggested he rent his car somewhere else — but she had chosen to rent cars for a living and sending a customer elsewhere isn't really consistent with that decision — and it would have *made the situation worse.*

- Perhaps if she had been a bit older she could have drawn herself up to her full height, stared the customer in the eye, and announced that she would not tolerate such behavior and demand an apology. That might have worked — or it might have set off even more fireworks, creating embarrassment for the other customers — *and made the situation worse.*

- She could have called her supervisor, but that wouldn't have solved the problem. It would just move the problem to her superior.

- What she chose to do was to deal with her problem — an irate customer — as best she could.

[13] Jane Wallace, "Why Waitresses Cry," *Restaurants and Institutions,* April 18, 1990, p. 3. Ms. Wallace urges employers to "have a plan in place that will provide caring support to the employee who has just been emotionally assaulted."

Indeed, even a pleasant customer can be difficult if you have to deal with that person when you are tired, having a bad day, or otherwise not really in the right mood. Your mood, however, is really not the guest's problem. And, the guest's mood *is* your problem if you have chosen to work in hospitality.

If we recall that the product the guest is purchasing is *an experience,* then your reaction to her or him *is* a part of what the guest is purchasing. A part of the job of service employees, then, is what has been called "emotional labor."[14] An extended study of the work of airline flight attendants notes:

> The smiles are *part of her work,* a part that requires her to coordinate self and feeling so that the work seems effortless. To show that (her enjoyment of her work) takes effort is to do the job poorly.[15]

Emotional labor is defined as "the management of feeling to create a publicly observable facial and bodily display."[16] Such work is widespread in our society because work that involves people interacting with other people instead of machines or other material things has become so common.

> The secretary who creates a cheerful office that announces her company as "friendly and dependable" and her boss as "up-and-coming," the waitress or waiter who creates an "atmosphere of pleasant dining," the tour guide or hotel receptionist who makes us feel welcome, the social worker whose look of solicitous concern makes the client feel cared for, the salesman who creates the sense of a "hot commodity," the bill collector who inspires fear, the funeral parlor director who makes the bereaved feel understood, the minister who creates a sense of protective outreach but even-handed warmth—all of them must confront in some way or another the requirements of emotional labor.[17]

DEALING WITH EMOTIONAL LABOR

Stress management is an everyday fact of life in many occupations and certainly a necessary part of work for people rendering personal service in hospitality. The study we have quoted is not intended as a manual on how to render personal service. In fact, it is concerned primarily with the "commercialization of feeling" and its psychological consequences for people in service work.[18] Nevertheless, the techniques developed by the airline personnel and

---

[14]Arlie Russell Hochschild, *The Managed Heart* (Berkeley, Calif.: University of California Press, 1983), p. 7. The discussion in this section draws extensively on Ms. Hochschild's work.

[15]Hochschild, *The Managed Heart,* p. 9.

[16]Hochschild, *The Managed Heart,* p. 7.

[17]Hochschild, *The Managed Heart,* p. 11.

[18]Hochschild's concern is to define what emotional labor actually is and, in her words, to reflect on "what are the costs and benefits of managing emotion, in private life and at work?" (p. 9). The characterizations below, then, of when and how various kinds of acting are appropriate are the conclusions of this author rather than of Hochschild.

other service workers whom the author studied can provide us with some insights into how people "manage" their feelings in public contact work. There are two general approaches that she labels "surface acting" and "deep acting."

Surface Acting

Surface acting is intended to create an impression on others through manipulating outward appearance. We see every day the host who greets us with a quick smile; the bartender who pretends to listen; the clerk who sympathizes with us in our troubles as a traveler as she registers us. All of these are probably just surface acting to create the necessary impression in a passing moment—and a moment generally characterized by low stress.

Deep Acting

The term *deep acting* is drawn from "method acting"—this is the kind of acting prominently associated with actors such as Marlon Brando and James Dean. The direct object of deep acting is, in effect, to deceive yourself rather than the public. At first blush, this will seem pretty far-out—and yet a moment's reflection suggests that deep acting is a common part of everyday life.

Often our feelings are not the ones that we think appropriate to our situation. A person going to a party when they don't really feel like it may "try to feel" in a party mood to avoid being a wet blanket. Someone else burdened with a lot of responsibilities—perhaps at work, or a student during exam period—may be inclined to feel preoccupied. If they are to attend a wedding, however, they are likely to want to "put out of their mind" their own concerns and join wholeheartedly into the festivities. Someone who is elated over a large order (or a scholarship) they have just won would probably move other thoughts into the forefront of their mind if they were about to attend a funeral.

The object of everyday deep acting, then, is to get into a mood that suits your circumstances so that your outward behavior will also fit the circumstances. At work, however, this mood change is *part of the job*. A waitress who has a sick child at home will be worried. Nevertheless, she will realize that putting that worry out of her mind and concentrating on giving a pleasant impression is more likely to earn the tips needed to pay the doctor bills!

To a significant degree, the *roles* we assume in hospitality and the roles of the guests we encounter dictate the "parts" we will play. (A role can be thought of as a coherent pattern of behavior that others will recognize which identifies and places the person in that role in society more generally.) The role of waitress or waiter, for instance, is generally socially subordinated to that of the guest.

While a degree of friendliness may be appropriate in many service settings, there is a line beyond which this probably becomes an unacceptable familiarity. A shade of deference to the guest is almost always appropriate. Notice, however, that this is true at work but has nothing to do with general life circumstances. The deferential maître d' may be earning more money than the executive he seats. Students paying their own way through college may be future Nobel Laureates, entrepreneurs, or captains of industry. For the moment, however, they accept their roles and act them.

Deep acting may be especially appropriate in high-stress situations. In the study quoted earlier, flight attendants report making up "little stories" to explain the behavior of passengers who were hard to deal with. The passenger who demanded a lot of attention was thought of as an anxious victim of fear of flying. Drunks were thought of as children whose tantrums had to be withstood. When confronting an obnoxious passenger, one stewardess reported reminding herself of a man whose unusual obnoxiousness turned out to be the result of stress over the death the previous day of his son. Phrases flight attendants used in describing their "emotion management" included, "I psyched myself up," "I squashed my anger down," "I tried hard not to feel disappointed," "I got in gear," "I got revved up," "I got plugged in."[19]

Another technique used by the people Hochschild studied was "self-prompting." Employees reminded themselves that the problems experienced at work were *not* a reflection on themselves, much in the way the young woman in Jane Wallace's story that began this section was able to say, "I didn't do this to you." In other cases, stewardesses reported thinking "I don't have to go home with him" or "This flight will only last another X minutes." When confronted with obnoxious passengers, some repeated to themselves, "Don't let it get to you. Don't let it get to you. Don't. . . ."

There are many ways that people deal with the particular kinds of stress found in hospitality service roles, and it is not our purpose to chronicle all of them here. It will be enough to establish that the interpersonal side of service work embodies not only surface behavior but the absorption of a certain amount of stress that we have called emotional labor. This side of your work calls for understanding—and coping—whether you are doing the service work yourself or supervising or managing others in that work.

MANAGING THE SERVICE TRANSACTION

Most activities in the economy that managers are responsible for are focused by a process and conducted in a central place. To take a hospitality example, a kitchen is organized around the process of cooking, usually following written or unwritten recipes. If the food is acceptable, the process is being managed correctly. Hospitality *service,* however, is made up of transactions that are numerous, diverse, and often private. In a dining room, each server-guest interaction is a separate unique event. The problems of managing the process are made more complex by the fact that the product is the guest's experience. The problem of producing a favorable *feeling* about an operation in numerous guests is a difficult challenge for supervisors and managers.

---

[19] Hochschild, *The Managed Heart,* pp. 39 and 133.

Two somewhat different basic approaches to this challenge of managing service have developed.[20] The most common, which we can call the *product view of service,* focuses on controlling the tasks that make up the service. An increasingly important alternative is the *process view of service,* which concentrates on the guest-server interaction. The two views are not necessarily mutually exclusive. In practice, some of the elements of control that underlie the product view are found in any well-run service unit. In addition, attention to the way we treat people, that is, a process orientation, is necessary in any operation.

THE PRODUCT VIEW OF SERVICE

The product view looks at service as basically just another product that businesses sell to customers. The product view concentrates on rationalizing the service process to make it efficient and cost-effective — as well as acceptable to the guest. The focus is on *controlling* the accomplishment of the *tasks* that make up the service. Employee behaviors that are a part of that task are prescribed, often in considerable detail.

Perhaps the best example of the product view of service is McDonald's and fast food, generally.[21] Theodore Leavitt has described old-style, European service as a process anchored in the past, "embracing ancient, pre-industrial modes of thinking," involving a servant's mentality and, often, excessive ritual. Leavitt contrasts this with the rationale of manufacturing, where the orientation is toward efficiency and results — and where relationships are strictly businesslike. Leavitt sees the key to McDonald's success as "the systematic substitution of equipment for people, combined with the carefully planned use and positioning of technology."

The fast-food formula for success is a simplified menu matched with a productive plant and operating system designed to produce just one specific product line. Leavitt suggests that giving employees choices in their tasks "is the enemy of order, standardization, and quality." The classic example of the simplification and automation is the McDonald's french fry scoop that permits speed of service and accurate portioning with no judgment or discretion on the part of the employee. A McDonald's unit, Leavitt says, "is a machine that produces, with the help of totally unskilled machine tenders, a highly polished product."[22]

Detailed control of procedures and process is, however, not limited to fast food. Carol King, the president of QualityService Group, a quality-assurance consulting firm, advocates setting measurable "service levels [as] the

[20] Peter G. Klaus, "Quality Epiphenomenon: The Conceptual Understanding of Quality in Face-to-Face Service Encounters," in Czepiel, Solomon, and Surpenant, *The Service Encounter.*

[21] Theodore Leavitt, "Production Line Approach to Service," *Harvard Business Review,* September/October 1972, reprinted in *Service Management* (Cambridge, Mass.: Harvard University, n.d.), pp. 20–31.

[22] Leavitt, "Production Line Approach to Service," pp. 22–25.

Services must be suited to the differing needs of many market segments. Achieving service goals for each segment will be based on well thought out procedures. (Courtesy of Wendy's)

equivalent of setting manufacturing product standards," which in turn must "be related to the customer's requirements and the properties' desired image." As examples of service standards, she suggests, "one might limit to five minutes the maximum amount of time a guest should wait in a check-out line. Human needs can be met by such performance standards as 'every guest is greeted on arrival'; 'eye contact is made at least once during the transaction'; 'when guests give their names, as when checking in or claiming a reservation, they are subsequently addressed by name'. . . .Procedures must be thoroughly defined and documented, specifying how each task should be performed." Measurement of the system's performance, King advocates, should include guest evaluations, operating audits, and inspection.[23]

The product view faces obstacles on two different fronts. First of all, the pool of employees that hospitality service firms draw from has been shrinking for several years. In the light of this scarcity, employers have begun to look for means to make service jobs more attractive. Because many employees prefer to be able to use their own judgment rather than just follow the rules, the close control of behavior required by the product view is increasingly called into question. Perhaps even more significant are guest reactions, particularly in upscale markets.

[23] Carol A. King, "Service-Oriented Quality Control," *Cornell Hotel and Restaurant Administration Quarterly,* November 1984, pp. 95–97.

Widespread application of the production view of service has led guests to "ask where the *service* has gone from the service industries," as one writer put it. "They [i.e., the hospitality industry] have perfected training methods to provide the guest with adequate but impersonalized attention and unvarying hamburgers. . . . Especially in the hospitality industry, some managers and customers feel that the loss of the personal touch is too severe a penalty to pay for productivity gains through 'production line' approaches."[24]

THE PROCESS VIEW: EMPOWERMENT

The product view of service, as we have just noted, sees service as a product that can be controlled efficiently in a production process that is typical of manufacturing. The process view, on the other hand, focuses on the interaction between the service organization and the guest.[25] The key contrast between the two approaches, as we will view them, is between *control* and *empowerment*. The process view of service calls for satisfying the guest's desires as the first priority. Service employees increasingly are being given the discretion—that is, empowered—to solve problems for the guest by making immediate decisions on their own initiative and discussing these later with management. Three examples from the experience of Four Seasons, a premier hotel chain, illustrate the kind and degree of impact this approach is having on hospitality companies.[26]

- A guest ordered a dinner of linguini and clams. When the order came, the dish was divided into white and black (squid ink) linguini. The guest ate the white linguini but left the black half untouched on the plate. The server inquired if the dinner was all right, and the guest responded, "I just don't like squid ink linguini." The incident came to light because the guest was a "spotter" employed by a firm retained by Four Seasons to "shop" their hotels and report on the quality of service.

  In reviewing the incident, management learned that the description "squid ink linguini" was *not* indicated on the menu. Since the guest had no way of knowing that something she didn't like was going to be served, the waiter should have removed the charge for this item from the guest's bill even though she didn't complain. The waiter did not do so, however, because the property's accounting procedure would have required a lengthy process and management authorization for taking the charge off the guest check.

[24] D. Daryl Wyckoff, "New Tools for Achieving Service Quality," *Cornell Hotel and Restaurant Administration Quarterly,* November 1984, p. 78.

[25] Klaus, "Quality Epiphenomen," p. 21.

[26] James Brown, senior vice-president, Four Seasons Hotels, personal communication to author, May 31, 1990.

The key to empowerment is giving the employee the authority to solve the guest's problem. (Courtesy of La Quinta Inn)

As a result of this incident, the property's accounting rules were changed to make it possible for a server to void an item on a bill immediately and account for that action later. (The menus were also reprinted to identify the squid ink linguini specifically.)

- A guest called the desk and asked to have a fax machine installed in his room. The property did not have a fax machine available for this purpose but the clerk undertook to rent one from an equipment supply house. Since the supply house required a sizable cash deposit, the clerk asked the guest for the cash.

    When the front office manager learned of this, she told the clerk to pay the deposit out of hotel funds and charge the guest's account for the "paid out." She then used this incident to teach not only this clerk but the whole front office as part of the hotel's constant retraining process to heighten everyone's sensitivity to the need to *solve the guest's problem* with a minimum of inconvenience to the guest and clean up the paper work later. (The property also added fax machines to the equipment available for guest use.)

- A guest's reservation had identified a preference for a club floor room with a king-sized bed and an ocean view. When the guest arrived, he found the room had all the requested features but was too small for his working needs. He called the concierge and told him of his problem.

Looking at room availability, the concierge indicated he could meet all of the guest's requirements only with a room that was not on a club floor. That would mean the guest would not have concierge services available. The guest decided to stay where he was. A few minutes later, however, the concierge called the guest back. After studying his reservations, the concierge had been able to juggle some arrivals so as to make a room on the club floor available, one that had the ocean view and adequate space. The concierge offered the guest the room at the same rate although it was an executive suite which normally carried a higher rate. The concierge was able to do this because of a recent change in procedure giving him the authority to make decisions to satisfy guests—and account for them later. The guest accepted the concierge's offer and, not surprisingly, later wrote to compliment the hotel's management on its superb service.

In these examples, we have seen how one luxury hotel group is trying to make its employees more concerned for the guest. It is changing operating and accounting rules and procedures to help employees do what they have to do to satisfy guests. This is precisely what is meant by the term *empowering*.

We can take another example—a training program developed by the Marriott Corporation to provide greater discretion to waitresses and waiters.[27] The new program was substantially different in both content and procedure from more traditional programs.

Training was built around working groups of three or four employees who began by *discussing* key questions such as, What does good service to kids mean? What would be the best way of serving coffee? When do you think the check should be presented? Who should get it? Often discussion questions covered a wide variety of service situations ranging from taking orders to handling criticisms and complaints. Results from the small groups were then brought to the whole departmental group to serve as a basis for general discussion by the department.

Procedures, too, were viewed differently from more conventional programs.

There is no formula for greeting guests or introducing yourself. Servers are encouraged to come up with their own way of meeting the customer. The guideline is how to make the customer feel welcome. How you do it is your

---

[27] The discussion of training in the process view of service is based on David L. Romm, "The Quiet Revolution at Allies," *Cornell Hotel and Restaurant Administration Quarterly,* August 1989, pp. 26–34. Allies was intended to be a vehicle for converting a number of midscale family units that Marriott operated, including their own Big Boy Restaurants, as well as some they had acquired, such as Howard Johnson and Wag's. The Allies concept presented a number of problems that were essentially financial, having to do with physical plant-conversion costs as well as food-cost and quality problems related to operating an extensive food bar on a week-long basis. Allies was one of several restaurant concepts that was sold by Marriott when the company exited the commercial restaurant business.

choice. The trainer emphasizes that how you do things is more important than what you do. There are no rigid rules or routines because the idea is to avoid routines.[28]

PRODUCTION OR PROCESS VIEW?

Clearly some kinds of operations are ideally suited to the "production line" approach to service. Fast-food restaurants, amusement parks, and hard-budget motels come to mind as having the need for the cost-efficiency of the production approach. Patrons of upscale operations, however, demand the personal attention and individualized service that is facilitated by the process view of service, and midmarket operations are increasingly interested in empowering employees to achieve the competitive advantage that comes from committed service people.

As we noted at the outset of this discussion, some attention must be paid to the quality of personal interchanges in the most bare-bones economy operation. Similarly, basic tasks must be accomplished with competence and dispatch in the most luxurious of operations. It is not a matter of choosing between two different approaches but of adapting each approach to the needs of particular operations. The reliance on rule setting and the product approach is associated with mass market operations, but we should note that Hampton Inns, a limited-service hotel chain, has built a "satisfaction guaranteed" program for guests around employee empowerment with excellent results. Figure 13.3 summarizes key characteristics of the two views of service discussed.

HOW COMPANIES ORGANIZE FOR SERVICE

In the first section of this chapter, we defined what service was. In the next section, we turned our attention to the emotional labor that delivering guest experiences can entail. In the section we just finished, we were concerned with two approaches to managing numerous and diverse service transactions. These approaches were based on either control of the tasks or empowerment of individual servers to solve problems for guests. In this final section, we will consider the steps necessary on a companywide basis to achieve excellence in service.[29] To do this, we will consider what underlies a service strategy, the development of a service culture, the importance of people to service organizations, and the development of a service system as a competitive advantage.

SERVICE STRATEGY

The basis of service strategy is market segmentation. Market segmentation identifies groups of customers and prospects who share sufficient characteris-

---

[28] Romm, "The Quiet Revolution at Allies," p. 31.

[29] This section draws extensively on Davidow and Uttal, *Total Customer Service: The Ultimate Weapon.*

PRODUCT VIEW OF SERVICE

Emphasizes service as a task

Controls
   employee behavior
   cost of transaction/process
   objective, measurable standards

Concentrates on what *we* do

PROCESS VIEW OF SERVICE

Emphasizes interaction with the guest

Empowers employee
   to satisfy guest's needs and desires
   to solve guest's problem

Concentrates on what the guest wants

FIGURE 13.3 Managing the service transaction: two approaches.

tics in common that a product and service can be designed and brought to market for their needs.[30] A wide variety of service levels and types are available in hospitality. In food service these stretch from fast food to coffee shop to dinner house to haute cuisine. Each of these levels of service denotes a different style—counter service; fast, simple table service; informal, unhurried table service with multiple courses; and, with haute cuisine, most probably formal European-style service. Each level denotes a particular price level and, most probably, a distinctive ambiance, as well.

We said earlier that "zero defects" is the standard that service organizations must set. This very high standard, however, is set in the context of customer expectations for a particular segment and operation type. The *level of service* is an intrinsic part of the service segmentation strategy. A leading management book on customer service points out, *"Segmenting by customer service,* rather than by customer, often reveals that it is possible to give great service to a wide range of people who share a narrowly defined set of expectations."[31]

A rising young executive may take clients to the haute cuisine restaurant, his or her spouse to a casual dinner house, and the kids to a fast-food shop. When alone, the executive may lunch at a nearby family restaurant because it is convenient, fast, and offers a suitable selection. The needs of the same person and that person's expectations of the operation vary according to occasions. Similarly, different people in each of these situations will have

---

[30] For an extended discussion of market segmentation for the hospitality industry, see Thomas F. Powers, *Marketing Hospitality* (New York: John Wiley & Sons, 1990), especially Chap. 3.

[31] Davidow and Uttal, *Total Customer Service,* p. 70. Emphasis added.

The level of service is an important part of a service strategy. The key is that it must be matched to guest expectations. (Courtesy of Stouffer Hotels)

different needs. The primary business of a restaurant, is, of course, serving food. Second only to that, however, restaurants are in the business of providing guests with experiences that meet their expectations. Consider how outlandish it would be if you dropped in to the local Kentucky Fried Chicken and were met by a maître d' and served your fried chicken, mashed potatoes, and gravy by a tuxedoed waiter.

It would be equally ludicrous if you were expected to wait to pick up your Duckling Montmorancy at a service window at "Chez Haute Cuisine." A point to consider is that there is no intrinsically "better" kind of service: only service that fits the setting and is designed to meet guest needs and expectations. With service level, of course, go other factors such as price, atmosphere, and location. Indeed, these are crucial to the zero-defect goal of a service operation. A Four Seasons room rate is roughly 10 times that charged by Motel 6— and that rate differential is necessary to fulfill the luxury guest's expectations. On the other hand, Motel 6 customers are not disappointed by the service level they encounter. It is what the budget guest expects.

Marriott Hotels have segmented the market broadly into two groups, "upstairs" and "downstairs" customers. The upstairs customer is seeking a room (i.e., upstairs) for the night and minimal supporting service. For this customer, Marriott offers the Courtyard concept, with limited food and beverage facilities in the property, and Fairfield Inns, which have no food and beverage facilities but are located near other restaurants. Courtyard and Fairfield both offer top-flight guest rooms and highly competitive rates for

Choose market segment or segments.

- Determine appropriate service level and standards.
- Don't overpromise.
- Fulfill expectations.

FIGURE 13.4 Setting a service strategy.

their segment. These properties have eliminated some services but, because of that, have been able to keep their rates low. Most significantly, the service level they do offer fits the guest's expectation for that kind of property.

On the other hand, some guests do want the "downstairs" services of a full-service hotel. These include the luxurious lobby and a range of restaurants and bars as well as shops. Meeting and banquet facilities are important to the "downstairs" guest, too. Marriott targets the "downstairs" guest with its Resorts and Hotels Division—and a quite different price range. For each price and service range, operating standards are set to meet the target segment's expectations.

It is important to pay careful attention to the *level of expectation* your advertising arouses in your customer and not to overpromise. "Embassy Suites ads feature Garfield, a plump, scruffy cartoon cat known for his self-indulgence, to send the message that the 'suite life' costs no more than staying in a traditional hotel."[32] By poking a little fun at themselves with Garfield, Embassy Suites avoids evoking images of grand luxury and Old World service and adjusts their guests' expectations to the fairly narrow range of services they actually offer.

Strategy in service, then, involves picking a distinct segment and crafting facilities and services specifically to fit the expectations of that guest. Care must be taken not to overpromise because anything less than the service your guest expects will result in disappointment, lost sales, and unfavorable word-of-mouth reputation. Figure 13.4 gives an overview of setting a service strategy.

SERVICE CULTURE

A company's culture can be defined "as a set of assumptions or an ideology shared by members of an organization. These assumptions are used by people to identify what is important and how things work in that company. When these assumptions become formalized, rules for behavior are established so that people know how to act."[33]

To establish a strong service culture, an absolute prerequisite is top management commitment.

[32] Davidow and Uttal, *Total Customer Service,* p. 114.
[33] Kareen H. Tidball, "Creating a Culture Adds to Your Bottom Line," *Cornell Hotel and Restaurant Administration Quarterly,* May 1988, p. 63.

"There's a sign on my desk that reads 'What have you done for your customer today?' " says Hervey Feldman, President of Embassy Suites. "I worship at my sign every day, and all my hotel managers worship at theirs" — Bill Marriott writes thank you letters to his hotels' best guests, volunteering to fix anything they're unhappy with, and so do the managers of Marriott Hotels."[34]

The visible commitment of top management to the service culture sets the tone for the rest of the organization. The following conversation, overheard in a restaurant's dining room just after the breakfast rush, between a young trainee and the restaurant manager, illustrates the logic of management commitment to service. During the rush, the restaurant manager had been on the floor almost continuously, generally pouring coffee and water refills for guests and occasionally even busing dirty dishes.

TRAINEE (jokingly): Hey! I thought you said managers weren't supposed to work stations. You looked like one of the bus boys out there this morning.

MANAGER (smiling): Well, I know what you mean but you have to understand another truth. We want our customers to be happy with our service so they'll come back — and send their friends here, too. So, when there's a big rush like that I like to pitch in and please a few customers. When the rest of the service staff sees me hustling, they *know* what I think is important and they tend to reach a little harder to please people, too.

Say It and Mean It

Research on company culture in the hospitality industry suggests that where there is a wide divergence between what company officials say and what they do, employees will be cynical and indifferent to the quality of service. On the other hand, where there is a close relationship between what the company publicly claims its service policies are and the way things actually happen within the organization, employees' ratings of managerial competence tend to be high. The evidence is "that there is a higher profitability in restaurants where what *should* happen [according to company policy] *is* happening."[35]

Communication

Top management must not only take a position but must communicate it to employees. Department meetings and general employee meetings are important.

A popular tool in companies that have many low wage employees in constant contact with customers is the employee council. Employees from each department elect a representative and the representatives meet weekly

[34] Tidball, "Creating a Culture Adds to Your Bottom Line," pp. 64 and 67.

[35] Tidball, "Creating a Culture Adds to Your Bottom Line," pp. 64–67.

The assumptions that underlie a service culture must be accepted as important by all of the players on the service team. (Courtesy of the Hilton Hotel Corp.)

with the general manager. He updates them on everything he's doing; they ask questions, offer suggestions, voice opinions, and then go back to their departments to explain what's going on.[36]

Other media such as employee newsletters, posters, or an "Annual Report to Employees" such as ARA publishes help create and maintain a climate of enthusiasm for service.

Manager as Helper

Service America! made famous the motto, "If you're not serving the customer, you'd better be serving someone who is."[37] This approach sees employees as internal customers whose needs must be met. In effect, managers treat the

[36] Davidow and Uttal, *Total Customer Service,* p. 103.

[37] Karl Albrecht and Ron Zempke, *Service America!* (Homewood, Ill.: Dow Jones-Irwin, 1985), p. 96.

employees as they'd like to have them treat the guests. The intention is that employees follow management's example. The philosophy underpinning this view is that "a manager's main responsibility is to remove obstacles that keep people from doing their jobs."[38] To quote an often-restated position of J. Willard Marriott, the Marriott Corporation's founder, "You can't make happy guests with unhappy employees."[39]

Restraining Bureaucracy

Bureaucracy is a "bad word" for most North Americans, but it is actually a name for the kind of structure necessary to serve any large organization. In other words, in large companies, a certain amount of bureaucratic structure is needed. Nevertheless, a consistent effort needs to be made to resist the bureaucracy's tendency to achieve internal efficiencies by making rules that, in their total effect, can strangle the service out of a service organization. With too much bureaucracy, employees quote the rules of the operation rather than satisfy the customer's requests.

It is useful to recall, here, the experiences cited earlier at Four Seasons. That company decided to reformulate a lot of its rules to make it possible for servers to make exceptions to the rules to satisfy the guest on their own judgment—and account for their decisions later.

Figure 13.5 summarizes the development of a service culture.

THE EMPLOYEE AS PRODUCT: THE IMPORTANCE OF PEOPLE

Because the service employee (and often the back-of-the-house employee, too) is involved personally in transactions with the guest, the employee usually comes to represent the operation to the guest. Managing, it has been said, is getting results through people, and that is doubly true of managing service. The tools that are being used to undertake this job at the company level are employee selection, training, motivation, and employee "award and reward programs." Each is discussed briefly below.

Selection

Employee recruiting has become, for many firms, a marketing activity with "jobs for sale." In spite of vigorous recruiting to fill positions, operations have to choose their hires with care, especially in public contact service jobs. At Four Seasons, all employees hired must first be interviewed by the general manager or the executive assistant manager as well as division and department heads. At Guest Quarters, prospective employees pass through four interviews, one of which is with the general manager. The key point for both

---

[38] Davidow and Uttal, *Total Customer Service,* p. 106.

[39] G. M. Hostage, "Quality Control in a Service Business," *Harvard Business Review,* July-August 1975, reprinted in *Service Management* (Cambridge, Mass.: Harvard University, n.d.), p. 101.

Developing a service culture in a company requires:

- Commitment of top management
  In word and policy
  In action

- Policy and practice to be the same
  High profitability is achieved when what *should* happen *does* happen.

- Constant, clear communication, up as well as down the organization

- Employees to be treated as customers
  Manager's job: service to employees

- Restraining bureaucratic tendencies
  Customer is more important than rules.

FIGURE 13.5 Developing a service culture.

companies is the fit of the person with the company and the particular service team they will be working on.[40]

Training

Companies that lead their industries in service tend to share two unusual characteristics. First of all, most such companies emphasize cross-training. Embassy Suites, for instance, encourages employees to master several jobs. The wider training not only gives the property a more flexible employee but also heightens the employee's understanding of the total operation. As well, the added training can add to the interest and excitement of the work.

A second characteristic is that all employees share certain core training experiences. McDonald's Hamburger University has a special four-day program through which staff, head office, and other nonoperations employees gain an understanding of the company's operations, products, and policies. Thus, all responsible employees pass through some Hamburger University orientation to the company. Virtually all senior executives at McDonald's, too, have store-operating experience. Similarly, "Everyone at Embassy Suites understands how to inspect a room for cleanliness."[41]

Motivation

Embassy Suites has a system called Skills Based Pay (SBP). SBP encourages all employees to learn the 10 basic jobs that are necessary to operate the hotel. After being in a job for a probationary period of 90 days, an employee can apply for certification that is based on a written test and a work sample. The

[40] Davidow and Uttal, *Total Customer Service,* p. 123.
[41] Davidow and Uttal, *Total Customer Service,* pp. 128–129.

For the guest, the employee represents the organization. In a sense, the employee is the product. (Courtesy of Pizza Hut Inc.)

work sample is passed on by both supervisor and the employee's co-workers. Certification means an immediate pay increase (usually 25 cents an hour) and the chance to train for a different job one day a week. In time, this permits the employee to win further certification and pay increases. The result is increased job interest and a clear career path. In fact, half of the people in Embassy Suites' management training program came up through the ranks through SBP.[42]

Embassy also has a bonus program called Success Sharing. When a hotel meets or exceeds targets that are set quarterly for occupancy, customer satisfaction, and cleanliness, employees get a bonus that amounts to about $100 per month based on the number of hours worked and their hourly rate. Roughly 90 percent of Embassy's properties achieve the levels of performance necessary to receive the bonus.[43]

Like many companies, Embassy Suites also has an employee-of-the-month award to recognize outstanding performance. Moreover, workers get frequent feedback on their performance in terms of how they are contributing to the property's success. The Success Sharing and SBP programs link individual and corporate success in a way that reinforces team building.

[42] Davidow and Uttal, *Total Customer Service,* p. 116.
[43] Davidow and Uttal, *Total Customer Service,* p. 117.

Employee Awards

Awards programs "are formal expressions of encouragement and praise that effective frontline supervisors mete out continually. By creating service heroes and service legends, the programs charge up all employees, not just the winners." To succeed, programs must have "credibility, frequency and psychic significance" to the employee. The process of selecting winners, if it is to have that credibility and significance to employees, must be "careful, obviously meritocratic and tightly linked to customer perceptions of service quality." Awards need to be made soon after the performance they are intended to recognize so that the linkage is clear; to have tangible value like a day off; and to involve active recognition and applause, "not just a name on a plaque." Otherwise nobody will care.[44]

Participation in Planning

Workers must have "ownership" of service standards and procedures if the standards and procedures are to be accepted in the workplace. The necessary step to secure acceptance is to involve employees in planning either by consulting them fully in the planning process or by asking them to actually do the planning themselves.

When Rusty Pelican Restaurants set out to improve sales per employee hour without hurting service quality, for instance, work groups in the restaurants were asked to set targets for themselves. Productivity improvements were seen almost at once, partly because the employees wanted to see how much improvement they could bring about. Management's original targets for productivity improvements were easily met and sustained. In informal interviews, customers also rated the service quality as being higher.[45] The process of making the employee a key part of the product is summarized in Figure 13.6.

SERVICE AS A SUSTAINABLE COMPETITIVE ADVANTAGE

The products sold in hospitality are strikingly similar. One hotel room is very much like another. While there are important differences between food service segments, within each segment there is considerable similarity—often, almost uniformity. Service offers the most important opportunity to differentiate one product from another. When a service system is established at the chain level, the ability to operate multiple units across a wide territory successfully gives the company an advantage over newcomers to the field. The company's reputation for a dining experience or night's (or week's) stay is an invaluable resource. Almost certainly, it is based on personal interaction with company employees. That is, the company's reputation, its sustainable competitive advantage, is most likely based on its service—and that means, its service employees.

---

[44] Davidow and Uttal, *Total Customer Service,* p. 131.

[45] Wyckoff, "New Tools for Achieving Service Quality," p. 79.

REQUIREMENTS

Employees selected who fit the team.

Training emphasizes
cross training,
basic shared experience.

Motivation offers
reward for desired performance,
frequent feedback for team building.

Awards provide
formal public recognition based on guest service.

Participation in standard setting creates "ownership" of
standards.

FIGURE 13.6 Making the employee the product.

SUMMARY

Service is an intangible experience of performance that the guest receives along with the tangible side of the product purchased. Because the service is performed and consumed at the same time, there is no inventory—such as, for instance, of unused rooms from last night—that can be sold at a future date. Both server and guest are a part of the transaction, which makes quality control difficult. Service quality has two sides: the task and the interpersonal interaction. Different planning and control problems arise for mechanical, indirect, and personal service transactions, with personal service the most difficult to manage.

People who work in personal service do "emotional labor." They smile when they'd rather cry—or snarl. People cope with the stress of giving service to people with surface acting or, where service is more intense and stress more likely, deep acting. Deep acting involves controlling your moods so your reaction to the guest is natural.

The service transaction is the heart of service in hospitality. Controlling the details of task performance fits well with a *product view* of service, while a *process view* focuses more on the personal interaction between guest and server. In the process approach, servers are *empowered* to solve problems for the guest.

The basis of *service strategy* is market segmentation, largely based on consumer expectation. Successful service companies develop a service culture based on top management commitment, consistency between policy and practice, and well-developed channels of communication. Since service people are a part of the product, a good service team is essential. Service teams are based on careful selection and training and built on motivational programs that include rewards and involvement in service planning. Because most hospitality products are strikingly similar, service is the most significant sustainable competitive advantage.

KEY WORDS AND CONCEPTS

To help you review this chapter, keep in mind the following:

Service as
    customer's experience
    operation's performance
Characteristics of service
Zero defects
Mechanical interactions
Indirect interactions
Face-to-face interactions
Aspects of service
    task
    interpersonal
Helping skills

Emotional labor
Surface acting
Deep acting
Process view of service
Product view of service
Empowering
Service strategy
Market segmentation
Customer expectations
Service culture
Employee as product

REVIEW QUESTIONS

1. What does "zero defects" mean in service? Does it mean perfection?

2. Discuss the three types of service transactions. What are the considerations managers need to take into account in planning for them?

3. What are the two aspects of service? Which is more important in your opinion?

4. How do you feel about "acting" in a service role? Can you think of a time when you found deep acting appropriate at work? In other parts of your life?

5. What are the two views of managing the service transaction? Can you think of examples from your own experience where each was appropriate?

6. How is a service strategy designed? What is its basic determinant? What other considerations are important?

7. What do companies need to do to develop a service culture?

Courtesy of Hyatt Hotels International

MANAGING
INTERNATIONAL HOSPITALITY

THE PURPOSE OF THIS CHAPTER

Transportation is faster and less expensive, and instantaneous communication has become common; along with these trends, world travel has increased dramatically. The hospitality industry has become a global industry. Investment by foreign companies in North America has risen significantly and American brands are going overseas. To understand today's hospitality industry, you need to recognize its international dimension. When you do so, you may decide you want to work abroad. This chapter introduces you to an exciting and still-developing aspect of hospitality and to the possibility of a career in international hospitality.

THIS CHAPTER SHOULD HELP YOU

1. Recognize the forces that are making hospitality an international business.

2. Consider what attracts foreign investors to the North American hospitality industry.

3. Know the methods by which American firms have moved into the international environment.

4. Understand how U.S. hospitality firms are organizing foreign operations.

5. Become familiar with the major foreign firms that are investing and operating in the United States and that compete with U.S. firms overseas.

6. Acquaint yourself with what is required of someone who seeks a career in international operations and some possibilities to begin to move your career in that direction.

THE IMPETUS TOWARD INTERNATIONALIZATION

In the trade press and at hospitality meetings across North America, we hear increasingly of a global hospitality industry. Gregory R. Dillon, executive vice-president of Hilton Hotels, speaking at a conference on hospitality investment put it this way:

> The world is getting smaller and smaller and smaller. We're no longer living in a world of seven far-flung continents with close to 200 independent countries living to some extent isolated and independent of each other. Today—and even more tomorrow—whether we like it or not—believe it or not—the economies of the world, though still decidedly competitive, are beginning to interact more and more.
>
> The philosophies of the world's peoples are coming closer and closer together. The language barriers are beginning to crumble. By virtue of fast intercontinental travel, telecommunication advances, and computerization we are only hours or minutes away from every place in the world. As has been said earlier, the world is becoming globalized.[1]

While we will use the words *global* and *globalization* in this chapter, it is more accurate to speak of internationalization.[2] That is, while we have already begun to move toward a single world economy—and perhaps even someday a world government—that is a process that is still in its early stages. Although countries are increasingly involved in regional economic and political alliances, there is, in fact, continuing stiff competition between nations. Given the potential for "tariff wars" and other restrictions of trade growing out of rivalry between trade blocs, it is perhaps too early to think of the globe as one world. Moreover, the actions of the blocs are typically dictated by the will of the strongest nation or nations within the bloc. While we will use both terms, we will prefer the word *international* to *global* because it emphasizes the degree to which *nations* are still the principal actors on the international stage. It is useful, as a starting point, to try to understand what forces lie behind the internationalization of hospitality. They are summarized in Figure 14.1.

---

[1] Gregory R. Dillen, Remarks made during a panel discussion, "International Hotel Operators: What is the Outlook for the Future?" 11th Annual Hospitality Investment Conference, New York City, June 5, 1989.

[2] The distinction was suggested by Simon Crawford-Welch during his remarks at the Conference on Hotel, Restaurant and Institutional Education, August 1990.

Decreasing significance of national boundaries
 Common markets
 Free trade areas

Increasing indifference of consumers to national identity
  of goods and services.

Free flow of capital

Ease of evading regulation in international business

Immigration—legal and illegal
 "South" to "North"

Ease of communication
 Phone
 Fax
 Computer networks

FIGURE 14.1 Forces for internationalization.

DISSOLVING NATIONAL BOUNDARIES

During the 1980s, the 12 nations of the European Economic Community (EEC) resolved to develop a single regional economy by 1992.[3] They acted in response to increasing competition from the United States and Japan as well as to their own self-interest in working more closely together. The increasing success of this union was one of the forces that gave impetus to the aggressive development of other trading blocs such as the Canada–United States free trade agreement and similar agreements in other regions of the world. A trading bloc made up of the U.S. and Canada, as well as Mexico, and perhaps, much of Latin America seems a realistic possibility.

The European Economic Community is removing restrictions not only on trade but on the movement of capital and labor. As a result, the 1992 EEC marketplace for sellers is made up of 320 million consumers. If we look at the probable future size of the European economy, the outlook for that area is even stronger. If the countries belonging to the European Free Trade Association (EFTA), which has close trading relations with the EEC, are included, the total market measures 350 million.[4] Beyond that, there are 140 million East Europeans, the 285 million inhabitants of the former Soviet Union and 50 million Turks all hoping to join or at least achieve a close working and trading relationship with it.

Whether it is 320 million, 350 million, or the nearly 1 billion people that can be envisioned in the next generation, the European market is huge com-

[3] The EEC is made up of Great Britain, Ireland, Germany, Denmark, The Netherlands, Belgium, Luxembourg, France, Portugal, Spain, Italy, and Greece.
[4] The EFTA is made up of Iceland, Norway, Sweden, Finland, and Austria.

pared with even the largest European national market, namely, Germany, with 78 million people. The very size of the market, then, is an inducement to economic cooperation because of the economies of scale that the much larger market offers. The competing bloc in North America will have over 350 million consumers if only the United States, Canada, and Mexico are included. Brazil, Chile, Argentina, and Venezuela have also indicated an interest in participating in an "Americas" trading bloc, creating the potential for an even larger market further into the future. The Pacific Rim (more an idea at this point than a trading bloc) nevertheless has a population of nearly a billion without China and roughly 2 billion with that country.

Attractions other than just a large market explain why national economies are giving way to regional and international marketplaces. One very strong force is the increasing *indifference of consumers to the national identity* of goods and services. As one international consultant put it:

> It does not matter to you that a British sneaker made by Reebok (now an American-owned company) was made in Korea, a German sneaker made by Adidas in Taiwan, or a French ski by Rosignol in Spain. What you care about most is the product's quality, price, design, value, and appeal to you as a consumer. My observations over the past decade seem to indicate that the young people of advanced countries are becoming increasingly nationalityless and more like "Californians" all over the Triad Countries—(that is) the United States, Europe and Japan—that form the international economy.[5]

Today we see KFC in Tiananmen Square, Nathan's Famous (hot dogs) in Red Square, and a British company that struggles to revitalize a flagging Burger King here in North America.

Increasingly the *flow of international capital* ignores national boundaries. The mobility of financial assets is helped along by almost instantaneous worldwide communication. This mobility of capital helps further break down international boundaries or render them increasingly irrelevant. Burger King, for instance, and Holiday Inn are both brand names as "American as apple pie," yet they are now British-owned companies, just as that pride of grand hotels, Westin, is now controlled by Japanese. In these circumstances, we have to wonder what, if anything, national identity means in the business world—or the world of hospitality.

National governments from time to time become alarmed at the advantages that seem to accrue to one trading partner, and they try to bring pressure to bear to right that perceived imbalance. Pressure from the U.S. government, for instance, to increase shipments of beef to Japan became intense in the late 1980s. At that point, "Japanese importers such as Zenchiku Ltd. [began] aggressively buying up American ranches, feedlots, and packing plants. They

---

[5] Kenichi Ohmae, *The Borderless World* (New York: Harper Collins, 1990), p. 3.

Increasingly, international capital flows ignore international boundaries. Shown here is the Hyatt Sanctuary Cove in Australia. (Courtesy of Hyatt Hotels International)

and many other traders will soon be shipping in more beef from the United States than Americans do today, but it is not clear in what sense that represents a real increase in American exports, since these are really Japanese exports from America."[6] Once again, we see that commerce can easily get around national boundaries.

Another factor undermining national boundaries is immigration, both legal and illegal, from the less-developed countries of the "South," such as Mexico, southern Europe, Africa, and Southeast Asia, where population is plentiful, wages low, and unemployment high. More developed nations in the "North," the United States and Canada, Western Europe, and Japan, need labor in good economic times and admit immigrants to supply that need. Because wages and opportunities are better in the "North," illegal immigration is a continuing problem. The U.S. immigration service estimates, for instance, that 2 million Mexicans enter the United States illegally each year.[7] In the European Economic Community, moreover, immigration from southern member states such as Spain, Portugal, and Greece to their more prosperous northern neighbors will be entirely legal. Europe, too, faces massive illegal immigration from North Africa, the Middle East, and Eastern Europe. Some

[6]Ohmae, *The Borderless World,* p. 140.
[7] *The New York Times,* March 31, 1991, p. E3.

estimate that up to 30 million Soviet citizens are ready to move, for instance.[8] Clearly, with continuous legal and illegal migration of huge numbers of people each year, the meaning of borders becomes questionable.

Finally, the ease of communication by phone, fax, and computer networks has made possible the information flows needed for the management of worldwide companies. Management reports, transfers of funds, and company directives can all be transmitted almost instantaneously. The world, as we are all fond of saying, has become smaller.

THE INTERNATIONALIZED MARKET FOR HOSPITALITY

We have just noted some large U.S. companies whose foreign ownership could open their "national status" to question. We will add to that list here—and often again as the chapter unfolds. For instance, the largest "hard-budget" motel chain in the United States, Motel 6, is owned by France's aggressive lodging company, Group Accor. But the United States is not the only country so penetrated. Fully 45 percent of the British budget lodging chains will be in foreign hands by 1992.[9] Canada's, Japan's, and Europe's largest fast-food chains are all 50-percent owned by—and franchisees of—an American company: McDonald's.

One of the largest Kentucky Fried Chicken franchisees worldwide is a Canadian firm, Scotts Foodservice. In turn, Scotts, which does business in both the United States and Canada, was until recently the fourth largest *U.S.* franchisee of KFC. The hospitality industry in virtually all developed countries has become internationalized. Companies foreign to the host country own some operations, but host country investments control operations in other countries, too. Increasingly, consumers buy what they want; investors invest where they wish.

Advantages to Foreign Investors in North America

There are a number of factors that lead companies to invest in North America. We will look briefly at some of the principal ones: fluctuating currency values, large market size, security of investment, and the availability of management skills and systems.

Currency fluctuations have made the purchase of assets in the United States attractive to foreign investors. (You may want to review the discussion of the impact of exchange-rate fluctuations that appeared in Chapter 9, page 295.) When the dollar is low relative to, for instance, the yen, the purchase price of dollar assets—when stated in yen—look very attractive to Japanese investors. Because the dollar's value does fluctuate, that is, *both* up and down, Japanese investors can assume that their investment will be worth more—in yen—when the dollar rises. In effect, foreigners have been buying North American companies with what were—for them—50- and 75-cent dollars.

---

[8] *The New York Times,* March 31, 1991, p. E3.

[9] *Hotels and Restaurants International,* September 1989, p. 49.

Currency fluctuations are only a part of the story, however. Because of the relatively high standard of income, the U.S. market of some 245 million people has been for a long time the largest market in terms of *buying power*. The United States will retain this distinction because of its continuing high average income even after 1992, although the European Community (and, for that matter, the former Soviet Union, China, and India) will have larger populations. Buying into the profits of the huge and prosperous U.S. market has made a lot of sense for overseas investors.

Not only is the North American market more prosperous than most, it offers a more secure haven for international investment. A truly radical government or even the violent overthrow of a government is a distinct possibility in many countries — or in their next door neighbor's. In contrast, the United States seems like a steadier ship politically and one possessed of vast natural resources. This makes the United States less subject to foreign pressure than many smaller countries. While the U.S. dollar fluctuates in value against other currencies, the U.S. Federal Reserve System "is the closest thing there is to a worldwide central bank," and the U.S. dollar "accounts for more than one third of the world's supply of usable money."[10]

Foreign buyers are often satisfied with lower rates of return than American asset holders expect. The Japanese, for instance, have become famous for their willingness to accept modest returns from the early years of an investment in order to secure a strategic position and, they hope, larger returns in the future. Moreover, foreign tax rules can make a seemingly expensive purchase a good investment after sorting out the tax consequences of the purchase in the home country of the buyer.

In buying North American companies, many overseas companies seek to gain the advantage of North America's highly developed management systems in accounting and cost control, reservation referral systems, and marketing. North American hospitality brands, moreover, have worldwide appeal and can be used to spearhead expansion in other parts of the world. To give just one example, after Grand Metropolitan bought Burger King, it proceeded to acquire 20 Wimpy operations in Great Britain from a restaurant company there. The purpose of the acquisition was to convert those units to Burger Kings and use the converted units to take advantage of the power of the Burger King brand name.[11]

U.S. Investment Abroad

Whenever the value of the dollar is low compared with other currencies, U.S. firms have been less active in purchasing foreign firms. Nevertheless, a great deal of acquisition activity was carried out by U.S. firms in the 1960s and 1970s. Even in the face of a lower dollar, U.S. companies have not been entirely absent from the market in recent years, particularly in "gateway cities." These are cities that have a dominant position in a country in the way

---

[10] *The Economist,* October 28, 1989, p. 19.

[11] *TRA Foodservice Digest/Chicago Tribune,* January 9, 1990, S3, p. 4.

U.S. investment is made in key cities in the world's many markets. Shown here is the Park Hyatt in Sydney, Australia. (Courtesy of Hyatt Hotels International)

that Paris has in France or Tokyo in Japan. In these markets American firms have been active as buyers. More often, however, American firms have entered the market either as franchisors or through a joint venture with a partner firm from the host country where the venture is located, thus securing advantage in adjusting to the local market as well as local social and political environments.

In the balance of this chapter, we will look first at international activity to identify trends in competition and to give the reader a chance to become briefly acquainted with a few of the key players who have come to North American shores. We will also examine the somewhat different ways in which American brand names and concepts have entered foreign markets.

AMERICAN HOSPITALITY ABROAD

Competition in the international environment makes it a rapidly changing marketplace. We cannot hope to report here all the actions of individual corporations, but we can outline the major directions in which U.S. firms are expanding abroad. We will look, as well, at the impact on hospitality of foreign firms' purchases of assets in North America.

METHODS OF EXPANSION

U.S. firms are, indeed, expanding into the international environment. As we noted a moment ago, a relatively small number are expanding through outright ownership. More are moving abroad through franchising, joint ventures, strategic alliances, management contracts, or some combination of these.

Ownership

When a company moves into a foreign market, all the rules change. Employment practices differ. Supervisory skills need to take account of the local culture. Government rules and procedure, ranging from zoning to sanitation to labor as well as to many other key areas of concern, all are different. As you can see, there is good reason to do whatever can be done to minimize problems arising from national differences.

One way to do this is to choose a country that has a high degree of similarity to the United States—which probably explains why Canada is often the first country chosen by U.S. firms for expansion. Even in a country with as many similarities as Canada, however, culture, laws, and practices differ, so a key step is to hire local nationals, wherever possible, who have the necessary local contacts as well as the required business skills. For instance, when General Mills expanded its restaurant division into Canada, it hired an executive staff of seasoned Canadian executives and undertook an aggressive management training program to develop Canadian unit-management staff. In fact, there are very few U.S. nationals employed in the company's Canadian headquarters or in its numerous Red Lobster and Olive Garden Restaurants in Canada.

Wendy's entered Japan some years ago in a joint venture (see below for a discussion of joint ventures) with a Japanese company. In 1989, however, the company announced that it would begin opening company-owned units in Japan to gain more control over the Japanese operation's marketing program.[12] Ownership of an operation does confer tighter control over the business.

A different way to bridge the gap to operations in another country is by obtaining the management know-how when the assets of a company are purchased, that is, by acquiring a company and convincing its management to remain in place. U.S. travel agencies, for instance, are expanding into Europe by acquiring large firms,[13] and many European and Japanese firms have chosen this method to enter the U.S. market, as in Grand Metropolitan's purchase of Burger King.

Franchising

Probably the most common U.S. approach to overseas expansion is franchising. Kentucky Fried Chicken operates more restaurants outside the United

[12] *TRA Foodservice Digest/Chicago Tribune,* March 5, 1989, S7, p. 13C.
[13] *The Wall Street Journal,* September 26, 1989, p. B1.

States than any other U.S. chain, virtually all of them franchised. Roughly 40 percent of KFC's stores are outside the United States. In 1989, the 3,000th KFC outlet outside the United States was opened by KFC's Korean franchisee in Seoul, South Korea.[14] The company's largest unit is in Beijing, China, and the company's second highest-volume store is in London, England.[15] The overseas market has clearly been a rich one for them.

A wide variety of companies have moved their concepts overseas by franchising. Chi Chi's is active in Canada, England, Kuwait, and Luxembourg.[16] Like so many companies expanding into the international market for the first time, Rax Restaurants has begun in Canada, granting area franchises to two companies whose territories will cover the whole country.[17] Domino's Pizza operates over 350 stores in 22 countries. In the Japanese market, Domino's finds its *speedy* delivery to be a unique competitive advantage even though this is a market where food service delivery has been available for centuries. Their delivery service, moreover, uses uniformed drivers, achieving an upscale image for the company in that market.[18]

Hotel franchise companies are well represented overseas, too. For instance, in Japan, Quality, Ramada, and Holiday all have franchised operations. All three of those brands are conventionally "American," but, you may recall, two of them are now foreign owned.

Even U.S. regional companies find that they have the know-how to sell overseas. Carl Karcher Enterprises, a regional restaurant chain concentrated in the southwestern United States, has licensed a Malaysian company to open Carl's Jr. stores in nine Pacific Rim countries. The first stores will be in Malaysia, Singapore, Australia, and Hong Kong.[19] Trendy American-style restaurants such as Ed Debevic's casual dining operation and Spago, an haute cuisine restaurant owned by chef Wolfgang Puck, have been successfully franchised in Japan.[20]

Concepts developed in the United States often need to be adapted to local conditions. Bonanza's English operations, for instance, look like the U.S. outlets—except for a closed-circuit television screen located at the restaurant's entrance to tell first-time diners how to place their order and how to use the salad bar.[21] TGI Friday's franchisee in England is a brewer, Whitbread. In Friday's English operations, the decor is identical but a number of Mexican dishes have been replaced with the more familiar (in England) curried Indian

[14]*Nations Restaurant News,* November 13, 1989, p. 24.

[15]*TRA Foodservice Digest,* January 1989, p. 7.

[16]*Nations Restaurant News,* August 14, 1989, p. 67.

[17]*TRA Foodservice Digest,* June 1989, p. 8.

[18]*Adweek,* December 12, 1988, p. 14.

[19]*The Wall Street Journal,* March 19, 1990, p. B7.

[20]*The Wall Street Journal,* November 14, 1988, p. B5.

[21]*TRA Foodservice Digest/Chicago Tribune,* June 25, 1989, S7, p. 3.

Overseas tourism attractions offer many advantageous opportunities for American companies to join with foreign investors in joint ventures, such as the Stouffer Presidente shown here. (Courtesy of Stouffer Hotels)

dishes, and salad is served *after* the entrée, as is the custom there. In addition, "TGI Fridays has made special efforts to train the naturally reticent British to be outgoing and service oriented."[22] In Japan, McDonald's has introduced a Teriyaki McBurger in response to local competition,[23] while in France they serve wine—and in Germany, beer. The key in all these situations is to maintain the core values of the company while bending enough to offer local customers a product and service that meets their needs and preferences.

Joint Ventures

Joint ventures are separate enterprises formed between two (or sometimes more) companies to undertake a specialized venture. Usually each company involved has some ownership interest. Very commonly each brings different assets to the enterprise. One partner may bring financing, real estate, or other fixed assets while the other partner brings know-how, expertise, a marketing or an operating system. One partner's advantage may be know-how and contacts *in an area* while the other's may be know-how and management ability *in a specific business.* For instance, Marriott's in-flight catering division formed a joint venture in 1988 with Kuwait Airways, Saudi Airlines, and Gulf Air. The joint venture was aimed at establishing Marriott as an acceptable provider of Islamic meals—although it is a Western company.[24] Another

---

[22] *TRA Foodservice Digest,* April 1989, p. 7.

[23] *TRA Foodservice Digest,* October 1989, p. 7.

[24] *Nations Restaurant News,* October 24, 1988, p. 2.

venture was formed between a Texas franchisee of Dairy Queen and an Italian company to operate "Continental Dairy Queen," initially in Italy and, in time, in Spain and Portugal as well. The new company, of course, was a franchisee of International Dairy Queen.[25]

The international division of Hilton Hotels, Conrad International, is building luxury hotels in a series of joint ventures with local partners in places such as London, Dublin, Hong Kong, and Monte Carlo.[26] (Note that Hilton International and the rights to the Hilton name outside the United States were sold some years ago by Hilton-U.S.)

With the opening of Russia and Eastern Europe, some joint-venture partners have been government agencies. Nathan's Famous formed a joint venture between the Lenin District Catering Trust and Ziegler Enterprises, a New Jersey company specializing in business ventures in the Soviet Union. Nathan's sells the hot dogs, for which it is justly famous, from trailers in Moscow's Red Square.[27] Perhaps the most widely noted entrant into Eastern Europe in recent years, however, was McDonald's.[28]

McDonald's in Moscow. Doing business in the context of an entirely different economic and social system certainly raises the level of complexity of an international business venture to a high level. In 1976, George Cohon, president of McDonald's Canada, itself a joint venture owned by Canadian stockholders and McDonald's U.S., opened discussions during the Montreal Olympics with Soviet officials with the aim of bringing McDonald's to the USSR. These discussions lasted through the governments of three different Russian premiers. McDonald's joint venture partner was the Food Service Administration of the Moscow City Council. The value of local contacts was illustrated when the venture received an assist from then Premier Mikhail Gorbachev, who introduced new legislation in the Supreme Soviet permitting joint ventures with non-Soviets.

"The same quality, service, cleanliness, and value that exist wherever there are McDonald's restaurants will prevail in Moscow," Cohon said. "A Big Mac is a Big Mac; it will taste the same whether it is served in Canada, the United States, Japan, or the Soviet Union." Indeed, according to Cohon, what ultimately sold the Russians on McDonald's was the business system—quality, service, cleanliness, and value—that the company had to offer. Nevertheless, McDonald's made more than modest adaptations in its business system to deliver the standard McDonald's menu.

While preserving the core values offered to the consumer, McDonald's found that the needed foodstuffs just would not be available in Russia. Accordingly, although the company relies on outside suppliers elsewhere,

[25] *Restaurants and Institutions,* September 4, 1989, p. 1.

[26] *TRA Foodservice Digest,* August 1989, p. 7.

[27] *The Wall Street Journal,* August 23, 1989, p. B-1.

[28] The information regarding McDonald's Moscow operations was supplied to the author by McDonald's Canada unless otherwise noted.

McDonald's and its joint-venture partner constructed a 110,000-square-foot food production and distribution center that can supply McDonald's basic products to the company's specific, very-high-quality standards. The output of the center is prodigious: 10,000 meat patties per hour, 14,000 buns per hour, and 5,000 pies per hour. The processing center will be able to supply products to other joint-venture hotel and restaurant operators — and export pies to other Eastern European countries. The processing center is sized to provide the products for the 20 McDonald's units projected for the Moscow area.

To provide the raw product the center requires, McDonald's installed an agronomist on a local collective farm to supervise the growing of potatoes from planting to harvesting and persuaded farmers to grow iceberg lettuce and pickle cucumbers from imported seed.[29] Milk is collected from a local collective farm in McDonald's own refrigerated dairy trucks and is pasteurized at the Food Production Center.

The first Moscow unit to open is the largest McDonald's unit ever constructed. Located on Pushkin Square, it offers seating for 700 people on four levels (with room in the summer for another 200 in an outdoor terrace) and has the capacity to serve over 25,000 people per day. Not surprisingly, the crew of 630 people is also the largest McDonald's unit staff in the world.

McDonald's, however, has been limited to sales in rubles, a currency that has little value outside the Soviet Union. Profits are being used to build a second operation, but McDonald's still faces the problem of bringing its profits home in dollars.

Strategic Alliances.   Strategic alliances in the hospitality industry are a type of joint venture that is aimed at a specific geographic region. These are typified, for instance, by the arrangements Radisson used to move swiftly into international markets. In Switzerland and Germany, Radisson is allied with Movenpick. These hotels are known as Movenpick-Radissons. In Hong Kong and the Far East, a similar arrangement has been made with Park Lane Hotels and in Australia with Argus Hotels International. In India, the strategic alliance for that country is with the Indian Tourist Development Corporation, while in Mexico it is with Banamex — the National Bank of Mexico.[30] Choice International is seeking strategic partnerships with airlines and other travel-related companies as well as with other hotel groups. The local partner brings such advantages as its knowledge of operations and labor-force conditions in its country or area as well as contacts with government suppliers. The U.S. partner brings an international brand name, the technology of an international reservations system, and management expertise.[31]

---

[29] *The New York Times,* January 21, 1990, p. E1-7.

[30] Robert J. Pearce, senior vice-president of development, Carlson Hospitality Group, Remarks made during a panel discussion, "U.S. Chains in the International Market," 12th Annual International Hospitality Investment Conference, New York City, June 5, 1990.

[31] Frederick Mosser, Remarks made during a panel discussion, "U.S. Chains in the International Market," 12th Annual International Hospitality Investment Conference, New York City, June 5, 1990.

Management Contracts

A management contract is an arrangement between a management company and a hotel owner that provides for the management company to operate a hotel either for a fee or for a share of the profits. Some management contracts provide for fees whether a profit is earned or not and may or may not require investment in the property by the operator. Limiting investment is customary where the "country risk" (i.e., political and economic instability) is high. Naturally, on the other hand, the owners prefer an arrangement where the operator shares in the investment risk. This kind of arrangement is common where the long-run outlook justifies either a start-up investment by the operator or investment of a portion of the management contract fees in the purchase of an ownership interest. Thus, for example, Stouffer's has entered into a joint-venture management company with Mexico's second largest chain, the Presidente Hotels. Presidente will own 51 percent of the joint-venture management company and Stouffer's will have 49 percent. In addition, Stouffer's will gradually acquire a share in the ownership, up to 25 percent of each Presidente Hotel. Stouffer's interests are clear. While Mexico's economic situation has been volatile for some years, its government has been basically stable. Six million tourists visit Mexico each year, mostly from North America. New markets are clearly opening, moreover, and European visitation has been growing at 25 percent annually since 1987. Thus, Mexico offers both Stouffer's and Presidente excellent prospects for growth.[32]

Combinations of Arrangements

As the foregoing discussion suggests, combinations of franchising, joint venture, strategic alliance, and management contract are common. Arrangements are flexible. Indeed, while an international franchise is a fairly standardized document, and a degree of standardization is appearing in international management contracts, most partnerships and alliances are concluded on the basis of the specific interests, abilities, and needs of the partners. Thus, the wide variety of combinations of arrangements is hardly surprising.

ORGANIZING FOREIGN OPERATIONS

The best way to view the development of foreign operations abroad is to see them as passing through four stages. This usually begins with one or a small number of units, run as simply as a "51st state"—that is, an extension of the regular operations—that happens to be in another country. In a second stage, an "international division" is created which responds to particular opportunities overseas but is still essentially an extension of the domestic operation. In a third stage, international development acquires a strategic focus of its

---

[32] *Hotels,* October 1989, p. 68.

own, and international markets are seen as separate entities to be developed on their own merits rather than as extensions of the domestic activity. In a fourth stage, a company moves to what one international consultant calls "insiderization"—that is, the development of a company whose overseas subsidiaries act so much like domestic companies that they become literally "insiders" in their host countries.[33]

Figure 14.2 shows one possible set of organizational arrangements. In stage one, foreign units report to operations just as does any other unit. In stage two, foreign operations report to the same person as do other operating districts but their separate needs are recognized by a special place in the organization. In stage three, international operations has a separate reporting relationship to top management. In stage four, fully developed companies are deployed in each major national market.

Choice International has passed through the first two stages and is moving into the third stage. Frederick Mosser, executive vice-president of development, described that process in this way:

> International expansion began in the 1970s fairly typically in Canada and Mexico. Canada was treated, more or less as the 51st state. . . . In 1985–86, we decided to really get serious about the international expansion. The "global triad" (North America, Western Europe and the Pacific Rim) was our first priority, . . . Organizationally we had a very conventional approach to setting this up. We were essentially a U.S. corporation with an international division.

The results of this organization, however, were recognized as unsatisfactory. As Mosser put it:

> We have come to recognize that to get to where we want to get to in terms of numbers of properties and truly being a global lodging company, . . . we're going to have to undertake a more comprehensive strategic approach.[34]

It is interesting that, in 1991, Mosser moved his office to Germany to better direct Choice's expansion in Europe.

Turning to another company, Marriott, after a slow start internationally, moved quickly to stage three. The head of Marriott's International Lodging Division put it this way:

---

[33] These stages follow very loosely those set out by Kenichi Ohmae in *The Borderless World,* p. 91. Note, however, that he is dealing principally with manufacturing companies that are concerned with, initially, overseas distribution of goods, hence my treatment of the early stages is somewhat different. In addition, I do not discuss the "country neutral" stage that he cites, as that stage of development is not yet apparent in hospitality and, according to Ohmae, rare in any industry.

[34] Frederick Mosser, Remarks made during a panel discussion, "U.S. Chains in the International Market," 12th Annual International Hospitality Investment Conference, New York City, June 5, 1990.

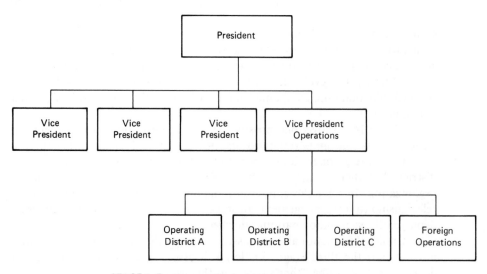

STAGE 1: Regular operations — but in another country

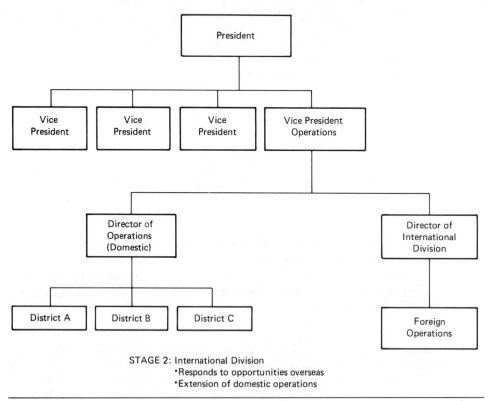

STAGE 2: International Division
  •Responds to opportunities overseas
  •Extension of domestic operations

FIGURE 14.2 Stages in the development of international involvement.

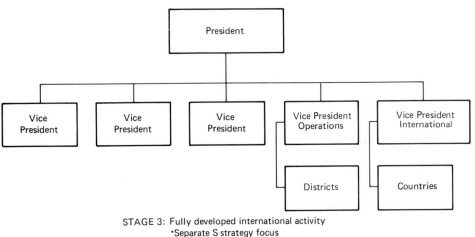

STAGE 3: Fully developed international activity
•Separate S strategy focus
•Developed on own merits

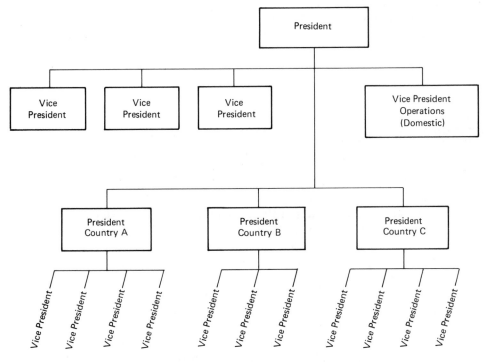

STAGE 4: Fully developed International activity in each major foreign market

FIGURE 14.2 Continued

> We were so busy taking advantage of opportunities in the U.S. that we didn't do a lot internationally until about five years ago. [Then] last year [i.e., 1989] we made the decision to become a full-fledged international lodging company.

As a result of this decision, an international development group was created consisting of a group vice-president and five development executives backed by teams drawn from the disciplines of project finance, feasibility, tax, design management, and construction management. In spite of this considerable commitment, in 1991 only 17 of 500 lodging properties were international, with another 23 scheduled for opening or in development. It seems reasonable, using the framework developed earlier, to characterize Marriott as a stage-three company even though only a "small part of the company's profit comes from international operations."[35]

McDonald's, clearly a stage-four company, is the leader in fast food in a number of countries such as Japan and in regions such as Western Europe. McDonald's makes long-term commitments, as it has done in the Soviet Union, and is able to wait patiently for them to pay off. Because it relies on local partners, the company has excellent contacts in all parts of government and society. It is able to fully play the role of the true insider. In fact, our earlier discussion of McDonald's in Moscow is a good illustration of what "insiderization" means in practice.

FOREIGN INVESTMENT IN THE U.S. MARKET

We have used the word *foreign* from time to time. We should pause, here, to consider once again how limited the meaning of a national designation is in today's world. Table 14.1 gives a partial list of well-known "American" firms that had "foreign" owners in 1991. That list includes the two U.S. pioneers in international hotel keeping, Intercontinental and Hilton International, as well as a number of famous American brand names like Burger King and Holiday Inn. In using the word *foreign,* we are really victims of the limitations of language to deal with a rapidly changing world. It is convenient to use the word, but its meaning is much less clear today than it was even 5 or 10 years ago.

Most of foreign direct investment (FDI) in the United States has been spent on acquiring existing companies. In 1988, for instance, $60 billion was spent in the total U.S. economy by foreign companies for acquisition, and only $5 billion to start up new companies.[36] We can assume that the propor-

---

[35] Ronald E. Eastman, Remarks made during a panel discussion, "U.S. Chains in the International Market."

[36] *The Economist,* December 16, 1989, pp. 63–64.

National identities have become blurred in an increasingly global marketplace. Here an "American brand" owned by a British company flourishes in Dresden, Germany. (Courtesy of Burger King)

tion spent on new enterprises in hospitality is even less than for the economy as a whole. Given the level of development of the U.S. hospitality industry relative to that in other countries, as well as the size and competitiveness of the market, it takes a very large investment to enter the hospitality industry in the United States. Companies that can afford to make that size of investment

TABLE 14.1   American Brands with Foreign Owners

Company Name	Nationality of Ownership
Burger King	Great Britain
Baskin Robbins	Great Britain
Dunkin Donuts	Great Britain
Hilton International	Japan
Holiday Inn	Great Britain
Intercontinental	Japan/Sweden
Omni	Hong Kong
Ramada	Hong Kong/United States
Restaurant Associates	Japan
Westin	Japan

quite reasonably conclude that going concerns—purchased with their management expertise and successful, consumer-accepted concept—make the best investment.

The largest investors in the United States are the British, who control 30 percent of foreign-owned assets; Japan is a distant second, with 16 percent. Foreign ownership of assets in the United States is at a proportionate level significantly *lower* than foreign ownership in other developed countries—about two-thirds the level experienced in Great Britain and Germany, for instance.[37]

MAJOR FOREIGN COMPETITORS IN U.S. AND WORLD MARKETS

It is interesting to identify some of the most important international companies, although a listing of all of them would be impossible. What is attempted below is a brief look at a few of the leading companies, particularly those that are—or are likely to be—a factor in the U.S. hospitality industry, or which will provide direct competition on a worldwide scale to U.S. operators. Since overseas multiunit firms have been more significantly active in lodging than in food service, most of the discussion pertains to hotels although some of the companies discussed also have large European food service operations.[38]

Accor

One of the largest international hotel operators—the (third) largest chain in the world—is the French-based company, Accor. An innovator, Accor began offering specialized hotel products aimed at specific market segments in the 1970s. Accor, then, can take credit for being the first segmented lodging company. The company's brands and lodging segments served are summarized in Table 14.2.[39]

Accor is represented in virtually every international hotel market, with nearly 1,600 hotel properties having 180,000 rooms in 55 countries in 1991. In addition to being Europe's largest hotel chain, it is the largest hotel chain in Brazil and a major force in several other national markets. Eighty-five percent of its hotels, however, were in Europe until its acquisition of Motel 6. With that acquisition, the distribution changed to roughly 55 percent in Europe, with Motel 6 and Accor's other U.S. properties accounting for something

---

[37] *The Economist,* December 16, 1989, pp. 63–65.

[38] Students who are interested to learn more about current developments in international hospitality can follow them in the trade journal, *Hotels,* which is a magazine devoted not just to the hotel business, but in large part to the international lodging industry. The magazine reports current developments each month and usually features two or three in-depth portraits of international hotel companies. Unfortunately, there is as yet no similar forum devoted to food service.

[39] *Hotels,* September 1989, pp. 52–53.

TABLE 14.2 Accor Brands and Segments Served

Brand Name	Market Segment
Sofitel	Luxury market
Mercure	Luxury market
Novotel	Midrange market (similar in many ways to Holiday Inns)
Compri	Limited-service hotel developed in North America under license in a joint venture with a subsidiary of Metropolitan Life Insurance Co.
Ibis/Urbis	Economy market, with Urbis properties located in urban areas, Ibis in suburbs, smaller cities, and outlying areas, mainly in Europe
Motel 6	A hard-budget motel, presently centered in the United States
Formula 1	A hard-budget motel offered only in Europe
Hotelia	A chain of residence hotels for the aged offered only in Europe

under 35 percent of its hotels.[40] Accor, unlike most U.S. chains, owns 50 percent of the hotels it operates and franchises only 20 percent. The remaining 30 percent are operated by Accor under management contracts. This pattern of ownership and limited franchising permits tight control of its operations. This tight control over operations is an important policy difference between this company and many North American hotel companies, which have a much greater proportion of franchised properties where detailed control of operations is more difficult. Only 50 percent of Accor's revenues come from hotel operation. The balance comes from contract food service and restaurant operations.[41]

Wagons-Lits

This Belgian-headquartered company is in the process of merging with Accor as this text is written. It has a network of almost 300 hotels, including 157 upscale properties under the brand names Pullman, Altea, and PLM Azur. In addition, the company operates 79 properties under the Arcade brand in the upper end of the European budget market. Primo, a hard-budget brand, is still in test. The hotel division of Wagons-Lits, operating under the name Pullman International Hotels, has a total of 262 hotels in 35 countries, principally in Europe, Africa, and the Middle East. Pullman has two North American operations—one deluxe hotel in New York City and an economy property in Montreal. The company has regarded the North American market as significantly overbuilt and not an attractive area for expansion.[42]

[40] *The Economist,* January 27, 1990, p. 72; *Hotel-Motel Management,* May 27, 1991, p. 3.

[41] *Hotels,* September 1989, pp. 52–53.

[42] Jean Paul Champlain, general manager of Arcade Hotels, Remarks made during a panel discussion, "Foreign Hotel Companies' Views of U.S. Operations," 12th International Hospitality Industry Investment Conference, New York City, June 4, 1990.

Wagons-Lits derives only 15 percent of its revenues from hotel operations and 40 percent from restaurants. The balance of its revenues, however, also come from tourism-related industries including sleeping car rail operations (12 percent), travel agency and car rental operations (18 percent), and travel-related retailing and vending (15 percent).[43] When the Accor and Wagons-Lits merger was completed at the end of 1991, it became one of the largest international hospitality companies in the world.[44]

Trust House Forte

Another very large operator in the United States whose ownership is based in England is Trust House Forte (THF). In the United States, the Forte name is not as well known as that of its largest operating group, Travelodge. Originating in the United States, and still predominantly located in North America, Travelodge was purchased some years ago by THF in one of the earliest major transnational lodging-chain acquisitions.

Travelodge makes up somewhat more than 50 percent of THF's rooms. The bulk of these are in the United States. THF's operations outside England, comprising 550 properties with 52,600 rooms, significantly outweigh its 274 United Kingdom properties with 25,000 rooms. In spite of the size of its international operations, however, THF is more limited than Accor in its geographic scope, operating hotels principally in the United Kingdom and the United States. The company operates two dozen hotels in Europe, seven in the Caribbean region, and three in the Middle East. THF is also implementing development agreements in Mexico.

While its largest group of hotels, Travelodge, is in the upper level economy market, the company's "Exclusive Group" of five-star hotels includes some of the most famous names in international hotel keeping, such as the Plaza Athenee in Paris and in New York, the Hyde Park in London, and the George V, also in Paris. At the other end of the scale, the company is developing a hard-budget chain, Thriftlodge, for expansion in Europe, the United Kingdom, and North America. THF derives two thirds of its profits from hotel operations and the balance from its food service division.[45]

Club Mèditerranèe

Well known to American tourists as Club Med, this company pioneered the all-inclusive resort package featuring no-frills accommodations and a very active sports, entertainment, and activities program. Although headquartered

---

[43] *1989 Annual Report* (Brussels: Compagnie Internationale Des Wagons-Lits et du Tourisme, 1989).

[44] *Travel Agent,* June 17, 1991, p. 12.

[45] *Hotels,* February 1989, pp. 36–42.

in France, the company operates a subsidiary with headquarters in New York City. Guests at Club Med are known as *gentil membres* (GMs) — honorable members — while the staff, who mix socially with GMs, are known as *gentil organisateurs* (GOs). The company's success relies to a large degree on the social interaction between GM and GO. Known principally as a young singles resort to many North Americans, the company actually targets very successfully a large spectrum of markets, including couples, families with children, and the business-meeting market.

Voluntary Chains

These groups, similar to Best Western in North America, have a large role to play in the international market, particularly as European independents scramble to deal with mounting chain competition in their market. Reservation referrals, joint marketing programs, and joint purchasing activities are some of the principal values these groups offer their members. The largest voluntary chain internationally is Best Western with 260,000 rooms in 3,300 properties in 36 countries. Best Western is expanding aggressively in Europe, the Pacific Rim, and South America. The company has a target of representation in 50 countries by 1994. The next largest voluntary group, *Logis et Auberges* (4,660 properties), has been in business in France for 40 years and is well known there. The third largest, Flag International (500 properties), headquartered in Australia, operates principally in Australia, New Zealand, and the Asia Pacific region. The somewhat smaller (375 inns), upscale *Relais & Chateau* has properties in 36 countries and a number of properties in the United States.[46]

Many foreign airlines operate associated hotel companies. Japan Air Lines affiliate, Nikko Hotels, operate luxury hotels in major gateway cities in the United States. Meridian, an affiliate of Air France, and Penta, an affiliate of Lufthansa, also operate hotels in the United States.

Canadian Companies

A number of Canadian hospitality brands have moved into the U.S. market, particularly in northern states that share a border with Canada. Swiss Chalet, a barbequed chicken and ribs restaurant operation, has moved across the border from their Ontario base into upstate New York. Journey's End Motels, a Canadian budget chain, operates properties in the northeastern United States. Delta Hotels seeks to serve its Canadian clientele with operations in Florida, a major tourist destination for Canadians, as well as in border states. Four Seasons, a premier luxury chain, operates in many U.S. cities and in Europe, Japan, and the West Indies as well, serving, however, an international clientele rather than principally a Canadian one.

---

[46] *Hotels and Restaurants International,* July 1989, p. 87.

International competition involves many European chains that have a significant presence overseas. Shown here is the Southampton Princess Hotel in Bermuda. (Courtesy of Princess Hotels International, Inc.)

OVERSEAS EXPERIENCE AND EMPLOYMENT

There *are* reasons to hire North Americans to work in hospitality overseas. Some countries do not have a large enough source of trained managers. Moreover, particularly in responsible positions, a good fit with the rest of the firm's executive staff is important—and often easier for an American firm to achieve with someone from North America. The relevant operating experience and background may not be available to people living outside the United States and Canada. For all these reasons, there are opportunities abroad for Americans who are adequately prepared. American employees, however, are more expensive to hire to most companies operating abroad than are local nationals. Normally, expatriate benefits to senior managers include cost-of-living and foreign-tax allowance, children's tuition in English-language schools, and housing allowances. Companies, not surprisingly, have been making efforts to reduce overseas employment by using shorter term assignments and often by reducing overseas benefits, especially for junior employees.[47]

Cost is not the only reason for hiring people from the host country. Local people have an understanding of the culture of the employees in a particular country, to say nothing of fluency in the language. Local managers, moreover, do not arouse the resentment that sometimes is directed at a foreign manager. Thus, there are several reasons for a company to prefer to develop and advance local managers. Foreign-owned firms operating in the United States seek U.S. managers and supervisors in their U.S. operations for similar reasons.

While most positions in operations outside the United States *are* filled with people from those countries, many American companies with significant foreign operations do have opportunities for overseas employment. The manager of college relations with ITT Sheraton notes that one of the obstacles to immediate employment overseas is the immigration restrictions of other countries (similar to restrictions that the United States enforces). Employment of foreign nationals is usually permitted only if the employer is able to show that the prospective employee has special skills that are not otherwise available in the country. It is not surprising, therefore, that many employees who do receive overseas assignments have been employed by the company for a few years and thus have significant operating experience.[48]

Another major problem facing Americans who want to work overseas is lack of language skills. In fact, many hospitality programs are now encouraging students to select the study of at least one foreign language as part of their curriculum. The ability to adapt to a different culture is also important and probably the only way to get it is to have some experience of living abroad.

Summer or short-term work or study abroad not only give students experience in living in another culture but also may offer them an opportunity to build up contacts that will help them in securing employment abroad upon graduation. Opportunities to study abroad are plentiful in summer programs offered by many HRI college and university programs. Some institutions also maintain exchange programs with institutions in foreign countries. The University of Wisconsin at Stout, for instance, holds an annual four-week short course for students from Instituto Tecnologico de Estudios Superiores de Monterrey in Monterrey, Mexico. The language of instruction is English and the subjects covered include Front Office Procedures, Developmental Tourism Awareness, Fast-Food Operations, and Quantity Food Production.

The *value to Stout students* is twofold. First of all, a midwinter visit to the Monterrey campus by the Wisconsin students is greatly facilitated by the close working relationship that has emerged between the two institutions. In

---

[47] *The Wall Street Journal,* December 11, 1989, p. B-1.

[48] Brett Hutchens, manager of college relations, ITT Sheraton, personal communication to author, August 1990.

Overseas operations offer attractive and interesting opportunities but securing overseas employment requires considerable investment of time and effort on the part of the interested individual. (Courtesy of Hyatt Hotels International)

addition, a special course has been organized in multiethnic management at Stout's summer school. In this course, the Stout students work with the students from Mexico as a means of preparing themselves to meet the demand of an increasingly international marketplace as well as the changing composition of North America's work force.[49]

Graduate study in hospitality management is available in France at the Institut de Management Hotelier International (IMHI) offered jointly by the

[49]Prof. Donald Dinkelman, University of Wisconsin-Stout, personal communication to author, August 1990.

Cornell Hotel School and France's leading business school, Ecole Superieur Science Economique et Commerciale (ESSEC). Although the language of instruction is English, IMHI students are generally at least bilingual, and ESSEC offers a wide and varied language-studies program as well as its courses in hospitality administration. Virtually all IMHI students have industry experience and are drawn from all over Europe as well as from Asia and the Americas.

Obtaining work abroad is more difficult because work permits are required to be legally employed in a foreign country, and these are not easy to come by. The Association of International Students in Economics and Commerce (AISEC) operates student work exchanges, but they provide only a very limited number of positions. Some colleges and universities have begun to arrange for exchange programs for summer employment but, unfortunately, many do not yet have such a program.

As a student seeking overseas work, you should begin with your own institution's placement office and international center. The consulate or embassy of the country you seek to work in may be aware of exchange programs or other means to obtain a work permit. Probably the best source of information is other students who have worked abroad. Talk with students at your own institution or those you may be able to meet at gatherings of students such as regional or national restaurant or hotel shows. They know the ropes and can give practical advice on getting jobs and what to expect in the way of pay and working conditions.[50] Whether you are interested in overseas work as a career or not, work, travel, and study abroad can all be unique educational experiences that broaden your cultural background, increase your sophistication—and enhance your resume.

The hospitality industry, always a competitive one, is becoming more so with an influx of firms from overseas. On the other hand, new opportunities are presented by markets outside the United States, and many *personal* opportunities are presented to individuals by the presence of such aggressive and successful firms as Accor and Grand Metropolitan as employers in North America. Though we must still use it here from time to time, the word *foreign,* it seems, may be on the way out of fashion.

SUMMARY

We identified six factors (Figure 14.1) that are increasing the internationalization of all businesses, including hospitality. We noted the

---

[50] I am indebted to Prof. Jo Marie Powers, whose experience coordinating international activities for the School of Hotel and Food Administration at the University of Guelph I draw on here. Conversations with Prof. Patrick Moreo at Penn State University and Prof. Donald Dinkelman at the University of Wisconsin-Stout also provided useful insights.

advantages to investors in the U.S. market to include currency fluctuations, large markets, security of investment, and management skills and systems. U.S. firms have moved abroad by purchasing assets there, but increasingly the mechanisms used are franchising, joint ventures, strategic alliances, management contracts, and combinations of all of these. Developing overseas operations can be seen as a four-stage process (Figure 14.2), ending in the kind of "insiderization" achieved by McDonald's in Moscow. The limitations to the word *foreign* in today's internationalized market were also discussed. We noted that most foreign direct investment was in going concerns and that the proportion of assets owned by firms from outside the United States is less than for other developed countries. The major foreign companies active in the U.S. market that we discussed are Accor, Wagons-Lits (the two have merged), Trust House Forte, and Club Mèditerranèe as well as a number of voluntary chains of independent properties.

There are opportunities for employment abroad, but they are limited because of costs and because local managers are more familiar with local conditions. Preparation to work overseas should include language skills and experience in living abroad as well as operating know-how. While work-permit requirements make working abroad difficult, there are numerous opportunities for study abroad.

KEY WORDS AND CONCEPTS

To help you review this chapter, keep in mind the following:

International/global
Forces for internationalization
Advantages to foreign
    investors
Methods of U.S. investment
    abroad
  ownership
  franchise
  joint venture
  strategic alliance
  management contracts

Foreign Direct Investment (FDI)
Stages of development in
    expanding abroad
Insiderization
Limitations of the meaning of
    foreign
Voluntary chains
Expatriate benefits
Immigration restrictions
Language skills
Adapting to other cultures

REVIEW QUESTIONS

1. What are the forces increasing the internationalization of the hospitality industry?

2. What attracts foreign investors to U.S. markets? What attracts U.S. companies to foreign markets? What form are those investments taking?

3. Discuss the four phases of international organization.

4. Discuss the operations of the major foreign companies covered.

5. What does *insiderization* mean?

6. If you are interested in working abroad, what steps do you need to take to prepare yourself for such a move?

Courtesy of Stouffer Hotels

VIEWS OF THE FUTURE

THE PURPOSE OF THIS CHAPTER

This chapter brings together some of the major themes and concerns that we have explored in previous chapters and speculates about their meaning for the near future. We will look at how basic forces—demand, supply, and the environment—may interact to create opportunities in hospitality. You will not be surprised, however, to find that where there are opportunities, there are also risks.

We have noted at several points in this text that you are really in business for yourself, whether you are self-employed or work for the largest company in town. Your career *is* your business, and we will conclude with consideration of where you may want to fit in the industry's future and how you should prepare for it.

THIS CHAPTER SHOULD HELP YOU

1. Identify major themes of the text and draw them together into a coherent picture.

2. Review the basic forces that cause changes in consumer demand.

3. See the importance of education in shaping consumer demand.

4. Identify favorable and unfavorable trends in the hospitality industry's factors of production.

5. Assess trends in the hospitality industry's social, physical, and technological environments.

We study the future, to paraphrase the historian, to understand the present. Looking ahead forces us to think in an orderly way about the forces at work today that are likely to affect tomorrow. Thus, we are really *not* trying to prophesy in this chapter but, rather, to identify the forces visibly at work today that are important to our industry. Even if the future this chapter envisions may be off the mark here and there, the identification of significant trends will still be important to you. As you shape your own career plans, the forces we examine in this chapter will continue to command your attention in the years to come, when you will be making your own estimates of their likely effects.

Looking back over the material we have covered in earlier chapters, we can identify several recurring themes. The consumer ultimately determines what the industry will be—and hospitality's consumer base is changing dramatically. Key demographic facts of the 1990s will include the aging of the baby boomers and the emergence of a large senior citizen population that will continue to grow for the foreseeable future; a continuing shortage of younger workers; a high level of female participation in the work force; and the continuing growth of two-income families.

Another point that has recurred throughout the text involves competitive conditions. The hospitality and travel industries have reached maturity. This means, in most sectors of the businesses, growth at about the rate of the national economy *and heightened competition*. The internationalization of the world's economies has certainly included the North American hospitality industry. Internationalization adds the force of foreign investors to the competitive picture in North America. It also means, however, heightened opportunities for U.S. firms overseas and new markets for American hospitality as the United States grows as an international *destination*.

The hospitality industry, then, faces growing competition from other, parallel industries such as C Stores, from overseas firms, and from changes within the industry itself. Successful firms will be the ones that can establish a real competitive difference. The single best means to achieve that competitive edge, it appears, is *service*. Whether personal, indirect, or mechanical, guests will choose the firms that come the closest to the zero-defects goal of successful service systems.

The hospitality industry in the last decade of the twentieth century must face the environmental concerns that dominate public discussion and concern. We have earlier noted the problems of solid-waste disposal as adding both cost and complication to operations. In this chapter we will want to consider, as well, the threats to the global environment that are claiming an increasing share of both the public's and governmental agencies' time and attention. We also need to consider other aspects of the industry's environment and will do so later in the chapter.

The best way for us to organize our consideration of these major themes is to look at them in terms of demand, supply, and the changing social, physical, and technological environments in which supply and demand operate. With so many variables at play, we can make no precise forecasts, but some general directions seem clear.

THE DEMAND FOR HOSPITALITY SERVICES

Ultimately, the hospitality industry is shaped by its consumers and the products and services they need and want. Demand is affected by factors such as consumer demographics and population trends, income and employment trends, the education of the population, and the changing culture we live in. In the following sections we will look at both the quantitative and qualitative aspects of demand from the point of view of demographics, employment and income, and education.

CONSUMER DEMOGRAPHICS

As we have looked at the sectors of the hospitality industry, we have repeatedly examined population trends, particularly in reference to our customers' ages. One conclusion we have reached is that the middle-aged segment of our population is growing rapidly. This is the age when people are most likely to travel and when their spending on eating out reaches its highest point. The increase in the affluent middle-aged population represents a major opportunity for the hospitality industry. The late middle years provide an even wealthier consumer. Dubbed the "Ultras," consumers aged 50 to 64 spend over 20 percent more of their income on nonessentials than does the average consumer.[1]

One of the keys to attracting older patrons, clearly, will be superior service. Because these customers generally spend more when they dine out, they will be paying for a service-intensive experience and, as value-conscious consumers, they will expect the best in service.

For the rest of the hospitality and travel field, a middle-aging population is a rich potential for a booming business. This is especially true for people over 50, who have higher disposable incomes, less demands on that income, fewer family obligations, and more leisure to travel. In fact, they are prime customers for hotels and other travel and transportation services.

The over-65 population, particularly up to the age of 75, are another prime customer segment for travel. Since most are retired by this time, their incomes are somewhat lower. On the other hand, a better measure of their economic position is total *wealth*. Many in this segment have their mortgages paid off, significant assets in savings and pension plans, and very few if any outstanding obligations—or dependents. Thus, while they have lower incomes, they have less need for income, and many are very secure economically. They also have plenty of leisure time.

[1] *Restaurants and Institutions,* January 7, 1987.

Senior citizens are value conscious, not price conscious. As shoppers, in fact, they tend to buy known top brands, and will not be attracted just by a low price. They are quality- and value-conscious customers who are attracted, for instance, by the superior value of off-peak pricing for meals or accommodations. Their willingness to patronize operations outside their peak-demand times, whether an early bird dinner or a fall or spring vacation, makes them valuable customers because they represent a net addition to business for operations that run at full capacity in the busy times. Once again, service will probably be a key consideration.

People over age 65 often have special service needs. Many suffer from some loss of hearing. Accordingly, it is best to avoid speaking rapidly or changing subjects quickly or unexpectedly. Eyesight also is a problem for many older guests so it is best to seat them in a well-lighted area of a dining room. Above all, avoid condescension or making an obvious fuss over any disability. Most older people, psychologists and market researchers tell us, have a *perceived age* of 35 to 40; that is, they feel the same as they did when they were younger. They don't want some young whippersnapper giving them a bad time.

Another significant set of demand factors are the dual-income family, smaller family size, and the delay in having children. Dual-income families have, on average, roughly half again as much income as single-income families. As long as the family are "DINKs" (Dual Income, No Kids), their disposable income is much higher and they—along with prosperous singles—are the restaurant industry's best customers.

Families with children are an important target, too. The industry has long since learned how to provide service to families with children, and it is important that we not forget about children's menus, toys, and special attention. For the two-income family, time away together is scarce and they are seeking "quality time." That, too, requires attentive service.

We must also note the less fortunate side of the changing family structure outlook. Single parents constitute a large, lower income group. This segment is the target for lower priced food service, such as fast food, and for social programs such as school breakfasts or free or reduced-price school lunches.

With more women working, in any case, many of the "service functions" of the family, such as feeding children at school and sometimes caring for the elderly, have been moved to social agencies such as schools and congregate meal programs. The next decade will likely see the continuing expansion of day-care services as more mothers of young children move into the work force.

Paralleling these developments, commercial food service, too, has benefited as women and families are more inclined—and more financially able—to eat out. The growth *rate* for working women is slowing, but female employment continues to rise. With more than half of North America's mothers already in the work force, food away from home has become a *necessity rather than a luxury*.

These pictures point out the contrast in needs of key population segments who are at different stages in their lives. The senior citizens dining in Hyatt's Classic Residences have quite different needs from the baby boomer parents of young children shown at the Key Biscayne Sonesta. [Courtesy of Hyatt Hotels Corp. (top) and Sonesta Hotels (bottom)]

Lack of time is a fact of life for families with both parents working. This "poverty of time" results in a tendency to eat out and in a demand for relatively fast service. Fast food, we can expect, is here to stay, but it has continually redefined itself and is likely to continue to evolve and change to serve the needs of a "middle-aging" population.

With both parents working, the long vacation trip is becoming less common and shorter "minivacations," often combined with business travel, are becoming the rule. Generally, this means shorter trips and more business near home.

EDUCATION'S IMPACT ON HOSPITALITY DEMAND

The North American population is the most highly educated in history in terms of its years of formal schooling. The average educational achievement is about 12 years, implying that at least half the population has somewhat more than a high school education.

But formal education is far from the only educational influence. If we include the pervasive effect of television and the increase in travel as educational, we can see that today's hospitality consumer is a sophisticate. Attractions like Walt Disney World and other theme parks have done a great deal to raise consumers' entertainment expectations.

The educated consumer is health and nutrition conscious, and as the baby boomers move into middle age, their health concerns are likely to heighten. Consumer concerns about nutrition are a permanent part of the food service landscape.

Consumerism is a movement that educates the public. Consumerists want the guest to have a part in setting businesses' agendas, not just in deciding whether or not to patronize a business. Concern, for instance, about "passive smoking," that is, the smoke that nonsmokers inhale when there is smoking around them, continues to heat up as more data come in and the U.S. Surgeon General calls for a smoke-free society by 2000. Under the circumstances, no-smoking sections in restaurants will continue to grow in number, whether voluntarily or by law. In some areas we are already seeing entire restaurants that are smoke free. Indeed, the greater demand for smoke-free guest rooms in hotels also suggests a trend that will continue to grow in importance in lodging.

Similarly, concerns over truth in menu will continue, and voluntary nutritional labeling to avoid legally mandated labeling may well spread.

Educated consumers are people who demand value in terms of quality of product, service, and entertainment. They value themselves, want to protect their health, and are responsive to consumer groups that seek to represent those kinds of interests. Educated consumers are in the driver's seat in our marketing-oriented civilization.

SUPPLY CONDITIONS

Food and labor costs are the major factors of production that we will examine in this chapter.[2] Although the cost outlook is favorable for food itself, food service workers are likely to grow scarcer and more costly.

FOOD

The Reverend Thomas Malthus—an early nineteenth-century English economist and probably the man most responsible for economics being labeled "the dismal science"—offered some pessimistic conclusions about population growth and the food supply. He predicted that as the population grew faster than the food supply, worldwide famine would result. As it turned out, the crisis that Malthus foresaw did not materialize, but his argument has been repeated ever since. Each time, however, the prophets of doom have been disproved by advances in agricultural technology.

Barring a natural catastrophe, however, it appears likely that food supplies will continue to the point of posing a problem of *surpluses*. Indeed this oversupply is presently a problem in all developed countries. The European Community, for instance, is often described as having "wine lakes" as well as "butter and grain mountains." In any case, poor crop conditions in a year in one area will almost certainly be offset by global surpluses in the marketplace. This should mean that raw foodstuffs such as grains will continue to be relatively inexpensive, barring an unexpected worldwide climate catastrophe. (Of course, government intervention in the marketplace, which has been fairly common and problematic in both North America and Europe, could change the outlook. Intervention could take the form of restricting growing, artificially propping up prices, or both.)

More expensive beef has been only one cause in the decline of beef sales. Perhaps more fundamentally, consumers' nutrition concerns have been a big factor in the marketplace. Concerns about fat and cholesterol have led to a greater consumption of chicken and, though to a lesser degree, of pork. (Pork has less saturated fat than beef.)

Despite the falling price of some foodstuffs, when significant processing value is added, as is required for convenience foods, the cost of labor and capital are more likely to dominate, and prices may rise. These processed foods—and the contents of the grocer's freezer case, generally—are directly competitive with food service. Any upward price trend in convenience foods in the grocery stores offers some help to food service in maintaining its compet-

---

[2]Capital is usually considered as a basic resource but is excluded here because it is beyond the scope of this text. There is, however, every reason to believe that capital will be in short supply worldwide. The United States, because of low savings rates, may face an especially difficult capital shortage. A shortage of capital could mean increased interest rates and greater difficulty in attracting capital to the hospitality industry, especially for smaller firms.

itiveness. As more of food service is take-out or delivery, and thus more directly competitive with supermarket delicatessen counters, it is interesting to recall that the biggest advantage restaurants have in the off-premise market is their service culture, a factor grocery stores haven't emulated successfully as yet.

LABOR

You will recall that the number of younger workers, on whom the hospitality industry normally draws, has been declining since the late 1970s. That decline will continue in the 1990s, although at a more moderate pace; and even when the trend is reversed, the shortage of people in that age bracket is likely to continue through most of the decade. The demand for food service workers, for instance, is projected by the National Restaurant Association to increase half again as fast as the growth of the labor supply in the economy generally. Hospitality will need to succeed in attracting a larger share of the work force. Under these circumstances, even as older workers are sought to fill the gaps, in many markets wage rates will continue to rise, and some companies may base their expansion plans on whether they can find the staff they need to operate. Most probably labor costs will continue to rise, the use of part-time workers will grow, and the skills needed to motivate workers will become more important. So, too, will skills in scheduling, work simplification, and other measures aimed at alleviating labor costs.

We earlier noted the high average educational attainment of today's population. But we should also be aware that that poses some problems regarding hospitality labor supply. Many people regard work in hospitality as too demanding, too dull, or beneath them. Although students in hospitality programs are aware of the challenge and excitement of hospitality industry careers, many people do not share those values.

Child Care as a Fringe Benefit

The number of mothers of young children who are working continues to grow rapidly. To attract these women as employees, companies are adopting a range of benefits related to child care. The proportion offering on-premise day care is still small but is growing in labor shortage areas, and some employers are subsidizing outside day-care arrangements.[3] Other forms of help for working parents are flexible scheduling (sometimes called flextime); availability of part-time status on a temporary basis; job sharing (where two or more working parents split the time commitment of one full-time position); and flexible leave policies.[4]

Marriott offers its employees a range of services. One company publication, *Child Care Choices,* provides parents with information about child care

[3] *Hotel and Motel Management,* December 17, 1990, p. 1.

[4] *American Demographics,* May 1985, p. 16.

in their community and a toll-free number that any employee can call to discuss specific problems with a child-care specialist. A second program makes available a discount for Marriott employees who use any of a number of child-care programs that have agreed to provide special prices to the company's employees. The company will also establish Family Care Spending Accounts for employees that allow workers to take advantage of tax breaks for child and elder care.[5] In addition, the company has contracted for on-site day care for employees at its national headquarters and acquired an interest in a day-care company, Corporate Child Care.[6] Marriott's response to the problems of working parents is directed by the company's Department of Work and Family Life.

Employers who provide day-care programs reduce absenteeism, strengthen hiring and retention rates, and experience a noticeable rise in morale as well as favorable public relations.[7] The logic, obviously, underlying these kinds of programs is to treat an employee group as a target market and create a package of benefits that goes well beyond pay to attract and keep employees in a tight labor market.

Work Force Diversity

Three changes that are forecast from today's work force are that workers will be older, more likely to be women, and composed of a higher proportion of minorities.[8] In fact, dominance of the work force by white males is coming to an end. By the year 2000, one in four employees will be from a minority group[9] and approximately 47 percent will be women. Sensitivity to the points of view of minorities, women, and older workers will be an absolute necessity for managers. Men who have problems working with—or for—women will, in truth, have a problem working at all. With greater diversity, more and differing points of view will affect all aspects of the workplace, including such factors as scheduling (more flexibility), selection (a "balance" based on affirmative-action programs), and even humor in the workplace (sexist and racist jokes will be even more "out" than they are today). These developments, of course, apply not just to hospitality but to the entire North American economy.

The obvious factor that will make the work force older will be the aging of the population's largest group, the baby boomers; but another, oddly enough, a characteristic holding aging back, may be the increasing cost of higher education. *American Demographics* suggests that increasing tuition and other costs will make it necessary for many young people to go to work for a

[5] *Marriott World,* Summer 1990, p. 18.

[6] *TRA Foodservice Digest/Foodservice Director,* February 15, 1990, p. 8.

[7] *Hotel and Motel Management,* December 17, 1990, p. 41.

[8] *American Demographics,* February 1988, p. 34.

[9] *American Demographics,* December 1990, p. 23.

Employees are crucial to providing effective service. Increasingly, to attract and hold good employees operators are treating them as a target market that needs to be sold on their jobs. (Courtesy of Bob Evans Farms)

few years before they go to college, adding more young people to the work force. By the year 2000, they forecast, half of all college students will be 25 or over.[10]

THE ENVIRONMENT

Demand and supply are, indeed, determining forces, but they operate within the constraints of the social, physical, and technical environments. Our discussion of the changing age distribution and family structure covered an important element of the social environment of the 1990s, and now we need to consider another aspect of the social environment — competition. We will then turn to the physical, technical, and built environments.

THE COMPETITIVE ENVIRONMENT

We have already noted that most of the hospitality industry is at the mature stage of development, a time when entrenched, established competitors face

[10] *American Demographics,* December 1990.

each other in the marketplace. The mature stage of the competitive cycle, we ought to note, is likely to be a good time for well-prepared managers because sharp management, good service, and close control of costs become more important in this tougher competitive environment. Your education, then, in preparing for your career is, as we have said before, a good investment.

In both food service and lodging, operators are paying more attention to market segmentation. That is leading to much greater differences between operations in the industry. In lodging, for instance, the middle-of-the-road hotel, such as a Holiday Inn or Ramada, were once the backbone of the industry. They provided all the basic services: lodging, food, beverage, and meeting and banquet facilities. These properties are challenged today by limited-service properties such as La Quinta, Hampton, and Fairfield Inns. As well, they face competition for their upscale customers from all-suite properties charging rates only slightly higher. These operations provide significantly more plush guest room accommodations but less extensive food and beverage facilities and services to keep rates in line. The extended-stay all-suite property carries targeting even further—and acquires a tight grip on an important market segment.

In the face of this competition, many midscale properties are being converted to less service-intensive formats such as Days Inns, Holiday Inn Express, and HoJo Inns. Lodging, then, is likely to continue fragmenting into upscale, limited-service, and hard-budget segments at the expense of the traditional midscale operation.

Food service is following similar trends. Fast food is threatened by lower cost competition from take-out operations. Value pricing, too, is whittling profit margins in fast-food and popular-priced restaurants. The result of slimmer operating profits may well be reduced expenditures on physical plant and even more emphasis on self-service and other cost-reduction moves. In all, then, the lower priced end of the spectrum is likely to emphasize price and reduce service.

On the other hand, the product of the casual dinner house *is* service. And, with the middle-aged market taking center stage, operations that specialize in service are likely to give even greater emphasis to the service dimension of the dining experience. In food service as in lodging, there is a fragmenting into service-intensive and limited-service concepts, with the middle ground that seeks to serve everybody occupying a less and less attractive competitive position. As we noted in the chapter on service, by the way, the service-intensive operation offers especially attractive opportunities to the independent. Once again, the key appears to be personal service.

Recalling that service is designed to fit customer expectations rather than some abstract model of perfection, it is not surprising that limited-service concepts still emphasize *good* service. Hampton Inns guarantees customer satisfaction, for instance, and McDonald's insists on fast and courteous service. While the definition of service, then, varies with the needs and wants of

Hotels and restaurants face competition from consumers' many options. There are many ways people can satisfy their need for food and shelter away from home, so tourism dollars cannot be taken for granted. (Courtesy of Kampgrounds of America)

the customer group served, it will be a vital consideration in competitive differentiation for any hospitality organization.

The Home as Competition

Another set of competitive concerns for hospitality involves alternatives to going out to eat or to traveling. Consumers *can* choose to spend their money on putting in a sauna instead of taking a vacation—or to forego their accustomed weekend dinner at a nice restaurant for a couple of weeks and buy a VCR. In addition to choices about money, consumers can also select how they will use their scarce time. With all the amenities and amusements available in today's home, they may find they prefer not to face the hassle of crowded roads or lost luggage and delayed flights. Competition with the home is of special interest to food service because of the large number of people who will be entering later middle age over the next few years. The evidence we have so far, as you will recall, suggests that these people may not be as prone to dining out once they are much over age 50.

THE PHYSICAL ENVIRONMENT

In Chapter 5, we looked at an aspect of the environment whose direct impact on hospitality will be increasingly significant, the solid-waste problem. Gar-

One way to respond to the home as a competitor for food service is to provide a service that meets that specific need as Domino's and other delivery operators do. (Courtesy of Domino's Pizza Inc.)

bage used to be just a nuisance and a minor cost, but in the not-too-distant future it will be a problem of crisis proportions for many communities. In the United States, nearly a half million tons of garbage have to be disposed of daily.[11] The basics of the solution to solid waste, you may recall, are *reduce, reuse,* and *recycle.* The complexity in practice of dealing with the solid-waste stream is illustrated by the many disputes over appropriate solutions and cost-effectiveness. To *reduce,* for instance, one state banned asceptic plastic juice containers, which add bulk that is hard to recycle to the waste stream. In fact, however, these packages require half the energy needed to fill glass bottles and much less energy to transport. (It takes 15 times as many trucks to transport bottles.)[12] Permanent tableware creates much less trash—but much more water pollution. Finally, while recycling is desirable, it can be very expensive, drawing on already stretched civic budgets. The good news here, however, is that the next decade will almost certainly see a much clearer consensus on such

[11] *American Demographics,* July 1989, p. 16.
[12] *The Wall Street Journal,* January 14, 1991, p. 23.

issues. Managing the solid-waste stream is only a few years old as an issue, after all, and still in the experimental stage regarding many applications. We can expect waste management to present rising costs and require increasing concern on the part of managers. Almost certainly, most of the uncertainty will be removed and waste problems will be handled by routine rather than innovation by 2000.

Global Concerns

The much larger issue of the global environment, on the other hand, is likely to increase both in urgency and controversy as the decade wears on. Our concern here is not to enter the debate on the global environment but to consider its probable impact on the hospitality industry in the 1990s.

William Nordhaus, a professor of economics at Yale University and former member of President Carter's Council of Economic Advisors, in an article on "Greenhouse Economics" identifies four major global environmental risks: acid rain, ozone depletion, deforestation, and the greenhouse effect.[13] While deforestation involves the hospitality industry only indirectly, the other three have direct impacts on our industry.[14] Acid rain and ozone depletion are both interrelated with the greenhouse problem. That is, the processes and chemicals that result in acid rain and ozone depletion are also involved in creating the greenhouse effect. Certain gases, especially carbon dioxide, collect in the upper atmosphere and reflect back to earth heat that would otherwise escape into space, resulting in temperature increases. We will concentrate our attention here principally on the greenhouse effect.

According to *The Economist,* "Scientists now broadly agree that the buildup of a number of gases in the atmosphere, including carbon dioxide, will cause world temperatures to rise."[15] In the year 1800, the atmosphere contained 280 parts per million (ppm) of carbon dioxide. Geologists studying the polar ice caps tell us that the range in carbon dioxide in the atmosphere over the last 160,000 years has been, until very recently, between 190 and 290 ppm. In 1991, however, that count has risen to 353 ppm.[16]

The best estimates are that the greenhouse effect will result in a rise in average global temperature of somewhere between two and seven degrees Fahrenheit (one to four degrees Celsius) during the twenty-first century. This, in turn, could mean a rise in sea level of about one foot over the next 100 years due to melting of the polar ice caps. For most of the economy, the impacts of these changes will be manageable, according to Nordhaus. He notes, however,

[13] William Nordhaus, "Greenhouse Economics." *The Economist,* July 7, 1990, p. 21.

[14] In limiting our attention to the impacts of environmental changes on hospitality, I do not intend to indicate indifference on my part *or* on the reader's to the broader implications of environmental degradation; they are simply beyond the scope of this text. There is, in any case, no shortage of commentators on the subject.

[15] *The Economist,* September 15, 1990, p. 85.

[16] *The Globe and Mail,* June 13, 1991, p. A6.

Degrading the environment raises serious business problems for many hospitality operators. (Courtesy of Stouffer Hotels)

that industries "dependent on unmanaged ecosystems—on naturally occurring rainfall, runoff and temperatures" will be more extensively affected. Nordhaus mentions "agriculture, forestry and coastal activities."[17] Anyone who has worked in a resort during a week of rain or watched a restaurant's best night be destroyed by bad weather will understand why we should add hospitality and tourism to that list.

There is, as Nordhaus puts it, "immense uncertainty" regarding the degree of change we can expect and the impact of those changes on our lives and our economy. For instance, it seems clear that the change in temperature will be more extreme at the poles, but it is a distinct *possibility* that the greenhouse effect may disturb the way air masses circulate, resulting in a hotter, drier climate in midcontinent areas such as the U.S. grain belt. (Thus, at some point in the future, the outlook for food supply discussed earlier may change dramatically as a result of the greenhouse effect, but almost certainly not in the next decade.) In fact, over the very long term (a hundred years), there may be a shifting of popular vacation spots as regional weather changes.

The degree of change is hard to forecast, as we have said, and the impact of those changes is even harder to foresee. In the coming decade, however,

[17] Nordhaus, "Greenhouse Economics," p. 22.

what is almost absolutely certain is that our customers and our governments at all levels will be increasingly concerned about the problems. The *impact of that concern* is not as hard to foresee, at least in its general direction. Pollution will be seen as a more important problem, and polluting activities may become subject to much greater regulation. The automobile is a number one polluter. There is a distinct possibility of restrictions on auto use, particularly in cities, and much higher gasoline taxes to discourage auto use. A shift to more rail transportation, particularly between major population centers, is also possible.

Another regulatory possibility is that refrigeration and air-conditioning may require major changes that will add to both investment and operating costs for hospitality operations. Most refrigeration today is based on chloro-fluorocarbons (CFCs), and CFCs are both a major contributor to ozone depletion and a significant factor in the greenhouse effect. The technology to replace CFCs is in development, and alternatives are already available. They would, however, be expensive to purchase and install and, because they are less efficient, they would be more costly to operate.

Almost certainly customers will have a heightened awareness and concern for environmental issues. Operators will do well to display their own concern through public relations efforts that let customers and the public know what they are doing to be environmentally responsible.

Petroleum Resources

Another way of viewing environmental problems is in terms of using up the world's scarce resources. Certainly one of these is petroleum. The United States has become heavily reliant on petroleum from the Middle East and will have to buy two thirds of its oil from abroad by the end of the century.[18] While fuel supplies for the next decade are adequate, the cost of fuel may well rise. Both because of pollution and because of issues related to the balance of trade—oil imports account for approximately 40 percent of the U.S. trade deficit—heavy gasoline taxes, the mandated use of alternative fuels, and the restrictions on travel mentioned a moment ago are all possibilities. These pressures, too, could contribute to greater use of rail transportation between cities and mass transit within cities. Any pronounced change in travel and transportation patterns could, of course, create major opportunities for some hospitality entrepreneurs—and enormous dislocation for many existing operations in lodging, food service, and recreation.

THE TECHNOLOGICAL ENVIRONMENT

Computers and communication systems have already had a pronounced effect on hospitality operations. Point-of-sales systems have led to an explosion in management information for both operational and marketing planning. Com-

---

[18] *The Economist,* May 26, 1990, p. 23.

puter chips—microprocessors—are used to automate the control of heating and air-conditioning costs. Satellite-transmitted company "meetings" have become possible if not yet common. Computers "talk" to each other, and a national or worldwide company can, using its computer, make a realistic estimate of what its sales, costs, and profit were for one day before the office opens the following morning. Fax machines transmit management communications around the globe instantaneously. Car phones and other personal communications permit managers to keep in constant touch with events. The end of these changes, however, is not in sight.

Lap-top computers have helped us to view the computer as a portable device, and increasingly user-friendly, specialized software such as spreadsheets and word-processing programs make computers more readily accessible to everyone. Now early versions of the "notebook computer" suggest we will soon be free of the keyboard, as this device permits people to write on a computer screen with an electric pen (actually to print carefully—computers that can read individual handwriting are still in the future). The pen-based computer may replace many business forms and eliminate data-entry chores, speeding information even more quickly and easily to users.[19] Ultimately pen-based computers are slated to become much smaller and more portable, and to have built-in communication capabilities. *The New York Times* put it this way:

> This vision of the coming computer/communicator has more than a touch of Star Trek about it: a handheld gadget that can effortlessly send and receive messages and faxes, store and retrieve computer documents, recognize handwriting and someday even respond to voice commands.
>
> More powerful than today's desktop computers, the nomadic computer is also expected to be less visible and may not even be thought of as a computer. Instead, it could augment many everyday tasks, functioning as an appointment calendar, a tape recorder and a gateway to information ranging from the day's news to vast digital libraries.[20]

Imagine going on your rounds as a food production manager, writing your orders for food on the screen of a device about the size of a calculator that would transmit the summarized order to purveyors on command and print out a summary in your office for reference later.

The worldwide information network that is emerging through the linking of travel company central reservation systems (CRS) will give travel agents and other travel intermediaries (principally airline and car rental CRS) a much larger role in the selling of hotel rooms. It may also change drastically the way hotel prices are set.

[19] *The Economist,* September 15, 1990, p. 88.

[20] *The New York Times,* December 23, 1990, p. E6, col. 1, L38–50.

Room Inventory Auctioning

One of the impacts of the linked CRS is the possibility that a computerized auction market will be formed for guest rooms. Let us suppose a business person is planning a trip two weeks hence. He calls his travel agent and indicates the travel and room reservations he wants and the price he is willing to pay. The traveler would indicate how long his bid is good for—let's say 10 days. The agent enters the bid into a computerized auction market that keeps track of guest bids for rooms and hotels' offers of rooms. Hotels in the destination city review the level of demand for the days in question as well as this bid and other bids for this time period. If the bid is below regular rates, they may or may not accept the bid, depending on whether they expect to sell all their rooms or not. If at the end of 7 days (to continue our hypothetical example), the guest has not received a confirmation, he may want to make a new, higher bid to be sure of having the required accommodations.

Let's look at the transaction from the other side of the market. Suppose that, because of a cancelation, a convention hotel loses a 1,000-room convention without enough time to book another large group. That hotel could go to the auction market through its own CRS terminal and offer the 1,000 rooms, or some portion of them, at a discount. This would, after all, be a better solution than 1,000 empty rooms. Rate-sensitive discretionary travelers such as retirees or students might wait for a low-price availability date and make their travel plans on short notice when a bargain became available, postponing their travel if one was not.

Obviously, such an auction market could have a destabilizing impact on rates. It seems most likely that the result would be lower average daily rates. Whether an advantage to hotels or not, if and when this development comes into effect (and informed opinion is that it is quite likely), it will take quick minds familiar with computers to cope with the resulting changes in reservations procedures.

Technology will continue to change not only the way we work but the way we play. A toy manufacturer has already developed a "Power Glove" that gives players of video games a view of the game that is more realistic and three dimensional. In more advanced applications, the user wears a visual display that looks like bulky flying goggles, which is so close to the eyes that the user appears to be surrounded by the image. An electronic glove is used to indicate movement and direction. Similar technology is used (at enormous expense) to give aircraft simulators a realistic feel. Several computer firms in the United States, Europe, and Japan are working on advancing this "virtual reality" technology. For instance, NASA proposes to use it, along with data from space probes, to create "virtual" models of other worlds. At least one company has begun to develop a DataSuit that can map movements of the whole body.[21] If people can visit the moon, Mars, or Alpha Centauri without ever leaving

---

[21] *The Economist,* September 15, 1990, p. 108.

home, the home entertainment center may be an even more powerful competitor in the future than it is today.

THE BUILT ENVIRONMENT

Roads, bridges, airports, air-traffic control, and other travel facilities are essential to tourism. Unfortunately, the outlook for this travel infrastructure is not bright. Every reader of this text has probably had some experience with traffic jams, poor roads, and seemingly endless detours. Those who live and drive in large cities find such experiences a part of everyday life. The number of cars, according to the American Automobile Association (AAA), is growing twice as fast as the number of people. Airline passengers have doubled since airline deregulation in the late 1990s. From a current level of approximately 500 million, the number of passengers is expected to soar to 800 million by the year 2000.

At the same time that travel is growing, the North American travel infrastructure is decaying, and its capacity is being stretched beyond reason. Sixty percent of America's roads need resurfacing and 40 percent of its bridges are structurally deficient or functionally obsolete. The last major airport was built in the United States in 1974, and only one new airport (in Denver) is presently under construction, yet today's air traffic is *25 times* the 20 million passengers of 1974. The prospect of gridlock faces both auto and air transportation. The cost to bring roads up to standard would be $100 billion, a level of spending that is 50 percent higher than the current level. At the present rate of repair, it would take 83 years to clear up the current backlog of bridge repairs. And expert opinion is that building new airports will take 20 years from proposal to the finish of construction because of overlapping jurisdictions and the customary local opposition.[22]

If there was ever an area where civic activism and the interests of the hospitality industry and its members came together, it is in the need to respond to the coming crisis in travel-support facilities (and in lobbying for change). AAA data suggest that people are already replanning travel to try to avoid transportation delays, and some are postponing or reducing travel. The vast majority of people feel that auto travel is worse than it used to be, and half have reached that conclusion regarding air travel.

Rail travel may well increase as a part of the effort to deal with the growing crush of travelers on existing systems. High-speed trains are being seriously studied for 23 corridors between major cities in North America.[23] Traveling at speeds of 250 miles per hour or more, high-speed trains connected to major air terminals and downtown centers could help solve intercity traffic jams both on roads and in the air. In fact, air travel is least efficient on trips of

---

[22] J. Kay Aldous, "Roads Not Taken," a presentation to the 1990 Travel Outlook Forum, October 3, 1989.

[23] *The Economist,* June 13, 1991, p. A16.

between 100 and 600 miles,[24] distances such as those between Boston, New York, and Washington; Chicago and Cleveland; or Los Angeles and San Francisco. Displacing travel by car or air would also lessen fuel consumption and pollution. The very extensive investment required to bring higher speed trains into service, however, poses serious problems as to feasibility.

Another step that is being considered is the development of new downtown facilities "that can accommodate vertical takeoff aircraft/helicopter hybrids that could substantially reduce downtown-to-downtown intercity commute time." For longer distance travel, huge rural airports, called superhubs or wayports, as many as 20 of them, have been proposed. These very large airports would be located far away from city congestion where land costs and noise-pollution problems would both be reduced. They would be linked to the nearest major cities by regional airlines and high-speed rail and road transportation.[25]

Certainly, any change in the basic patterns of transportation poses both risks and opportunities to hospitality operators. It *is* clear, however, that we risk, at the very least, injuring the health of North American tourism if we do not stop neglecting our transportation infrastructures.

THREATS

War, pestilence, and famine have been a threat to every civilization, and that continues to be true today. On the other hand, we have passed through one of the longest periods in modern history without a major war—nearly 50 years. Pestilence (epidemic disease) becomes less of a problem with every advance in modern medicine. Famine is the unhappy lot of some, particularly in Africa, but it, too, seems unlikely as a major problem in North America. The environmental threats we have considered do pose the possibility of global disaster at some point in the future. As well, the threat of another oil crisis looms, though not as a result of any current shortage of that resource. Oil is not just a commodity but also a political weapon and hence unpredictable. Since earlier energy crises have abated, the United States' consumption of foreign oil has increased substantially; and as prices have fallen, U.S. oil production and exploration have fallen as well. Thus, the United States is vulnerable to another energy crisis.

Should a new crisis develop, we know from experience that, in the short run, the hospitality industry would be badly disrupted. In the longer run, higher fuel prices seem to have resulted in a rearrangement of travel destinations that favors regional centers closer to home. But people still travel. We might expect another energy crunch to give further impetus to plans discussed

---

[24] *The Economist,* October 13, 1990, p. 92.

[25] Aldous, "Roads Not Taken."

above to improve rail transportation. To date, support for more rail passenger transportation has been brought on largely by highway congestion.

Perhaps these two possibilities are most useful to us, though, in raising *the issue of uncertainty* in any look at the future. In this chapter we have looked at what is called a "surprise-free projection"; that is, we have assumed that there will be no overwhelming unforeseen developments, either good or bad. We've said that the future will probably be a continuation of trends already in place and, usually, it is. When presenting this kind of reasoning, however, it is incumbent on the writer to note that if there *is* a surprise, some bets may be off.

THE FUTURE AND YOU

We began this volume with an exploration of your interests in the industry and some consideration of how you might make a place for yourself in it. This is also an appropriate note on which to end. From our consideration of career planning for managers and supervisors in the hospitality industry, three points particularly deserve summary consideration: an industrywide view, the notion of retained earnings, and the need to develop a personal strategy.

THE HOSPITALITY INDUSTRY

Your interests may lie today in a particular area of the industry. They will necessarily become specialized as you take your first job after completing your schooling. Although you certainly must specialize to do an excellent job at whatever you are doing then and concentrate your energies there, it will also help you keep a view of the whole industry in mind. As the industry changes and evolves, you may encounter opportunities that suit your goals better in, say, club work or institutions. The reverse might just as easily be true. The hospitality industry is, and will continue to be, characterized by a good deal of movement from one segment to another.

In charting a career, you should keep your goals clearly in view. If they involve advancing through supervision into senior management, your early jobs should probably be in areas that prepare you for the variety of opportunities in the hospitality industry now and in the future. Thus, experience in food service offers a background useful and often essential to practically all of the industry's components. Although front-office work (for example) is extremely rewarding, it offers limited opportunities for growth and little basis for a move to other sectors of the industry.

RETAINED EARNINGS

The notion that what you have learned is something no one can take from you is central to this text. The idea that you can learn a great deal more from every job than just the job itself is equally important. As anyone (whether as a student in a summer dishwashing job or as a graduate in a junior assistant manager's position) moves through a career, he or she occasionally finds a job that does not make the fullest use of his or her abilities. For these jobs to be profitable in the fullest sense, they must be explored from the perspective of what you can learn to make them really productive *for you.*

Consider the many changes that appear to be in store for the industry and the possibility of opportunities presenting themselves from unexpected quarters. This consideration should make clear the importance of a broad fund of knowledge of people, management techniques, and guest relations, to name just a few areas. What this suggests is that what you learn through study and experience are the most important assets you can develop early in your career.

STRATEGIES AND GOALS

Career goals differ from person to person. Not everybody needs or wants to be a Henry Ford. Some people seek fame and fortune in a career; others want enjoyable work and an adequate income. To some, income is most important; to others, helping other people is the key. The main thing to realize is that whatever your objectives are, you are more likely to attain them with consciously developed plans that move you toward definite goals.

Of course, setting goals is never easy and is always harder for some than others, so you must be patient. You may decide that, for now, your goal will be to form goals as soon as you can! If you cannot realistically set lifetime goals at the moment, you can adopt a policy of exploration and set intermediate goals that support that policy.

Although long-range goals are important, so are medium-range and short-range planning. These may even be more important for people early in their careers, because long-range goals have a way of evolving with experience and opportunity. Thus, it is important to ask yourself what you want to get done *this* week! What can you learn from your new job besides the job itself? How much should you be earning a year from now? What is the next job you want to seek with your current employer?

It is important to have goals, but it is equally important to develop the strategies and tactics for moving toward your goals. This notion invites you to see yourself as an active element in your career, not as someone who waits for things to happen but as someone who makes his or her own place in the world. Remember, no matter who your employer is, you are in business for yourself. It is your life!

KEY WORDS AND CONCEPTS

To help you review this chapter, keep in mind the following:

Internationalization	Mature industry
Environmental concerns	Competitive differentiation

Service-intense operation
Demographics
Demand factors
Supply factors
Child-care benefits
Work force diversity
Competitive environment
Market segmentation
Physical environment
Solid-waste stream
Greenhouse effect
Energy (petroleum) crisis

Technological
Pen-based computers
Room inventory auctioning
Virtual reality
The built environment
Travel infrastructure
High-speed trains
Wayports (Superhubs)
An industrywide view
Retained earnings
Strategies and goals

REVIEW QUESTIONS

1. What is the impact of the internationalization of the hospitality industry?

2. What are the most important demographic changes we face in the 1990s? What are their effects on demand? On supply?

3. What is the meaning of the term *work force diversity*? What impact will work force diversity have on employee recruitment?

4. What long-term impacts would you foresee from the greenhouse effect on tourism in your community or region?

5. How would the use of the pen-based computer change managers' work in an operation you are familiar with?

6. What are the impacts on tourism of the travel infrastructure crisis? Are any aspects of these problems visible in your community? What should leaders in the hospitality industry do about these problems?

7. What are the arguments for high-speed trains? What impact might they have on your community's travel business?